620

D

THE DRAMA OF CHEKHOV, SYNGE, YEATS, AND PIRANDELLO

F. L. LUCAS

Fellow of King's College, Cambridge
Emeritus University Reader in English

THE DRAMA OF

CHEKHOV, SYNGE, YEATS, AND PIRANDELLO

CASSELL · LONDON

CASSELL & COMPANY LTD
35 Red Lion Square, London WC 1

and at

MELBOURNE . SYDNEY . TORONTO . JOHANNESBURG
CAPE TOWN . AUCKLAND

———

© F. L. Lucas, 1963

First published November 1963
Second edition April 1965

TO MY SON OLIVER

CONTENTS

Part I—Anton Chekhov

Part II—John Millington Synge

Part III—William Butler Yeats

CONTENTS

Part IV—Luigi Pirandello

CONTENTS

LIST OF ILLUSTRATIONS

ACKNOWLEDGEMENTS

Permission to quote from the works of W. B. Yeats has been kindly given by Mrs. W. B. Yeats and Messrs. Macmillan.

The two portraits of Chekhov are reproduced by permission of D. Magarshack from his book *Chekhov: A Life* (Faber 1952); the pastel of Synge, by permission of D. H. Greene from his book *J. M. Synge* (Macmillan, New York, 1959); the portrait of Yeats 1902 from *Images of a Poet* (Manchester University Press 1961), by permission of Professor D. J. Gordon and Mrs. W. B. Yeats; and the photograph of Yeats broadcasting, by permission of the B.B.C. The portrait of Pirandello is by courtesy of *Theatre Arts Magazine*.

PART I

Anton Chekhov

'God, what a sad country is our Russia!'
PUSHKIN (after laughing over the first
two chapters of Gogol's *Dead Souls*)

'O God, grant me simplicity of style!'
TOLSTOY (youthful diary)

LIFE

Anton Chekhov was born in 1860 as the third son of a shopkeeper in Taganrog, at the north-east corner of the Sea of Azov. Taganrog had originated with a fort built by Peter the Great in 1698; and the military stores there had recently been thought worth attack by our naval forces in the Crimean War; but its shallow harbour suffered from silting, and it had become what the Russians picturesquely called 'a deaf town'. 'Completely Asiatic'—so Chekhov himself was to describe it—a community where people 'do nothing but eat, sleep, and multiply'—'filthy, empty, lazy, illiterate, and uninteresting'—in fine, the same sort of depressing backwater as Chekhov's Three Sisters were one day to fill with nostalgic sighs for the far-off life of Moscow. This dull port seems an even less promising cradle for genius than that other dull port of Skien, at the opposite extremity of Europe, which thirty years before had brought forth Henrik Ibsen.

Chekhov's grandfather, Yegor Chekh, was a serf.[1] By a curious coincidence, this serf's master was a landowner called Chertkov, whose son Vladimir became a well-known disciple of Tolstoy (and, in Countess Tolstoy's eyes, his evil demon). From his master, Yegor Chekh bought freedom for himself, his wife, and three sons at 700 roubles apiece (say £70). Indeed the landowner was so generous as to throw in a daughter free of charge. Later, the liberated Chekh gained some prosperity as bailiff to Count Platov.

But this servile ancestry, and his own harsh childhood, left deep marks on Chekhov's memory. He too had, in a sense, to win his own emancipation; and the struggle this cost him is revealed, despite his usual reticence, in a letter to his friend Suvórin (January 1889).

---

[1] It is hard for Western minds fully to realize the primitive barbarism of Russia and of serfdom at the time. For example, according to Tolstoy, when a gentleman stayed the night, the serf-butler might be put first into his bed, to blunt the appetites of the creatures infesting it.

What upper-class writers receive 'gratuitously', by right of birth, plebeians purchase only at the price of their youth. So try to write the story of a young man, who has had for father a serf; who has served in a shop, sung in a choir, attended high school and university—one who has been trained to bow his back, and to kiss the hands of priests; submissive to other people's opinions; grateful for every crust of bread; a hundred times whipped; running, miserably ill-shod, to give a few lessons; a brawler; fond of tormenting animals; accepting with gratitude the dinners of rich relations; a hypocrite before God and men, without the least need for it, simply from a sense of his own nonentity. Describe, then, how this young man struggles to free himself, drop by drop, from the slave within him; and how, waking one fine morning, he realizes that there flows in his veins, no longer *the blood of a slave*, but the blood of a real human being.

Suvórin, himself the grandson of a serf, might well understand. But if Chekhov's labours were long and painful, they attained astonishing success. For in the writings of his maturity there seems no trace of the crude or the vulgar; more than many better-born writers, Chekhov became free, proud, and a gentleman.[1]

On the other hand, he still recalled the life of the poor too vividly to be blinded, like the aristocratic Tolstoy, by sentimental idealizations of the peasant. Chekhov had many sympathies; but few illusions.

Chekhov's father, Pavel, born in serfdom, later became a clerk, then a shopkeeper in Taganrog, where he married a cloth-merchant's daughter. He was enterprising enough to teach himself to play the violin, and to paint icons. Indeed Chekhov once said of his family, 'we get our talent from our father, our soul from our mother'. But at other times Chekhov's filial feelings were less indulgent—his father, he said, was 'a mediocrity'. And though the old man ended his days peacefully in the home of his famous son (1898), the son retained memories ineffaceably bitter. 'In my childhood I had no childhood.'

For Pavel Chekhov seems to have been a testy husband and a callous parent. 'I want you to remember,' wrote Anton at twenty-

---

[1] Compare his complaint that Russian actors possessed everything except good education, culture, and 'gentlemanliness in the good sense of that word'. Like Ibsen (another bankrupt merchant's son who yet forced his way to the top), and unlike some modern rebels, Chekhov was convinced that 'the good sense of that word' was something real.

nine to his elder brother Alexander, who had taken likewise to bullying his wife and his servant, 'I want you to remember that tyranny and lies killed your mother's youth. Tyranny and lies spoiled our childhood to such a degree that it is sickening and terrible to recall. Remember the horror and disgust we used to feel when father at dinner-time raised a row because the soup was too salt, or called mother a fool. . . . Tyranny is thrice criminal.' All his life Chekhov, like Byron, kept an implacable hatred for any form of despotism.

'I remember,' he writes again, in an autobiographical passage of his story *Three Years*, 'father began to teach me or, to put it more plainly, to whip me, when I was only five. He whipped me, boxed my ears, hit me on the head; and the first question I asked myself at waking every morning was—"Shall I be whipped again to-day?"' And so it was stunning to the little Anton to be told by a school-friend that *he* had never been flogged.

All this Chekhov could never forget. 'Do you know,' he said to Nemiróvich-Dánchenko, 'I could *never* forgive my father for whipping me as a child.'[1]

Apart from beatings, the boy's schooling was hindered by having often to do his homework sitting in the icy shop, where the very ink froze, so that he might keep a dragon's eye on the two shop-apprentices. Summer and winter, that shop opened at 5 a.m., to shut only at 11 p.m. Life in Taganrog was tough.

But Pavel Chekhov, besides being harsh and irritable, had also a curious mania. Though by no means a paragon of Christian un-worldliness, he was yet possessed by a passion for church ritual and music. So he formed a church-choir from his own family and fellow-townsfolk; and made his sons sing as a trio in church, where Anton felt 'like a little convict'. No matter how starved of sleep, these wretched children might even be hauled from bed at two or three in the morning. Further, not content with such public exhibitions, Pavel liked also to dress himself up as a priest, and conduct inter-minable services at home. 'Singing,' he purred, 'strengthens little chests, and going to church develops little souls.' But the 'little

---

[1] Another vivid picture of a domestic hell will be found in the story *Difficult People* (Vol. V of Constance Garnett's translation).

chests' were *not* strengthened. His children became consumptives. And the 'little souls' reacted violently. They became sceptics.

The eldest son, Alexander (also a writer), turned, when he grew up, to women and vodka; and the second son, Nikolai (said to have shown real gifts as a painter), took likewise to women and vodka, till he died young of tuberculosis. Anton, indeed, proved tougher, and less neurotic. But his attitude towards religion became double. He could still feel the beauty of the Orthodox ritual; he could write with sympathy and understanding about poor priests, or monks, or bishops. But his own mind was settled—'I have long lost my faith, and can only look with consternation on an intelligent man who believes.'

'Why are you so fond of church-bells?' asked his friend Vishnevsky. 'It is all,' he answered, 'that is left me of religion.' Like Matthew Arnold and Thomas Hardy, Chekhov still found beauty in a worship where he could no longer find truth.

With his more worldly eye, however, Pavel Chekhov had noted the prosperity of the Greek merchants in Taganrog. Therefore, he decided, his three eldest sons must go to the Greek school. A mere folly. For not only was the teaching conducted in Greek—it was also bad. And so, in the end, the boys had to be transferred to the ordinary gymnasium.

This was at least better; but not without its odious features. For example, Mr Urban, the Latin master, sought to advance himself by denouncing the boys to the masters, the masters to the headmaster, and the headmaster to the Ministry. Once, for example, he reported that the staff had committed the horrid outrage of smoking, at a staff-meeting, 'in the presence of some icons and the portrait of his Imperial Majesty'. Such was Russia, then also.

At this school Anton remained ten years (1869-79). He was no prize-pupil. His home-life was a constant hindrance; and examinations cost him agonies. Yet the works of his maturity remain strangely free from any signs of defective culture or education. Some of his early humour may be crude; but he became in the end extremely fastidious. 'Never,' he wrote to Lydia Avílov, 'use rough, clumsy words found only in colloquial speech' (a point often forgotten now by the inverted snobbery of translators who cannot resist the cheap and ephemeral charms of contemporary slang). Similarly, much though he liked and admired Maxim Gorky, Chekhov felt forced to warn him of the eternal need for grace, and for reserve—'the only defect,' he says of one of Gorky's works, 'is lack of restraint, lack of grace. When a man uses the minimum of movements for a given action, *that* is grace. In *your* expenditure one feels excess.' And again—'Lack of restraint is felt also in the descriptions of women . . . and the love-scenes. It is not vigour, not breadth of treatment, just plain unreserve.'[1]

It grows evident, then, that Chekhov was mainly self-educated. Certainly he read voraciously. And often there is no education more effective than self-education. Yet self-made men do not always make themselves very attractive. There must also, one feels, have been in Chekhov an inborn delicacy of feeling. For the sort of atmosphere he grew up in can be judged from an incident recalled by his brother Alexander. In 1877, when Anton was seventeen, for the first time he visited Moscow. Alexander, a top-hatted student of twenty-two, made the odd attempt of trying to impress the boy by belching in the face of an old lady in the street—a flourish which aroused in Anton mere disgust.

But perhaps none have an intenser loathing for vulgarity than some sensitive characters whose youth has seen the thing at close quarters.[2]

---

[1] Cf. Charles Chaplin to Max Eastman: 'You have what I consider the essence of all art—even of mine, if I can call myself an artist—restraint.' Restraint and reserve—there seem to me no qualities that the literature of our century more commonly forgets. But one may hope they will some day return.

[2] Compare Chekhov's indignant letter to Alexander (2/1/1899), reproaching him for his loutishness to his wife and his cook: 'I hope you will forgive my saying so, but to treat women like that, whoever they may be, is unworthy of a decent man. . . . Language of the foulest kind, shouts, reproaches, rows at breakfast and dinner, constant complaints of your hard life and your damnable work—are these not expressions of the coarsest despotism? However worthless or culpable a woman might be—however intimate your relations with her might be—you have no right to sit in her presence without trousers, or be drunk in her presence, or utter words which even factory-workers would not use in the presence of women. . . . You claim that decency and good manners are prejudices; but one must have some regard at least for something—a woman's weakness, or one's own children.'

It becomes abundantly clear that Chekhov was fundamentally civilized; but that much in his own family was not.

Even in these early years Chekhov showed also a delight in drama—both at home where, for instance, he would act dentist and extract with a pair of tongs an immense tooth, represented by a cork, from the jaws of his brother Alexander; and in the Taganrog theatre, which was out of bounds for the school, so that the boys might have to creep thither disguised in dark spectacles and false beards. Perhaps some memory of this survives in the good-hearted, grotesque schoolmaster, Kulígin, of *The Three Sisters*, who has obsequiously shaved off his own moustaches to please his clean-shaven Director, but agonizingly chooses the moment when his wife is plunged in gloom, to start clowning to her with a false beard —'Yesterday I took these whiskers and beard from a boy in the third class. . . . Don't I look like the German master? Don't I? The boys *are* amusing!'

Meanwhile, however, Chekhov's eccentric father Pavel found his business decline. By 1876 he was bankrupt. He had to abscond, hidden at the bottom of a cart, to the next station up the line from Taganrog and take train for Moscow, where his two elder sons were now students.

Creditors formed designs on the family-home; a false friend, Selivánov, pretending help, finally turned out to have bought the house himself, at a bargain-price. (Just as Lopákhin—though in his case quite honestly—buys the Cherry Orchard.) The rest of the family then joined Pavel Chekhov in a Moscow slum; while Anton, aged sixteen, was left to fend for himself in Taganrog for three years more of school. In the intervals of schooling the boy earned for himself and his impoverished family by schooling others. Thus in return for coaching a nephew he received board and lodging from the sly Selivánov. But at least and at last he was free from his father's tyranny.

So, like Ibsen, Strindberg, Trollope, the young Chekhov had to bear the hardships and humiliations of parental bankruptcy. But such early troubles, where they do not break a young spirit, may toughen it.

In 1879 Chekhov passed his final school-examinations, and received from the town-council of Taganrog a scholarship of 25 roubles a month. With this he too migrated to Moscow, to help support his family, and to pursue at the same time his five-year studies for a medical degree. But 25 roubles a month did not go far with a hungry household. And so, following his elder brother Alexander, Anton began in 1880 to write short stories for papers in Moscow and St Petersburg. A grim grind—simultaneous journalism and medicine, in a crowded, noisy, stuffy household, nine persons in five rooms.

Further, since his father was hopelessly incompetent, and his two elder brothers drunken wastrels, he now became the real head of the family. Little wonder if he could exclaim sardonically in after-life, 'Relations are a race in which I take no interest.'

But the young Chekhov was resolute, gay, and vital—the very reverse of those moaning, ineffectual intellectuals that throng his plays and stories. For several years he wrote over a hundred tales annually—an average of two a week. What fertility and facility! By 1887 he had produced some six hundred!

This early work, however, had no literary pretensions—it was honest, unashamed pot-boiling.[1] Not that the pot was easy to boil—even when he had earned payment, he had still to extract it from impecunious and evasive editors. Like Johnson, Chekhov early came to know all too well the bleak climate of Grub Street.

At last, in 1884, he graduated as doctor; but now fate suddenly revealed in him (as in that other humorist, Laurence Sterne) a malady that neither he nor any other doctor then could cure—tuberculosis. This year, in November, he had his first haemorrhage. Five years later the same disease killed his brother Nikolai. It is easy to see the parallel with Keats; who likewise cured himself so wonderfully of early vulgarities, but whose consumption nothing could cure. Only—luckily for us—Chekhov was twenty years in dying;

[1] Anyone curious to see how badly Chekhov *could* write, even as late as 1885, can turn to his crime-novel, *The Shooting Party* (English version by A. E. Chamot, 1926), with its crude and improbable plot, its thin descriptions, its characters who behave with much more of that spasmodic, neurotic, un-accountable impulsiveness one has come to think of as 'typically Russian', than the figures of Chekhov's maturity.

Similarly with some of the early stories translated by A. Yarmolinsky in *The Unknown Chekhov* (1959). 'Oh, with what trash I began,' said Chekhov once, 'my God, with what trash!'

and, for most of these, remained marvellously alive. None the less it should be remembered that his lifework was accomplished in a brief forty-four years by a man suffering, towards the end, not from consumption only, but also from haemorrhoids, heart-trouble, eye-trouble, and, finally, tubercular diarrhoea. His will must have been of iron.[1]

In 1885, however, on a visit to St Petersburg the honest young pot-boiler was suddenly amazed to find himself fêted as a literary eminence. He met the prosperous Suvórin (1833-1911), twenty-six years his senior, who has been described as a sort of Russian North-cliffe, and in whose paper *Novoye Vremya* (*New Times*), much of Chekhov's work was later to appear. Soon afterwards, he was over-whelmed by an enthusiastic letter from the veteran novelist Grigoróvich (1822-99); the same who once said, with typical Russian exuberance, about one of Chekhov's rivals—'He is not worthy to kiss the trail of the flea that has bitten Chekhov.'

This turning-point proved decisive. Suddenly the young author of twenty-five realized that he possessed a real talent, deserving self-respect. Hitherto, 'I wrote lightheartedly, as though I were eating pancakes: but now I write and tremble.' He acquired, in short, an artistic conscience. His apprenticeship had been rough and rude; yet his scribblings had at least taught him fluency; just as Dryden gained his easy mastery of the heroic couplet by writing them in thousands, often worthless. Chekhov is an instance in support of Johnson's dictum that one may learn to write well by writing quickly; whereas Quintilian had maintained the opposite—that one should learn to write quickly by writing well. Further, from Tagan-rog, from the steppes to north of it, from the streets of Moscow, and from passing love-affairs, Chekhov had begun to gain his multitudinous knowledge of human character; a knowledge that he could put to the fullest use because he possessed also, more than most men

[1] In 1899 he estimated that, in addition to articles, journalism, and so forth, he had published, in twenty years of literary activity 'over 4,800 pages of tales and stories'. He is said to have jestingly observed that the only kinds of writing he had *not* produced were poems, novels, and informers' reports.

But of 117 longer pieces written in the years 1880-3 he is said to have retained only twenty in his collected works (M. Slonim, *Modern Russian Literature*, 1953, p. 57).

and most writers, a passion for naked reality, an incorruptible contempt for all distortions of the truth. Here, perhaps, his medicine also helped. It made him scientist as well as artist. Medicine, he said, was his lawful wife; literature, his mistress. And it may well be that this scientific side of him helped him to become one of the most relentlessly honest among the world's writers, scornful of all parade or pretence, all comfortable conventions or wishful delusions.

Together with this scientific scepticism, Chekhov learnt also the scientist's patient self-control. Yet the lesson proved long and hard. 'Animal-training' he called it. For lack of such self-discipline, his father and his two elder brothers had come, like so many Russians, to frustration and ruin. 'I must tell you,' he wrote, years after, to his wife, 'that by nature my character is very harsh; I flare up easily, etc., etc.; but I am accustomed to restraining myself, for no decent person should let himself go. The devil only knows what I used to do in old days.' A Shelley may often seem too unreal; a Zola, too squalid; a Bridges, too chilly; a Strindberg, too mad and malignant. But Chekhov avoided these excesses. He became a most admirably civilized person. Very few of the world's writers have been characters as balanced and as fine. Men abnormally gifted are often abnormal, also, in ways less pleasant. He was not.

It is the last nineteen years of Chekhov's brief forty-four that matter to the world—the period 1885-1904. (Though born thirty-two years after Ibsen, he died two years sooner.) His output of short stories now decreased in quantity, just as it increased in quality. With these Chekhov had begun; and to the end the short story remained, I think, his most successful field. He liked stories short. One might imagine that it was his frail health which kept him so conscious of the swiftness and shortness of time. But it seems to have been still more a matter of temperament. When he did attempt a full-length novel, it was only to abandon it. He developed a consuming passion for brevity.

But there is another literary form which likewise, at least in comparison with the novel, enjoys this advantage of brevity—the drama. And towards drama Chekhov felt drawn by temperament also—though not without a certain repulsion as well. For, just as he had called medicine his wife, and literature his mistress, so, within the field of literature, he regarded fiction as his wife, the stage as 'a noisy, impudent, and tiresome mistress'. The theatre, said a contemporary, was fonder of Chekhov than Chekhov of the theatre. Still his last four plays have left their mark on European drama; and these are here our main concern.

In 1887 *Ivánov*, badly produced at Moscow, caused almost a pitched battle among its bewildered and divided audience; but two years later, in 1889, a revised version won a great success at St Petersburg. Yet the same year saw the failure at Moscow of his *Wood-demon*, the first form of *Uncle Vanya*.

But in 1890 came an abrupt diversion. Amid general amazement Chekhov suddenly betook himself to the other end of Siberia, in order to study convict-life on the island of Sakhalín. It seemed an incomprehensible freak for a successful writer—imagine Tennyson dashing off to investigate convicts in New South Wales! And it seemed, also, an insane adventure for a consumptive. For the journey across Siberia was frightful; and the northern part of Sakhalín itself is permanently frozen, even though it lies on the latitude of London (such are the blessings of our Gulf Stream). Actually Chekhov developed one haemorrhage before starting; and another before he was far on his way. However, it is hard to be sure how clearly he as yet realized, or could bear to realize, the seriousness of his malady. For it is notorious that the tubercular are apt to be over-optimistic about their condition. Chekhov's own brother Nikolai was convinced almost to his last breath that he would recover, and paint again.

It is also hard to be sure of Chekhov's real motives for going. First, perhaps, a longing for fresh experience? Certainly he had no patience with inert intellectuals. Two years before (1888) in an article on Przhevalsky, a Russian explorer of Central Asia (1839-88), he had written—'in our sick time when . . . even our best men sit about doing nothing, and justify their idleness and debaucheries by the absence of a clear purpose in life, such pioneers are as necessary to us as the sun itself'.

Of Chekhov's own admirable energy it remains uncertain how far it was the hectic drive of a consumptive, like a flame burning in pure oxygen; how far it was natural, healthy vitality. But it was certainly intense. 'What a luxurious thing Nature is!' he has written. 'I could just take her and eat her up.' And again to Suvórin (1894): 'I feel I could eat everything: the steppe, and foreign countries, and a good novel.'[1] And yet again, to Gorky, in 1900: 'In your place I would go off to India or the devil knows where; I would take two more university degrees.' 'I have sailed,' he concluded after the Sakhalín journey, 'more than a thousand versts on the Amur; have seen a million landscapes. . . . Truly, I have seen such riches, and have enjoyed so many pleasures, that even death does not seem so terrible now.' At other times he formed equally venturesome ideas of going to Africa, Persia, India, America, Nova Zembla; and only a little while before his death he still thought of serving as a doctor on the Manchurian front in the Russo-Japanese War. His was the unconquerable spirit of Dante's, and of Tennyson's, Ulysses.[2]

But, secondly, Chekhov's energy was not always thus spontaneous. Here, as in many other ways, he was a man of very varying moods. (Probably this helped him, as a writer, to create his rich diversity of characters.) Energy alternated in him with indolence. But such indolence his will was determined to dominate. 'This journey,' he wrote to Suvórin, 'represents an uninterrupted labour, physical and mental, of six months: therefore it is indispensable for me, for I am a southerner, and I begin to grow lazy. One must discipline oneself.'

Thirdly, he was scientist as well as artist; and his professional conscience told him that medicine still remained his 'lawful wife'. 'I want to write a couple of hundred pages, and so atone in some degree for my medicine which, as you know, I have piggishly neglected.'

Fourthly, Chekhov's journey to Sakhalín was due also to his

[1] Compare the exuberant Browning: 'I have such a love for flowers and leaves that I every now and then in an impatience at not being able to possess them thoroughly, to see them quite, satiate myself with their scent—bite them to bits.'

[2] Ilya Erenburg quotes a passionate protest of Chekhov's provoked by the morbidity of Tolstoy's parable, 'How much earth does a man need?—'Six feet of earth are the need of a corpse, not a man. . . . A man needs, not six feet of earth, nor a country estate, but the whole round world. the whole of nature.' ('Erenburg', I gather on good authority, is a correcter form than 'Ehrenburg'.)

social conscience; reinforced at this time by the influence of Tolstoy. He felt he must do something for these 'criminals'—men mentally sick—who were so mishandled by the Russian state. 'It is evident that we have let *millions* of people rot in prison—rot to no good purpose—barbarously, without giving the matter a thought.'

Fifthly, it has been conjectured that he wished also to cure himself of a trouble of the heart—to deaden and kill his own passion for Lydia Avílov.[1] In the words of Baudelaire's *Le Voyage*:

> Un matin nous partons, le cerveau plein de flamme,
> Le coeur gros de rancune et de désirs amers,
> Et nous allons, suivant le rhythme de la lame,
> Berçant notre infini sur le fini des mers:
>
> Les uns joyeux de fuir une patrie infâme;
> D'autres, l'horreur de leurs berceaux, et quelques-uns,
> Astrologues noyés dans les yeux d'une femme,
> La Circé tyrannique aux dangereux parfums.
>
> Pour n'être pas changés en bêtes, ils s'enivrent
> D'espace et de lumière et de cieux embrasés;
> La glace qui les mord, les soleils qui les cuivrent,
> Effacent lentement la marque des baisers.[2]

This last theory of Chekhov's motives may, indeed, be merely the romanticism of biographers. But not necessarily.[3] Anyway, whether

---

[1] See pp. 53-5.

[2]
> One dawn we take the road, with brains a-fire—
> With rankling hearts and bitter fantasies
> We set adrift our infinite desire,
> Cramped in the narrow cradle of the seas:
>
> Some wild to leave a country they have found
> Too vile, or homes grown hideous; some to flee
> (Astrologers a woman's eyes have drowned)
> Chains of some Circe, perfumed perilously;
>
> Lest they be changed to beasts, they turn and run
> To drink of space and light and flaming skies;
> Beneath the biting frost, the bronzing sun,
> Slowly the brand of ancient kisses dies.

[3] It is at least curious that, according to Olga Knipper, he was thinking early in 1901 of a play about a love-crossed scientist going on an expedition to the Arctic: ice-bound there in the last act he sees, against the Northern Lights, the woman's shadow.

or no his journey was meant to cure him of Lydia Avílov, it did help to cure him of the Tolstoyanism that had influenced him for six or seven years. For these Siberian convicts had, perforce, to practise the completest Tolstoyan non-resistance. And much good *that* did! 'Before my Sakhalín journey,' he wrote to Suvórin, '*The Kreutzer Sonata* was an event in my life; but now it just seems to me silly and ridiculous.'

At all events, whatever his reasons, Chekhov plunged off into Siberia, equipped, among other things, with a sheepskin, a revolver, and a penknife ('for cutting sausages and killing tigers'); but with no official authorization or documents, apart from his journalist's card. However, the tyranny of the Tsars was mild compared with the tyranny of Stalin; and on his arrival Chekhov was allowed surprisingly free access to all except political prisoners.

None the less this trip of nearly three thousand miles was a drastic ordeal for an invalid. There existed as yet no Trans-Siberian railway. The traveller must face ramshackle conveyances, foul inns, bugs, bone-shaking roads, rivers in spate.[1] On Sakhalín itself, 'a perfect hell', Chekhov spent three months; making a census, on cards, of ten thousand convicts, each one personally interviewed. Few writers have been in less danger of drooping into unpractical aesthetes.

After his return by way of Singapore and Ceylon, his account of Sakhalín, published partly in *Russian Thought*, and later in book-form, is said to have brought *some* reforms, especially in the physical punishments inflicted; till the twentieth century plunged Siberia into new horrors.

Chekhov had now (December, 1890) less than fourteen years to live. Yet despite worsening health he produced a further host of stories, and four outstanding plays—*The Seagull*, a disastrous failure at St Petersburg in 1896, a resounding success at Moscow in 1898; *Uncle Vanya*, produced at Moscow in 1899; *The Three Sisters*, produced at Moscow in 1901; *The Cherry Orchard*, produced at Moscow in 1904. The last three were not immediate triumphs; yet they grew like his beloved trees—slow, but sure.

[1] A. Yarmolinsky's *The Unknown Chekhov* includes a part-description of the journey; so vivid that the reader shivers.

With all this went also an amazing practical activity. From 1892 to 1899, at Melikhovo in the Moscow province, he ran a large estate, which he bought in ruinous condition, and then improved by tireless toil. Here he planted trees as fanatically as his Dr Astrov in *Uncle Vanya*—a thousand cherries, pines, elms, and oaks; doctored sick peasants by hundreds; undertook census-work; and built three schools.

Driven south at last by tuberculosis to Yalta in the Crimea, there too he recommenced the same eager building and planting— cherries, mulberries, palms, cedars.[1] Chekhov was the exact opposite of his futile character, Laevsky, in *The Duel*, whose utter emptiness is summed up in the words—'all his life he had never planted one single tree in his own garden, never grown one single blade of grass; living among the living, he had never saved a fly'.

'Do you see?' said Chekhov to Kouprin at Yalta; 'it was I that planted every tree here, and you can understand they are dear to me.' All had been nothing but stones and thistles. 'Then I came and transformed this lost corner into a place of civilization and beauty. Do you know?—in three or four centuries the whole earth will change into a flourishing garden. And life will be, then, astonishingly light and easy.'

It grows clear that the Utopian dreamings of Chekhov's idealistic characters were also, at times, Chekhov's own. Who knows? They might even be true.[2]

Add to all this a lavish hospitality at home, and the provision of an Art Museum, a Library, and a statue of Peter the Great for his native town of Taganrog. Such endless exertion may have been bad for his illness; it may have been, partly, a symptom of his illness; but how not admire it? Chekhov lived up to the advice he had given his feckless brother, Nikolai, in 1886—'What one needs is constant

---

[1] After Chekhov's death, his sister (who preserved the house just as he left it, and remained curator of its museum till her own death in 1957) appropriately planted outside his study-window a cypress, which has since grown vast.

[2] But one must always remember that, at other times, he could also be much more sombre—'On the whole, life gets every day more and more complex, and moves on at its own sweet will, and people get more and more stupid, and isolated from life—like crippled beggars in a religious procession.'

work, day and night, incessant reading, study, and exercise of will. Every hour is precious.'

All this needs stressing because the notion even now persists that Chekhov was himself a pessimistic son of futility and defeat, whimpering idly in the shade. The truth was the exact reverse. 'I despise laziness,' he said, 'as I despise weakness and sluggishness of spirit.'

In 1898, at a rehearsal of Count Alexey Tolstoy's *Tsar Fyodor* in the Moscow Art Theatre, Chekhov was struck by the actress who played Irina—'If I remained in Moscow,' he wrote, 'I should fall in love with Irina.' He did fall in love with her. She was a young German, of Alsatian origin, ten years his junior, called Olga Knipper; the daughter of an engineer and factory-manager. Soon afterwards she played Arkádina in Chekhov's *Seagull*. Chekhov's love for her led in May 1901 to a marriage which, in his hatred of publicity and ceremonial, he celebrated with only four witnesses, concealing it till the last moment even from his own family. From church the married pair drove off to spend their honeymoon in a sanatorium.

He had now only three years to live. Half their time the two were separated. For he was imprisoned by his health in Yalta (which, ruefully remembering Dreyfus, he called 'my Devil's Island'); and she was kept in Moscow by the stage. From his humorous, affectionate letters, it is clear that Chekhov often suffered intensely from loneliness; while his wife on her side felt a sense of guilt at leaving him lonely. But she felt too, like Shakespeare's Portia with Brutus, that she did not know nearly all that went on in his mind. She has been criticized for not giving up the theatre. But how can one presume to judge relationships so personal? Least of all can one judge lovers. For they alone know all the facts (except that even they inevitably forget half of them); but they cannot judge dispassionately. And those who *could* judge dispassionately, cannot know even half the facts.

But one may suspect that Chekhov was a lonely soul who yet dreaded loneliness. 'I simply cannot live without visitors,' he wrote in 1899. 'When alone, I am for some reason terrified, as if I were a castaway in a small boat in mid-Pacific.' He would pack his house like a hotel, till there were visitors sleeping even on the sofas. His invitations were imperiously pressing in their eagerness; and he would keep his guests for weeks on end. He was lavishly hospitable. He would speak of people with heart-felt warmth—'a delightful fellow', 'a splendid chap', 'a darling man'. He would even invite quite unsuitable partners to abortive literary collaborations. And yet that haunting sense of loneliness remained.

'Just as I shall be laid alone in the grave,' says his notebook, 'so, at bottom, I live alone.' And he wore on his watch-chain a seal, which he used for his letters to Lydia Avílov—'To the lonely the world is a wilderness.' At times, like Byron, he suffered from nocturnal terrors.

And yet, while part of him thus shrank from solitude, another part of him clung to it. In 1895 he had written, of imagined marriage, that his wife, whoever she might be, 'will have to live in Moscow, and I shall go to see her now and then. . . . I promise you to be an excellent husband; but give me a wife who, like the moon, would appear in the sky not every day.'

Loneliness, indeed, he came to accept as an essential necessity of human life. How often in his plays, especially in *The Cherry Orchard*, when characters do not even listen to each other because they are too wrapped up in their own thoughts and desires, one recalls that grey conclusion of Proust—'nous sommes irrémédiablement seuls'![1] And how desolate is that entry in Chekhov's notebooks—'If you fear loneliness, do not marry'!

None the less, reading his often gay letters to Olga Knipper with their odd endearments—'my sweet goose'—'marvellous dog'—'pony'—'pet'—'poppet'—'popinjay'—'little crocodile'—'whale'—'beetle', one feels also that of Chekhov's last years, as of his last plays, it is a mistake to think *too* gloomily. Despite his pessimism, there still remains the same splendid gaiety and tenderness, humour and courage. 'To marry a girl,' he had written to his brother Mikhail, three years before meeting Olga Knipper, 'just because she is nice, is like buying yourself something you do not want, merely because *it* is nice. The most important thing in family life is love, sexual desire, one flesh; everything else is unimportant,

---

[1] 'We are irremediably alone.'

Chekhov in the year he died (1904)

Chekhov and Olga Knipper

however clever your calculations might be. So, you see, it is not a question of finding a nice girl, but one with whom I should fall in love—just a little thing like that!'

It was a great grief to him that their only child was born dead. But essentially, one hopes, in Olga Knipper Fate gave Chekhov what his heart needed.

His end was characteristic. In June 1904, after receiving an ovation, marred by his extreme physical weakness, at the first production of *The Cherry Orchard*, he left Moscow, seriously ill, for Badenweiler in the Black Forest. But even there the invalid's keen eyes still watched with humour the queer foreign types about him. On his very last evening he made his wife curl up with laughter by his imaginary description of fat bankers and pink-faced Englishmen or Americans, at some fashionable resort, left suddenly to dinnerless consternation by finding the hotel-cook decamped.

That night, as he never had done before, Chekhov asked for his doctor; and said to him, in a loud, firm voice, 'Ich sterbe'—'I am dying'. When ice was put on his chest, 'you don't put ice,' he remarked, still ironic, 'on an empty heart.' When ordered champagne, he smiled—'It's long since I drank champagne.' Then his mind began to wander. He talked deliriously of his countrymen struggling against the Japanese far away in Manchuria. Then the end. About the room where he lay dead, there fluttered a huge black moth.

Chekhov's body was brought home to Russia by rail. But, through some oversight, it arrived in a dingy-green refrigerator-van, labelled 'Fresh Oysters'. By a further mistake, part of the crowd that had gathered at the Moscow station to honour him, trooped off behind the coffin, not of Chekhov, but of a General Keller, killed on the Manchurian front; much though they wondered why their quiet dramatist should be escorted to his rest by the blarings of a military band—such a band as dies away into the distance at the close of *The Three Sisters*. Meanwhile Chekhov's own body was followed along the hot, dusty road by only some hundred people. At their head jogged majestically a plump police-officer on a plump white horse. Irony to the last.

Maxim Gorky was outraged by the banality and vulgarity of it all.

That this 'marvellous man', he raged, should have been brought home to Russia in an oyster-van, and interred beside the tomb of some Cossack's widow, Olga Koukaretkina! 'These are mere details, and yet when I think of the oysters, or of Koukaretkina, it wrings my heart, I could howl aloud, weep like a calf, flog myself with indignation and fury. It does not matter to *him*—they could have brought back his body in a dirty-clothes basket; but it is ourselves, our whole Russian community, that I cannot forgive for that oyster-waggon.' Generous indignation. But perhaps Gorky had a little forgotten his dead friend's warning about the need, always, for restraint. Chekhov himself would only have smiled his usual ironic smile. He could so well have afforded to say (but he was far too modest), like Gibbon in his testament, 'Shall I be accused of vanity if I add that a monument is superfluous?'

Thirteen years later, in 1917, came the Red Revolution; and the Cherry Orchard of the Russian upper and middle classes was felled with a resounding crash.

Yet Chekhov survived. Lenin liked him, especially his satire of bureaucrats. Stalin quoted him at a party congress, as a bitter castigator of the petty vices of the bourgeoisie. All this, however, might have brought smiles still bitterer from the man who wrote with such compassionate irony of his decaying gentlefolk, and with such irreconcilable loathing of all tyrannies.

In 1933 Chekhov's body was exhumed, and removed from the side of his father to the part of the cemetery assigned to actors of the Moscow Art Theatre—a sort of Actors' Corner. Olga Knipper came. What must her thoughts of those twenty-nine years have been?

But the Russian Communists are too concerned with corpses—witness their pickling of Lenin and Stalin. A form perhaps of 'dialectical materialism'? Had they only read Chekhov a little more closely, they might have liked him less. Still they have had the grace to surround his grave, one gathers, with appropriate cherry-trees.

MAIN DATES

1841 Chekhov's serf-grandfather buys freedom.

16/1/1860 Chekhov born.

1861 Serfdom abolished by Alexander II.

1862 Turgenev's *Fathers and Sons*.

1865-6 Dostoievsky's *Crime and Punishment*.

1869 Tolstoy's *War and Peace*.

1876 Chekhov's father bankrupt.

1877 Tolstoy's *Anna Karenina*.

1879-84 Chekhov's medical studies at Moscow; combined with story-writing to support his family.

1880 Dostoievsky's *Brothers Karamazov*.

1881 Alexander II assassinated. Political reaction. Dostoievsky dies.

1883 Turgenev dies.

1884 Chekhov's first haemorrhage. *Tales of Melpomene*.

1885-6 Recognition by Suvórin and Grigoróvich.

1886 *Motley Stories*.

1887 *Ivánov* dubiously received at Moscow.

1889 *Ivánov* a success at St Petersburg. *The Wood-Demon* a failure at Moscow.

1890 Sakhalín journey.

1891 Travel in Austria, France, Italy with Suvórin.

1892 Chekhov buys estate of Melikhovo.

1894 Nicholas II succeeds—the last of the Tsars. Second trip to Austria, Italy, France with Suvórin.

1896 *The Seagull* a fiasco at St Petersburg.

1897 Foundation of Moscow Art Theatre. Serious haemorrhage. Trip to Biarritz and Nice.

1898 Chekhov builds his house at Yalta. Meeting with Olga Knipper. *The Seagull* triumphant at Moscow.

1899 Sale of Melikhovo. *Uncle Vanya* at Moscow (Olga Knipper as Helen).

1900 Chekhov elected to the Academy of Sciences, St Petersburg. Trip to Austria, Italy, France.

1901 *The Three Sisters* at Moscow (Olga Knipper as Masha). Marriage to Olga Knipper.

1902 Chekhov resigns from the Academy in protest against the annulment of Gorky's election (by order of Nicholas II).

1904 *The Cherry Orchard* at Moscow (Olga Knipper as Mme Ranevsky).

2/7/1904 Chekhov dies at Badenweiler.

Chekhov, like Pirandello, seems to me best in his best short stories. For these can reveal more of the author's own most attractive personality (as do the best of his later letters). Further, the stories lend themselves less than the plays to elaborate misinterpretations by silly-clever critics. Therefore even those concerned with Chekhov the dramatist should on no account neglect Chekhov the story-writer.[1]

[1] To those who do not know this side of him I would particularly recommend the following in the thirteen-volume translation by Constance Garnett:

Vol. I   *The Darling, Ariadne.*
Vol. II   *The Duel, Neighbours.*
Vol. III   *The Lady with the Dog, An Anonymous Story.*
Vol. IV   *The Party, The Kiss, A Trifle from Life.*
Vol. V   *The Grasshopper, A Dreary Story.*
Vol. VI   *In the Ravine, Peasants.*
Vol. VII   *A Nightmare.*
Vol. VIII *The Chorus-girl, Verotchka, My Life.*
Vol. IX   *Misery, In Exile, The Bet.*
Vol. X   *Ward 6.* (This story filled the young Lenin with a kind of terror, so that he had to leave his room and walk out into the night. 'I felt as if I too were shut up in Ward 6.')
Vol. XI   *Enemies.*
Vol. XIII *Lights.*

These can be read, and re-read, and re-read.

DRAMATIC WORKS

Chekhov's dramatic work consists mainly of some short pieces, largely farcical, which do not seem to me worth spending time on, in a world crammed with more good literature than life is long enough to read; and five important plays—*Ivánov, The Seagull, Uncle Vanya, The Three Sisters*, and *The Cherry Orchard*.

Of the short pieces the best, perhaps, are *On the High Road*, which points forward to the low-life scenes of Maxim Gorky; and *The Bear*, which won a great and lasting success with its picture of a testy middle-aged landowner who comes to dun a widow for a debt; grows furious to the point of nearly fighting a pistol-duel with her; and then falls into her arms. But these are hardly the Chekhov that matters. The humour of his farces seems often strangely clumsy compared with the delightful humour of his letters.

His first full-length play was apparently written in the early eighteen-eighties and his own early twenties, with a hope of performance at the Moscow Maly Theatre; was shown to the actress Yermolova, who disapproved; rewritten; and then lost to sight till in 1920 the manuscript was rediscovered (without any title). Russian texts appeared in 1923, 1933, 1949; an English translation by B. A. Ashmole was published in 1952, with the title *Don Juan (In the Russian Manner)*; and a fuller version by Dmitri Makaroff in 1961, with the title *Platónov*. It is a burlesque melodrama about the philanderings of the said Platónov, whose feeble impulsiveness in some ways foreshadows Ivánov. But, as in Chekhov's novel *The Shooting Party* (p. 9), the characters tend to baffle the English reader much more than the figures of Chekhov's maturer work—they run to such Russian extremes, unbalanced and bizarre, inconsistent and illogical, incalculable and unaccountable. At all events *Platónov* seems to me chaotic, unconvincing, and tedious. It has been pleaded that the play is largely farce (though it ends with the hero's being shot by one of the ladies he has trifled with). But nothing is more melancholy than a farce that fails to amuse. Its main interest lies, I think, in again showing how much its author's

23

ultimate greatness was due, not to effortless genius, but to infinite pains.

Chekhov's later and more characteristic dramas read as if written in deliberate defiance of Aristotle. For Aristotle laid it down that 'drama' (as is implied by its very etymology—'a doing') consists essentially in *action*—and in a *single* action; and that, accordingly, plot is more important than character. Chekhov seems to me to confirm my flatly opposite conviction that often character proves far more vital than plot.

In his most typical plays the characters are often Hamlet-types, who find it hard to achieve any action at all. They drift. Aristotle's Unity of Action becomes replaced by a whole series of trivial actions, listlessly performed by a number of more or less helpless characters, who feel no unity either with each other or with themselves. One of the earliest comments evoked by *The Three Sisters* was that it seemed not so much a play as the outline of a play. The men and women of most tragic drama, from Aeschylus to Ibsen, crash; those of Chekhov drift and rot, in a mist. From the active drama of Aristotle he has moved closer to the 'Static Drama' of Maeterlinck (though Maeterlinck remains far more mystical, and less warmly human). With Greek tragedy Chekhov has little in common; except that such few drastic actions as do occur, occur mainly behind the scene.

Inevitably, then, Chekhov's characters, often incapable of considering or even comprehending one another, but endlessly absorbed in themselves, become far more important than the tenuous plots which merely bring them together for a moment before they float apart again. For unity of action there is substituted a certain unity of mood. The persons come to seem more like performers in an orchestra; each playing his own instrument, yet combining to build up a symphony of ironic sadness. And so the audience at a Chekhov play such as *Uncle Vanya* tends to grow like the contemplative Gods of Tennyson's *Lotos-Eaters*, as they lie beside their nectar and watch the painful earth—

> But they smile, they find a *music* centred in a doleful song,
> Steaming up, a lamentation and an ancient tale of wrong,
> Like *a tale of little meaning* tho' the words are strong;

Chanted from an ill-used race of men that cleave the soil,
Sow the seed, and reap the harvest with enduring toil,
Storing yearly little dues of wheat, and wine and oil;
Till they perish. . . .

Often, indeed, Chekhov's characters are lotos-eaters themselves.

Mood, then—what the Russians called *nastroénie*—seems often the ultimate effect of his dramas; as also of his tales. For even his characters, though more important than the plot, have about them nothing dominating or decisive. Chekhov has left us no Clytemnestra, no Hamlet, no Brand or Peer Gynt; no demon, even, like the Laura of Strindberg's *Father*. His plays and stories are memorable, rather, for their total atmosphere—the muted melancholy and irony that hang over the lake of *The Seagull*, over the sombre forests round Uncle Vanya's hopeless home, over the dusty provincial streets of *The Three Sisters*, or the bridal whiteness of the blossoming Cherry Orchard before its final fall.

It was shrewdly remarked by de Tocqueville that in a democratic society the poets, no longer believing in great actions by great men, tend to concentrate rather on mere moods, feelings, and impressions. For these can be felt by characters far from heroic; even by the humblest. Hence, perhaps, the tyrannical predominance of lyric in modern poetry; and the tendency of modern literature to become excessively, indeed unhealthily, subjective and introspective—the unheroic musings of nonentities, the meditations of marionettes, the antics of *little* men. Romantic tempest and earthquake have yielded place to still, small voices—often to mere squeaks.

In the same way the plays of Chekhov are not a-glitter with stars; what remains is misty twilight on flowery steppe, or autumn woodland, or wintry snowfield, amid the brooding immensities of Russia. Both the later Ibsen and Chekhov are profound poets disguised in prose. Their successors have often failed because they were *not* poets, not even hidden poets, but merely prosy; because they neither possessed characters, nor produced them; being mere puppet-pullers in this modern age that, with its scientific and industrial wizardry, its artistic barbarisms, its spawning over-population, suggests at times a Twilight of the Dwarfs and Gnomes, a Pandemonium of pygmies.

In many ways Stanislavsky may have misunderstood, and misinterpreted, and irritated Chekhov; but at least in this one important respect author and producer remained united—in seeking, not overpowering figures that bestride the stage, but rather the total effect of a whole troop of human beings, working in all their diversity, as a united team, to build up a general impression, by simple, scrupulous truthfulness of speech and gesture, of setting and stage-effects—a kind of artistic collectivism; a kind of communism that is *not* barbarous.

Ivánov
(produced 1887)

'For I have lost the race I never ran.'
HARTLEY COLERIDGE

Between 1887 and 1901 Chekhov altered this repeatedly. Seven revisions exist. Here it will suffice to deal with its final form. For it seems not a very good play—its main interest is historical, as a stage in Chekhov's development.

Its hero, Nicholas Ivánov, is a country gentleman of thirty-five, whose youth had been fired with idealism and enterprise. But, the author wrote to Suvórin (30/12/1888), 'Russian idealism possesses one specific quality—it is quickly followed by fatigue'. No such tendency to swift fatigue has been conspicuous in the Soviet Union. But in the Russia of the nineteenth century it seems to have been often all too true.

In such a state of nervous exhaustion a man drifts, with brief spasms of resurgence, ever downward. Ivánov is like an athlete who has permanently overstrained his back. He is crippled like Hamlet—that character as deeply interesting to Chekhov as to Turgenev (who even wrote an essay unfavourably contrasting the impotent Prince of Denmark with the at least active Don Quixote).[1]

Five years ago, when still a buoyant idealist, Ivánov fascinated a Jewish girl, Sarah Abramson, so that she forsook her rich parents and her faith, like another Jessica, to marry him. But her angry parents cast off the renegade 'Anna', as she now called herself; she grew consumptive; and for the last year Ivánov has succumbed to fits of melancholy during which he finds the poor woman's presence unendurable. He was not, Chekhov passionately insisted, *always* a hopeless character—he has *become* one, under the stress of exhaustion, boredom, loneliness, financial worry, and emotional conflicts.

---

[1] See note on p. 42.

Act I[1]

Ivánov, now practically bankrupt, sits reading at a table, in a melancholy dusk where the owls will soon be hooting. But his peace is brief. His drunken estate-manager, Borkin, tiptoes in from the garden and jestingly points a gun at Ivánov's face—a fore-shadowing of the play's end.[2]

Ivánov is not amused. And the pair proceed to quarrel over the workmen who cannot be paid, and over the hare-brained schemes of Borkin to raise money. Then Ivánov is further exasperated by the arrival of his decadent old uncle, Shabelsky, whose one con-solation in life lies in pronouncing mankind to be either fools or knaves; and of his wife's doctor, the young Lvov, who pesters Ivánov with angry warnings that Anna's very life depends on her removal to the warmer climate of the Crimea. Ivánov fully realizes that this is true. It tortures him with guilt. But he has become, as it were, depersonalized—as helpless to lift a finger as a man lost in a nightmare.

> The sum of it is, my dear Doctor—(*hesitates*)—that, in a word, when I married her, I was passionately in love, and swore to love her always, but—well, after five years, she loves me still, but I—(*waves his hands*). Now you tell me she will soon die; and I feel neither love nor pity, only a sort of weariness and indifference. To anyone else it must seem horrible; what is happening to me, I don't myself understand.

Indeed Ivánov so suffocates in his dismal home that now he cannot bring himself to forgo an evening visit to his neighbours and creditors, the Lébedievs, despite the appeals of his lonely and suffering wife. (One may recall Boswell leaving his consumptive Margaret, or Rossetti leaving *his* consumptive Lizzie Siddal, for evenings of amusement in London.)

[1]

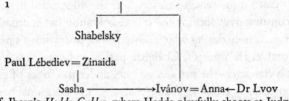

Shabelsky

Paul Lébediev = Zinaida

Sasha ⟶ Ivánov = Anna ← Dr Lvov

[2] Cf. Ibsen's *Hedda Gabler*, where Hedda playfully shoots at Judge Brack with the pistol that she will finally use to kill herself.

ACT II

The Lébedievs are having a party. A drab affair. For the wife,
Zinaida, is a comic miser. Paul, the husband, drinks. And their
guests are equally third-rate—concerned only to chatter of lottery-
tickets, to wrangle over cards, or to backbite their neighbours'
characters. At this very moment, as it happens, they are maliciously
busy with the character of Ivánov himself. But the Lébedievs'
daughter, Sasha—the party is in honour of her twentieth birthday—
bursts into passionate defence of the absent victim. A moment
later—enter Ivánov.

Soon the bored guests troop out to fireworks in the garden. Left
alone with Sasha, the weary, unheroic hero pours out to her his
domestic miseries, tied to a sick wife he can no longer love. Sasha's
consolation is highly practical—she throws herself at his head.

At first, in dismay, Ivánov begs her to be silent. Then he grows
bewitched. He dreams of growing young again. But meanwhile the
lonely Anna has forced her Dr Lvov, despite the cold night air, to
bring her too to the party. She walks in from the garden just in time
to see Sasha in her husband's arms. She faints. (At this date Chekhov
was still ready to employ 'strong curtains'—in contrast to those
muted endings that he later came to prefer.)

ACT III

A fortnight has passed. Sent by his stingy Zinaida, Lébediev comes
to dun Ivánov for what he owes them. But Ivánov cannot pay; and
Lébediev, touched with pity for his old student-friend, offers to pay
the sum himself, without Zinaida's knowledge. Ivánov refuses.

Then reappears Dr Lvov. This honest prig, underbred and over-
bearing, is the louder in his righteous indignation for being himself
in love with Anna. Again he curses Ivánov for killing his wife with
neglect. Ivánov in reply is as full of guilt as a Communist in a
Russian purge. But he cannot, cannot change his ways.

Next, by a backway (to avoid Anna), enter Sasha, handsome in
her riding-dress. She reproaches Ivánov for a fortnight's absence;
and it grows clear that this passionate young girl is really one of
those masterful, maternal women who like setting themselves to

reform rakes or moral cripples. For to reform is to dominate. And power is what, like Chaucer's Wife of Bath, they most desire.

Ivánov. . . . My antics are absurd enough to make anyone die of laughter—and *you* want to play guardian-angel. . . . Do you actually think it worse to be wife of a strong man with courage, than nurse to some whimpering failure?

Sasha. Yes, it *is* worse. . . . Any girl would rather love a failure than a man who succeeds, because every girl wants her own love to be *active.* A man has his work. . . . But, for *us*, love is life.

Then she takes her leave—'Well, God bless you! You must forget me altogether. In two weeks you must send me a line, and I shall be content with that. But I shall write to you——'

One may be sure she will. What feminine logic! 'You must forget me—we must correspond.' The play is wrecked if poor Sasha is misinterpreted as a noble young heroine. She is a sort of girlish vampire; endowed with far too much will, as Ivánov with far too little.

But Ivánov's wife, the sick Anna, has glimpsed Sasha stealing away. She bursts in on her husband in fury; and there follows one of those hideous exchanges where jealousy can make even civilized people ugly, mean, and cruel. She taxes Ivánov with being faithless, thankless, fraudulent, mercenary. Now he is coquetting with Lébediev's daughter just to shirk paying his debts. At this unfair calumny even Ivánov's weakness suddenly flares into fury—'Hold your tongue, Jewess!' Again she taunts him. And his retort becomes horrible—'Then realize that you are dying! The doctor has told me—you are dying!' Anna collapses in horror.

Ivánov (clutching his head with both hands). . . . Oh, how guilty I am! How guilty!

Again the strong curtain, so unlike the later Chekhov.

Act IV

An evening a year later. Already the grass is growing over poor Anna. But tonight the house of the Lébedievs is lively with guests in full dress. For Ivánov is wedding his Sasha. The act opens with a raging soliloquy of the self-righteous Dr Lvov, more infuriated than ever—'Failing to rob Sarah, he has tortured her to death. And now he has found another victim to dupe, until he has robbed *her*.' As others enter, it grows clear that seldom was a wedding less gay. For Lébediev is against it; his miserly Zinaida is inconsolable as a bereaved Rachel, at the thought of all the dowry to be disgorged; and even Sasha has misgivings at Ivánov's coldness. Then, against the strict Russian convention that the groom must not see his bride on his wedding-day before the actual wedding, Ivánov himself bursts in. (In real life Tolstoy, tortured by like doubts, had committed the like impropriety.)

> Listen!—as I was dressing just now for the wedding, I looked in the glass and saw how my temples were grey. Sasha, this must not happen! Let's end this mad comedy, before it is too late.

Then, while Ivánov, Sasha, and Lébediev are wrangling and wringing their hands, once more Dr Lvov charges in—'Nicholas Ivánov, I denounce you before the world as a cad!'

Sasha turns on this meddler in fury. But Ivánov has had enough. 'Wait a moment. I'll soon end it all. My youth is awake in me again; the former Ivánov is here once more.' He pulls out a revolver, runs off, and shoots himself.

Little wonder that the first-night audience in Moscow was lost in bewilderment. The play's chief interest today lies in the violent contrast it presents to Chekhov's later and finer work. For *Ivánov* is still close to conventional melodrama; particularly in the way that at the end of each act, as Chekhov put it, 'I give the spectator a punch on the nose'. Act I closes with Anna's sudden impulse to follow her husband to the party; Act II, with her discovery of Sasha in his arms; Act III, with Ivánov's exasperated revelation to his wife that she is doomed; Act IV, with his own exasperated suicide.

We are still remote from the later Chekhov whose theme was to become the strange importance of little, humdrum, haphazard things, the deep meanings of what seems meaningless; whose vision pierces the grey disguises of the passing day; whose keen ear seems to listen to the grass growing on the fields—and on the graves—of human life.

As he himself wrote: 'After all, in real life people don't spend every minute shooting each other, hanging themselves, and making declarations of love.[1] They don't spend all their time saying clever things. . . . Life must be exactly as it is, and people as they are—not on stilts. Let everything on the stage be just as complicated, and at the same time just as simple, as in life. People eat their dinners, just eat their dinners, and all the time their happiness is being established, or their lives destroyed.'

But *Ivánov* is still prentice work. Though it contains more than enough of trivial talk, melodrama it largely remains. Its plot seems to me mediocre; its hero a bore; its other characters unsympathetic; its crises lacking in real tension. For it is hard to care much what becomes of these dreary, futile, rather vulgar people. Why trouble to meet on the stage persons just as dull as those of real life? Why go to the theatre for talk as tedious as tea-parties? From drama or novel we want, unless we are merely killing time (which is stupid), something made to seem, underneath, more significant, more real than the transient trivialities of every day.

What did Chekhov mean *Ivánov* to mean? In early days he had taken, like Ibsen, the line that it was a writer's business merely to formulate questions, not to answer them—answers to his problems the public must find for themselves, like a jury at a trial.

And yet, as years pass, Chekhov makes his intentions clearer. Presumably he came to see that, however impartially a writer may present his facts, still by the very facts he chooses, by the very events he selects, he cannot help implying his own scale of values. For example, naturalistic and dispassionate though Flaubert tried to be in *Madame Bovary*, none the less, in fact, few tracts have ever pointed a more telling moral—'Beware of false, day-dreaming romance!'

Naturally, however, the first audiences of *Ivánov* were left groping in a fog. Were they to sympathize with the tortured Ivánov, or with

[1] Compare Byron: 'I can never get people to understand that . . . there is no such thing as a life of passion any more than a continual earthquake. . . . Besides who would ever shave themselves in such a state?'

the resolute young Sasha, or with the pathetic Anna and the right-
eously indignant Lvov? But, for us, in the light of Chekhov's letters
and later works, it becomes far clearer what he meant. Compassion
for human weakness in general did not alter, for him, the blunt and
simple facts that Lvov is a pharisaical prig, 'cliché incarnate', seeing
all men as either saints or scoundrels; Sasha, a man-hunting and
man-driving young Amazon; Anna, hysterical; Ivánov, a demoral-
ized intellectual.

Shakespeare, I believe, felt liking and sympathy for Hamlet,
however paralysed by the collapse of his maternal ideal. Few but
critics would dream of doubting that. But Chekhov shows in the
play little sympathy for Ivánov (though so clearly a descendant of
Hamlet); or for Ivánovs in general. He saw in them a type of
weakling dangerously common in the Russia of his day.

'Excessive excitability,' he writes (with a good deal of exaggeration), 'the sense of guilt, weariness, are purely Russian.' Similarly
in 1889 he expressed his irritation with so-called 'advanced' authors
of his day—'they make France degenerate, and in Russia they help
the devil to beget *the woodlice and molluscs we call "intellectuals"*.
The drowsy, apathetic, lazily philosophizing, cold intelligentsia . . .
who have no love of country . . . who refuse to marry and rear
children and so on.'

The object of his plays (though often misinterpreted by Stanislavsky) was, Chekhov said, 'to make people realize *how bad and
boring were their lives*'.[1] It would be hard to speak more clearly.
Ivánov, then, is not so much a sympathetic hero, as merely a
drunken Helot. Fine he may have been once; but fine he has long
ceased to be.

Yet why, asks the Western reader, if Chekhov was himself so
feverishly active, and wished to make others so, did he continue,
year after year, to fill both his stories and his plays with whole
processions of Ivánovs? The ineffectual Konstantin in *The Seagull*

---

[1] Turgenev, another creator of will-less types, gave the same verdict—'He
should deem himself happy who has not lost faith in goodness and the power
of the will, and keeps a taste for action.' 'What platitudes!' some may cry.
But often life's main truths *are* platitudes; only, because so unpleasant, they
are constantly forgotten; and therefore in constant need of re-utterance.

shoots himself like Ivánov; the ineffectual Uncle Vanya, after shooting at (and of course missing) his pedant of a brother-in-law, relapses at the play's end into the same melancholy frustration with which he began; at the close of *The Three Sisters* all three women are not an inch nearer their longed-for Moscow; the owners of the beloved Cherry Orchard cannot lift a finger to save it—and it falls.

A strange contrast to the Napoleonic energy that pulses in the heroes of Balzac or Stendhal.

Now one or two drunken Helots may be effective; but why, one must ask, do whole queues of them thus droop their way across the stage of Chekhov?

No doubt the explanation is partly historic. Such flabby molluscs, such 'superfluous men', were, in fact, all too common in the Russia of Turgenev and Chekhov. And for this there were special historic reasons. Not only was Tsarist Russia a Bastille of half-oriental tyranny, all the more stifling for being next-door to a free Europe. Not only was Russia a prison and, at that, a prison rat-ridden and worm-eaten with corruption and incompetence. In addition, Russia had become still more depressing because liberal stirrings had repeatedly recurred, only to be crushed out, again and again, by ruthless reaction. Catherine the Great had been influenced by the Enlightenment; yet the French Revolution frightened her back, and she put away her bust of Voltaire. Alexander I had dreamed of liberal ideals; yet he became a pillar of the Holy Alliance. The 1825 conspiracy of the Decembrists was followed by the insane despotism of Nicholas I. After the Crimean War Alexander II again moved towards reform. But in 1881 this emancipator of the serfs was rewarded with a bomb; and yet again autocracy returned. Indeed autocracy was to persist until the abortive Revolution of 1905 (only twelve years before the great upheaval of 1917) brought yet another false dawn of freedom; to be followed yet once more by the gloom of fresh repression. 'Hope deferred maketh the heart sick.' Just because the sixties in Russia had raised new hopes with the emancipation of the serfs, and other reforms, it was only natural and inevitable that the eighties should become all the more deeply disillusioned.

But this historic explanation may not be the whole story. Even if paralysed intellectuals *had* become so common in Chekhov's

Russia, one still asks why Chekhov himself, who was by no mea ns a paralysed intellectual, but hated and despised them, should yet have been so fond of portraying such human marsh-mallows. Shakespeare created Hamlet; but he created also Fortinbras and Othello and Macbeth. Beside his wavering Richard II he set also the resolute Henry V and Hotspur. Ibsen, again, might depict prevaricators like Peer Gynt and Hjalmar Ekdal; but he depicted also the drive and energy of Brand and Rebecca West. Or think of the infinite variety of characters in Balzac. Why, then, did Chekhov continue to mobilize—or immobilize—these stage-armies of hollow men? Why does so much of his strength lie in vividly depicting human weakness?

One may wonder if the reason was not partly, also, that Chekhov felt a touch of their malady in himself; though in himself he cured it, partly by writing it out of him (just as Goethe, instead of commit-ing suicide, made his Werther commit it, and broke the spell of women who too much haunted him by embalming them in books); and partly by a deliberate effort of 'over-compensation' (as the stammering Demosthenes made himself in the end a master-orator).

It is worth noting that both Chekhov's elder brothers had actu-ally sunk into tippling ineffectuals. 'It's impossible,' he writes of his brother Nikolai,[1] 'to find anyone more of a balalaika-hound. . . . A good, vigorous Russian talent is going to the dogs.' And his brother Alexander, twice married, twice proved a hopeless husband. Even Anton himself, despite his tireless labours, yet had moods when he could exclaim—'I believe that real happiness is impossible without idleness. For me the greatest delight is to walk, or sit, or do nothing.' And again—'Life disagrees with philosophy, there is no happiness without idleness; only the useless is pleasurable.' Like his Trigórin, he was never happier than when quietly fishing.

Both in love and in life, indeed, Chekhov had perhaps a dual temperament—on the one hand, the eager energy of the West; but on the other the disillusioned quietism of some Asiatic minds. Constantly though he overworked, he could yet write to Suvórin in May, 1889: 'In this world, it is indispensable to be indifferent.

---

[1] In a photograph of the two brothers Nikolai looks a curiously ugly, spectacled owl, in contrast to the strikingly handsome young Anton.

Only indifferent characters are capable of seeing things clearly, capable of being just, and working. . . . In me, the flame burns with indolence and uniformity, without sudden flare-ups. That is why it never happens to me to write three or four sheets[1] in a night or, carried away by my work, not to go to bed as soon as I am sleepy. And that is why I commit neither notorious follies nor actions of remarkable intelligence. . . . I lack passion.'

Always, in trying to understand Chekhov's moods, views, and attitudes, there remains the difficulty that there are so many of them. The critic is wrestling with Proteus. But it seems clear that there was, as well as the energetic Chekhov, an indolent Chekhov. And in portraying so many human oysters, Chekhov may also, in part, have been sitting in judgement, like Ibsen, on one side of himself. But, if so, it was a side of himself that he sternly disciplined. The oyster laboured and brought forth pearls.

However that may be, *Ivánov* remains, despite all its revisions, a far less satisfactory play than its successors. Apart from other things, its characters and atmosphere seem commoner; as if Chekhov had still not quite squeezed out of him, to use his own image, the blood of the serf.

Even its style appears less distinguished—too wordy and repetitive; hard though it remains, if one does not know Russian, to judge from translations.[2] It is a play that can be saved only by

---

[1] Presumably in the printer's sense of the word (for example, in an octavo book, a 'sheet' = 16 pages).

[2] Constance Garnett's version of Chekhov's stories seem to me at least to read admirably; but with this and other plays of his she is, I think, less happy. There are too many needless words; and too many sentences that tail off with phrases of no importance. The reader or hearer sees them coming. Therefore his interest flags—he ceases to listen with tiptoe eagerness and zest. In any good style, I believe, the sentences are so ordered as to bring the emphasis, quite naturally, on the words that are really emphatic. But this is particularly vital on the stage.

'The players, Sir,' growled Johnson, 'have got a kind of rant, with which they run on, without any regard to accent or emphasis.' Garrick himself could say, it appears, 'I will speak *daggers* to her; but use *none*', instead of 'I will *speak* daggers to her; but *use* none'. (Boswell's *Johnson*, ed. Birkbeck Hill, I, 168; V, 127.)

Again, Marian Fell's versions of Chekhov plays seem to me often too bookish; those of Elisaveta Fen and others often too wordy, or too fond of

excellent acting; in the hands of well-meaning English amateurs it can acquire tedium intolerable.

In fine, it has seemed worth dwelling at length on *Ivánov*, only because it is Chekhov's, and something of a landmark in his career.[1]

---

slang, such as 'loony-bin' for 'asylum'. This seems hardly appropriate to an author who explicitly condemned 'rough, clumsy words found only in colloquial speech'.

[1] When performed at St Petersburg in 1889 it was said to have driven one young man to suicide; but this is no great proof of merit.

The Seagull
(produced 1896)

'Enfin, mon conseil permanent est celui-ci: *voulez*! . . . Ne soyez pas lâche envers vous! Mais non, vous caressez votre douleur comme un petit enfant chéri que l'on allaite et qui vous mord la mamelle. J'ai passé par là et j'ai manqué en mourir. Je suis un grand docteur en mélancholie. Vous pouvez me croire.'

(FLAUBERT to MLLE LEROYER DE CHANTEPIE, 11/7/1858.)[1]

This play, when first acted at Petersburg in 1896, inadequately rehearsed and insensitively cut, proved a dismal fiasco. The critics were mercilessly malevolent—'a shocking, unheard-of scandal'— 'decadent weariness'—'every act exuded terrible boredom'. True, subsequent nights went better. But after five performances the play stopped. This new wine had burst the crude old bottle of Russian stage-tradition. Chekhov must wait for the new style of Stanislavsky and the Moscow Art Theatre.

Konstantin Stanislavsky (1863-1938), son of a rich Moscow business-man, had early developed a passion for amateur drama. In 1885 and 1890 Moscow was visited by a German theatrical company belonging to the Duke of Saxe-Meiningen. The Meiningers (who had enjoyed marked success in staging Ibsen) pursued, in a rather pre-Raphaelite way, both naturalism and simplicity. They also stressed team-work, as against the dominance of stars. 'Im Ganzen, da sitzt die Macht.'[2] From them Stanislavsky learnt much. At the first night of his production of *The Seagull* everything, it is said, seemed so natural, quiet, and unstrained that 'the audience felt

---

[1] 'In fine, my permanent advice is—Will!...Do not be cowardly towards yourself. But no!—you fondle your grief like a little darling child that one nurses—and it bites your breast! I have been through all that, and it nearly killed me. I am a specialist in melancholy. You can believe me.'

[2] 'In the *whole*, there lies the power.'

almost embarrassed at being there—as if they were eavesdropping, or peeping through a window'.[1]

To carry out his dramatic principles, Stanislavsky had founded in 1888 a Society for Art and Literature, which included a group of amateur actors. In 1897 he met the novelist and dramatist Nemiróvich-Dánchenko, who shared his views. With Russian vitality the two men talked for eighteen hours on end (from 2 p.m., 22/6/1897, to 8 a.m. next day). Out of their decision to join forces arose the Moscow Art Theatre.

As a beginning, in October 1898, after a whole summer of rehearsals in a country barn, they put on Alexey Tolstoy's *Tsar Fyodor Ioannóvich*. Success was immediate. Then, after much pleading, Nemiróvich-Dánchenko got permission to do *The Seagull* from the reluctant Chekhov, in whose memory there still rankled the laughter and booing of the Petersburg disaster, which had made him vow to write no more for the stage, 'were I to live seven hundred years'.

Stanislavsky, more classical in his dramatic tastes, did not at first regard the play with much favour. 'The characters seemed to him half-and-half.' But after working on the *mise-en-scène* he too warmed to characteristic enthusiasm. And Chekhov, visiting a couple of rehearsals in September, 1898, was surprised and charmed by the young actors' culture. They might not be great artists; but they were youthful, fresh, and keen. And yet he was also (most justifiably) alarmed by Stanislavsky's passion for minute and multitudinous realism—barking dogs, croaking frogs, chirping grasshoppers. As Chekhov tellingly remarked, it would not improve a picture to stick on a painted face a real nose.

Further, there was Chekhov's delicate health. In November, 1898, he had a five-day haemorrhage; in December, his sister Mary went and begged Nemiróvich-Dánchenko to postpone the performance. For she feared that a repetition of the Petersburg failure might kill her brother. Luckily she was too late.

On December 17, 1898, the play was performed. A tense moment for the whole company as well as for the author. *Tsar Fyodor* had,

---

[1] One may be reminded of similar tributes to the naturalness and sincerity of the acting in Dublin's Abbey Theatre.

indeed, been a great success. But that was a historical costume-play, elaborately spectacular. Could they hope the like from this grey contemporary drama, dependent on the most delicate nuances of meaning and mood? And with *The Seagull* they must do or die; for *Tsar Fyodor* had been followed by five failures.

The sequel was strikingly Russian in its emotionalism. From the start the actors were tense with anxiety; when the curtain fell on Act I, they listened behind it to a deathly silence in the audience. One actress swooned. Olga Knipper, who was playing Arkádina, burst into hysterical weeping. In a mute stupor the cast began slinking off the stage—till suddenly there burst from the unseen auditorium a thunderous tumult of applause.

'After the third act,' wrote Nemiróvich-Dánchenko to Chekhov, 'the mood behind the scenes was one of intoxication. Someone said very truly that it was just like an Easter morning. Everybody was exchanging kisses with everybody else, everybody was throwing himself on everybody's neck.'

Similarly Stanislavsky: 'Everybody kissed everybody else; even perfect strangers who forced their way back-stage. Someone writhed on the floor in a fit of hysteria. Many, myself included, were so overjoyed that they threw themselves into a wild dance.'

And according to a correspondent of Chekhov's, 'at the end (I tell you this in dead earnest) it was quite possible to walk up to a lady you did not even know, and remark "Well! What a play, eh?" '

Indeed, it must all have made a spectacle as remarkable as the play itself.[1]

In memory of this fateful first night of Chekhov's play, a seagull became the permanent emblem of the Moscow Art Theatre. It appeared on programmes, curtain, attendants' uniforms. When the company came to London in 1958, the symbolic bird was still there. And yet, reading *The Seagull*, one may find these wild ecstasies a

---

[1] One need hardly add that Russian audiences have very different standards of emotion from ours. We hear, for instance of the famous actress Kommis-sarevskaya (who also played Nina in the first, Petersburg performance of *The Seagull*) being on one occasion recalled by her weeping audience no less than fifty times. Finally she appeared in hat and coat. 'Don't go! Don't leave us!' cried the spectators. 'I am yours,' she replied, weeping. And ladies swooned.

little astonishing. An interesting and moving play—yes; but quite
so wonderful? It seems clear that the delirious enthusiasm of that
night in 1898 was aroused in large part, not by the novel strangeness
of the play alone, but by its combination with a new type of staging
and acting.

The Seagull might have for sub-title *The Egoists*; or, *Of Human
Loneliness*; or, *Artistic Vanity and the Vanity of Art*. For such are
its themes. It is about lonely people, unhappy in love, and making
others unhappy; obsessed with art, yet unconsoled by it.

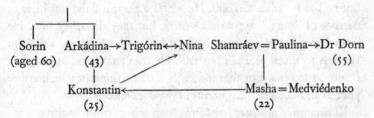

In the original version it was made clear at the close of Act I
that Masha was really the daughter of Dr Dorn. But this theme of
her illegitimacy was never developed; and Chekhov was later
persuaded to excise it.

The plot is built on a whole series of triangles—but triangles
unlike those of Euclid, in that all their angles are both acute and
obtuse.

First, Paulina, wife of the estate-manager Shamráev, is in love
with the not unkindly, but bleak Dr Dorn, aged fifty-five.

Secondly, Masha, Paulina's daughter, aged twenty-two, loves
Konstantin, who is indifferent to her; she marries the poor schoolmaster Medviédenko; whom she then callously neglects.

Thirdly, Konstantin, loving both his mother, who is a cold egoist,
and Nina, who flings herself at his mother's lover, loses the only
two women that matter to him in the world.

Finally, Trigórin betrays his mistress Arkádina for the young
Nina; tires of Nina, and betrays her; only to return, or be dragged
back, to the feet of Arkádina.

In short, lots of highly sensitive, but futile persons, living in a
dank, stuffy little jungle, mutually devouring and being devoured.

As Chekhov himself drily put it (to Suvórin), the play contains 'landscape (a lake), a lot of talk about literature, little action, and five poods[1] of love'.

Konstantin Trepliev, the hero, like Ivánov, is another Russian Hamlet. Indeed he and his mother both quote Shakespeare's play. For Konstantin's mother, like Queen Gertrude, has kindled her son's lasting resentment by taking a lover; and Konstantin's own love, Nina, fails him even more disastrously than Ophelia failed Hamlet.[2]

Konstantin remains, indeed, a little less ineffectual than Ivánov. But he too is rather a rabbit. He writes a play; it fails, and he is in frenzies of despair. He writes stories; but they dissatisfy him. He loves Nina; but she deserts him for her mother's lover, Trigórin. He tries to shoot himself; but fails. He tries again; and at last, like Ivánov, succeeds. But that indeed is the one thing in which either poor Ivánov or poor Konstantin ever does succeed.

Konstantin's mother, Arkádina, is an actress of forty-three, with all the grasping self-absorption of some ageing actresses—in Chekhov's own words, 'a foolish, mendacious, self-admiring egotist'. She is ruthlessly possessive about *her* money, *her* successes, *her* dresses, *her* lover (who, one feels, is in fact merely one more of her elegances). She has no time to read her son's stories. She is callously ironic about her son's play. She is jealous of her son's beloved, Nina; seeing in her, first, a potential rival on the stage, as her son's heroine; and, soon, an actual rival, as her lover's mistress. But, being the one strong-willed character among all these weaklings, Mlle Arkádina ends, as she began, not only as Trigórin's mistress, but also as complete mistress of Trigórin. She is not

[1] Russian weight=about 36 lb.: 5 poods= 13 stone.
[2] Chekhov's letters, it is said, contain more allusions to Shakespeare than to all other literary classics put together. There are also frequent quotations from him in Chekhov's works. In 1887 he planned a one-act skit on *Hamlet*; in 1891 he wrote *A Moscow Hamlet*. Compare too his story *The Duel*: 'My indecision reminds me of Hamlet, thought Laevsky on the way. How truly Shakespeare describes it! Ah how truly!'

On the other hand, parallels between *Hamlet* and *The Seagull* should not be overstressed. Trigórin, Arkádina, Nina, even Konstantin, are not much like their Shakespearian counterparts. And, except for writers of dissertations, it might well prove tedious if they were.

wholly without feelings—indeed she is only too full of them; but they are so centred on her own beauteous self that there is little left over for the rest of humanity.[1]

On Trigórin himself we are again lucky enough to have Chekhov's own verdict. Stanislavsky had begun, quite mistakenly, by picturing Trigórin as an aesthetic, dandiacal author of the nineties, in elegant white trousers and fancy beach-slippers. 'You act very well,' said Chekhov, in his terse, cryptic way, 'but that is not *my* character. *I* did not write *that*. . . . *My* character wears check trousers, and has holes in his shoes. . . . And he smokes a cigar *so*. . . .' Only later did the puzzled Stanislavsky fathom Chekhov's meaning—that Trigórin was really a rather dowdy person, who bewitched poor Nina, not by any glamour of personal appearance, but simply by that romantic halo which can so gloriously transfigure a successful writer in the fantasy of an idealizing girl.

Pure illusion. For Trigórin is not meant to be remarkable even as a writer. He is only a sort of minor Turgenev, who despite his successes honestly knows himself second-rate. His writing, however it may satisfy his public, does not satisfy *him*. It merely rides on his back as relentlessly as the Old Man of the Sea on Sinbad.

The adoring Nina may naïvely picture great writers as radiantly enthroned on beds of roses. But one of the most vivid and human passages in the whole play is Trigórin's opposite picture of the writer's galley-slavery. For here one seems to catch the disillusioned accents of Chekhov himself.

Nina. How wonderful the world is! If you only knew how I envy you! Men's fates are so different. Some people drag out dim, dreary, narrow lives, all alike, all unhappy; but others—like you, for instance—one in a million—find existences that are interesting, bright, happy—lives full of meaning, and worth while. You are *very* lucky!
Trigórin. I, lucky? (*He shrugs his shoulders.*) Hm. You talk of fame, and happiness, and bright, interesting lives; but all these fine words of yours mean as much to me (forgive my saying it) as sweetmeats—which *I* never eat. You are very kind, and very young.
Nina. But *your* life must be wonderful!

[1] Mme Arkádina is said to have been modelled (though such statements need to be treated with reserve), like the heroine of Chekhov's story *Ariadne*, on the actress Lydia Borissovna Yavorskaïa.

Trigórin. Must it? I see nothing particularly fine about it. (*He looks at his watch.*) Excuse me, I must go, and do some more writing. I am in a hurry. (*He laughs.*) You have stepped, as they say, on my pet corn; and I am getting excited, and a little cross. However—let us discuss this bright and beautiful life of mine. (*After a few moments' thought.*) There are obsessions that people get—for instance, a man may think, night and day, of nothing but the moon. Well, I too have such a moon. Day and night I am obsessed by one tormenting thought—that I must write, write![1] Hardly have I finished one book than, for some reason, I have to start another; then a third, a fourth—I write ceaselessly. And I cannot stop. Well, what is there bright and beautiful in *that?* . . . I look over there, and see a cloud shaped like a grand piano.[2] Instantly it occurs to me that I must remember to mention in some story a cloud floating by in the shape of a grand piano. Or I smell heliotrope; I mutter to myself: 'A sickly scent, a colour worn by widows; I must remember *that* in my next description of a summer evening. . . .' As soon as I stop work, I rush off to the theatre, or go fishing; and there at least I ought to be able to relax and forget. But no! Something like a heavy iron cannon-ball comes rolling through my brain—an idea for a new story. . . . I feel I am consuming my own life—that, to make honey for people whom I do not even know, I am brushing the bloom from my best flowers, tearing them from their stems, trampling on their roots. Am I not crazy? . . . As a beginner, the best years of my youth were made one continual torment for me. . . . I was mortally afraid of the public; and whenever a play of mine appeared, I felt as if all the dark-haired people in the audience were hostile[3]; and all the blond ones coldly indifferent. Oh, how terrible it was! What torment!

Nina. But doesn't your inspiration—the act of creation—give you moments of ecstatic happiness?

Trigórin. Yes. Writing *is* a pleasure to me; and so is reading the proofs; but no sooner is my book published than I find it odious.[4] I realize

---

[1] Compare Chekhov himself to Leeka Mizinov (27/3/1894): 'I am bored . . . because the thought never leaves me for a single minute that I am obliged—compelled—to write. To write, write, write. I hold the opinion that true happiness is impossible without idleness. My ideal is to be idle and love a plump girl.'

[2] Another distant echo of *Hamlet*.

[3] Compare Chekhov to Suvórin, of *Ivánov* (4/1/1889): 'the thought . . . that all the dark-haired people in the boxes will seem hostile, and all the blond ones cold and indifferent'.

[4] Cf. Montesquieu: 'J'ai la maladie de faire les livres, et d'en être honteux quand je les ai faits.' 'I have the malady of writing books, and then being ashamed when I have written them.' (Yet few writers have had less reason to be ashamed than Montesquieu.)

that it is not what I meant; that it's a mistake; that I should not have written it at all. I feel angry and depressed. Then the public reads it, and says: 'Yes, clever and charming; but a far cry from Tolstoy'; or 'It is a fine thing; but not as good as Turgenev's *Fathers and Sons.*' And, to my dying day, so it will always be. 'Clever and charming; clever and charming'—but nothing more. And when I'm dead, my friends will say, as they pass my grave: 'Here lies Trigórin, a good writer, but not so good as Turgenev'. . . . So I write about everything, always in a hurry, pushed from every side. People get angry with me; and I race and dodge like a fox, with a pack of hounds at his heels. I see life and knowledge forging ahead before me, while I drop behind, like a peasant running after his train; and I end by feeling that all I am fit for is to describe landscapes; and that in whatever else I write I am false to the marrow.

Nina. You have been overworking—you haven't the time, or the wish, to realize your own importance. What if you *are* dissatisfied with yourself? Others think you great and wonderful. If *I* were a writer like you, I should give my whole life to the service of the people; knowing at the same time that I should have them harnessed to my chariot.

Trigórin. A chariot! Do you think I am Agamemnon? (*They both smile.*)

Zola has put a strangely similar cry of exasperation against literary life into the mouth of the author Sandoz in his novel *L'Œuvre* (1886). One is reminded, too, of the old Ibsen, feeling that all his glory was mere vanity of vanities—a shadow for which he had sacrificed life's substance; and putting his disillusion, his regret for all the roses he had never gathered, into the mouth of the disenchanted Dr Rubek of *When We Dead Awaken* (1899).

But how vividly alive this Chekhov passage is!—real people, talking real talk, about a subject that is real. It is also a wonderful picture of Young Lady making up to Famous Artist. A vast advance on the futilities of *Ivánov.* Trigórin should not be mistaken for Chekhov himself. Nemiróvich-Dánchenko believed Trigórin was based on a real writer, facile and inferior, called Potapenko.[1] Yet much that Trigórin says in this particular passage *is* clearly an utterance of Chekhov's own feelings about writing; just as Trigórin's search for tranquillity in catching fish is also Chekhov's own.

An old-fashioned, classical critic would have objected to this long

[1] See p. 56.

discussion of literary sorrows as an episodic and irrelevant excrescence on the plot. But it is a typical example of Chekhov's interest in bringing a character to life, by simple human truth. Trigórin does live; and he *is* interesting. Naturally he is not the sort of person, nor are these speeches the sort of speeches, that you are likely to find in most fashionable dramatists. But Chekhov, to me, seems much more intelligently civilized.

Further, it is typical of life's ironic tragi-comedy that this second-rate writer, Trigórin, with his weak character, will yet be quite enough to wreck the lives of both Nina and Konstantin. Trigórin does not mean harm. He is merely an angler. His life's labour is to fish for ideas; and his only real happiness to fish, literally and much more lazily, for unfortunate little fishes. (One is moved to remember Johnson's description of angling—'a string with a worm at one end and a fool at the other'.) Trigórin is no fool. But he fishes. And if on his hook there throws herself a charming young girl. . . .

Act I

The opening words strike the note that is to prevail throughout. They strike it comically. But tragedy was never the worse for irony. Irony only deepens it.

Medviédenko. Why do you always wear black?
Masha. Because I am in mourning for my life. I am unhappy.

An encouraging young woman to woo! A wiser man than Medviédenko would at once have turned and fled. But this poor wretch can only enlarge on the greatness of his love, and the smallness of his salary.

Masha, for her part, vainly sighing for Konstantin, has acquired the habit of drugging her unhappiness with snuff; soon it will appear that she reinforces the snuff-box with the bottle also. A futile pair. But such pathetic futilities make up much of human life, much of the human race, and very much of Chekhov's plays.

This evening Konstantin's play is to be performed—for here, as in *Hamlet*, we have a play within the play. And now Konstantin enters with his maternal uncle of sixty, Sorin, one more of Chekhov's futile, yet not uncharming country-gentlemen.

Konstantin (straightening his uncle's cravat). Your hair and beard are all untidy. Shouldn't you have them trimmed or something?

Sorin (smoothing his beard). That's the tragedy of my life—my appearance. Even young, I always looked as if I drank, and so on. Women never liked me. (*Sitting down.*) Why is my sister in such a bad temper today?

Konstantin. Why? She is bored. (*Sitting down beside Sorin.*) And jealous. She is against me—and against the performance—and against my play, because *she* is not acting in it, and Nina *is.* She hasn't read my play; but all the same she hates it.

Sorin (laughing). Really! What an idea!

Konstantin. Yes, she is furious because on this little stage there is going to be a success for Nina, not for *her.* (*Looking at his watch.*) My mother is a psychological curiosity. Brilliant and gifted, no doubt; she can sob over a novel, recite all the poetry of Nekrasov by heart, or nurse the sick like a heavenly angel[1]; but see what happens if you start praising Duse![2] Oh no, no! She and she only must be praised, written about, raved about—and her marvellous acting in *La Dame aux Camélias* exalted to the skies. Because, here in the country, she cannot get all this flattery, she grows cross and peevish, and thinks we are all against her, and it's all our fault. And then she's superstitious—frightened of lighting three candles, terrified of the number thirteen. And she's mean. She has 70,000 roubles in an Odessa bank—that I *know.* But, just ask her for a loan, and she'll burst into tears.

Sorin. You've got it into your head that your mother dislikes your play; and the idea has upset you; and so. . . . Calm down; your mother worships you.

Konstantin (pulling off the petals of a flower). She loves me—loves me not. Loves me—loves me not. Loves me—loves me not. (*Laughing*)

[1] Curiously like the familiar lines of Scott's *Marmion*—

> O, woman! in our hours of ease,
> Uncertain, coy, and hard to please,
> And variable as the shade
> By the light quivering aspen made;
> When pain and anguish wring the brow,
> A ministering angel thou!

[2] Chekhov saw Eleonora Duse (1859-1924) in March, 1891, at Petersburg as Shakespeare's Cleopatra; and wrote that night to his sister that he had never seen anything like it (contrast his coldness towards the artificiality of Sarah Bernhardt). 'I kept looking at this Duse, and was harassed to the point of anguish to think that we have to exercise our temperaments and tastes on such wooden actresses as N. and her like, whom we call "great" because we have not seen any better. Watching Duse, I realized why one feels so bored in the Russian theatre.' (This passage was duly deleted by Soviet patriotism in the edition of 1944-51. See p. 127.)

You see! She does *not* love me. And why should she? She wants life—love—gay clothes; and I'm already twenty-five—a reminder that she is no longer young. When I'm away, she's only thirty-two; when I'm there, she's forty-three—and loathes me for it. And then she knows I despise the theatre. *She* adores it, and imagines herself working there for the good of humanity and the sacred cause of art; but to me the theatre is just prejudice and conventionality. When the curtain goes up on its artificially lighted little room with three walls; when those vast geniuses, those high-priests of sacred art, exhibit to us a lot of people eating, drinking, making love, walking about, and wearing clothes, and try to squeeze some cosy little domestic moral from their empty scenes and vapid talk; when I am offered, under a thousand different disguises, the same, same, same old stuff—then I just have to run from it, as Maupassant ran from the Eiffel Tower, which crushed him by its vulgarity.

Sorin. But we can't do *without* the theatre.

Konstantin. No. But we need new forms.

One begins to suspect that Konstantin (though he may be, in part, expressing Chekhov's views) is one of those frustrated young men who talk with endless disparagement of the established past, and in praise of some future revolution, when in fact the whole trouble lies in their own lack of talent.[1]

Now appears Nina, daughter of a neighbouring landowner. She creeps in stealthily, for her father and stepmother have forbidden her to go near this too Bohemian household. So she has merely darted over to act her part in Konstantin's play—then vanish again.

Now there gathers Konstantin's audience—his mother Arkádina, good-looking, ironic, resolved to be bored; her lover Trigórin; her old brother Sorin; Paulina, with her impassive lover, Dr Dorn; the unhappy Masha, with her despised lover, Medviédenko.

Konstantin's play is, I suppose, meant to seem decadently absurd; but still with that absurdity of the imaginative young at which it is cruel and callous to laugh. Yet Arkádina, though a mother, remains pitilessly callous.

The prologue is spoken by Nina, in white; impersonating the

[1] Chekhov had no use for novelty-mongers, trying to become original by being studiously eccentric. Compare his letter to Bunin: 'All this new Muscovite art is mere folly. I remember seeing at Taganrog a notice-board—"Establishment for Artificial Mineral Waters". It's the same thing. The only novelty is talent.'

world-soul of a creation whose life has now lain a thousand years extinct.

Men, lions, eagles, and partridges, horned stags, geese, spiders, dumb fishes that dwell in the waters, starfish and creatures no eye can see—all living things, all living things, all living things—their cycle of sorrow ended, are extinct.

By this point the Petersburg audience of 1896 were already rocking with contemptuous giggles.

Arkádina. It's something decadent.[1]
Konstantin (imploring and reproachful). Mother!

But when across the lake there appear two glowing points of red—the eyes of Satan, father of eternal matter—accompanied (as now in the latest type of olfactory cinema) by an infernal stench of sulphur, then Mlle Arkádina's scorn becomes so biting that her son in fury shouts to lower the curtain. Again as in *Hamlet*, the play within the play breaks off amid general tumult.

Sorin, Trigórin, and Dorn are all a little horrified by Arkádina's maternal callousness. Masha, agonized by the misery of her beloved Konstantin, only infuriates him still more by pursuing his flight about the park. Nina reappears for a moment and is introduced by Arkádina to her lover Trigórin; whom, for a brief while, Nina will bewitch. Then the curtain falls on Masha's despairing confession, to her mother's lover, Dr Dorn, of her own hopeless love for Konstantin.[2]

ACT II

It is noon, in the garden, a few days later. The moods of the characters flit and change before us like the dancing air of this summer heat—Arkádina, proud of looking younger at forty-three

---

[1] It may seem a little strange that Mlle Arkádina should hit on this particular term of abuse. Tolstoy would have judged her passably 'decadent' herself. Presumably a parrot-word that she has picked up. (We are here in the mid-nineties.)

[2] In the original version, it will be recalled, Dr Dorn was definitely her father.

than Masha at twenty-two; the old Sorin, sentimentally fond of the young Nina; Masha still woeful over the woes of Konstantin; Paulina, Masha's mother, jealously tearing in pieces the flowers innocently given by Nina to Dr Dorn, whom Paulina has just vainly begged to run away with her. (Dr Dorn, however, thinks fifty-five a little late for romantic elopements.) Then comes a key-scene. Konstantin enters with a gull he has just shot.

Konstantin. Today I was vile enough to kill this gull——I lay it at your feet.
Nina. What is the matter with you? (*She picks up the gull and stands gazing at it.*)
Konstantin (*after a pause*). Soon, in the same way, I shall kill myself.

A histrionic youth.

Women, says Konstantin, never forgive failure. (A foolishly sweeping generalization; one has only to contrast Chekhov's own Sasha, who loved Ivánov just because he *was* a failure.) Already Konstantin has burnt his play. Now he catches sight of the hated Trigórin, who approaches, deep in a book.

Here comes real genius, stalking like Hamlet—with a book too! 'Words, words, words'. . . . Look, this shining sun of yours is still miles away, but already you smile—your glance melts in his radiance. Good-bye—I won't be in your way.

Nina is indeed all too ready to adore the supposed genius. There follows the already quoted passage where Trigórin describes the trials and tribulations of a writer's life. Then he sees the shot seagull. Out pops the inevitable notebook.

Nina. What are you writing?
Trigórin. Oh, nothing. Just making a note. . . . An idea for a short story. A young girl has grown up by a lake, like you. She loves the lake, as gulls do—is free and happy like them. Then by chance comes a man, sees her and, for want of anything better to do, destroys her, like the seagull here.

An unconscious prophecy about himself and her. It can very well happen that a writer's works become unconsciously prophetic: for the Unconscious is at work alike in his books and in his life.

The curtain falls, as the musing Nina murmurs 'A dream!' Often, indeed, it is in a desert of dreams that Chekhov's characters seem to wander, with their gaze vainly fastened on mirage beyond mirage.

This symbolically slaughtered seagull recalls, of course, Ibsen's *Wild Duck*—yet only remotely. The gull had much closer antecedents in Chekhov's real life. In 1892 the painter Levitan,[1] visiting Chekhov at Melikhovo, wounded a woodcock. The poor bird, picked by Chekhov out of a puddle, gazed up at him with wondering eyes. Levitan begged him to put it out of its misery; and Chekhov forced himself to wring its neck. 'There,' he comments, 'was one beautiful, amorous creature less in the world; and two fools went home to supper.' (Chekhov, though a passionate angler, had a great tenderness for animals; and, when forced to trap mice, would release the creatures out of doors. Even for plucking flowers he shared the compassionate dislike of Walter Savage Landor.)

ACT III

A further week has passed. Konstantin has tried to shoot himself; but with no result beyond a wound in the head.

Here again, Chekhov was drawing on real life. In July, 1895, his friend Levitan, who had gone to paint in the Novgorod lake-district, tried to shoot himself (whether from melancholia or because of some love-trouble with his hostess); but likewise incurred only a wound in the head. Summoned by wire, Chekhov at once rushed to join him.

According to Mikhail Chekhov, there were further similarities. For Levitan likewise, 'during an explanation with the ladies', tore off his bandage; then went down to the lake, shot a gull, and threw it at his mistress's feet.[2]

[1] His picture *Haystacks in Moonlight* is said still to be in Chekhov's study at Yalta. It was empanelled under the mantelpiece.

[2] See D. Magarshack, *Chekhov*, p. 284. Chekhov had already, in 1892, drawn freely on Levitan's life for his story called *The Grasshopper* (from the fable of 'The Grasshopper and the Ant'), which has been excellently filmed. This tale contained vivid, but all too recognizable details from Levitan's liaison with Sophia Kuvshinnikov, the frivolous, pseudo-artistic wife of a

The desperate Masha, to cure herself of Konstantin, has now resigned herself to marry her poor schoolmaster. Konstantin, jealous of Trigórin, plans challenging him to a duel. But both these efforts to escape prove equally vain.

The now infatuated Nina enters and gives Trigórin a medallion as a parting remembrance of her; for he and Arkádina are about to leave. When Nina has gone, Trigórin finds engraved on the medallion the title of one of his own books, followed by a reference —'Page 121, lines 11 and 12'. At once he rushes out to look it up.

Sorin, entering with his miserly sister Arkádina, suggests to her that she should at least allow her son a little money to lead a life of his own. But of course she protests that her purse is empty. A moment later, Konstantin enters with his head bandaged. Sorin goes. As his mother prepares to dress his wound, Konstantin in his turn suggests that she should give at least old Sorin a little money, so that he can escape for a while to town, away from this country-side where he moulders. But of course the miserly mother again protests her poverty. Yet for a moment, as the actress in Arkádina gives place to the maternal nurse, Konstantin's childish love for her reawakens. All in vain. A moment later he is bitterly reproaching her with being Trigórin's mistress. She flares up; and he flings out of the room as Trigórin returns, reading to himself the passage referred to by Nina's medallion. It is a frank declaration of passion— 'If ever you need my life, come and take it.'

At once Trigórin begs Arkádina to postpone their departure, just for a single day. But with equal quickness she guesses his motive—Nina. He begs Arkádina to release him as lover; but she only storms—pleads—falls on her knees before him. Once more,

<hr>

police-surgeon, who would cry to her ill-used husband in front of her artistic coterie—'Dmitry Kuvshinnikov, let me shake your honest hand. Ladies and gentlemen, look what an honest face he has!' Exactly like Chekhov's heroine. The forty-two-year-old Mme Kuvshinnikov easily recognized her counter-part of twenty-two in Chekhov's story; was naturally angered; and made Levitan quarrel with Chekhov. (The break lasted over two years.) But *The Grasshopper* remains particularly fascinating for the way it shows the scientist in Chekhov grinding scornfully underfoot the snobberies of artists—and yet, in the very act, creating a work of art. One sees yet again how widening it was for him to be both artist and scientist in one.

in his weakness, Trigórin yields. Their carriage is at the door. The economical Arkádina bestows at parting on the cook a single rouble (say two shillings) to be shared with two other servants. A moment later Trigórin comes back, alone, for his walking-stick. There stands Nina, waiting. Her mind is made up—she will run away from home, and go on the Moscow stage. Hurriedly Trigórin gives her a Moscow address. The curtain falls on their parting kiss.

Behind this small incident of Nina's medallion lay a serious chapter in Chekhov's own life. In January, 1889, at Petersburg, he met Lydia Avílov, four years his junior, the not very happily married wife of a civil servant. Their mutual impression was immediate; and time, despite separation, only deepened it; though as yet, perhaps, it was hardly more than a dream. In any case the obstacles were daunting—Chekhov's conscience; his health; his difficulties in providing even for his own family. After his return from Sakhalín (whether or no he went there to forget her),[1] they met again at a party on January 1, 1892. But some lying tale-bearer made her husband furious. For privacy, Chekhov wrote letters to her 'poste restante'. When they met again (October, 1892?), she realized that she was definitely in love. We hear of two more meetings in February, 1895; the second, at her house, was ruined by the unexpected intrusion of two merciless bores. When these at last had gone, Chekhov recalled to Lydia their first encounters— 'Do you know I was deeply in love with you?' But he had felt that his love must remain Platonic. Next day she received his latest book of stories, dedicated 'To L. Avilov'.

At this point passion seems to have swept her away. Exactly like Nina in *The Seagull*, she sent Chekhov an engraved message. It was on a watch-chain pendant, in the shape of a book, which had on one side, 'Short Stories by Chekhov', on the other, 'Page 267, lines 6 and 7'. This reference was to a sentence in *Neighbours*:[2] 'If ever you need my life, come and take it' (exactly as in the play). But Chekhov was no Trigórin. He did not answer. Perhaps he had

---

[1] See p. 14.

[2] A melancholy story about a brother whose sister has gone off to live with a weak-kneed fool of an idealist, a married man separated from his wife. It is he who says to the brother: 'If ever you need my life . . .' Not a very encouraging picture of free love for Lydia Avílov to quote from.

cooled, or had resolved on renunciation. Indeed in a letter to Suvórin the following March (1895), he remarks that he could endure marriage in general only if his wife lived in Moscow and he himself in the country, with meetings merely at intervals.[1] 'For happiness which goes on day after day, from one morning to another, is something I shall find unendurable.'

In November, 1895, he finished the first draft of *The Seagull*. About the same time Lydia Avílov published a book dedicated to Chekhov—'To the proud master from his apprentice, L. Avílov.' In February, 1896, they met by chance at a masked-ball. But she was sure that he recognized her despite her mask. (Indeed this seems obvious.) He said his new play (*The Seagull*) would contain a message for her. At its disastrous first night (October 17, 1896) she naturally recognized as her own the message of Nina's medallion— 'If ever you need my life, come and take it.' But how odd!—the reference in Chekhov's play was different—not 'Page 267, lines 6 and 7', but 'Page 121, lines 11 and 12'. Looked up in Chekhov, the reference hardly made sense. But then it occurred to Lydia to look up her own book, *The Happy Man*. Result—'It is not proper for young ladies to go to masked balls.'

A piece of Chekhov's whimsical humour. It has been supposed that he meant to imply, 'We must give up all improper ideas of belonging to each other'; and that Nina's tragic fate was meant as a reinforcement of the same 'message'. But this interpretation seems to me a little laboured. It would not be a very gracious form of lover's farewell. Nor does Lydia Avílov seem to have taken it at all as a rebuff. Nor, even allowing for Chekhov's variable moods, is it easy to reconcile this supposition with what actually ensued.

In March, 1897, he arranged to meet her in Moscow. But, when she went, he was not at his hotel—he had been seized, that very evening, by a violent haemorrhage. With difficulty, she was allowed to see him in the clinic. Forbidden by his doctor to speak more than a few words, Chekhov scribbled a note asking her to bring his proofs, and something of her own for him to read; then added the Russian equivalent of 'I lo ... thank you very much'; then, with a smile, crossed out the 'lo'. Next day she saw him again, and

[1] See p. 18.

he begged her to come on the morrow. But she had been wired for by her husband. Just outside the hospital she met Tolstoy—a formidable apparition to one whose own thoughts had travelled so far down the road of Anna Karénina.

In the train to Petersburg she *says* she dreamed of walking with Chekhov by the sea. A little boy ran dancing happily towards them. But Chekhov screened her from the child, crying that there was blood on his mouth. 'We must throw him into the sea. But I can't.' (A symbol of Love, sealed with the fatal mark of Death?)

Yet their passion had now passed its climax. They still corresponded; but only as old friends. Chekhov's story *About Love* (1898), based on their relationship, hurt her because it was so brief, and because it seemed to write 'Finis'. Yet in 1899 she toiled gladly for him at digging his old stories from magazine-files, and trying to buy him a house in Moscow for his mother and sister. In May they again met briefly in a Moscow station. It was the last time. By now Olga Knipper had come into his life—the brief life that was left him. The love-story of Chekhov and Lydia Avílov remains a very typical Chekhov love-story, in its melancholy frustration and inconclusiveness.

In 1942 Lydia Avílov died, aged seventy-eight. Some years later appeared her brief book, *Chekhov in my Life*. By some Chekhov scholars it was greeted with a curious scepticism. For it disturbed their preconception of him as one whose heart had never been deeply involved with anybody. But Bunin, his junior by ten years, who had known and admired both him and Lydia Avílov, though surprised, was convinced. 'Biographers,' he decided, 'must reckon seriously with the memories of Mme Avílov.' Clearly her discretion does not tell the story completely. But it seems hard to doubt what tallies so well with other evidence.[1]

Yet this is not all. The unhappy romance of Nina and Trigórin had a further basis in actual fact. In 1888, through his sister Mary, Chekhov got to know Lydia ('Leeka') Mizinov, aged eighteen; an ash-blonde swan-princess so beautiful that people turned round in

---

[1] See L. Avílov, *Chekhov in my Life* (Eng. translation, 1950); D. Magarhack, *Chekhov* (1952); C. Wilczkowski, "Un Amour de Cechov" in *A. Čechov*, ed. T. Eekman (1960); and Chekhov's own story, *About Love*.

the street to look at her. By 1892 she had fallen vainly in love with him. In 1893 she became the mistress of Potapenko, a third-rate writer, whom Chekhov none the less found an amusing companion. With Potapenko she went off to France and Italy; had a child (which later died); and was deserted by her beloved (1894). That October Chekhov wrote to his sister Mary, 'Potapenko is a swine'. Yet he continued his friendship with both the lovers. Leeka too was at the disastrous first night of *The Seagull* (October 17, 1896) in Petersburg; and Potapenko visited him next morning. Later she married an actor and assistant-producer in the Moscow Art Theatre.

It will be seen that Chekhov's writings, like Ibsen's and Strindberg's, sometimes contain a lot, not only of life, but of real life.

ACT IV

The first three acts covered only a few days. But now comes a gap of two whole years. Indeed Act IV seems almost an epilogue.

The wind and rain of evening rattle the windows of the solitary house, and flap like a ragged banner the curtain of the derelict stage in its garden, where Konstantin's play, two years ago, found a grotesque and premature end. Konstantin has settled down to write mere magazine-stories, and to keep company with his old uncle Sorin, much feebler and frailer now. Masha has married her schoolmaster, Medviédenko, and borne him a son; yet loves him no better than before. Mme Arkádina, recently arrived to visit her sick brother, has gone to the railway-station to meet Trigórin. For after Nina had borne him a child, which died, Trigórin went back to his old mistress; leaving Nina to become a struggling actress on the provincial stage.

Trigórin and Arkádina arrive. The party sits down to a futile game of lotto, with talk no less futile; then troops out to supper. Konstantin, whom Trigórin's hated presence has robbed of all appetite, is left alone. A tap at the window. The lost Nina has returned. For a moment poor Konstantin's heart leaps up. But no, Nina still loves her faithless Trigórin; and still loves the stage. 'I am a real actress now. I enjoy acting. I revel in it. The stage intoxicates me. I feel I am—superb.' (One may doubt it.)

Then, after a last wild embrace, she darts away into the night. Konstantin tears up his manuscripts, and goes out. Returning from supper, the party resume their lotto, with tea, beer, and claret. Shamráev shows Trigórin in a cupboard the slaughtered seagull of long ago, now stuffed, as Trigórin had ordered. But Trigórin's memory of the whole affair is now a blank—'I don't remember a thing about it—not a thing'.[1] All passes, like reflections in a looking-glass.

Then a detonation.

Arkádina. What was that?
Dr Dorn. Oh nothing—something must have exploded in my medicine-chest.[2]

Dorn leaves the room; comes back; leads Trigórin to the front of the stage, on the pretext of discussing some magazine-article—and whispers: 'You must get Mme Arkádina away somehow. The fact is—Konstantin has shot himself.'

The most deliberately untheatrical of stage-suicides—the extreme opposite to Othello's gorgeous eloquence, or the frenzied dance-music before Hedda Gabler's end. Imagine Dolabella merely entering to tell Octavius—'Excuse me. But Cleopatra has just killed herself.' Curtain.[3]

Konstantin may be closer to those Greek heroines—Jocasta, Dejanira—who quietly withdraw to hang themselves. But, even so, their muted endings are not left to form the end and climax of a whole play.

Chekhov's is an effective novelty. But the method would hardly

[1] Compare the forgetfulness of the old Pontius Pilate at the end of Anatole France's story, *Le Procurateur de Judée*—'Jésus? murmura-t-il, Jésus, de Nazareth? Je ne me rappelle pas.' ('Jesus? he murmured, Jesus of Nazareth? I do not remember.')

[2] A detail destined to be curiously repeated in Chekhov's own last hour. As he lay dead at Badenweiler, says Olga Chekhov, 'the cork shot out of the champagne-bottle' (the last champagne he had drunk) 'with a report that sounded terrifyingly loud in the airless, silent gloom.'

[3] When Chekhov read *The Seagull* to friends in December, 1895, the theatre-manager Korsh was much dismayed by this ending.—'My dear fellow, but it isn't dramatic! You make your character shoot himself behind the scene, and don't even give him a chance of making a speech before he dies.'

bear much repetition; whereas, if Shakespeare is full of dramatic deaths and suicides, their variety yet remains infinite. Antony, Cleopatra, Lear, Hamlet, Macbeth, Coriolanus—no two resemble each other in their ends. And this variety they owe, not merely to differences of plot, but largely also to the vastly wider range possessed by poetry. Prose realism has today established itself. It can be powerful; as modern attempts to escape from it seldom are. But often, as here, realism does enforce a bleak reticence; and one grows conscious of its inevitable limitations.

Yet it should be noted, that though the death of Konstantin is so deliberately flattened (where that of Ivánov had been melodramatic), Chekhov does not repeat this flatness in his last three plays. The endings of *Uncle Vanya, The Three Sisters, The Cherry Orchard* are much more imaginative. For Chekhov learnt, like Ibsen, to mingle his prose realism with touches of poetry—as, indeed, in earlier passages of *The Seagull* itself. The *dramatis personae* of Chekhov or Ibsen may be seldom poetic. But, at moments, the dramatist *is.*

The most interesting English edition of *The Seagull* is D. Magar-shack's translation[1] of 1952, which gives on opposite pages Stanis-lavsky's original notes for its production.

Stanislavsky, whatever his faults, had two great merits. Firstly, he took infinite pains; secondly, in training his actors he insisted on their becoming a united team, loyal to each other and their art, 'There are,' he would repeat, 'no small parts—only small actors. Today Hamlet, tomorrow a super; but, even as a super, an actor must be an artist.' This admirable view was far from prevailing on the Russian stage of the time. But anyone who has watched the players of the Moscow Art Theatre can see how faithfully this finer tradition has been maintained.[2]

---

[1] The translation itself, whether rightly or wrongly, gives me a certain impression of being rather too colloquial. A natural reaction, perhaps, from some older translations, that have been too bookish. But I suspect that Chekhov himself might have felt the same dislike of its colloquialisms.

[2] When the Moscow Art Theatre acted *The Cherry Orchard* in London (1958), one of the most perfect performers was that minor character, the deaf old servant Fiers.

Stanislavsky's weakness, on the other hand, was a passion, not uncommon in producers, for preposterous excess in stage-business and stage-effects. For example, at the opening of *The Seagull* Act I, Chekhov had written the simple stage-direction—'The sun has just set. Yakov and other workmen are busy on the stage[1] behind the lowered curtain; sounds of hammering and coughing.'

In Stanislavsky this becomes fantastically elaborated.

The play starts in darkness, an August evening. The dim light of a lantern on top of a lamp-post, distant sounds of a drunkard's song, distant howling of a dog, the croaking of frogs, the crake of a landrail, the slow tolling of a distant church-bell, help the audience to get the feeling of the sad, monotonous life led by the characters. Flashes of lightning, faint rumbling of thunder in the distance. After the raising of the curtain a pause of ten seconds. After this pause Yakov knocks, hammering in a nail (on the stage[2]); having knocked the nail in, he busies himself on the stage, humming a tune.

On the next page, Konstantin and Sorin, entering, 'walk through some bushes on to the path, pushing the branches out of their way, bending down, climbing over garden seats. Half-way between the stage and the path Sorin starts talking'.

At the end of Act I, 'Masha bursts into sobs and, kneeling, buries her head on Dorn's knees. A pause of fifteen seconds'. (Stanislavsky was great on pauses.[3]) 'Dorn is stroking Masha's head. The frenzied waltz grows louder' (from inside the house); 'sounds of the tolling of a church-bell, of a peasant's song, of frogs, of a corncrake, the knocking of the night-watchman, and all sorts of other nocturnal sound-effects.'

In his young days Stanislavsky had himself loved to sit for hours on the veranda at Lyubimovka, listening to the noises of the night—frogs, corncrakes, and so on. All the same, it is surely better to sow one's seed by the handful than by the whole sack.

Typical is a letter from Stanislavsky to Chekhov about *The Cherry Orchard*, Act II (19/11/03): 'In the distance you see the flash

---

[1] For Konstantin's play.

[2] Again, of Konstantin's improvised theatre.

[3] So indeed was Chekhov himself. The stage-directions of his reflective, reticent plays are full of 'Pauses'. See note on p. 96.

of a stream and the manor-house on a slight rise, telegraph-poles and a railway-bridge. Do let us have a train go by with a puff of smoke in one of the pauses. That might turn out very well.' (One wonders.) 'Before sundown there will be a brief glimpse of the town and, towards the end of the act, a fog: it will be particularly thick above the ditch down-stage. The frogs and corncrakes will strike up at the very end of the act.' Trust them to!

When the Moscow Art Theatre company performed the play in London in 1958, I do not recall their employing any of these embellishments. They and their scenery were pleasantly realistic. (I have no great love for modernist stage-settings with planks and scaffoldings that make it look as if the theatre itself had been abandoned half-built, owing to a builders' strike.) But the minutiae of Stanislavsky seem preposterous. As with Gordon Craig, the producer encroaches on the dramatist. Too much staging or too little—both alike tend to disturb, by distracting attention from what really matters, the actors and the words they speak. So in the eighteenth century Vaucanson invented a mechanical asp to bite Marmontel's Cleopatra—but this mistaken marvel simply distracted the audience.

No wonder that Chekhov, with his usual good sense, once teased Stanislavsky by saying: 'I will write a new play and it shall begin—"Oh, how marvellous! One does not hear either dogs, birds, cuckoos, owls, nightingales, clocks, bells, or even crickets."' And again, according to Nemiróvich-Dánchenko, Chekhov would remark, half jesting, half serious,—'In my next play I shall stipulate: "The action takes place in a country with neither mosquitoes nor crickets to hinder conversation between human beings."'

But nothing could parody Stanislavsky better than his own production of Shakespeare's *Julius Caesar* (1903).

Here the Roman streets were embellished with such extras as a Jewish merchant; a Gaul with a donkey; flower-girls; a Roman matron with sons and slaves; and a Syrian damsel doing a stomach-dance to the flute, before a barber's shop where customers were shrieking while the hair was plucked from their arms, chins, and chests. In Brutus's orchard lay the toys left there by his playing children; and the sight of these playthings deeply moved the Roman during a pause in his soliloquy. On a branch of his orchard swayed a parrot; from behind one of its bushes appeared the head of a stork, which squawked when one of the conspirators tried to catch it. There was a shower of shooting stars; and of course frogs, corn-crakes, etc. Another stage-direction reads—'noise of a babbling brook and, if possible, the splashing of a fountain on the stage; in the distance the barking and howling of dogs, and from time to time the roaring of tigers and other animals in the circuses; distant shouts of sentries in different voices, approaching and retreating (gramophone); the knocking of night-watchmen (comes through excellently on a gramophone); cries of southern frogs like high-pitched bells (accidentally got this sound on a record). Other nocturnal noises.'

Even Beerbohm Tree never went to such fantastic lengths. How right was Aristotle in putting spectacle (important though it can be) *last* in importance of the six elements of drama!

Again, Stanislavsky himself has somewhere written, of a rehearsal of a Chekhov play: 'There we were, sitting disconsolate in semi-darkness. Everyone was dejected. Nothing would go quite right. Suddenly we heard something nibbling—a mouse. We listened in silence, and felt the right atmosphere had been created.' One has heard of mountains producing mice; but seldom can a mouse have produced such a mountain.

The Russian producer Vaktangov wrote in his diary in 1922, the year before he died young: 'Meyerhold calls a performance "good theatre" when the spectator does not forget for a moment that he is in the theatre. Stanislavsky, on the contrary, *wants* the spectator to forget that he is in the theatre at all. We all know that Chekhov's plays cannot be staged successfully without chirping crickets, orchestra-music, street-alarms, cries of pedlars, chiming clocks. . . .'

Yet Stanislavsky himself in the end grew wiser. 'Realism on the stage,' he wrote, 'becomes naturalism only when justified by the actor from within. Only, when thus justified, realism either becomes wholly unnecessary, or you simply do not notice it.'

Surely, a far truer view. In Stanislavsky's favour, however, it must at least be granted that he was passionately sincere, and endlessly painstaking. In producing Byron's *Cain*, for example, he had

160 rehearsals—though the play only survived, alas, eight performances.

The best, perhaps, of many books about him, N. M. Gorchakov's *Stanislavsky Directs*,[1] gives an impressive picture of the old producer as he was in the nineteen-twenties—no longer thus obsessed with stage-effects, but still tireless in his energy and concern for absolute precision, team-work, study of the dramatist's intentions, imaginative conception of character. The ironic question 'How many children had Lady Macbeth?' may be justified by some critical pedantries. But, as a producer, Stanislavsky (like Ibsen) would have thought it essential to have a clear idea on such a point. Indeed he would have made even the actor who played Macbeth's Porter, imagine for himself a complete biography of that personage, so as really to *live* the part.

On *The Seagull* Tolstoy's verdict was both sharp and blunt—'It is absolutely worthless; it is written like Ibsen. Words heaped on words. Heaven knows what for.' Always Tolstoy was exasperated that Chekhov's plays and tales should lack that sense of purpose which he himself had come to demand so passionately from life and literature alike. 'I detest Shakespeare,' he said to Chekhov. 'But your plays, dear Anton Pavlóvich, are even worse. Shakespeare at least takes the reader by the scruff of his neck and drags him to a definite end. . . . But where is one to go with *your* heroes? From the sofa they lie on, to the closet and back?' (Relating this, it is said, Chekhov with his charming freedom from vanity would laugh till his pince-nez fell off.)

But Tolstoy's judgement seems hardly very perceptive. Chekhov's values in life are clearly enough implied in his plays, for anyone who troubles to look; and are all the more persuasive for being implied, not preached. Whereas a work like Tolstoy's own *Kreutzer Sonata*, for example, has a morality that some find both repulsive and repulsively obtruded, like bones sticking through its flesh. Even *War and Peace* (as, despite his admiration for it, Chekhov complained) is marred in places by silly belittlements of Napoleon as merely a lucky nonentity—in which case his good luck was most

[1] 1950. Eng. translation, New York, 1954.

improbably frequent. (Marbot has pointed out, on the contrary, how often the Emperor's own victories were nullified, particularly in 1813, by the failures of his Marshals.) Such crabbed moralizings seem not only perverse, but also artistically self-defeating.

Nor, whatever Tolstoy said, does *The Seagull* seem to me much like Ibsen; nor by any means worthless. But it does not seem, either, a very great work. Its outstanding success in 1898 may well have been largely due to the novelty of its excellent acting and elaborate production—frogs and corncrakes included.

For the plot is not outstanding; nor the characters. Minor writers who shoot themselves for minor actresses are liable to remain somewhat minor, except by some miracle of treatment.

Modern criticism has, indeed, stressed that Chekhov called his play a comedy. But this can be overstressed. It seems a little curious to say that the suicide of a failure has 'an element of the ludicrous'; that 'to Chekhov, who could contemplate death dispassionately and, as a doctor, almost clinically, it was not Konstantin's suicide that mattered, but Nina's perseverance on the road to success'.

If I thought that Chekhov found Konstantin's death 'ludicrous', I should cease to read him. A man who kills himself in self-disgust and despair, as a hopeless failure, is likely to suffer an anguish far deeper than the character who meets his end in the high Roman fashion with a proud feeling that he passes still unbowed and undefeated from the stage. And anyone who finds such anguish a matter for laughter has sunk to the level of those higher beings whom Soame Jenyns imagined as diverting themselves with human agonies. To the angry humanity of Johnson this did not seem a very fine sort of fun. 'Some of them, perhaps, are virtuosi and delight in the operations of an asthma, as a human philosopher in the effects of an air-pump. To swell a man with a tympany is as good sport as to blow a frog. Many a merry bout have these frolic beings at the vicissitudes of an ague, and good sport it is to see a man tumble with an epilepsy, and revive and tumble again, and all this he knows not why.'

When Dr Astrov in *Uncle Vanya* has a poor railway-hand die on his operating-table, *he* is far from viewing the matter 'dispassionately and almost clinically'. He is haunted by it.[1] And in Astrov there is a great deal of Chekhov himself.

This kind of criticism has today become something of a fashion. Pundits have similarly discovered that the last act of Ibsen's *Doll's House* is hugely amusing; and *The Wild Duck* a comedy from start to finish; and *Hedda Gabler* a most tickling farce. One wonders that they have not yet discovered *Lear* to be a side-splitting entertainment, with its funny madmen and its conspicuous Fool. Such minds do not seem to see that life's ironic grotesqueness can make its sorrows only bitterer; that it can become only the more tragic for lacking the consolations of high tragedy. 'Comic relief' need not be merely 'relief': it can, on the contrary, deepen tragic intensity— as in *Troilus and Cressida*. Any actor who acted Konstantin's end as merely 'ludicrous' would kill not only himself, but the whole play. Such critics would be wiser to recall Chekhov's own maxim that an author must be, 'to his very finger-tips, humane'.

Nor is it so certain that we are meant to contrast the ineffectual Konstantin with a resolute Nina, whom suffering will develop into 'a great artist'. Why are we to be so sure of her coming triumph? No doubt Konstantin says enviously, '*You* have found your way, *you* know where you are going.' But that may mean only that the disillusioned Konstantin envies one who keeps faith in herself—as yet. We are merely told that, after beginning in Moscow, Nina has been touring provincial towns, with a delivery that was 'harsh and monotonous', and gestures that were 'heavy and crude'. Konstantin thinks she *may* have talent; but 'I could never make out'. Nothing here to show that Nina would become another Duse. Chekhov leaves her future, at best, quite obscure. And obscure it might well have remained.[2]

---

[1] See pp. 70-1.

[2] A view shared, I find, by A. Luther in his *Geschichte der Russischen Literatur* (Leipzig, 1924, p. 385). One may also note that Chekhov does not seem to have thought very hopefully of the stage-aspirations of 'Leeka' Mizinov, the original of Nina. 'There are,' he wrote from Milan in 1894, 'many foreign girls à la Leeka here, who come to learn singing in the hope of fame and riches. The poor things scream at the top of their voices from morning till night.' Later (1902) Leeka gave up her hopes of becoming an opera-singer.

Further, Nina is symbolized by the shot seagull. Shot seagulls are not phoenixes. They do not rise from their ashes. They perish.[1]

The Seagull seems to me, not what *we* call 'a comedy', but an ironic, tragi-comic slice of life. Chekhov in some moods could well have spoken, like Flaubert, of 'ma nature bouffonnement amère';[2] might have said, like Flaubert, 'le grotesque triste a pour moi un charme inouï'.[3] (This is particularly true of *The Cherry Orchard*.) *The Seagull* seems a considerable advance on *Ivánov*; but it lacks, I feel, the deeper sympathy, the finer personalities, which animate *Uncle Vanya* or *The Three Sisters*.

---

[1] Lydia Avílov reports Chekhov as saying to her: 'The Seagull. It has such a desolate cry. When it cries, one can't help thinking of something sad.'

[2] 'My temperament of mingled buffoonery and bitterness.'

[3] 'I find a charm without equal in the grotesquely mournful.'

Uncle Vanya
(published 1897, produced in Moscow, 1899)

'J'en reviens toujours à Candide: il faut finir par cultiver son jardin; tout le reste, excepté l'amitié, est bien peu de chose; et encore cultiver son jardin n'est pas grande chose.'[1]

VOLTAIRE TO D'ARGENSON

This is a recasting of an earlier play, *The Wood-Demon*, which failed at Moscow in 1889, and was later regarded by Chekhov with detestation. 'I hate it, and am trying to forget it. . . . It would be a serious blow to me if it were dragged into the daylight and revived.'

Needless to say, since his death it *has* been dragged into the daylight, and translated into English.[2] But, as with *Platónov*, this dredging of writers' drawers is usually disappointing. *The Wood-Demon* seems as poor as Chekhov said it was—melodramatic, confused, tiresome. The character corresponding to Uncle Vanya shoots himself, like Ivánov and Konstantin (these suicides grow monotonous), instead of trying to shoot the Professor; and the play ends with the conventional marriages of four characters for whom one cares not a pin. All this is far inferior to the poignant bleakness of the final version, where Sonia and her uncle are left alone to face their remaining years of desolation.

Yet in 1899 Prince Urusov wrote to Chekhov lamenting that *Uncle Vanya*, far from being an improvement, had merely spoilt *The Wood-Demon*. So subjective are tastes. And so conservative. It is very human to dislike any revision of a work once loved; as can be seen with the public antipathy to new versions of the Bible (though in this case, unfortunately, the antipathy is often all too justified).

[1] 'Always I come back to Candide: one must end by cultivating one's garden; all else, except friendship, matters little; and even cultivating one's garden is no great matter.'

[2] It will be found in the Everyman edition, *Tchekhov's Plays and Stories* (1958).

Uncle Vanya was finished in 1896, published in 1897, successfully performed in the provinces during 1898, and acted in Moscow in 1899. In Moscow Chekhov first offered his play to the Maly Theatre. But the Maly Theatre Committee, which contained several professors, objected to anything so sacrilegious as the scene where the sacred person of an ex-professor is actually shot at. (In Tsarist Russia ex-professors enjoyed the exalted rank of generals!) So Chekhov transferred *Uncle Vanya* to the Moscow Art Theatre. It was not immediately a great success; but it soon established itself.

Like *The Seagull*, *Uncle Vanya* is a study of frustration and futility. The great difference is that its characters are more interesting; and its construction better.

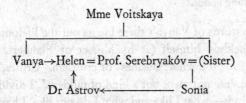

Uncle Vanya is a man of forty-seven who realizes, too late, that he has wasted his whole life in a sterile, altruistic drudgery, barren alike of love and of ideas. In youth, twenty-five years before, he had been passionately devoted to his sister. When she married the famous Professor Serebryakóv, her father bought her, as dowry, an expensive estate.

To pay for that dowry, her brother Vanya forewent his own inheritance and became merely the Professor's estate-manager; toiling year after year for a miserable pittance, to finance his famous brother-in-law. Quixotic? But one must suppose that for this adored sister there was nothing Vanya would not do. Further, he fondly imagined his brother-in-law to be a great man.

Vanya's sister bore her Professor a daughter, Sonia; then she died. And after a time the widower married a second wife, the beautiful Helen, now twenty-seven. Rather like George Eliot's Dorothea with Dr Casaubon,[1] Helen was dazzled by Serebryakóv's

---

[1] This unhappy union of pedantry and beauty in *Middlemarch* was partly suggested by the marriage (1862) of Mark Pattison (1813-84), Rector of Lincoln, Oxford, with Emilia Strong, later Lady Charles Dilke.

learned reputation into imagining that she loved this pedantic, shifty egoist.

Now, retired from his chair, the Professor has come to settle on his dead wife's estate. And now, in close contact with him, Uncle Vanya realizes with horror that he and his niece Sonia have sacrificed their best years for a shallow charlatan who can think only of his own importance, his own comfort, and his own ailments.

> The man has been lecturing and writing on art for twenty-five years, and does not know the first thing about it. For twenty-five years he has been chewing other men's ideas about 'realism', 'naturalism', and all such nonsense. For twenty-five years he has been lecturing and writing on what intelligent men knew all the time, and stupid men care nothing about.

In these words of Vanya's there bursts out the lifelong contempt felt by Chekhov himself (as by Musset or Flaubert, Morris or Tennyson) for the whole business of criticism. 'Critics,' Chekhov once wrote, 'are not men, but a kind of mildew.' 'I divide all work into two kinds—what I like and what I do not like. I have no other criterion.' And, again, to Gorky—'Critics are like horseflies which hinder the horse from ploughing. The horse is toiling, with every muscle taut as the strings of a double bass; and then the horsefly settles on its rump, buzzing and tickling. . . . And what does the fly buzz about? The fly itself hardly knows; it is just because it feels restless and wants to proclaim: "Look, I too am alive on the earth. See, I can buzz too, buzz about anything." For twenty-five years I have read criticisms of my stories, yet I cannot remember a single useful remark, or one word of valuable advice.' Indeed the only comment that remained in his mind was the bland prediction of one expert that Chekhov would die drunk in a ditch.[1]

It is likely enough that few writers have ever learnt much from printed criticisms. Most writers teach themselves; helped only by an occasional hint from friends or fellow-writers. Still it might be pleaded that Chekhov's denunciation of critics mistakes the real function of criticism. For its true task is not to help writers to write

---

[1] Compare an entry in Chekhov's notebook: 'A professor's opinion: no Shakespeare, but the commentaries on him are the thing.'

better; it is to help readers to read better—to read with fuller understanding. That *can* be useful.

To this, however, Chekhov might have retorted that if he was mistaken about the critics' true business, that mistake was too commonly shared by the critics themselves. For they *are* inclined to impose on the public by a pompous self-importance; to resemble not only 'horseflies', but also La Fontaine's 'mouche de la coche'; which congratulated itself on bringing the coach so finely up the hill, when it had really done nothing but buzz in the coachman's eyes and the horses' ears.[1]

At all events Vanya's rage with this dilapidated old bookworm is made bitterer still by his having fallen hopelessly in love with the bookworm's beautiful wife, Helen.

So too has the local doctor, Astrov; who seems to embody much of Chekhov himself. For Astrov likewise is a clear-sighted, ironic, yet passionate mind; a lover of nature and of trees; a victim of the crushing burdens that the rural life of Russia imposed on those labouring to better it.

Already at the opening of the play one seems to catch the very voice of Dr Chekhov when Dr Astrov pours out his bitterness to the old nurse Marina.

Astrov. Have I changed much since then?

Marina. Yes, a lot. You were young and handsome then; and now you've aged. You've lost your looks. And another thing—you take a drop of vodka now and then.

Astrov. Yes, ten years have made me a different man. And why? Because, nurse, I am overworked. I am on my feet from dawn to dusk. I get no rest. At night I tremble under my blankets, for fear I shall be dragged out to a patient. All these years you have known me, I've not had one free day. How could I help growing old? And then the life is tedious, stupid, squalid. . . . It drags one down. One is surrounded by queer people—a queer lot, all of them—and after living two or three years with them, one grows queer oneself, without noticing. (*Twisting his long moustache.*) See what a huge moustache I have grown! A stupid

---

[1] On the other hand Chekhov valued literary history. To Suvórin he wrote (23/12/1888): 'Many races, religions, languages, civilizations have disappeared without trace because there were no historians, no biologists. In the same way numbers of lives and works of art vanish before our eyes owing to the complete lack of criticism.'

moustache. Yes, nurse, I've grown a queer fellow. But not stupid yet, thank God! My brain still works; but my feelings are somehow dulled. I ask nothing, I need nothing, I care for nobody[1]—except you perhaps. I believe I'm fond of *you* (*kisses her hand*). When I was a child, I had a nurse just like you.

As so often, how spontaneous, unstrained, and lifelike Russian dialogue can be!—less bothered with relevance or consistency, with logical connexions, or conventions of behaviour, than the usual style of writers further west.

Marina.   Wouldn't you like something to eat?
Astrov.   No. In the third week of Lent I went to Malitskoe, because of the epidemic—spotted typhus. The peasants were all lying in their huts. Everywhere filth, stench, smoke. Calves on the ground among the sick—and young pigs. I worked all day, without a moment to sit down, or a morsel to eat. But when I got home, there was still no rest. They brought me a pointsman from the railway—I laid him on the operating-table—and he went and died on me under the chloroform. And then, when I least wanted it, my feelings seemed to wake up again, and my conscience tortured me, as if I had killed the man on purpose. I sat down and shut my eyes—like this—and thought: 'Will the people who live a hundred or two hundred years from now, the people for whom we are breaking the road—will they remember and give us a good word?' No, nurse, indeed they won't!

No wonder Dr Astrov seeks refuge in vodka. Still he remains a far stronger character than poor Uncle Vanya, who is lovable, pathetic, but hopelessly weak. Where Vanya weeps, Astrov still whistles.[2] He has at least his demonic passion for forests, his loyalty to this Russia whose beauty (like that of most modern lands) is being so recklessly and brutally ruined by human greed and folly.

Astrov.   Oh I don't object to cutting wood that's really needed; but why wreck the forests? The forests of Russia are groaning under the axe. Millions of trees are being destroyed; the homes of birds and animals laid waste; the rivers dwindling and drying up; lovely landscapes vanishing for ever. And all because men are too lazy and stupid to stoop and pick up fuel from the ground. (*To Helen*) Am I not right,

---

[1] Cf. Chekhov's own sombre saying: 'In this world it is indispensable to be indifferent.'

[2] Cf. Chekhov's own stress on this, p. 76 below.

Madam? One must be a stupid barbarian to burn this beauty in a stove, and destroy what we cannot create. Man is gifted with reason and creative power, so that he may increase what is given him; yet till now he has not created, but destroyed. The forests grow fewer, the rivers run dry, the wild creatures are being exterminated, the climate ruined, and every day the earth gets poorer and uglier.[1] (*To Uncle Vanya*) I see irony in your eyes; what I say, you don't take seriously . . . and, after all, maybe it is just crankiness. Yet when I walk past peasants' woods that I have saved from the axe, or hear the rustling of young trees that my own hands have planted, I feel that to some extent the climate *is* in my power; and that if in a thousand years mankind is happy, I shall have done a little for their happiness. When I plant a little birch, and see it growing green and swaying in the wind, my heart swells with pride and I—(*sees the workman who has brought a glass of vodka on a tray*) however—(*drinks*) I must be going. Probably it's all my crankiness.

Despite these ironic doubts, there is here too a lot of Chekhov himself, that tireless planter of trees at Melikhovo and Yalta. And what he says of ruined forests, and the ruin they bring, is truer than ever today. Our age has had to coin the grim word—'dust-bowl'.

Yet even the sensible and far-seeing Astrov falls likewise under the spell of this baleful, useless woman who has come, with her stupid, exacting, old husband, to upset everybody's hard-working existence. For Astrov, Helen's attraction is merely physical; none the less, it has become a distracting, paralysing obsession.

Astrov. I love no one—and don't believe I ever shall. What still moves me is beauty. That *does* stir me. I fancy that Helen, if she wanted, could turn my head in a day. But *that* isn't love, *that* isn't affection—(*He covers his face with his hands, and shudders.*)
Sonia. What's the matter?
Astrov. Nothing. . . . In Lent one of my patients died under chloroform.

Such is the stupid irony of things that, while Astrov is fascinated

---

[1] Chekhov would have appreciated that poem of Ronsard which execrates the fellers of the Forêt de Gastine (1584); and the bitter 'Dirge of the Munster Forest, 1581' by Emily Lawless—

> Soon shall my sylvan coronals be cast;
> My hidden sanctuaries, my secret ways,
> Naked must stand to the rebellious blast;
> No Spring shall quicken what this Autumn slays.

by the beauty of this shallow woman—a glamour as real, and as
unreal, as the reflection of a star in a puddle, which a mere pebble
can destroy—yet he cannot respond to the real love of poor Sonia,
who would have made him a perfect wife. (The same situation as
recurs with Lopákhin and Varya in *The Cherry Orchard.*)

Even to Helen herself all this passion brings no happiness either;
only an indolent, yet guilt-stricken titillation of her vanity.

Helen (*to Uncle Vanya*).   And at lunch you quarrelled with Alexander
again. How petty it all is!

Vanya.   But if I hate him?

Helen.   There is no reason to hate Alexander. He is like everyone else.
He is no worse than you.

Vanya.   If you could only see your face, your gestures! Life seems too
much of an effort for you. . . . Ah, what an effort!

Helen.   Yes, it *is* an effort, and a bore. Everyone blames my husband;
everyone looks at me with pity. 'Poor thing,' they think, 'with that
old husband!' How well I understand it, that pity! As Astrov said just
now, you all wantonly destroy the forests, so that soon there will be
nothing left on earth. In the same way you destroy human beings; and
soon, thanks to you, there will be no loyalty, no integrity, no capacity
for sacrifice left on earth. Why can't you look at a woman with indifference, unless she is yours? Because—yes, the doctor was right—you are
all possessed by a devil of destruction. You have no mercy on the
woods, the birds, on women, or each other.

Vanya.   I don't like this sort of philosophy.

Helen.   That doctor has a tired, sensitive face—an interesting face.
Obviously Sonia is attracted by him—she's in love with him, and I
can understand. This is the third time he has been here since I came;
but I'm shy and haven't had a proper talk with him, or been nice to
him. He thinks me disagreeable. Probably that's why you and I are
such friends, Ivan Petrovich—because we are both such tiresome
bores. Tiresome! Don't look at me like that, I dislike it.[1]

Vanya.   How else *can* I look at you, when I love you? You are my joy,
my life, my youth. I know my chances of being loved in return are
nil—non-existent—but I ask nothing. Only let me look at you, listen
to your voice—

Helen.   Hush! Someone will hear.

(*They go towards the house.*)

---

[1] How admirably lifelike is this speech of Helen's with its blend of lofty,
moralizing concern for Sonia, irritation with poor Vanya, and secret interest
in Dr Astrov as a male to be allured!

Vanya (*following*). *Let* me talk of my love—don't drive me away—just that will be my greatest happiness!
Helen. Oh, this is torture!

Well might Chekhov give this unfortunate doll the name of Helen, recalling that ancient beauty who made havoc of Homer's world. And yet how living they are—she and her victims!

ACT II

All this tangled situation has emerged in Act I.

In Act II the heavy autumn-afternoon has given place to a heavy autumn-midnight, in which the ailing, pain-racked old Professor can console himself only by becoming as much of a burden and nuisance to others as he is to himself. He girds at his wife; he girds at his daughter Sonia. And when at last the old nurse Marina has coaxed him away like a fretful child, the sleepless and half-intoxicated Vanya again makes hopeless love to the weary Helen.

Vanya (*falling on his knees*). My sweetheart, my lovely one——
Helen (*angrily*). Leave me alone! Really this has become too unpleasant! (*She goes out.*)
Vanya (*alone*). She is gone! (*Pause.*) Ten years ago I first met her—at her sister's house—when she was seventeen, and I thirty-seven. Why didn't I fall in love with her then, and propose? It would have been so easy. And now she would be my wife. Yes, the thunderstorm would have waked us tonight, and she would have been frightened, but I should have held her in my arms and whispered: 'Don't be frightened, I'm here.' On the enchanting dream!—so lovely, I laugh to think of it. (*Laughs.*) But, my God! My head goes round. Why am I so old? Why *will* she not understand me? I hate all her rhetorical speeches, that morality of inertia, that ridiculous talk about the world being destroyed —(*Pause.*) Oh how I have been cheated! For years I've worshipped this miserable, gouty professor; and worked for him like an ox. For him Sonia and I have squeezed the estate to the last drop. We've bartered our butter, and curds, and peas like misers—never left a bit for ourselves—all so that we could scrape together enough pence to send *him* thousands of roubles. I was proud of him and his learning— took all he said, and wrote, as inspiration—and now? Now he has retired, and what does his life amount to? A blank! He is completely obscure—his reputation burst like a bubble. I've been cheated—now I see it—foully cheated.

73

Finally, in her hopeless passion for Dr Astrov, the golden-hearted, plain-featured Sonia pours out her sorrows to her stepmother, Helen, while outside in the September darkness sounds the monotonous rattle of the night-watchman going his rounds.

ACT III

Helen, touched by Sonia's six years of suffering, offers to sound Astrov on Sonia's behalf. Then, if all is hopeless, he had better stop coming to the house. Already Helen realizes that Astrov is attracted to herself. Doubtless she half realizes too that, pleading for Sonia, she may provoke him, instead, to declare his real passion. But then ladies, even though they may reject such declarations, for some reason seldom scratch out the eyes of those who make them. Poor Sonia consents. So Helen now pretends she would like to see Astrov's sketch-map of the local deforestation. Unsuspecting, he asks nothing better than to show it. But it is very dangerous when A pleads with B to love C. It so easily turns into A capturing, or trying to capture, B for herself. That is likewise the central theme of Turgenev's most admirable play, *A Month in the Country*.

So now in his eagerness Astrov shows the Professor's fair wife the green tints on his map where fifty years ago the forests stood, with elk and wild goats in their shadow, swans and wild geese on their lakes; while today only spots of green remain, but elk and swan are tragically vanished. Yet he quickly senses that she is bored. She comes to the point—Sonia loves him. But what use?—his heart is elsewhere.

Astrov. Beautiful, sleek tigress, you must have your victims. For a whole month I have done nothing but pursue you eagerly. I have thrown over everything for you, and you love to see it. . . . (*Crossing his arms and bowing his head.*) I surrender. Here you have me—now eat me.

Helen. You are mad!

Astrov. *You* are afraid! . . . Don't you see we *must* meet—that it is inevitable? (*He kisses her. Uncle Vanya, with a bunch of roses, stops short in the doorway.*)

Such are life's cruelties. It was just so, in *Ivánov*, that Ivánov's wife entered just in time to see her husband in Sasha's arms.

74

But now appears the Professor, with half the household at his heels, to hold a family-council. He has conceived a brilliant scheme. The estate yields only 2 per cent. Very well. Let it be sold. In bonds, the capital will yield as much as 4 or 5 per cent. How simple!

But, for Uncle Vanya, this is the supreme outrage. He has just seen the woman he hopelessly adores, clasped in Astrov's arms. That was anguish enough. But now, to crown all, comes this horse-leech of a professor with a calmly monstrous proposal to sell out-right the estate which Uncle Vanya has slaved through a wasted life to keep safe and prosperous. Partly for this once admired Professor's sake; but also for the sake of Vanya's beloved niece, Sonia. For to her, by rights, the whole ultimately belongs. This estate is as much, or more, to Uncle Vanya as the Cherry Orchard to Mme Ranevsky. No wonder he explodes.

Amid frantic altercation the family-meeting breaks up. An excellent quarrel. A moment later there is the crack of a shot—and Professor Serebryakóv dashes in like a bolting rabbit, pursued by Uncle Vanya, revolver in hand. Again Vanya fires and misses.

The curtain falls.

In *The Wood-Demon* Uncle Vanya's counterpart had shot himself. But, as Johnson wisely said, 'suicide is always to be had, without expense of thought'. This later version seems vastly better, in its tragi-comic futility.

ACT IV

It is evening. Poor Uncle Vanya has missed winning the woman he loves. He has missed killing the man he loathes. However, he has not quite missed everything. For the gouty Professor has no mind to be chased about the house as a pigeon for a mad brother-in-law's target-practice. And Helen, too, is anxious to flee from Astrov before her resistance breaks. So the two unwelcome guests hastily prepare to depart. Things shall go back to the old system, with Vanya running the estate, and the Professor living *from* it, but not *on* it.

Astrov enters with Vanya, whom the doctor suspects of having stolen some of his morphia to kill himself. Astrov demands it back. Vanya refuses.

Astrov. Yes, my friend. In this whole province there were only two decent, educated persons, you and I. But ten years or so of this miserable routine, this trivial provincial life, have swallowed us up and poisoned our blood with their putrid vapours, till we too are grown as contemptible as all the rest. (*With sudden intensity*) But don't try to talk me out of it. Give me back what you took.

Now Sonia comes; and at last, coaxed by her, Vanya surrenders the poison.

Helen takes her final leave of Astrov. 'We shall never see each other again, so why hide it?—I *was* really a little in love with you. Come, shake hands, and let us part friends. Think well of me.'

Then the beautiful butterfly and her owl husband drive away. Astrov too prepares to go back to his duties, after a final glass of that vodka he had once promised Sonia to give up. On the wall there hangs—fit emblem of life's unutterably incongruous futility—a map of Africa. God only knows how, or to what end, a map of Africa ever came to find itself in this remote Russian house of heartbreak. Astrov stares at it.

Astrov. I suppose there in Africa the heat now's terrific.
Vanya. Yes, most likely.

Typical human inconsequence. What is Africa to them, or they to Africa? Futility of futilities, all is futility.[1]

Sonia lights Astrov with a candle to his carriage; then she returns, while Vanya buries himself mechanically in his long neglected accounts.

On this last act Chekhov made to Stanislavsky (who acted Dr Astrov) one of his typically curt, cryptic, yet luminous comments. 'Listen,' said Chekhov, of Astrov, 'he *whistles*. It is Uncle Vanya who whimpers; but Astrov *whistles*.' This, I imagine, is another

[1] Chekhov warned Olga Knipper that she was wrong to imagine Astrov clutching at his departing Helen as passionately as the drowning swimmer at the straw. No, it was not like that. Much less romantic. Astrov liked her; he desired her; but he knows that all is over. Already it has all become remote and unreal—as remote and unreal as the far-away sunlight beating down on tropic Africa. Once more the ultimate 'indifference'.

simple, yet revealing trait in common between Astrov and Chekhov himself. Chekhov could understand Uncle Vanya, sympathize with him, pity him; but he was himself a more reticent, more stoic type. He too had known suffering and heart-ache; but his impulse was to hide it under a mask of humour. He too whistled.

And so the play, like life, continues its relentless course.

Vanya (*stroking Sonia's hair*).   Oh, my child, how my heart aches! If you knew how it aches!

Sonia.   What can we do? We must go on living. (*A pause.*) We shall go on living, Uncle Vanya. We shall live through the long, long chain of days, the dreary evenings. We shall bear patiently the trials fate sends. We shall work for others—now, and when we are old—and find no rest. And when our time comes, we shall meet it patiently; and there beyond the grave we shall say that we have suffered and wept—that our life was bitter—and God will pity us. Ah then, dear, dear uncle, we shall see a life that is bright and lovely and beautiful. We shall rejoice, and look back on our troubles here with tenderness, with a smile—and we shall *rest*. I have faith, uncle, fervent, passionate faith. (*She kneels and lays her head on his hands; in a voice of weariness.*) We shall rest. (*Telégin plays softly on the guitar.*) We shall rest. We shall hear the angels. We shall see the heavens with their stars like diamonds. We shall see all our earthly evil—all our sufferings, swept away in the compassion that will fill the world. . . . Poor Uncle Vanya, you are crying. . . . You've had no joy in life; but wait, Uncle Vanya, wait. We shall rest. (*Puts her arms round him.*) We shall rest. (*There is heard the watchman's tap.*)

This is more moving than any pistol-shots. And it is made only the more moving by the irony that Chekhov himself—and presumably Uncle Vanya—felt no such faith as Sonia's. *They* did not look forward to golden floors and angels. What good would *that* be? But they could at least believe in a different, deeper rest, no less eternal.

It brings back to memory the words of a woman not less simple and good, not less unhappily in love, not less fervent in faith, than poor Sonia—Christina Rossetti.

> Rest, rest, a perfect rest
> Shed over brow and breast;
> Her face is toward the west,
>   The purple land.

> She cannot see the grain
> Ripening on hill and plain,
> She cannot feel the rain
> Upon her hand.

Tolstoy, naturally, liked *Uncle Vanya* no better than he had liked *The Seagull*. 'Why,' growled the disgusted sage to the actor who played Uncle Vanya, 'why do you pester another man's wife? Can't you get a farm-girl for yourself?'

A little crude; and not very intelligent. For what poor Uncle Vanya wanted was, not a body, but a heart. How Blake would have cursed the too moralizing Tolstoy!—as he cursed the too moralizing Plato.

More modern criticism seems to me sometimes no more satisfactory. 'The principal theme of *Uncle Vanya*,' it has been argued, 'is not frustration but hope. . . . It is as if a hurricane had swept through their lives and uprooted everything. And it is the young girl's faith and courage alone that will rebuild the ruins.'

How jolly! We have been invited to find a lot of comedy in *The Seagull*; now we are to find a lot of optimism in *Uncle Vanya*. But this picture of Uncle Vanya looking forward to spending perhaps his last twenty years of life in adding up bills for butter and buckwheat—all for the benefit of an old charlatan and his idle wife—till finally he collapses into the quiet of a forgotten grave, seems a most curious kind of optimism. As well mistake a funeral for a flower-show.

Maxim Gorky's impression was much less gay. 'I wept,' he wrote to Chekhov, 'like an old woman, though I am far from being sentimental. . . . I felt as if I were being sawn with a blunt saw. We are unhappy, tedious people—that is true. It seems to me that in this play you are colder towards mankind than the devil himself.' 'Maupassant,' added Gorky, 'is excellent; I like him very much . . . you I like better.'[1]

Here, surely, is the truth. Gorky was a Russian, and a personal friend. I suspect that he was a great deal better at understanding how Chekhov really thought and felt.

---

[1] Elsewhere Gorky records how, at a thirty-ninth performance of the play, the actors still wept, as well as the audience.

Uncle Vanya seems to me as great an advance on *The Seagull* as *The Seagull* on *Ivánov*. Partly for reasons of plot. When Konstantin shoots himself because he cannot win Nina, though in life such things only too often happen, yet one is left with a dreary impression of disheartening pointlessness. For it remains imbecile to shoot oneself for Ninas. Such pretty simpletons are simply not worth it. There is far sounder sense in the lines of our own Sir Robert Ayton (1570-1638):

> He that can love unlov'd again
> Hath better store of love than brain;
> God send me love my debts to pay
> While unthrifts fool their love away;

or, again, in the stoicism of A. E. Housman:

> Blue the sky from east to west
> Arches, and the world is wide,
> Though the girl he loves the best
> Rouses from another's side.

Often, no doubt, such calm, cold realism is hard to obey. But characters like Konstantin win pity rather than admiration, or even respect. He is too feeble, too quick to despair. For women, however, like Sonia in *Uncle Vanya*, or Olga in *The Three Sisters*, or Varya in *The Cherry Orchard*, condemned by social convention to wait passively for the love that may or may not come, life can indeed be far harsher. An old Chinese story illustrates the folly of passive expectation by the fate of a certain peasant who once saw a fleeing rabbit run into a tree so hard as to fall dead; and then died himself, of starvation, while hopefully waiting for more rabbits to oblige. But women have often to wait just as helplessly as that Chinese peasant, unless they are charming enough to be magnets for admiration, or clever enough to lay snares, or strong-minded enough to propose themselves. And therefore, I feel, Sonia, or Olga, or Varya may stir in us a deeper and more deserved compassion than any Konstantin.

More and more, the virtues of Chekhov as writer seem to me the virtues of the admirable doctor that he also was. And a good doctor is surely one of the finest of all human types. When Gorky cried out that Chekhov in *Uncle Vanya* saw humanity with the coldness of the devil, that seems to me simply not true. Chekhov was far from cold. His heart was warm; but, as a doctor's must, his brain kept cool. If a doctor were shaken with sobs as he operated, he would cut an artery; if he wept over his patients, he would make their wounds septic; if he let himself become distracted with sympathy, he might end by sewing up sponges in their insides. Chekhov's vision is sharp and clear, as the surgeon's knife must be sharp and clean. Had one been in his medical care, one would have known that he would never let one down, that he would spend sleepless nights to pull one through. But he would not indulge in idle tears; though he lets his characters shed theirs in cataracts. His compassion was deep and real; but it was the kind of compassion that faces life's ruthlessness, because that ruthlessness can be lessened and mitigated only by seeing things with a stern integrity that tolerates no wishful thoughts—that refuses to believe things merely because they would be so pleasant to believe. Chekhov's was the kind of compassion that acts.[1]

When Chekhov died, after twenty years of illness, he indulged in no self-pity. He knew life was full of things as bitter. On that last night at Badenweiler he jested to the end; though beside his bed was the woman he loved and must leave. Chekhov had much in common with our own Thomas Hardy—a vision both compassionate and stern; a pity that felt for the weak, but was never weak itself.

[1] Compare that noble figure of Dr Larivière (based on Flaubert's own father) who appears for a moment at the bedside of the dying Emma Bovary, like a being from a different world among the knaves and noodles that surround her end. 'Dédaigneux des croix, des titres et des académies, hospitalier, libéral, paternel avec les pauvres et pratiquant la vertu sans y croire, il eût presque passé pour un saint si la finesse de son esprit ne l'eût fait craindre comme un démon. Son regard, plus tranchant que ses bistouris, vous descendait droit dans l'âme et désarticulait tout mensonge à travers les allégations et les pudeurs.' ('Scornful of decorations, titles, and academies; hospitable, liberal, paternal towards the poor; practising virtue without believing in it—he might almost have passed for a saint, if the subtlety of his intellect had not made him dreaded like a demon. His glance, keener than his lancets, pierced straight to the soul, and cut through all phrases and evasions to the falsehood beneath.')

As in its plot, so also in its characters, *Uncle Vanya* seems a marked improvement on the plays before it, even *The Seagull*. Dr Astrov is far more living, interesting, and sympathetic than Dr Dorn; Sonia than Nina; Helen than Arkádina; Uncle Vanya than Uncle Sorin. Even Trigórin, perhaps the most vivid figure in the earlier play, became a little tedious in his passivity; a little too like the poor fishes it was his life's main pleasure to catch. Astrov with his disillusioned courage leaves a far deeper stamp on the memory. And, other things equal, a work with duller and less sympathetic characters remains a duller and less sympathetic work. A platitude? Would it were!

The men and women of drama or fiction cannot, indeed, be always admirable or awesome. But surely they are merely wasting our time unless most of them can vividly arouse our curiosity, our amusement, above all, our sympathy. To judge from many modern plays and novels, this is no longer the prevalent view. But I still cannot see why one should persistently go to look in literature for the sort of bores and mediocrities, rats and rabbits, tarts and toads, that one would flee like the plague in real life. Up to a point, no doubt, a real artist can make art even out of rats and rabbits. But that point is soon passed. Shakespeare's world, or Ibsen's, contains a due proportion of 'dull and muddy-mettled rascals'. But they are at least kept in their places, and limited in their numbers.

As for ideas, it may not be a very new or startling truth that the world's work has to go on, even if dreams fail, Sirens deceive, and hearts crack. Still it is true. And, though the same truth may be already implied in *Ivánov*, or *The Seagull*, yet in *Uncle Vanya* it is put with far more incisiveness. Again, though Gorky might talk of *Uncle Vanya* as written with the coldness of the devil, in fact this play seems to me far deeper in compassion than its two predecessors. At its close the quiet affection of uncle and niece rests like a last glint of autumn sunset over the dry stubble of their desolate and darkened world. That is what Tolstoy should have seen.

The Three Sisters
(begun 1900, produced 1901)

'Into this Universe, and *Why* not knowing
Nor Whence, like Water willy-nilly flowing;
    And out of it, as Wind along the Waste,
    I know not *Whither*, willy-nilly blowing. . . .

When You and I behind the Veil are past,
Oh, but the long, long while the World shall last,
    Which of our Coming and Departure heeds
    As the Sea's self should heed a pebble-cast.'

FitzGerald, *Omar Khayyám*

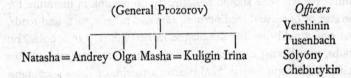

(General Prozorov)

Natasha ═ Andrey Olga Masha ═ Kulígin Irina

Officers
Vershinin
Tusenbach
Solyóny
Chebutykin

The Three Sisters is perhaps the finest of all Chekhov's plays. And, of all, the most tragic. One might wonder whether, feeling how moving Sonia had been in *Uncle Vanya*, he decided to have, this time, three Sonias—different, of course, but sisters to her as well as to each other.

A certain General Prozorov, an artillery-brigade commander, had a son and three daughters. The son, Andrey, was bookishly educated and became a schoolmaster in a provincial town, as dull and drab as Chekhov's native Taganrog.[1] The eldest sister, Olga, twenty-eight when the play begins, is likewise a schoolmistress there. The second sister, Masha, like the Masha of *The Seagull*, is married to yet another school-teacher—the worthy but ridiculous

[1] Chekhov said he was thinking of a town like Perm (later re-named Molotov). Its population in 1900 was about 45,000—Taganrog at the same period had about 56,000.

Kulígin; and, like her namesake in *The Seagull*, cannot love him. The youngest sister, Irina, is just celebrating her twentieth 'name-day', which is also the first anniversary of their father's death. But the family remains as unhappy in its provincial exile as poor Ovid when banished by Augustus to Tomi on the Black Sea two thousand years before. Just as Ovid sighed inconsolably for the life and light of Rome, so the sisters dream always of returning to the beloved Moscow which they left eleven years ago. For them, Moscow has become a Jerusalem, a Mecca, an Eldorado, a lost Eden. As legends of Adam's lost Paradise are said to be based on man's longings for the lost happiness and security of childhood, so this land of their childhood has become their lost Paradise.

Chekhov himself, when he wrote the play, was exiled by illness from Moscow to Yalta. And though to the English reader the thought of living in Moscow may suggest only repugnant shivers, the charm of the capital for Russian eyes is vividly drawn in a passage of Chekhov's story, *The Lady with the Dog*,[1] where the Muscovite Gurov has just come back from Yalta.

The frosts had begun already. When the first snow has fallen, on the first day of sledge-driving, it is pleasant to see the white earth, the white roofs, to draw soft, delicious breath; and the season brings back the days of one's youth. The old limes and birches, white with hoar-frost, have a good-humoured expression; they are closer to one's heart than cypresses and palms; and near them one does not want to be thinking of the sea and the mountains. . . . When he put on his fur coat and warm gloves, and walked along Petrovka, and when on Saturday evening he heard the ringing of the bells, his recent trip and the places he had seen lost all charm for him. Little by little he became absorbed in Moscow life, greedily read three newspapers a day, and declared he did not read the Moscow papers on principle.

But, being Russian intelligentsia portrayed by Chekhov, these unfortunate sisters can only yearn. The play's last act will merely find them further than ever from the Moscow of their dreams. More

---

[1] Published in 1899, the year Chekhov settled at Yalta, and the year before he began *The Three Sisters*. Cf. his own words in a letter to Lydia Avílov (February, 1899): 'We are having lovely weather in Yalta, but it is as dull as in Shklov. I am just like an army officer billeted in some god-forsaken provincial hole.'

practical and resolute persons, if they wanted Moscow so very, very much, would have taken the risk, and a train.

Andrey, the brother, is at first less torn by discontent. Not only has he hopes of becoming a professor; he has also fallen in love with an odious young woman, Natasha—egoistic, tasteless, dictatorial, grasping, and stingy—perhaps the nastiest woman in all Chekhov.

For the sisters, their dim provincial backwater is enlivened only by the officers of an artillery-brigade—such as Chekhov himself had got to know when staying with his brother Ivan, another schoolmaster, in the little town of Vokressensk near Moscow.[1]

Among these officers is the new Lieutenant-Colonel, Vershinin, a noble dreamer burdened with a neurotic wife who tries at intervals to poison herself. He too is one of those Chekhov characters who try to console themselves, not very convincingly, with visions of how beautiful life will become a few centuries hence. And yet he too has recurrent moments of disillusion. 'A Russian,' he exclaims, 'is particularly given to exalted ideals; but why is it he always falls so short in life? Why?' 'There can be no happiness for us; it exists only in our wishes.'

Then there is a lieutenant, Baron Tusenbach, of German origin, plain-featured, naïve, yet full of German idealism and conscientiousness, who vainly loves Irina. From his lips comes a prophecy truer than even Chekhov could know—'I shall work, and in twenty-five or thirty years every man will have to work. Everyone!' That was in 1900; in 1917 it was to become bleak reality.

Then, too, there is Captain Solyóny, also attracted by Irina; a neurotic, Byronic, Russian type, who fancies himself another Lermontov, but suffers in society from a gnawing sense of inferiority which exasperates him into a fatuous and vicious bully—a pygmy Mephistopheles. There is also a futile old army-doctor of sixty, Chebutykin, who reads nothing but futile newspapers, from which he makes futile notes, while content to forget what little medicine he ever knew.

But even Chebutykin, though now become an alcoholic nonentity, whose only philosophy is that perhaps all is illusion and, anyway,

---

[1] His story, *The Kiss*, had already in 1887 depicted the officers of an artillery brigade.

nothing really matters, was not always thus. Once he had loved the dead mother of the three sisters; and still he keeps a clumsy tenderness for Irina.

Like *Madame Bovary*, *The Three Sisters* is a tragedy of provincial life that seems too humdrum even to be tragic—but is not.

Chekhov's speciality, in his final phase, is to paint what are almost still-lifes, deathly in their stagnation; yet the trivial shadows in their background are alive with frustrated human passions, that only a vision sensitive as his could realize with full sympathy and understanding.

Indeed the essence of Chekhov's plays is largely summed up in Horace Walpole's wise saying that the world is a comedy to those that think, a tragedy to those that feel. In the theatre of Chekhov such thought and such feeling, such laughter and tears, alternate perpetually. Hence the constant wrangles whether his plays are meant to be tragic or comic. In reality they are both, ceaselessly passing from the poignant to the ridiculous and back again, as swiftly and imperceptibly as the colours change on an opal. Chekhov's atmosphere is, in short, as fitful as an April day—sunlight and storm, sunlight and storm.

ACT I

The opening lines already strike the note of life's eternal transience. For it is not only Irina's name-day, it is also the anniversary of General Prozorov's death. 'And now,' says Olga, 'a year has gone by, and already we think of it without pain, and you are wearing a white dress, and your face is happy.' That momentary happiness will soon have vanished; and only the eternal transience remain.

Just eleven years ago their father, appointed brigade-commander, rode out with the three sisters from Moscow. Now Olga herself is twenty-eight—prematurely aged, longing for a husband, longing for Moscow again. And all these memories are revived the more keenly by the entrance of the new Colonel of the local artillery, who recalls how he once knew the dead father of the family, and the three sisters themselves in their girlhood. Yet, as usual with Chekhov, this sadness is quickly mingled with the grotesque, in the person of the absurd, pathetic schoolmaster, Kulígin; who now finds to his dismay that he had already given Irina at Easter the name-day present he has just brought her again—a history of the High School, written by himself. So he presses his precious volume on the Colonel instead; while his wife Masha already feels attracted to this honest soldier, so unlike her absurd, good-hearted, pedant husband. For, as Irina observes, when Masha is out of the room, 'she married at eighteen, when he seemed the wisest of men. And now it's different. He's the kindest of men; but *not* the wisest.'

Finally there arrives the fatal Natasha, ill-dressed in clashing colours. On Andrey's embrace of her, unintentionally witnessed by two astonished officers, the curtain falls. The witch's cauldron of future trouble is already on the boil.

Act II

It is eight on a January evening, eighteen months later. Natasha has married her Andrey, and firmly established her foothold as invader in the home. This creature has a rage for dominance, and a grotesque ape-love for her first-born, Bobby; and so, though a kind of carnival-party had been arranged this evening for the officers, with some mummers due to arrive at nine, Natasha is dictatorially countermanding them, because 'Bobbee' has, possibly, a slight cold. Thus she informs Andrey; opportunely adding that Irina's room would be much nicer for her little darling. '*She* can share Olga's room . . . she only *sleeps* here, anyway. (*Pause.*) Andrey darling, why are you so silent?'

As for the spineless Andrey, he has already declined into a mere potterer. He fiddles; he makes picture-frames; he has become secretary of the local district-council—and might even become a member! All his finer dreams have faded to mere dreams. 'I to be a member of the local district-council!—I who dream every night that I am a professor at Moscow University, a famous scholar of whom all Russia is proud!' But one does not become a famous scholar by making picture-frames.

Andrey's district-council has for chairman a certain Protopopov. Protopopov never appears. But he too plays his part—behind the scenes. Once Natasha's suitor, he is now Natasha's lover. And poor Andrey (as the unloved are prone to do) tries to find in gambling a substitute for love—and, of course, loses disastrously.[1]

Curious, how many of Chekhov's characters are similar studies in degeneration—Ivánov, Konstantin, Uncle Vanya, even Dr Astrov. And in *The Cherry Orchard*, the heroine and her brother are already rotted boughs when it begins.

Masha, for her part, has by now wholly lost her heart to Colonel Vershinin.

Vershinin (kissing her hand). You are a splendid, wonderful woman. Splendid! Wonderful! It is dark here, but I see your eyes shine.
Masha (moves to another chair). There is more light here.
Vershinin. I love you, love you, love you. . . . I love your eyes, your movements, I dream of them. . . . Splendid, wonderful woman!
Masha (laughing softly). When you talk to me like that, I laugh; I don't know why, though I'm also afraid. . . . Please don't say it again. . . . (*In an undertone.*) No, go on, I don't mind. . . . (*Covers her face with her hands.*) I don't mind. . . . Someone's coming. . . . Let's talk of something else.

Hardly a conventional love-scene; but all the truer for that. The opal of tragi-comedy flashes; yet opals are said to bring ill-luck. Sure enough, the ill-luck will come.

It must be owned, however, that Vershinin is hardly an exhilarating lover. At moments he recalls poor Uncle Vanya with his Helen; though Vershinin is less ineffectual, and Masha less cold.

My hair is turning grey, I am almost an old man now; but I know so little, oh so little! Yet I think I know one thing that is true, and that matters most. I'm sure of it. And if only I could make you understand that for *us* there is *no* happiness, that there should not and cannot be. . . . We must simply work and work; happiness is only for our remote descendants. . . .

And again—

The other day I was reading the prison-diary of a French minister.

---

[1] As Chekhov himself generally lost (though with much more self-control than Dostoievsky) at the gaming-tables of Europe.

He had been condemned in the Panama Scandal.[1] With what joy, what rapture, he speaks of the birds he saw through the prison-window; as minister, he had never noticed them! Now, of course, that he is free again, he notices birds no more than before. In the same way, when you live in Moscow, you'll not notice it. We're not happy, and cannot be— we can only long for it.

A most disconsolate doctrine. But, rather curiously, the good Colonel does not apply this sceptical pessimism to the happiness he expects for posterity from some Utopian millennium. Yet, by parity of reasoning, that posterity must likewise cease to notice their blessings, and pine for something else; just as today in the most affluent of countries suicides can still multiply.

However, if Colonel Vershinin remains a somewhat sombre lover, that remains natural and excusable when we recall that he is married to a wife whose only recreation is to poison herself. In a moment comes news that she has just staged another suicide—of course, unsuccessfully. 'My wife has poisoned herself again. I must go. I'll slip out quietly. It's all awfully unpleasant. (*Kisses Masha's hand.*) My dear, fine, splendid woman. . . . I'll go this way, quietly.' Tragedy and comedy—comedy and tragedy.

As for Irina, she has now become a telegraph-clerk—and hates it; unconsoled by the patient wooing of the dog-like Tusenbach, who tonight, as every night, has faithfully escorted her home.

Then there is still Chebutykin, still at his eternal game of making notes. 'Chebutykin (*reading the newspaper*). "Balzac was married at Berdichev." (*Irina is singing softly.*) I must note that. (*Makes a note.*) "Balzac was married at Berdichev." '

Utterly futile, utterly pointless? Like the map of Africa in *Uncle Vanya*. Yet possibly, here too, there *is* a hidden point. For Berdichev is just such another provincial hole; yet even in that hole Balzac could crown his life's romance with his Polish countess. He did not need Moscow.

(Lovers of hidden meanings might add that, even so, Balzac's romance proved likewise an illusion, followed by bitter disillusion-

---

[1] 1892-3. Compare Chekhov to Suvórin (24/11/1897): 'I am reading *Impressions Cellulaires* by Charles Baïhaut, the former Panamist minister.' C. Baïhaut (1843-1905) was arrested in 1893; released from prison in 1896.

ment. For his Polish countess did not make him happy; and that same summer he died. But it would be too much to ask an audience to recall, and infer, all that.)

With empty bickerings and empty laughter the winter-evening drags on, till the guests, finding that there is after all to be no entertainment, drift away. In vain Solyóny makes a declaration of passion to Irina left alone.

Then Natasha, after informing Irina that she wants to annex Irina's room for little Bobbee, suddenly hears that at the door waits the troika of Protopopov. At once little Bobbee's chill, and the January night, are forgotten. Triumphant, Natasha rushes off for an evening drive with her lover.

The curtain falls on Irina's disconsolate cry—'To Moscow! Moscow! Moscow!'

All is futility. No, not quite all. These pathetic human puppets are still sometimes human; sometimes lovable; sometimes fine.

Act III

Another year and a half have dragged away. It is May once more. But now it is two in the morning, and the sisters' flat is reddened by the glare of a big fire in the town. Even in this backwater, it appears, sometimes something happens. And amid the clang of fire-alarms, under the crimson light of the burning, come glimpses of how much further these derelict existences have drifted, down the dull, sluggish river of Russian life.

Natasha is still busy burrowing under the household, like a parasitic insect. She has now been further blessed with a little daughter, Sophie—really, it seems, the child of Protopopov. And at this moment, while Olga with reckless generosity is throwing out clothes for the victims of the fire, Natasha suddenly demands the dismissal of the old servant, Anfisa, who is eighty-one, and has lived with the family for thirty years.

Natasha (*to Anfisa, coldly*). How *dare* you sit down in my presence! Get up! Get out! (*Anfisa goes. A pause.*)
(*To Olga*). I don't understand what makes you keep that old woman.
Olga (*confused*). Excuse me, I don't understand, either, how you. . . .

Natasha. She's no use here. She's a peasant from the country, she ought to be *there.* . . . Just spoiling her! I like order in the house. Not useless people about. (*Stroking Olga's cheek*) You're tired, poor darling! Our headmistress is tired!

If there was one of his characters that even the tolerant Chekhov really loathed, it was Natasha.

Andrey, for his part, to cover his gambling-debts, has mortgaged the house, though it belongs as much to his sisters as to him. His ambitions—his dreams of a professorship—are finally faded and gone. Enough that he *has* become a member of the district-council, whose chairman is—Protopopov, the lover of his wife.

Irina is no less unhappy now that she works in the town-council office, than she had been before as a telegraph-clerk. She cries out that her brain is addling.

> Yes, the truth is our Andrey is grown petty. He's ageing; and, living with that woman, his inspiration's gone. He used to be working for a professorship; and yet yesterday he was boasting that, at last, he had been made a *member* of the district-council! He a member, with Proto-popov for chairman! . . . The whole town talks and laughs, and he is the only one that sees, and knows, nothing. . . . Now everyone's rushed to the fire, but *he* just sits in his room, and takes no notice—merely plays his fiddle. Oh it's awful, awful, awful. (*Weeping.*) I can't, I can't bear it any more. . . . I can't, I can't. . . .
>
> Where—where has everything gone? Where *is* it all? Oh my God! I've forgotten everything—*everything*! There's nothing but muddle in my head. . . . I don't remember the Italian for 'window' or 'ceiling'. . . .
>
> Every day I forget more and more . . . ; and life slips by, never, never to return. . . .
>
> We shall *never* go to Moscow. . . . I can see we shall *never* go. . . .
>
> Oh, I am so unhappy. . . . I can't work, I won't work. I've had enough. First, I was a telegraph-clerk; now I work at the town-council offices; and I hate and despise every single thing they give me to do. . . .
>
> *Olga.* Dear, let me tell you something—as a sister and a friend. If you want my advice . . . why not marry the Baron? (*Irina cries softly.*)
>
> *Olga* . . . It's true he's not handsome; but he's so good and decent. . . . One doesn't marry for love, but just to do one's duty. I think so, anyway—I'd marry without being in love. . . .
>
> *Irina.* I was always waiting for us to move to Moscow—there I should meet the man I was meant for. . . . But it's all turned out nonsense—nonsense!

At this point there reappears the predatory, possessive Natasha prowling into the bedroom with a candle, in her anxiety to guard against burglars. Stanislavsky, as producer made her peer methodically under the furniture, and put out the lights. 'I think,' wrote Chekhov, 'it would be better that she should go straight across the stage, without looking at anything or anyone, like Lady Macbeth, candle in hand. That will be briefer and more terrifying' (2/1/01).

A typical contrast between the two men—Stanislavsky with his conscientious over-elaboration, Chekhov with his simple directness. Both were admirable characters; but how much more admirable is the wise simplicity, the subtle honesty of Chekhov! (Though one may feel that Natasha *should*, in passing, look sharply at *something*.)

After this fleeting vision of their hated sister-in-law, the sisters fall in talk again. And now it is Masha's turn to confess—she is hopelessly in love with Vershinin. Olga, horrified, refuses to listen. She shrinks behind a screen. But Masha is past caring.

> Oh, Olga, you are stupid. I love him—well, that's my fate. It means it's my destiny. . . . And he loves me. . . . It is all awful. Yes, it isn't good, is it? (*Taking Irina's hand and drawing her close.*) Oh my dear . . . how are we going to live through our lives?—what is to become of us? . . . When you read a novel, it all seems so old and obvious; but when you fall in love yourself, then you discover that no one knows anything, and you've got to make up your own mind. . . .

But now comes a deadly rumour that even the artillery-brigade is to be transferred, leaving this provincial town deeper than ever in its dusty desolation. And Irina cries that she *will* marry Tusenbach—'only let's go to Moscow'.

More ridiculous, or pathetic? Who shall say?

ACT IV

Another spring has changed to autumn. From these drowning fingers the last straws are about to slip. At moments, as with Hardy, one feels that Chekhov loads the dice *too* unfairly against his characters, and becomes more pitiless than life itself.

The brigade is going; and with it goes Colonel Vershinin, who alone made Masha's life endurable. Olga is now headmistress, as

she never wished to be, and has moved away to live at the school.
Irina has reconciled herself to marry, tomorrow, her good, ugly
German baron (who has quitted the army for a post in a brickworks).
And then she too will teach in the inevitable school.

But now, through old Chebutykin, comes a rumour that the
Baron, provoked by the insolent, jealous Solyóny, has insulted him
and been challenged to a duel. As doctor, Chebutykin must attend.
But all this hardly stirs the old man's oriental indifference.

Chebutykin.   The Baron is a good enough fellow; but one Baron more
or less in the world—what does it matter? So be it. It's all the same. . . .
Andrey.   In *my* view it's just immoral to fight duels, or to be present at
them, even as doctor.
Chebutykin.   It only *seems* so. . . . We don't exist—nothing exists—it
only *seems* to us that we do. And does it matter, anyway!

Tusenbach enters, carefully hiding from the anxiously suspicious
Irina that he is on his way to fight. But, though anxious about him,
she still cannot love him, poor, excellent man. Her soul, she sobs, is
like a costly piano that has lost its key.

Tusenbach.   In an hour I'll be back . . . here with you again (*Kissing her
hands.*) My treasure! . . . (*Gazing in her face.*) Five years ago I fell in
love with you, and still I can't get used to it—every day you seem more
beautiful. What lovely, wonderful hair! What eyes! To-morrow I'll
take you away. We'll work—we'll be rich—my dreams will come true.
You *shall* be happy. Only one thing, one thing—you don't love me.
Irina.   It isn't in my power. I'll be your wife—faithful and obedient; but
I can't love you. What am I to do? (*Weeping.*) I have never been in
love, all my life. Oh, I've so dreamed of it—dreamed of it for years,
day and night . . . but somehow my soul is like a costly piano, locked
up and its key lost. (*Pause.*) Your eyes are so restless.
Tusenbach.   I was awake all night. Not that there's anything in my life
to be afraid of, anything alarming—only that lost key torments me,
and will not let me sleep. Say something to me. (*Pause.*) Say something.
Irina.   What? What *can* I say? What?
Tusenbach.   Anything.

How could Chekhov make so hackneyed a situation seem so
new? Simply because his mind was so simply and incorruptibly true.

Between Masha and Vershinin likewise the time has come for a
bitter good-bye. Only the odious Natasha stalks triumphant. Now

the whole house will be hers to tyrannize; and all the trees in the garden hers to cut down. (One must remember how passionately Chekhov felt about trees.)

From the distance there begins to throb the music of the departing brigade. Chebutykin enters, exhausted, to whisper to Olga—in his duel with Solyóny the Baron has been killed. Once again, the drastic event happens *off* the stage—like Konstantin's suicide. For Chekhov, the *scène à faire* becomes often the *scène à ne pas faire*.

Fainter and fainter in the distance, the music of the marching column dies away—so proud, so confident, as if it at least never doubted whither it was going, and why men are born.

> Far the calling bugles hollo,
> High the screaming fife replies.
> Gay the files of scarlet follow:
> Woman bore me, I will rise.

But Olga clasps her two sisters, desolate as herself. 'The music is so gay, so joyful, and it seems as if in a little we should know why we live, why we suffer. . . . If we could only know, if we could only know!'

Most tragedies are about terrible things happening; but often in Chekhov the tragedy lies rather in the things that fail to happen— the dreams that die still-born. Most tragedies are about things that matter terribly; but here the tragedy is rather that nothing seems to matter at all. That is the refrain of the old surgeon Chebutykin, like some sad elder of a Greek chorus. And one thinks of a poem on a dead friend from Hardy's old age—a poem whose burden and whose title are just the same—'Nothing Matters Much'.

> Facing the North Sea now he lies,
> Towards the red altar of the East,
> The Flamboro' roar his psalmodies,
>   The wind his priest.

> And while I think of his bleak bed,
> Of Time that builds and Time that shatters,
> Lost to all thought is he, who said
>   'Nothing much matters'.

As usual Tolstoy disapproved—'I am fond of Chekhov, and value his writings highly. But I could not make myself read his *Three Sisters* through—where does it all lead us?'

A most Tolstoyan question. For Tolstoy's tragedy lay largely in his endless search for life's purpose; till that search, after turning his own home into a domestic hell, ended at last on the wayside station of Astapovo. The same problem forms the climax, in the heart of Levine, at the end of *Anna Karénina*. For Tolstoy could not possibly resign himself to answer—'But why should life have any purpose at all? Why should a man expect any purpose from life, beyond what he himself has the strength of will to put there?' That answer may be bleak. But it may be true.

Melchior de Vogüé, on the other hand, passes on this play a judgement no less typically French. For to the Frenchman there is apt to seem something irresistibly comic about the loves of garrison-life. 'Je redouterais,' says M. de Vogüé, 'un succès de fou rire pour les trois soeurs éplorées qui voient filer leurs militaires.'[1] And yet perhaps in *Les Grandes Manœuvres* of René Clair, along with this ironic Gallic laughter, there was also a touch of Chekhov's compassion for all the human hopes that life shatters to irreparable fragments.

After French gaiety, English solemnity. For an English critic has found, on the contrary, 'a gay affirmation of life in the final chorus of the three sisters to the accompaniment of an invigorating march by the band of the departing regiment'. One would imagine it was the end of a musical comedy. Surely even the poor corpse of Baron Tusenbach should be 'invigorated' by such a 'chorus' to leap to its feet and salute. 'Debout les morts!'

A similarly bracing interpretation of the closing scene was given by official Russian Communism at a revival in 1940. 'The sisters take each other by the hand. Their faces are stern and solemn. They speak little about what is in their hearts. Their eyes talk. Their eyes sparkle, not with tears, but with a stubborn belief in the future. And the three sisters here begin to show that they are great and strong . . .

---

[1] 'I should be afraid of shouts of wild laughter acclaiming the three tearful sisters who watch their military gentlemen march away.'

a magnificent type of Russian womanhood, with its suffering, self-renunciation, and moral strength.'[1]

Now it is of course true that Irina sobs, 'We must work, just work. Tomorrow I'll go away alone, and I'll teach and give my life to those who perhaps need it'; and that Olga echoes her with the usual vague hopes of building a happier future for posterity—'O dear sisters, our life is not yet ended. Let us live! The music is so gay, so joyful, and it seems that in a little while we shall know why we live and suffer.' But had Chekhov really wished to produce the sort of Marxist *Marseillaise* that critical Panglosses here thrust into his mouth, he needed only to drop the curtain on these closing words. Nothing easier. And then his meaning would have been beyond question. But he did *not* drop the curtain. He went on. Presumably, with *some* intention. The futile Andrey wheels out the pram with Bobbee. The futile Chebutykin hums sardonically over his futile newspaper—' "Ta-ra-ra-boom-de-ay.... It is my washing-day." It's all the same! It's all the same!' Then comes Olga's final, anguished cry—'If only we could know, if only we could know!'

A curious form of 'stubborn belief'. Chekhov was too ruthlessly truthful to be content with such glib consolations. He *had* to give also the other, gloomier, more sardonic side.

Of course one must work. The three sisters will go on working, as, doubtless, Uncle Vanya went on—as Voltaire's Martin went on. 'It is the only way to make life endurable.' But *Candide, ou l'Optimisme*—ironic title—is not usually taken as exuberantly optimist. In *The Three Sisters*, as in Voltaire, there breathes, rather, a disillusioned, stoical compassion for all human life.

Chekhov's plays contain plenty that is comic; but if, as wholes, they are to be called 'comedies', I can only say that they seem to me the saddest and most desolate comedies on earth. By comparison, even Molière's *Misanthrope* is gay.

Of this piece Chekhov himself wrote (13/11/1900): '*The Three Sisters* is ready. . . . The play turned out dreary, long, and inconvenient. I say "inconvenient" because it has, for instance, four heroines, and a spirit, as the saying goes, "gloomier than gloom itself".'

[1] N. A. Gorchakov, *The Theatre in Soviet Russia*, p. 393.

'Gloomier than gloom itself!' So much for 'gay affirmations of life' and 'eyes sparkling, not with tears, but with a stubborn belief in the future'.

Again, to Olga Knipper, who was to act Masha, Chekhov wrote, most revealingly: 'Do not look sad in any of the acts. Angry, certainly, but not sad. People *who have long carried sorrow within them, and grown used to it*, only whistle a little,[1] and are often lost in thought. So on the stage you must now and then grow lost in thought.'[2] Chekhov, one feels, is speaking here, at least in part, from his own experience of himself.

It is easy to make glib generalizations about the Slav soul and its passionate melancholia. But I do not think it all mere illusion. I can never forget the Jugoslav girl I once heard singing at midnight by the Gulf of Kotor, with a depth of inconsolable, irreconcilable despair such as I never heard from any Western lips. She at least might have understood *The Three Sisters*.[3]

On the night of June 21, 1941, Chekhov's tragi-comedy was being acted at the Moscow Art Theatre. Next day Hitler invaded Russia. But he found it no easier than the three sisters to reach Moscow.

[1] Cf. Dr Astrov in *Uncle Vanya*.

[2] In his later plays Chekhov made much use of 'Pauses'; where, as the Chinese say, 'the thought goes on'. A critic has counted 30 in *Ivánov*; 36 in *The Seagull*; 44 in *Uncle Vanya*; 66 in *The Three Sisters*; 35 in *The Cherry Orchard*. The predominance of *The Three Sisters* is revealing. (See Stender-Petersen, 'Zur Technik der Pause bei Čechov' in *A. Čechov*, ed. T. Eekman, 1960.)

[3] Though on its first night, in January, 1901, the play does not seem to have been fully appreciated, on the second night the audience sat spell-bound— 'weeping could be heard all over the theatre'. Not much 'gay affirmation of life', then either. 'I was not ashamed,' wrote one critic, 'of my tears.' Compare Ilya Erenburg (*Chekhov, Stendhal and other essays*, transl. Bostock and Kapp, 1962, p. 12): 'I have seen Soviet women—by no means sentimental, and certainly level-headed—weep as they shared the sorrows of *The Three Sisters*. . . . And engineers and doctors, grey-haired housewives and laughter-loving girl-students wept too.'

The Cherry Orchard
(produced 1904)

'Unwatch'd, the garden-bough shall sway;
  The tender blossom flutter down,
  Unloved, that beech will gather brown,
This maple burn itself away. . . .

We leave the well-beloved place
  Where first we gazed upon the sky;
  The roofs that heard our earliest cry
Will shelter one of stranger race.'

TENNYSON

The Cherry Orchard is a far less sombre play—it is a laughable, lamentable chaos. But though those who do not see its comedy are owls, those who do not also feel its sadness are hippopotami.

The Cherry Orchard is not, for me, the best of Chekhov's dramas —it was written, with heroic effort, by a dying man. But perhaps it is the most Chekhovian. Indeed at a first sight or reading it can bewilder.[1]

Perhaps it should be regarded as something between an ordinary play, and a ballet—such as *Petroushka*. In normal drama there is usually a considerable unity of action; but, very often, little unity of acting. In *The Cherry Orchard* the unity of action is largely lost in a diversity of themes; its real unity lies in the union of its actors to produce a total effect of mingled tears and laughter. When I say

---

[1] Somerset Maugham (*The Vagrant Mood*, 1952, pp. 199-200) has amusingly described Henry James at a performance of Chekhov's play—a much-perplexed James, explaining through the second interval to Maugham and a Mrs Clifford how, with his own French sympathies, he was repelled by this Russian incoherence. And yet, not a little incoherent himself, James was all the while groping for the right words to express his meaning; Mrs Clifford as constantly suggesting them; and James as constantly brushing aside her suggestions. A scene that may well have been as comic as any in the play.

that in ordinary plays the acting is often less unified, I am thinking partly of the tendency in the West for the star-actors to dim the lesser players. One may recall, for example, that story of the minor actor in *The Corsican Brothers* who ironically begged Irving to have at least a little of the moonlight directed on himself. 'Nature at least,' he pleaded, 'is impartial.' But Irving's kind of production is the exact opposite of the elaborately concerted team-work sought by Stanislavsky and the Moscow Art Theatre.

But there is also a tendency in drama for attention to be concentrated on the actor speaking at a given moment, while the others impatiently wait their turns to speak; whereas in ballet the dancers dance simultaneously. At all events, I repeat that there are scenes of carefully studied confusion in *The Cherry Orchard* which remind me of the crowd-scenes in a ballet like *Petroushka*.

Nowhere else in Chekhov's major plays is there such a whirl of boisterous humour and ludicrous absurdity. Yet the piece was composed by a man spitting blood, and tormented with tubercular diarrhoea—'I am writing four lines a day, and even that gives me unbearable pain.'[1] It was a feat as heroic as Walter Scott's, when he dictated *The Bride of Lammermoor* to Willie Laidlaw in like illness and pain—'Nay, Willie, only see that the doors are fast. I would fain keep all the cry as well as all the wool to ourselves; but as to giving over work, that can only be done when I am in woollen.' But, even so, *The Bride of Lammermoor* shows far less gaiety than *The Cherry Orchard*. Chekhov said himself that he tended to go by opposites. Just as some have held that a writer should deal with summertime in winter, with wintertime in summer, so, when he felt gay, he wrote dreary stories; and *vice versa*.

Because of this diversity of theme and mood *The Cherry Orchard* is one of the hardest of plays to memorize. Yet its main theme is staringly simple—indeed one might think it impossibly simple. A

---

[1] Tikhonov has left a grim glimpse of Chekhov in 1902, arriving from a railway-journey, grey, wan, worn, and carrying slung at his side a leather-covered flask into which he could cough. Wakened in the night by groans from the next room, Tikhonov found Chekhov with beard and moustache covered in blood, but gasping: 'I am stopping you . . . from sleeping . . . forgive me . . . mon petit.'

cherry orchard is threatened with sale; the only way to save it is rejected; and duly sold it is.

Long before, on a country-visit in 1888, Chekhov had described himself as surrounded by 'sad and poetical estates, shut up and deserted, where live the souls of beautiful women; old footmen, relics of serfdom, with one foot in the grave[1]; young ladies longing for the most conventional love'. This is exactly the world of *The Cherry Orchard*.

Its owner, Mme Lubov Andreyevna Ranevsky, is a feckless Russian widow. Six years ago her husband died—of champagne. A month later her little son was drowned. Lubov Andreyevna imagined this disaster to be a judgement on a love-affair of hers. So she fled from her guilty memories to France; but her lover followed, and fell ill. She bought a villa at Mentone; but it had to be sold to pay her debts. Next, in Paris, her lover robbed her of all she had left, and ran off with a new mistress; finally, after trying—ineffectually, of course—to poison herself, she has returned to Russia—penniless, but pursued all the time by telegrams from the now penitent lover.[2]

Yet this poor unpractical woman has only fled from debts abroad to debts at home. On these not even the interest has been paid. So, arriv'ng in May, she finds that her ancestral Cherry Orchard must be sold in August. And there she sits, paralysed and helpless, like a faded Marie Antoinette in a crumbling Petit Trianon.

Her beloved brother, Gaev, is equally butter-brained. He has not the faintest notion how to meet the crisis. His only idea is to borrow still more, so as to pay the interest on what is borrowed already; or else to sponge on a rich old aunt.

Through the whole play there moves only one competent character—Lopákhin, the rich business-man, whose father and grandfather were once serfs on the estate. (One thinks of Chekhov's own ancestry.) Lopákhin sees the obvious and only solution—to sell the Orchard in building-lots for villas (like Ibsen's Master

---

[1] Cf. Fiers in the play.

[2] Compare the Russian gentleman recorded in one of Chekhov's note-books, who sold his estate at Tula in Russia to buy a villa at Mentone; gambled away at cards all he possessed; became a railway-clerk; and died.

Builder). But Mme Ranevsky and her brother are appalled by such vulgar vandalism. Admirable of them—if only their own incompetence had not produced this situation where, despite them, the vulgar vandalism must triumph.

So in the end this glorious Orchard, which once even figured in the Encyclopedia, is bought up by Lopákhin himself; and in October Mme Ranevsky goes back to her lover in Paris and, one guesses, to final and irretrievable ruin; like Matthew Arnold's Marguerite,

> Flitted down the flowery track
> Where feet like thine too lightly come.

Stated so baldly, it might seem a plot of interest only to house-agents. But Chekhov seems to have had a special feeling for the sorrow of families driven from a home long loved. It recurs in two of his stories—*Other People's Misfortune* (1886) and *A Visit to Friends* (1898).[1] Perhaps he remembered from boyhood his own family's painful departure from Taganrog.

Still the essential life of *The Cherry Orchard* lies in its details, in the interweaving of its many minor threads. Thus there is the theme of Mme Ranevsky's daughter Anya, aged seventeen and buoyant with all the blithe heedlessness of a younger generation. She too is filled with emotion at seeing again, after five years, the old home of her childhood; yet to her young eyes the Cherry Orchard remains, after all, only a relic of the past—a past soon forgotten in the thrills of present and future, as embodied for her in Peter Trofímov, her drowned brother's former tutor. It matters little to Anya that Trofímov, though now twenty-six or seven, has become already a grotesque, bespectacled owl, a clumsy creature, spluttering half-baked ideals. In spite of his age, this 'eternal student' has still not passed his exams, having been twice expelled from the University (apparently for revolutionary principles). He may patter glibly about progress and hard work. But grotesque he remains. Even when he storms passionately from the room in wounded pride and anger at Mme Ranevsky's laughter, he inevitably tumbles, pride and all, headlong down the stairs. Even in the final chaos and desolation of the last act, the supreme tragedy for Trofímov is that he cannot

[1] Both included in A. Yarmolinsky, *The Unknown Chekhov*.

find his galoshes. Once *they* are retrieved, he gaily rushes off with his Anya—and pretty hard no doubt they will both tumble down the long stairs of life.[1]

Then there is the theme of Varya, Mme Ranevsky's adopted daughter, an affectionate, unhappy young woman of twenty-seven, recalling in some ways the Sonia of *Uncle Vanya*—for both girls alike bear on their young shoulders the burdens shirked by their feckless elders. Indeed Varya and Lopákhin are the only two rational persons in this blundering bedlam. It is Varya that has been left, with her hopeless uncle Gaev, in charge of the estate; Varya, that tries to keep *some* order among the insubordinate servants; Varya, that struggles to stop her mother from flinging away every rouble on futile gifts or futile loans; to stop her uncle Gaev from vapouring idiotic speeches; to stop Anya from getting entangled with the foolish Trofímov. And all the while her real dream is, rather, to wander away on pilgrimage among the holy places of Russia. In vain Mme Ranevsky tries to marry her off to Lopákhin. Varya would be willing; but Lopákhin typifies the too busy business-man. Some new project is always elbowing poor Varya out of his bustling mind.

And so at the end, when all is sold, Varya vanishes to become a housekeeper. For Lopákhin is too strenuous to think of love. He reminds one of the strenuous Balzac's rueful comment on some distracting love-episode—'Another novel wasted!'—'Encore un roman de perdu!'

So the play, like a bubbling mill-race, tosses and whirls away its pathetic human straws and bubbles—Mme Ranevsky, with her lover in Paris; the daughter Anya, clinging to her Peter Trofímov; the adopted daughter, Varya, longing for her Lopákhin. The poor

---

[1] It is a mistake, I think, to take Trofímov (as has sometimes been done) for a serious character, an idealist to be respected. One may compare that other character, likewise nicknamed 'the eternal student'—Kish, in Chekhov's story *Three Years*: 'He had been three years studying medicine. Then he went in for mathematics, and took two years over each year's course. . . . His stories were always long and tedious; and his jokes invariably raised a laugh just because they were *not* funny.' Trofímov seems to me meant as a comical incompetent, who (like Leigh Hunt) sometimes says something sensible, but has very slight success in acting sensibly himself.

straws may sink or swim: the mill-race churns on. And Chekhov delights to show also what queer fish swim in it.

There is, for example, Simeonov Pishchik, a Gogol-like elderly landowner, remarkable as his name, and strong as a horse, despite two paralytic strokes—an old rogue incapable of doing anything but fall asleep; borrow money; wait, like Micawber, for something to turn up; emit scraps of undignified reading, partly derived from his daughter Dashenka; and cry out, in constant astonishment—'To think of that, now!' (Here he becomes a distant relative of Jørgen Tesman in *Hedda Gabler*.) And such is, sometimes, the kindness of blind Fortune to fools, that at intervals something really does turn up to keep this reckless old monster's chin above water. A railway gets built over his land. Or some Englishmen buy from him a concession of white clay; thereby inspiring a flood of Pishchikian eloquence—

> A most extraordinary occurrence! Some Englishmen came along, and found on my land some sort of white clay. . . . I've let them the land and the clay for twenty-four years. . . . Men of enormous intellect, these English. . . . Never mind. . . . Be happy. . . . God will help you. . . . Never mind. . . . Everything on earth comes to its end.

The same flaccid philosophy as sustained that other improvident old wretch—Dr Chebutykin—in *The Three Sisters*.

This ludicrous creature is smitten at moments by attraction towards a being equally fantastic, the skinny, lorgnetted governess, Charlotta Ivanova, who knows neither her own age, nor whether her parents—circus-performers—were ever married, nor indeed who she is, nor why she lives at all. Only, from her circus childhood, she retains a fondness for juggling-tricks and ventriloquism. Actually Chekhov based her on a mannish English governess he once met—who must have made a very odd governess indeed. But then Chekhov found the English curious people.[1] 'The Englishman,' says one of his characters, 'is descended from a frozen fish.' Though that, at least, could never be said of Charlotta Ivanova.

---

[1] Compare the wooden English governess, 'Wilka Charlesovna Fyce', in his story *A Daughter of Albion* (in Vol. XIII of Constance Garnett's translation).

Then there are the servants. Epikhódov, the estate-clerk, is a melancholy noodle (somewhat like Shakespeare's Slender); nick-named 'Two-and-twenty troubles' because, as Sydney Smith put it, he is like a razor, always in hot water or a scrape.

> I'm a cultivated man, I read all sorts of remarkable books, but I can't seem to make out what I'm heading for, what I really want—to live or to shoot myself, I mean. Nevertheless, I always carry a revolver. Here it is. . . . Frankly speaking—to stick precisely to the point—I must explain that Fate, so to say, treats me without mercy, like a little boat in a storm. What I mean is—why, unless I am right, did I wake this morning, for example, to find on my chest an enormous spider? Big as this. Or if I pick up a jug for a drink of kvass, there's sure to be something most indelicate inside, such as a cockroach. Have you read Buckle?[1]

This mournful imbecile is in love with Dunyasha, the affected, over-dressed maidservant; but she at once forsakes him for Yasha, the intolerable, heartless lackey who has returned with Mme Ranevsky from Paris. There he has acquired only a French-polished insolence; and thither he pants to return. (At moments he recalls the more brutal lackey, Jean, of Strindberg's *Miss Julie*.)

In utter contrast to this flunkey is the eighty-seven years old Fiers, an ancient, deaf retainer who thinks himself still indispensable; still scolds his master Gaev like a little boy; hates the disrespectful modern world; and regards the emancipation of the serfs (which liberated himself among others) as a disaster comparable only with the Fall of Man.[2]

At the end when the house is shut up and deserted, it is intended that the old man should be packed off to hospital; but, with typical incompetence, even that is bungled. He always thought of his masters: but his masters cannot always think of him. And so the play closes with this tragi-comic old symbol of a régime for ever gone, locked by mistake into the empty house; while outside comes the dull thud of axes laid to the roots of the autumnal cherry-trees

---

[1] Epikhódov (like Fiers) may seem a minor part; but it was played by the famous Moskvin with memorable success.

[2] Cf. Chekhov's grandfather, the ex-serf Yegor Chekh, described by his grandson as 'a most rabid upholder of serfdom'.

which no spring will ever robe in white again.[1] Seldom, indeed, had a play a stranger ending. There are, indeed, very different ideas as to how this end should be interpreted. Thus it has been suggested that the forgotten Fiers provides a climax of high comedy, with an undertone of political seriousness. 'When he is left alone locked up in the empty house, the scales fall from his eyes. He suddenly realizes that his ideas of the good old days were false and that his life had been wasted.' (Is this really very comic?) 'The sound of the axe felling the cherry-trees is here merged with the dramatic realization of the born serf that the old order was wrong.' Doubtless the ending would have been more effective still if the old man had struggled to his feet and uplifted in a last quavering treble the strains of 'The Red Flag'! 'Expires. Curtain.' What an opportunity missed!

Yet other minds, less imaginative, may still wonder if it is not a little late—and sudden—for old Fiers to turn Marxist at eighty-seven. And if Chekhov meant Fiers to be seen as finally rebelling against his long servitude, why did he make it almost Fiers's last thought to worry devotedly because his master Gaev has gone off in his light overcoat, instead of his furs? 'Oh, these young people!' And why, one also wonders, if Chekhov meant this last episode to be so comic, and so invigoratingly revolutionary, did he add that final stage-direction?—'From far away, as from the sky, comes a sound like a breaking string, dying mournfully away. Silence follows; broken only by the sound, some distance off in the orchard, of axes falling on the trees.' It seems hardly a hilarious note on which to close the play—this mysteriously mournful sound, like a breaking string, above the slaughtered cherry-trees. 'Or ever the silver cord be loosed, or the golden bowl be broken.' Or one may recall, from Keats, those

---

[1] One should remember the rage and grief felt by Chekhov's Dr Astrov at the felling of woodlands. Chekhov himself had a special love for cherry-blossom; like Housman—

> Loveliest of trees, the cherry now
> Is hung with bloom along the bough,
> And stands about the woodland ride
> Wearing white for Eastertide.

> undescribed sounds
> That come a-swooning over barren grounds
> And wither drearily on barren moors.[1]

When this strange noise came before, in Act II, Mme Ranevsky *shuddered*. 'It's unpleasant somehow. (*A pause*.)'

Those, on the other hand, seem to me *too* gloomy who suppose that old Fiers actually dies in the deserted house, from hunger or exhaustion. This pathetically comic patriarch should not be melo-dramatically turned into a sort of Mistletoe Bride perishing in solitary confinement. The surrounding orchard is still full of wood-cutters. And surely it would be artistically incongruous suddenly to end this tragi-comedy of laughable incompetence in gruesome tragedy. With mere muddle it began: with mere muddle it concludes. Fiers is not Lear.

But though with all its minor characters, its subordinate themes, its jostling love-affairs, *The Cherry Orchard* seems a Masque of Anarchy, a ballet of marionettes, its figures possess one tragi-comic quality in common—that they have with one another no real communion at all. The whole is a 'sauve qui peut'—where none (except Lopákhin) seem likely to be saved. As the little marionettes whirl round, behind the forehead of each spins a little world which seems to itself the centre of the Universe. Yet to each other they remain little more than dummies, or phantoms. All of them are utterly lonely; though most of them never realize how lonely they are.

This disconsolate solitude is embodied with special vividness in the aged Fiers—that deaf spectre from a vanished age, who replies at cross-purposes to remarks that he has misheard, till finally he is

---

[1] *Endymion*, I, 285-7. When the mysterious sound occurs in Act II, Lopákhin thinks it perhaps caused by a bucket falling down a well; Gaev, by a heron; Trofímov, by an owl. And Fiers says a like sound once foreboded 'the misfortune' (the Emancipation of the Serfs). In Chekhov's melancholy story *Happiness*, shepherds hear something rather similar in the darkness of the steppe—' "It's a bucket broken away at the pits," said the young shepherd.' Why was Chekhov so fond of using this mysterious noise? It may not be too fanciful to suppose it associated in his mind with the aloof, melancholy indifference of external things to the hopes and sorrows of ephemeral human-kind.

left abandoned and alone; and, again, in the grotesque little governess, Charlotta, who is condemned to a like isolation by her origin,
her position, her eccentricities. But even the other characters, who
imagine that they communicate, attain no real contact.[1]

Two small children playing in a room together will conduct an
animated conversation in which neither listens to the other, yet each
feels happily that it has a hearer. Often Chekhov makes his characters much like such children.

> (*Dunyasha helps Anya to take off her hat and cloak.*)
> *Anya.* For four nights on the journey I haven't slept. I'm frozen.
> *Dunyasha.* You went away in Lent—there was snow, and frost. But
> now.... Darling! (*Laughing and kissing her.*) I could hardly wait for
> you, my joy, my pet! ... But I *must* tell you at once. I can't wait a
> minute longer.
> *Anya* (*wearily*). What is it now?
> *Dunyasha.* Epikhódov the clerk proposed to me, just after Easter.
> *Anya.* It's always the same thing with you. (*Putting her hair straight.*)
> I've lost all my hairpins. (*She is dropping with exhaustion.*)
> *Dunyasha.* I don't know *what* to think. He does love me—so much!
> *Anya* (*looking into her room, tenderly*). My own room, my own windows!
> —just as if I'd never been away.

Such is human sympathy. Such is comprehension. One thinks of
love; another of hair-pins.[2] 'We are irremediably alone.' And the
irony only deepens when one knows that soon the rapturous
Dunyasha will drop poor Epikhódov for Yasha, the Frenchified
footman; and that Yasha in his turn will drop Dunyasha, just as
indifferently, for his beloved Paris.

[1] The same bleak human solitude (recalling at times Proust and Pirandello)
recurs in such Chekhov stories as *Enemies* or *The Bishop*. In *Enemies* the
poor Dr Kirilov, whose child has just died, is dragged away, protesting, in
the middle of the night by the rich Abogin, whose wife has a heart-attack.
But the heart-attack proves a sham—the wife has run away with a lover. And
the two men, each fundamentally decent, yet each maddened by his own
despair, turn and rend each other. 'Unhappiness does not bring people
together, but draws them apart.' Even Chekhov never wrote anything more
masterly, or more desolate.

[2] Compare the grotesque wrangle in *The Three Sisters*, Act II, between
Chebutykin, who says that *chehartma* is a Caucasian meat-dish, and the
aggressive Solyóny who contradicts him—'*Cheremsha* is *not* meat!—it's a
plant rather like an onion'. And they go on quarrelling because they fail to
realize that each is talking about a totally different word.

The acting of the Moscow Art Theatre was concentrated team-work; but nothing could be less team-like, more self-centred and incoherent, more anarchic and chaotic, than the characters that here they acted.

Above this wind-tossed underwood of clutching, tangling, colliding bushes, the three main characters rise like trees—two of them rotten; one sturdy with promise of enduring growth.

Mme Ranevsky with her rattling, incoherent emotionalism would be hard to imagine as English or French; but she might just possibly be Irish. 'She was a good soul,' says Lopákhin. 'A good-natured, simple sort of person. I remember when I was a boy about fifteen, my father—he kept a little shop in the village then[1]—punched me in the face, and made my nose bleed. We were in the yard here, for something or other, and he'd been drinking. Lubov Andreyevna—I can see her now—she was young and slender then—took me to wash my face, in this very room—then, it was the nursery. "Don't cry, little peasant," said she, "it'll be well in time for your wedding."'

Perhaps Lopákhin feels a kind of love for her still. But she is weak as a rotten reed, and soft as a boiled turnip—like the lady whose mind Johnson described as incurably 'wiggle-waggle'. One more of Chekhov's many studies in fatty degeneration of the brain.

'It is not difficult to act Ranevskaja,' he wrote to Olga Knipper, 'only one must, from the very beginning, find the right key—one must find a smile, and a way of laughing; one must be able to dress.' Mme Ranevsky, in fine, must seem a lady of grace and style; yet with a certain fatal frivolity, as well as charm, in the way she smiles and laughs.

Mme Ranevsky (looking in her purse). I had a lot of money yesterday; but today there's very little left. My poor Varya feeds everyone on milk soup to save money; in the kitchen the old people get nothing but dried peas; and *I* spend recklessly. (*Drops her purse, scattering gold coins.*) There!—they're all over the place.
Yasha. Permit me, Madame, to pick them up.

He does so; and of course a lot of them slip into his pocket.

Further, Mme Ranevsky has that detestable Russian sense of guilt which treats past transgressions as puddles to wallow in, not

[1] Another echo of Chekhov's own boyhood?

as landmarks to learn from and march by. She feels guilty about her dead husband; guilty about her love-affair; guilty about her drowned son. Bombarded with telegrams from her faithless lover in Paris, she pours out her confession to the owlish Peter Trofímov.

> He begs forgiveness, and implores me to come; and I really ought to go to Paris and be near him. You look severe, Peter. But what *can* I do, my dear boy, what *can* I do? He's ill, he's lonely, he's unhappy, and who's to look after him? . . . And why should I hide it? . . . I love him, that's plain, I love him, I love him. . . . That love is a millstone round my neck; I'm going to the bottom with it; but I love that stone, and I can't live without it.

It is like Rossetti's *Orchard-Pit*:

> But I love her as in the maelstrom's cup
> The whirled stone loves the leaf inseparable
> That clings to it round all the circling swell,
> And that the same last eddy swallows up.

Only here Mme Ranevsky is the sodden leaf, in love with the stone that drags it down.

And so she goes back to the whirlpool of Paris. 'I'll live there on the money your grandmother at Yaroslav sent to buy the estate—bless her! Though it won't last long.'

It will not.

Gaev, her brother of fifty-one, is equally demented from every practical point of view—a loving brother, but an ass, who talks too much, drinks too much, eats too much—even sweets from a box carried in his pocket. Typical that the very first remark of this incompetent is to criticize the incompetent unpunctuality of the railway. 'The train was two hours late. What do you think of that! Is *that* the way to do things!'

Gaev has also a habit of bursting into emotional effusions, which his family, long sick of them, hastily interrupt. For example, he discovers a cupboard in the house to be a century old—and at once the romance of such antiquity inspires him to address this venerable cupboard in a tirade of rhetorical sentiment. And when such sentimental outbursts are met by his relatives with exasperated mockery, he falls back on his other nervous habit of describing imaginary strokes at billiards; just as Kosich in *Ivánov* loved recounting games of cards.[1]

In the end, when the family ruin is complete, poor Gaev has to enter a bank at £600 a year; and one may wonder whether even a Russian bank would have kept Gaev for even six months, at even £60 a year.

The character of Lopákhin is more intricate, and has caused dispute. Some critics took this upstart serf who buys the estate of his betters, to be the villain of the piece. Justly irritated, Chekhov himself pointed out to Stanislavsky that a girl like Varya would never have cared for a mere 'money-grubber'. 'It is true,' wrote Chekhov, 'that Lopákhin is a merchant; but he is a decent fellow in every respect. He has to behave, with perfect manners, like an educated man, without smallnesses and tricks.' Indeed Chekhov proposed that Stanislavsky should play this part himself.

A pity that we have not a few such letters from Shakespeare's hand, to explain as clearly how *he* saw his characters. But, of course, even then, there would be critics who knew better.

No doubt Lopákhin is self-made, and a little vulgar. No doubt he is tempted at times, as the angry Trofímov warns him at the end, to 'flap'—to show off (just as Tennyson complained of Browning that he 'flourished about').

Trofímov (searching for his galoshes). You know we may well never meet again. So let me give you a parting word of advice—don't flap your arms about. Get out of that way of flapping. Building villas, and reckoning on how your tenants will become freeholders—it's the same thing—it's all flapping.

Yet, even if he does 'flap', Lopákhin is kindly; and sane. Like Chekhov himself, he is a resolute character escaped from serfdom, to become a better man than his betters. His children, if not liquidated, might one day become Soviet commissars.

If the character of Lopákhin has caused perplexity, so has the intention of the whole play. Stanislavsky saw it as a tragedy;

[1] Up to what point one is amused by this sort of obsessional absurdity, remains a matter of temperament. Comic bores are dangerously apt to become more boring than comic; and Gaev's foolish tics require a very clever actor, if they are not sometimes to fall flat.

Chekhov, rather, as a farce. 'I am describing life, ordinary life,' he complained of the Moscow production, 'not blank despondency. They make me either cry-baby or bore.'

This controversy still continues. Yet it can be needlessly exaggerated. Why not see *The Cherry Orchard* as both tragic farce, and farcical tragedy?

'Farce' is too often assumed to mean nothing more than light-hearted buffoonery. But when the dying Augustus is reported as asking—'Have I played pretty well in the mime[1] of life?'; or the dying Rabelais as saying, 'Tirez le rideau, la farce est jouée'[2]; or the dying Beethoven as quoting, 'Clap now, good friends; the comedy is done', one is not compelled to suppose that these dying men felt uproariously funny. The tone is rather of wry, dry irony.

Such is the real mood, I feel, of this last drama by a doomed man. Chekhov on his death-bed at Badenweiler, like Heine on his mattress-grave in Paris, preferred sardonic humour to whining or whimpering.[3] Were they wrong? But those seem to me gross who see in *The Cherry Orchard* only the sort of heartless tom-foolery of which some critics today seem so inordinately fond.

At all events a rough count reveals in this play some thirty-five occasions on which characters indulge in sobs or tears.[4] Some, indeed, of these tears may be facile and ridiculous. But by no means all. It seems a lot of weeping for a pure 'farce'.

When Shakespeare speaks of human folly making 'the angels weep', he adds—

---

[1] The ancient 'mime' was a realistic sketch, often farcical.

[2] 'Draw the curtain, the farce is played.'

[3] So Rossetti in his last months composed not only *The King's Tragedy*, but also the grotesque ballad of the Dutchman, Jan Van Hunks.

[4] The scores are: Mme Ranevsky, 10; Varya, 10; Gaev, 6; Dunyasha, Trofímov, Pishchik, 2 each; Anya, Fiers, Lopákhin, 1 each. For laughter, the stage-directions are fewer—20. Compare Chekhov's story, *The Man in a Case:* 'I have noticed that Little Russian women are always laughing or crying—with no intermediate mood.'

Perhaps Chekhov himself did not fully realize how much tearfulness he had inserted. For he wrote to Nemiróvich-Dánchenko from Yalta (23/10/03): 'Why do you say in your telegram that there are many tearful people in the play? Where are they?'

It may be noted also that there are 35 'Pauses'. Chekhov made full and careful use of silences. (See p. 96.)

who with our spleens
Would all themselves laugh mortal.

This hardly suggests that the angels are mistaken, and inferior to men, because they weep rather than laugh. 'Life is a comedy to those that think, a tragedy to those that feel.' May it not be best *both* to think *and* to feel?

Today, of course, *The Cherry Orchard* has gained a fuller appeal, a deeper significance, by seeming so pathetically prophetic. For in 1917 the whole Cherry Orchard of Tsarist Russia was felled in blood. Though unfortunately the new owners proved far less human and humane than Lopákhin.

The play was revived by Stanislavsky's company almost on the eve of the Third Revolution in 1917, before a vast audience of common folk. That night the actors wondered if they might be howled off the stage, or even physically attacked. But, strangely enough, it proved one of their greatest triumphs; as if even that rough populace in the auditorium felt the wistful, poetic charm of the old life now vanished for ever. After giving the play a tremendous ovation, they drifted out of the theatre—many of them to the barricades. Soon, through the darkness, rang the crack of rifle-shots.

Again, on the fortieth anniversary of its first performance, *The Cherry Orchard* was revived in 1944. Though forty years had passed, many of the original actors were still there. Once more Chekhov's widow, Olga Knipper, played Mme Ranevsky. What artistic continuity, amid the cataclysms of war and revolution!

The Cherry Orchard is *said* to have been the most popular play in Soviet Russia after Gorky's *The Lower Depths*. If true, this seems extraordinary—and quite inconceivable in England.[1]

---

[1] In 1948 the Moscow Art Theatre published interesting figures of its Chekhov revivals in the previous half-century:

> *Ivánov*, 110.
> *The Seagull*, 63.
> *Uncle Vanya*, 347.
> *The Three Sisters*, 650.
> *The Cherry Orchard*, 1,190.
> (*Enciclopedia dello Spettacolo*, Rome, 1955, 'Čechov'.)

NOTE

The Cherry Orchard and *Heartbreak House*

In his preface (1919) Shaw suggests that his own play is a counter-part of Chekhov's. For Chekhov, he says, 'produced four[1] fascinating dramatic studies of Heartbreak House'—'the same nice people, the same utter futility'. In Shaw's view, the same type of intelligentsia inhabited 'all the country houses in Europe in which the pleasures of music, art, literature, and the theatre had supplanted hunting, shooting, fishing, flirting, eating, and drinking' (the pleasures of Horseback Hall). 'When they could, they lived without scruple on incomes which they did nothing to earn.'

But this seems already a little misleading. True, in *The Cherry Orchard* characters like Mme Ranevsky, Gaev, Pishchik (though hardly intellectuals) *are* idle parasites. But the other three Chekhov plays are full of people who may often be ineffectual, but certainly work—sometimes overwork—for their living; as writers, doctors, actresses, soldiers, teachers, housekeepers, estate-managers.

Shaw pictures both Russian and English gentry as blind to the abyss before them—in 1913, he says, 'only the professional diplomatists and the very few amateurs whose hobby is foreign policy even knew that the guns were loaded'. For those who lived through the ten years before 1914, or have read any history, this is certainly a new view of a period tense with international crises, naval building-races, popular clamours for more Dreadnoughts, and controversies about conscription.

Equally startling is Shaw's description of the doctors of the time as quack medicine-men, preying on the superstitions of Heartbreak House—'they prescribed inoculations and operations. Whatever part of a human being could be cut out without necessarily killing him, they cut out.' (One has visions of pre-war English society crawling about armless and legless.) 'The Inquisition itself was a liberal institution compared to the General Medical Council.'

It seems strange that *Ivánov* should apparently be more popular than *The Seagull*; and *The Cherry Orchard* so much more popular than *Uncle Vanya* and *The Three Sisters*. Possibly *The Cherry Orchard* lends itself particularly to Muscovite skill in acting and production.

[1] For some reason Shaw ignores *Ivánov*, which would make a fifth.

Nothing could better illustrate the real remoteness of Shaw, with his reckless generalizing and dogmatizing, from the Chekhov who valued science no less than art, his medicine no less than his writings; and was exasperated by Tolstoy's similar tirades against doctors.

The two plays seem really to have as little in common as their authors. *The Cherry Orchard* is a tragi-comedy of delicate nuances and compassionate ironies; *Heartbreak House*, a romp of farcical high-spirits, enlivened with paradoxical melodrama such as the capture of a burglar who wishes to be caught. The one ends with a mysteriously melancholy sound like a breaking harp-string; the other with a German bomb falling into a gravel-pit full of dynamite and blowing the burglar and a business-man hilariously to atoms. Shaw's play can still hold audiences, because he possessed an Irish gift for dramatic dialogue. But *Heartbreak House* seems to me no more like *The Cherry Orchard* than Hogarth is like Watteau.

STYLE, PERSONALITY, IDEAS

'What are my books but one plea against man's inhumanity to man, woman, and the lower animals? . . . Whatever may be the inherent good or evil of life, it is certain that man makes it much worse than it need be. When we have got rid of a thousand remediable ills, it will be time enough to determine whether the ill that is irremediable outweighs the good.'

THOMAS HARDY

Because the personality of Chekhov himself strikes me as both complex and exceptional in its charm, and wisdom, among the writers of the world, it seemed best to keep this to the last.[1]

With Turgenev, Chekhov is perhaps the most Western of the great Russian writers. From Tolstoy and Dostoievsky one may feel estranged at times by an emotionalism, extravagance, and exaggeration which, like much in Russian history, lack that sense of measure which has often been at least the ideal of the Greek mind, or the French, or the English. 'Russia,' said Lermontov, 'is a country where the most fantastic absurdities are ever and again renewed.' Some have attributed this barbaric exuberance to the infinite vastness of the Russian plains, or to the ruthless extremes of the climate, or to the proximity of Asia, or even, rather fancifully, to the tight swaddling of Russian babies, from which they were liberated only when suckled—thus alternating between crushing constraint and orgies of release.

But from this excessive and unpredictable vehemence of Russia, whatever its causes, Chekhov, like Turgenev, seems remarkably exempt. Mainly, no doubt, by inborn temperament; but one may suspect that his scientific training also helped to free Chekhov from fanaticism, and make him so insistent on self-discipline and restraint

---

[1] I am well aware that there is a modern school of criticism which regards such things as irrelevant and cries 'The text, the text, and nothing but the text.' But deliberately to clap a patch over one eye seems a curious sort of visual aid. We should have been spared endless misinterpretations of Shakespeare, had we only known more of his life, talk, and correspondence.

—far more so, indeed, than many West Europeans. He remained (in some ways like Ibsen) a good European liberal, with a dislike of nationalism, a loathing of despotism, and no blind beliefs in Slavs, 'noble peasants', or 'the Russian soul'.

He was, indeed, often highly critical of Russia; which he described to Suvórin, for example (24/4/1899), as 'an Asiatic country, where freedom of the press and freedom of conscience do not exist'. Indeed in 1882 he was nearly put under arrest by a furious Russian general who overheard him saying, after a railway disaster, that such a thing could only happen 'in our swinish Russia'.

Equally typical is his comment on the squalor of Dalmatian Abbazia—'here we have our brethren the Slavs'; or his delight in Venice (1891)—'It is not difficult for a poor and humble Russian to go off his head in this world of beauty, wealth, and freedom'; or his annoyance when Grigoróvich put it about that the Italian cities were 'nothing for Chekhov', and that he 'belonged to a generation that is obviously turning away from the West'. 'One must be an ox indeed,' he wrote to Suvórin, 'if, when one first sees Venice and Florence, one "turns away from the West". . . . What did he expect me to do?—roar with rapture?—break windows?—kiss the French?' Chekhov was by no means uncritical of Western Europe; but one cannot possibly imagine him a Pan-Slav.[1]

It was no less characteristic that (again like Turgenev, and Conrad), he disliked the daemonic, ultra-Russian Dostoievsky. He could recognize Dostoievsky's grasp of abnormal character; but found his psychology, in general, pretentious—an example of that Russian 'bone-laziness', which liked to meander in elaborate fantasies, like the intricate windings of the rivers of the Russian plain. *Crime and Punishment*, said Chekhov, 'did not impress me very much'. And Nemiróvich-Dánchenko adds: 'It was to be seen, from the way he said it, that he had no desire to go into details.' And when persuaded by Suvórin to re-read Dostoievsky's novels, he produced the typical comment—'They are all right; but much

---

[1] Compare a typical passage in a letter of his to Mme Suvórin from France: 'Nature here does not move me, but I am passionately in love with their culture—and culture oozes here from every shop-window and wicker-basket; every dog smells of civilization.'

too long and immodest.'[1] One more instance, in fact (the instances are endless) of that relativity and subjectivity in all aesthetic tastes which makes our aesthetic dogmatizings so pathetically stupid. The temperament of Dostoievsky was of a type that could not satisfy the temperament of Chekhov (just as Shakespeare could not satisfy Tolstoy). For Chekhov loved terseness and restraint; the scientist in him demanded sceptical detachment and objectivity; the liberal humanist in him loathed clericalism and reaction.[2]

Chekhov's own world, then, is a very different one; inhabited largely by a frustrated intelligentsia, sick with hopes long deferred of a Russia liberalized and civilized at last. None the less these characters of Chekhov's still remain, in many ways, Russian and un-English; particularly in the unashamed spontaneity with which they abandon themselves to their emotions and their moods. They strip their feelings; where an Englishman tends to go tightly muffled to the chin. They let these feelings change as fitfully as opals or kaleidoscopes; where an Englishman tends to keep in mind what he felt yesterday, and what he may feel tomorrow. For he is fearful of losing, by chameleon inconsistency, both the respect of others, and his own. It would be ideal, perhaps, if one could combine Russian vitality and spontaneity with English constancy and restraint. But that would be far from easy. Meanwhile we must be prepared often to find even Chekhov's characters unaccountably odd. But, after all, that can be part of their interest and their charm. For they are strange enough to excite new interest; but not so bizarre as to baffle and estrange. They are remote enough for novelty; yet near enough for sympathy. Above all, there is the attractive and admirable personality of Chekhov himself, which looks out between the lines of his maturer work with eyes that do *not* seem remote from our own. With all his gifts Tolstoy, I feel, can become at times exasperating; Dostoievsky can become forbidding and repulsive; but

---

[1] Similarly he wrote that mankind might attain a better future, 'not by guessing, not by seeking in Dostoievsky, but by seeing things clearly, as one sees that twice two is four'.

[2] Similarly Turgenev would observe, when something struck him as fantastically absurd, 'C'est du Dostoievsky'; while Dostoievsky, on his side, ridiculed Turgenev in *The Demons*, and would have liked Turgenev's *Smoke* burnt by the hangman.

Chekhov and Turgenev have qualities that, despite the gulfs of space, time, and nationality can still endear them to us, as if personal friends, like Horace or Montaigne.

*   *   *

Another most interesting feature in Chekhov's personality is its steady growth and development. This grandson of a serf was not one of those who ripen quickly to an early perfection. He developed far more slowly than Keats; but, like Keats, he was amazingly successful in curing himself of an initial vulgarity.

After his early period of pot-boiling, he developed a scrupulous artistic conscience. Thus, whereas in 1886 he had produced 115 short stories, in 1887 the number dropped to 65; in 1888, to 13!

Further, Chekhov became not only a conscientious artist, but a highly conscious one—the opposite of those galloping writers who can toss their first drafts, without even re-reading them, to the printer's devil. Like Wordsworth, he insisted on the need for composition in tranquillity—'I can write only from memory; not direct from nature. The subject of my story must first pass through the filter of my mind, so that only the typical and significant remains.' And, like Flaubert, he insisted also on the need for detachment. 'You should sit down to write,' he observed to Bunin, 'only when you feel cold as ice.' Similarly Flaubert had maintained —'One should write coldly. When Louvel wanted to kill the Duc de Berry, he drank a carafe of barley-water, and did not miss.'

This coldness did not mean callousness or apathy; it meant self-control and self-restraint.

Similarly Chekhov believed, in flat contradiction to Strindberg or Yeats, that an author should remain impersonal, and objective. Even in 1883, at twenty-three, he was blaming his brother Alexander for writing so subjectively. 'Throw your own personality over-board, don't make yourself the hero of your own story, renounce yourself for at least half an hour.' A writer, he believed, should draw things and people as they really are; not as he and his readers would like them to be. And again in 1889: 'Your play will be no good if all the characters are like *you*.' True, Chekhov could also use auto-biographical details; as in *The Seagull*. But he seems to me, very rightly, to use such personal experience in a discreet and transmuted form, like Ibsen; not, like the exhibitionist Strindberg, unashamedly undisguised. When Chekhov insists 'Give people people, and not yourself', he may seem to contradict Flaubert's 'Emma Bovary, c'est moi'. But the contradiction is only apparent. There is little visible likeness between the austere Flaubert and that poor, hysterical, self-indulgent wife. Yet he became Emma; he did not construct her out of newspaper cuttings, or mass-observation. The great creators of character are, it would seem, multitudinous personalities, with exceptional powers of sympathy and empathy. They can put themselves into remotely different minds and circumstances: yet it is part of *themselves* that they put; just as Goethe said there was no crime that he could not imagine himself, under certain circumstances, committing. They are like Homer's Old Man of the Sea who could transform himself into infinite shapes—

> to a lion with mighty mane
> He turned, to a snake, to a panther, to a huge boar; then again
> He shaped him as slippery water, and then as a towering tree;
> Yet all the while we gripped him, inescapably.[1]

For, through all his changes, Proteus was still himself.

This dislike of Chekhov's for intoxicated 'inspiration', this insistence on distance, detachment, impersonality were not mere caprices. They were part of his inflexible passion for truth. And this truthfulness, as already suggested, may well have been intensified by his scientific training. 'A man of letters,' he maintained, 'should be as objective as a chemist.' And to a chemist nothing is impure. 'If you would understand life, stop believing what is said and written; observe, and meditate, yourself.'

Like Crabbe, like Sainte-Beuve, Chekhov had begun as a medical student; all three writers may have gained thereby a keener sense of reality.[2] Similarly, Michelangelo said that all artists should

---

[1] *Odyssey*, IV, 456-9.
[2] Tolstoy, as one might expect, thought Chekhov would have been a better writer if he had *not* been a doctor. For to Tolstoy science was anathema. Chekhov himself, however, judged otherwise—that medicine had 'considerably widened the field of my observations and enriched my knowledge'. And he was irritated by the ignorant way in which medical matters were handled by Zola, and by Tolstoy himself.

have studied architecture (as Hardy, for example, actually did). For, like medicine, architecture also can be a remedy against the artist's (and the critic's) besetting temptation to allow beauty to obscure truth; fantasy to blur reality; intoxication to masquerade as inspiration. For no fine raptures will fool either bricks or bacteria.

It was natural, then, that Chekhov should be irritated by the common view—today still commoner—of science and art as antagonists. For him, they were not enemies, but allies.

'If,' he wrote to Suvórin (15/5/1889), 'a man knows the laws of the circulation of the blood, he is rich. If, in addition, he learns the history of religions and a romance of Tchaikovsky, he does not become poorer, but richer still.' And again—'Science and letters should go hand in hand. Anatomy and fine literature have the same enemy—the Devil. . . . In Goethe the naturalist lived in harmony with the poet.' And again, of Darwin[1]—'What a marvel! I like him terribly.'

It is not of course necessary to have a passion for science in order to have a passion for truth. The truth-loving Socrates came to regard as mistaken the scientific interests of his own youth. But science, even though it may not always make men love truth more, may help them to love truth better—more effectively. For it insistently brings home the danger of conclusions either too hasty or too wishful. 'When one is thirsty,' writes Chekhov, 'one feels one could drink the ocean—*that* is faith; but when one has started drinking, one cannot swallow above two glasses—*that* is science.'

And so, where a Blake, a Yeats, or a D. H. Lawrence cannot breathe without passionate beliefs, Chekhov, like Montaigne, Hume, or Flaubert, preferred the more open mind of the sceptic; and became, like Hardy, one of the most inexorably sincere of writers, with an irreconcilable loathing for the artificial, the affected, the rhetorical, the vague. He could not enjoy even Sarah Bernhardt,

---

Compare Sainte-Beuve: 'C'est à la médecine que je dois l'esprit de philosophie, l'amour de l'exactitude, et de la réalité physiologique.' ('It is to medicine that I owe a philosophic turn of mind, love of precision, and of physiological accuracy.')

[1] Darwin shared, it may be remembered, Chekhov's rational conviction that men need both art and science; and bitterly regretted his own loss of taste for literature.

because 'the whole charm of her performance was spoilt by her artificiality'.[1] Typically, he preferred Duse. Similarly he found the performers of his own *Seagull* (1896) too histrionic—'they act a lot. . . . I wish there were not so much acting.' To his players he would say, much like Hamlet, 'the chief thing, my dear fellow, is to play it simply, without theatricality'. Even the ballet he disliked, because too artificial.

In the same way he detested all 'acting' in real life. Most characteristic (with a memory, perhaps, of Andersen's fairy-tale) is the lover's comment on the heroine, in Chekhov's own story *Ariadne*: 'When she talked to me of love, it seemed as though I were listening to the singing of a metal nightingale.' Not for Chekhov the metallic, artificial birds of Yeats's Byzantium. And so, for all his gentleness, Chekhov himself could become almost Johnsonianly blunt towards any hint of pretence or pretentiousness; as when a plump, well-dressed lady treated him to what she doubtless imagined an appropriately Chekhovian tirade—'Life is so boring, Anton Pavlóvich, all is so grey . . . it is like a disease.' 'Yes,' he replied, 'it *is* a disease. In Latin it is called *morbus fraudulentus*.'[2] Or, again, there is his curt retort (recorded by André Maurois), when a friend started moaning, 'What should I do? Thinking is driving me mad.' 'Drink less vodka!' Or again, during the Greco-Turkish War, three silken-dressed and scented ladies tried drawing him on to politics— 'Anton Pavlóvich, how do you think the war will end?' But they got only the mischievous answer—'Probably in a peace.'

From this sincerity followed another of Chekhov's great qualities—his simplicity. 'Beautifully simple himself,' says Gorky, 'he loved everything simple, genuine, sincere; and he had a peculiar way of making other people simple.' Here Chekhov recalls another dramatist of his time, likewise cut off prematurely by incurable disease—John Millington Synge; who wrote, 'There is nothing so great and sacred as what is most simple in life.'

Simplicity, like grace and dignity, seems one of those qualities

---

[1] Chekhov wrote a criticism of her when she toured Russia in 1881. While recognizing that lazy Russian actors could well learn from her 'gigantic hard work', he yet objected that Sarah Bernhardt set out 'to strike, astonish, dazzle', by calculated tricks.

[2] 'Fraudulent illness'.

which our age least values—or even understands. We are too much oppressed by the multitudinousness of modern life, with its complexities piled on complexities. We grow like the dogs in the fable, trying to drink up the sea—and how sea-sick some of us get! Yet wiser minds and stronger characters, such as Chekhov, can see how futile and superfluous many of these complexities remain; just as Diogenes, confronted by all the futilities on sale at a fair, could exclaim, with astonished relief and contempt—'Immortal Gods, how many things Diogenes does *not* need!' But most of us do too much, talk too much, huddle too many fevered experiences into our fuddled lives; till there is no time left to think, or to be our real selves.

One should, perhaps, distinguish two stages of simplicity. First there is the innocent, unsophisticated simplicity of the child of nature, 'the peasant of the Danube'—of Man Friday, or Sancho Panza. Even this can at times be far more alive and effective than the efforts of sophisticated minds. 'It is very difficult,' said Chekhov, 'to describe the sea. Do you know what I found in a schoolboy's exercise book? "The sea is big." Just that! It seemed quite admirable.'[1]

Minds, however, that have outgrown this first simplicity, tend too often to fall in love with mere complexities and perplexities; delighting in the elaborately obscure, like bad 'Metaphysical' poetry, or much academic criticism, or the more twisted manner of Browning, Meredith, or Henry James.

But beyond the jungles of jargon and false sophistication there lies in its turn a simplicity of a subtler kind, reached only by those who have come to feel that life is too tragic, too comic, too brief, to be wasted in playing stupid games of cat's cradle with ragged words and tangled ideas. Naturally, in the eyes of fools, others may seem more profound. But what matter? What use in seeming and scheming? This second simplicity may be combined with as much real subtlety as is good for anyone. 'The nearer a man is to truth,' Chekhov wrote, 'the more intelligent and simple he is.'

[1] Cf. Peig Sayers, *An Old Woman's Reflections* (1962), p. 14: 'You were but a stone's throw from me then but the big watery sea is between you and me today.' (She was an old Irishwoman from Great Blasket Island.)

Of a piece with this candid simplicity was Chekhov's other growing passion, already mentioned, for brevity. For wordiness is often a mere form of self-importance, which cannot face the brevity, transience, and insignificance of most of the things men fuss about. Wordiness is, in fact, a form of 'flapping'. 'Odd,' Chekhov wrote, 'I have now a mania for shortness. Whatever I read—my own work, or other people's—it all seems to me not short enough.' In his notebook he copied a passage from Daudet—' "Why," a bird was asked, "are thy songs so short? Is it that thou art short of breath?" And the bird answered: "I have very many songs, and I should like to sing them all".'[1]

To the question what he would do if rich, Chekhov's reply was— 'Write the tiniest possible stories. Were I a millionaire I would produce works no longer than the palm of my hand.' And so we find him advising Schoukin to tear up the first half of his Tales[2]; and recommending Bunin, after finishing a short story, to cut out beginning and end. 'It is there that we authors do most of our lying.'

Similarly, to Lydia Avílov: 'you don't know how to economize ... one of your stories even gets lost among the masses of descriptive passages. ... Again, you do not work on a sentence. Every sentence must be carefully wrought—that is where art comes in. You must eliminate everything superfluous—clean it of "as much as" and "with the help of". You must think of its rhythm.' 'Write a novel. Spend a whole year on it; another six months on shortening it; and *then* publish.'

Brevity and simplicity. Not a multitude of details—for they weary. 'A single detail suffices'—provided it is the right one.

All this seems most admirable. For most of the world's books are far too wordy. I do not know what justification even *War and Peace* can claim for being such a dinosaur. And so, for me, the best of all Chekhov's work lies (even more than in his plays) in his short stories, and parts of his letters.

[1] Cf. Fontenelle, when Mme de Sergeville read his works to him at the close of his long life—'il l'interrompit quelquefois en lui disant: cela est trop long.' ('At times he interrupted her, saying "That is too long."')

[2] One recalls the Scottish professor who always asked his essay-pupils if they had remembered to tear up *their* first page.

'As a stylist,' says Gorky, 'Chekhov has no equal; and future literary historians, reflecting on the development of the Russian language, will maintain that this language has been created by Pushkin, Turgenev, and Chekhov.' Tolstoy himself, often critical of Chekhov's dramas and ideas, yet loving the man and the writer, could proclaim: 'Chekhov is an incomparable artist. Yes, yes, that is it—incomparable'. And again—'Chekhov is a Pushkin in prose.' In all this there is much that a non-Russian cannot even begin to judge; yet even through the smoked glass of translation it is possible to glimpse how much Chekhov's style owed to these three fundamental qualities of brevity, simplicity, and scientific truthfulness.

'On the dam, which was covered with moonlight, there was not a trace of shadow; in the middle of it the neck of a broken bottle glittered like a star.' This image, in his tale *The Wolf* (1886), must have pleased Chekhov particularly. For he repeats it in a letter to his brother Alexander; and repeats it yet again in *The Seagull.* Indeed the image is specially typical of him in its combination of contrasting elements—broken bottle, moon, and star—that are seemingly so commonplace, and yet transfigured by imagination.

Of course too many broken bottles would have led to that squalor found in extremer realists; who identify the 'real' with the disagreeable, and lead their readers up cul-de-sacs whose walls simply bristle with broken bottles. But from that danger Chekhov was saved by his equally intense loathing for everything vulgar and unrestrained. Like so many of the best writers since Homer, he merges in one the truth of the realist, the self-control of the classic, the imaginativeness of the romantic.

Imagery is one of the things that best survive even translation. And so a few other images of Chekhov's may illustrate, at least, his love of things objectively concrete, in preference to the vague abstractions of the woolly-minded.[1]

(Of a university lecturer.) 'He is in a nervous panic; he can hardly decipher his own manuscript; his poor little thoughts crawl along *like a*

---

[1] Compare an ironic sentence in Chekhov's story *Three Years*: 'The article was called "The Russian Soul": it was tediously written in *that colourless style with which people without talent, but full of concealed vanity, usually write.*' (And not only in Russia.)

bishop on a bicycle; and what's worse, you can never make out what he is trying to say. The deadly dullness is frightful—the *very flies expire*.'

'I myself ploughed, and sowed, and reaped, and was bored doing it, and scowled with disgust, *like a village-cat driven by hunger to eat cucumbers in the kitchen-garden*.'

'She was a pious woman, but who knows? *The soul of another is a slumbering forest*.'

'How early your soul has taken to its dressing-gown!'

'He was sitting up in bed, with a quilt over his legs; he had grown older, fatter, wrinkled; his cheeks, nose, and mouth all stuck out—*he looked as if at any moment he might begin grunting into the quilt*.'

'Now and then he would kiss his guest, always three times, put his arms round his waist, breathe in his face; it seemed as if he were *covered with a sweet glue*, and would actually stick to his companion.'

'The unseen waves broke languidly and heavily on the shore, as if saying "Ouf!"'

'Everything, everything recalled the approach of dreary, gloomy autumn. . . . The crows were flying above the Volga and *crying tauntingly "Bare, bare!"*'

'On the left *someone seemed to strike a match against the sky*; a pale phosphorescent streak glittered and went out. Then there was heard somewhere, very far away, someone walking on a zinc roof, doubtless in bare feet, for the zinc gave only a long dull rumble.'

Another quality of Chekhov's which even translation does not disguise is the compression by which a single vividly concrete phrase is made to convey more than whole pages of vague generalities.

'Even useless rubbish is collected in the courtyards nowadays, and used for some purpose; *even broken glass is considered a useful commodity*; but something so precious, so rare, as the love of a refined, young, intelligent, and good woman is utterly thrown away and wasted.' (Compare the supreme crime in Ibsen's eyes—killing the love-life in a human soul.)

(Of a greedy old man.) 'And every dinner left on Vera such an impression that when she afterwards saw a flock of sheep driven by, or flour being brought to the mill, she thought *"Grandfather will eat that".'*

(Of a corrupt one.) 'My father took bribes, and imagined they were given him out of respect for his moral qualities.'

'The telephone, too, was laid on in the local court; but it soon ceased to work, *as bugs and beetles bred in it.*'

(Of a Russian hospital.) 'Potatoes were kept in the baths.'

(Of Chekhov's Siberian journey.) 'The Irtysh neither booms nor roars, but seems to knock on the lids of coffins at its bottom. A dismal effect. . . . All night I listen to the snores of the ferrymen and my coachman, to the rain beating on the windows, to the roar of the wind, to the sullen Irtysh knocking on its coffin-lids.'

Naturally this vividness of phrase and image is more marked in the stories and letters; which reveal far more of Chekhov himself. But even in the plays there are such animated touches as the burdensome ideas for stories that come rolling through Trigórin's brain like heavy cannon-balls; his dodgings of the public like a hunted fox; his vain pursuit of life's happiness like a peasant running after a train; the locked heart of Irina, like a beautiful piano that has lost its key; Mme Ranevsky's 'Don't cry, little peasant, it'll be well in time for your wedding'; or Peter Trofímov's irritated rebuff to pretentiousness—'Don't flap!'

*   *   *

Just as the passage of years developed Chekhov's artistic conscience, so it did with his social conscience. He became, not an overtly moralizing writer, yet a writer with a keen moral sense. In 1888 he had written to Suvórin: 'You confuse two conceptions— the solution of a question and the correct statement of a question. The latter alone is an artist's duty. The judge's business is to put questions correctly; the jurymen must decide, each to his taste.' None the less, even then he had been mocked at in an anonymous story, 'The Tendentious Anton', for an inclination in his tales to lecture and to preach. And by 1892, in another letter to Suvórin, he was much more definite about the influence-value of the great writers. 'The best of them are realistic, and paint life as it is; but because every line is permeated, as with a juice, by awareness of a purpose, you feel, in addition to life as it is, life also as it should be. And we? We! We paint life as it is . . . beyond that, even if you lashed us with whips, we could not go. We have no aims either immediate or remote, and in our souls—a great emptiness.' Again, he compares the true classics with the ghost of Hamlet's father 'who did not come back for nothing, or trouble Hamlet's imagination for nothing'. 'He who wants nothing, hopes for nothing, and fears nothing cannot be an artist.'

Suvórin's own son was inclined to nonchalance about life's vital issues; and Chekhov's comment is again most characteristic—'He looks on at the cockfight like a spectator with no fighting-cock of his own. And one *ought* to have one's own fighting-cock, else life is without interest.' That seems to me very sound—though quite inconsistent with that other, more mournful mood in which Chekhov would stress the importance of 'indifference'. But such indifference can become crippling; far better the fighting-cock. 'There is plenty of phosphorus in our talent,' Chekhov observed of his contemporaries in 1888; 'but no iron. Maybe we are pretty birds, and sing well; but we are no eagles.' Writers need iron.

This problem of literature and morality is ancient. But Chekhov's rejection of purposeless writing seems to me right. A writer without values remains without value. He need not, indeed, invent new values. Creative writers are seldom philosophers. Often they have been poor enough at reasoning—Victor Hugo, for example. And they cannot prove anything. For the imaginary fortunes of imaginary individuals in imaginary cases cannot provide proof of any general laws. Even a play with moral ideas as pronounced as Ibsen's *Ghosts* cannot do that. But the creative writer *can* make men think again; he *can* make them feel anew.

The real question, then, is how writers can best use their unavoidable influence. Often they are unwise to preach. They are not priests. And as the wise artist conceals his art, so he will often conceal his moral. Better, as a rule, to imply. But that, at least, an author cannot help doing. All art involves selection; and the very subjects he chooses, the characters he thinks worth depicting, inevitably reveal his values, whether he will or no.

The influence of literature, in fine, may well be like that of radio-activity—hard to estimate and detect, yet deep in its effects, not only on the living, but also on the unborn.

Chekhov, then (unlike Tolstoy, for example), was wisely content to imply. But we have his own word for it that he became in the end well aware of his own purposes. Therefore it now becomes necessary to say something of his ideas. He was one of those not very numerous authors who have worked constantly, though unobtrusively, to make the world rather more civilized, more enlightened, more humane; where too many others have been, and are, irresponsible saboteurs, who spread only barbarism and decadence.

*   *   *

About party-politics, though essentially liberal in sympathies, Chekhov cared little; as he wrote to Suvórin in 1898, over the Dreyfus affair, 'great writers and artists must only engage in politics so far as it is necessary to defend oneself against them'. But about an issue like the case of Dreyfus, involving fundamental human justice, Chekhov did care—so strongly that there resulted a breach between him and Suvórin, who was an anti-Dreyfusard.

Needless to say, in Soviet Russia Chekhov's work has been approved for quite different reasons—for its satire of upper-class and bourgeois decadents. But there are other passages in him that, if squarely faced, would be much less congenial to official Communism.[1]

---

[1] A twenty-volume edition of Chekhov was published in Moscow during 1944-51. But, with typical Communist honesty, it is silently censored. Thus Chekhov wrote to Suvórin (1897): 'We should send our young writers on assignments abroad.' This is expunged. In 1894 Chekhov contrasted with the charm of the French Riviera the squalor of Dalmatian Abbazia 'and the whole of this uncivilized brotherly Moldavia. For here we have our brethren, the Slavs'. This is expunged. In 1890, after visiting Hongkong, he told Suvórin: 'Wherever you turn, you can see the tenderest solicitude of the British for their employees. . . . I grew angry at hearing my Russian fellow-travellers criticize the British as exploiting the natives. Yes, I thought to myself, the Englishman does exploit Chinese, Sepoys, Hindus, but in return he gives them roads, drains, museums, and Christianity; and what about you!—you

For Chekhov was, like Ibsen, far too individualistic to want to lose himself in masses, or become a good Party-member. 'I am not a liberal, and not a conservative, not an evolutionist, nor a monk, nor indifferent to the world. I would like to be a free artist—and that is all. . . . I cannot therefore nourish any specially warm feelings towards policemen, butchers, savants, writers, or youth. I consider trademarks or labels to be prejudices.' In fact, Chekhov was like Freud, who thought it better than being either 'red' or 'white', to be simply *'Fleischfarbe'*—'flesh-colour'—the colour of a healthy human face, which is *both* white *and* red.

Even literary 'togetherness' left Chekhov cold. When canvassed, for example, on the question of uniting young writers, his independent good sense replied—'I understand solidarity and that sort of thing on the stock exchange, in politics, in matters of religion; but the solidarity of young writers is impossible and unnecessary. . . . We cannot think and feel in the same way; our aims are different, or we have no aims at all. . . . And is it necessary? No.'

Like Ibsen, Chekhov was neither sheep nor jackal.

Nor could he share the herd-instincts of fanatical nationalism. 'There is,' records his notebook, 'no national science, just as there is no national multiplication-table; what is national is no longer science.' Here speaks the very antithesis of that Nazi aggressiveness which grotesquely proclaimed 'Aryan' and 'non-Aryan' mathematics to be, in some mystical manner, 'different'.

Above all, Chekhov had suffered enough from paternal tyranny in his own boyhood, to have a lifelong loathing of tyranny in any form. 'My Holy of Holies is the human body, health, mind, talent, inspiration, love, and the most absolute freedom—freedom from violence and falsehood, in whatever form they may be manifested.'

---

also exploit, but what do you give?' This of course is expunged. And a whole letter to the famous producer Meyerhold has disappeared; just as Meyerhold himself disappeared in 1939, for having dared to attack 'socialist realism'.

Thus one raises monuments to the great; and their 'dangerous thoughts' are then conveniently buried beneath. In his lifetime Chekhov was censored by the Tsardom (in particular, his story *Peasants* caused trouble): now he is censored anew by Communism after his death. (See G. Struve, 'Chekhov in Communist Censorship', *Slavonic Review*, XXXIII (1954-5), 327-41.)

And again, in talk with a friend: 'I love nature and literature, I love pretty women and I hate routine and despotism.'—'Political despotism?'—'*All* despotism, wherever it shows itself.' Landor and Byron could have said precisely the same.

Being, then, both individualistic, humane, and scientifically sceptical, Chekhov was the last person to be swept away by the mass-intoxication of revolutionaries. ' "Forward without fear or doubt!"—*that's* not politics. If you ask me to go forward, you must show me the way, the aims, the means. Nothing has so far been achieved in politics by "the frenzy of the brave".' It might have been safer, and truer, to say that *lasting* good has *seldom* been achieved by it. But *that* at least does, I think, remain extremely true.

How vivid, again, in Chekhov's tale, *The Duel*, when Laevsky describes Von Koren, is the glimpse of what Marxist intolerance was one day to put in practice.

He exerts himself for the improvement of the human race, and we are in his eyes only slaves, cannon-fodder, beasts of burden; some he would destroy or stow away in Siberia, others he would break by disciplinary measures—would, like Arakcheyev,[1] force them to get up and go to bed to the sound of the drum—would appoint eunuchs to preserve our morals and chastity—would have anyone shot who stepped outside the circle of our narrow conservative morality; and all this in the name of improving humanity!

Our century has seen more than enough Von Korens.

Elsewhere, the narrowness of Russian radicals wrung from Chekhov a prophecy grimmer still—'under the flag of science, art, and freedom of thought, we shall have such toads and crocodiles ruling Russia as were unknown even in Spain at the time of the Inquisition'.

In fine, Chekhov was that growing rarity in our mass-ridden world—a fearless, uncompromisingly independent individual.

[1] Count Arakcheyev (1768-1836), minister of Alexander I, was one of the maddest pioneers of totalitarianism. He tried regimenting and militarizing peasants in the Novgorod province, with a Chinese rigidity. Shaved, drilled, uniformed, housed in symmetrical villages, the victims must even do their agriculture to the word of command and the sound of the drum. Even sexual relations and birthrates were subject to strict controls.

It was not a success.

Yet to all this one can easily imagine a convinced Marxist replying in scorn: 'But this generalized hatred of despotism and inhumanity is so negative. Where does it take you? It is like being "against sin" —obvious, vague, and completely ineffectual. Chekhov himself has written—"A man with a hammer ought to stand behind the door of every satisfied person, and by knocking on it constantly to remind him that there are people unhappy; and that, however happy he may be now, sooner or later he too will feel life's sharp claws; and that, when misfortune overtakes him—illness, poverty, bereavement— no one will see or hear him, just as he does not see or hear others." Now that is precisely our point. It is by the hammer—and sickle— that the needed revolution must be, and has been, made. Not with powder-puffs.'

The truth remains, however, that Chekhov was in temper by no means a revolutionary. He was a gradualist; a Fabian. He believed— sometimes more, sometimes less—in evolution; not revolution. Though for a time he had been influenced by Tolstoy, in the end his common sense rejected Tolstoyanism.[1] He could not share Tolstoy's belief in non-resistance; nor Tolstoy's disbelief in 'progress'. 'From childhood,' he says, 'I have believed in progress...for the difference between the time when I used to be thrashed and the time when I ceased to be thrashed, was tremendous. Reason and justice tell me that in electricity and steam there is more love for mankind than in chastity and abstinence from meat.'

Perhaps a little optimistic? For one's childhood thrashings seem a rather narrow basis on which to theorize about human progress in general. But it is fair to remember that, even in 1914, European Russia (apart from Finland, Poland, and the Baltic provinces) had 80 per cent. of illiterates. Obvious room there for 'progress' of a sort; yet about the real furtherance of 'love for mankind' produced

[1] Chekhov, says Sergey Tolstoy, 'would listen to my father in silence, treating what he said with an interest that was respectful but sceptical'. Tolstoy thought Gorky *might* be converted, but that Chekhov was 'a perfect atheist'; none the less, when Chekhov died, Tolstoy could generously say, 'without any false modesty, I maintain that, from the point of view of technique, Chekhov is far superior to me'. And Chekhov, on his side, however exasperated by Tolstoy's ideas, could say, 'I have loved no man as I have him'.

by steam, electricity, and such scientific progress, our rattled century may feel less confidence.

Chekhov's real hope for the future lay rather in the obscure labours of individuals like his Dr Astrov (and himself)—doing the work that came to hand; building schools; fighting epidemics; planting trees. By such efforts, in a few centuries, human life might somehow, little by little, be transformed to happiness. Again, perhaps, optimistic? But here also Chekhov had too much sense of reality to be blindly so. In his grim story, *Ward 6*, such Utopian dreams of a happy future are put in the mouth of Ivan Dmitrich—who is *mad*! And in Chekhov's notebooks there occur entries of bleak disillusion—'We fret ourselves to reform life in order that posterity may be happy; and posterity will say, as usual: "In the past, things were better, the present is worse." ' And again—'The majority, the mass, will remain eternally stupid; let the man of intelligence, then, give up the hope of educating them up to his level; let him be content with building railways, telegraphs, telephones.' For that too is progress of a kind, and a possible kind.

In short, I take it, Chekhov really felt that in life one must simply do one's best, without fooling oneself to expect the best; that one should try to sow the seeds of a better world by cultivating, without undue optimism, the small garden around one.

Among that minority of mankind who think and care about the human future, there are indeed, two salient types. On the one hand there are doctrinaires, like the Communists, who feel absolutely certain how progress should go, and must go; and are quite ready, in furtherance of that great end, to justify no matter what means—tyranny, persecution, treachery, brutality, wholesale massacre. On the opposite side are those who doubt whether some sorts of means can be justified even by the most idealistic of ends; who feel, on the contrary, that the end needs often to be justified by the means—that it is both foolish and wicked to seek a more perfect civilization by way of barbarism, and to sacrifice for any problematical future those civilized values that, through long ages, men have so painfully and precariously acquired.

Such, one may suspect, was Chekhov. He could never have adopted the ruthlessness of his Von Koren. He had, for one thing, too keen a sense of justice. 'I don't dare ask you,' he wrote, in criticizing a story of Elena Shavróva's, 'to be fond of gynaecologists and professors; but I venture to remind you of justice, which to the objective writer is more precious than air.' Yet even justice could be over-rigid; Chekhov preferred an indulgent tolerance for the pathetic dreams, illusions, and frailties of mankind. 'Poetic love,' he wrote in another note, 'seems as devoid of sense as a mass of snow which stupidly tumbles down a mountain and crushes men. But when one listens to music, all seems majestic and serene, and even the mass of snow no longer seems stupid; for all in nature has now a meaning. And one gives one's forgiveness to everything, and it would be strange to refuse to give it.' Perhaps it was only in rare moments, as in listening to music, that Chekhov's mind could feel so; but sometimes at least it could.

*　　　　　*　　　　　*

All this leads up to the final and crucial question, which has caused such violent debate—was Chekhov, fundamentally, optimist or pessimist? Is the underlying tone of his writing more comic or tragic?

Tolstoy, on the one hand, was dismayed by what he considered Chekhov's gloom. He preferred Maupassant, as having 'more joy in life'. A very odd view of Maupassant. For Maupassant's general undertone seems to me even more desolate than Chekhov's; despite the Frenchman's superb vitality, which was to end, yet more tragically than Chekhov, in the shadows of a madhouse.

Still more pessimistic is the interpretation given by the Russian critic Shestov (1866-1939), when he sums up Chekhov's whole message in a single line of Baudelaire—

'Résigne-toi, mon cœur; dors ton sommeil de brute.'[1]

'I would say,' Shestov continues, 'that Chekhov was the poet of hopelessness. Stubbornly, sadly, monotonously, through all the years of his literary activity—nearly a quarter-century, Chekhov was doing one thing alone: by one means or another he was killing human hopes.' 'Art, science, love, inspiration, ideals . . . Chekhov

---

[1] 'Resign yourself, heart; sleep your brutish slumber.'

has only to touch them, and instantly they wither and die.' 'The real, the only hero of Chekhov is the hopeless man. He has absolutely no *action* left in life but to beat his head against the stones.'

This is the opposite extreme to those who discover in Chekhov's last three dramas the brassy enthusiasm of modern Moscow. But it seems equally preposterous. True, the landscapes and atmosphere of Chekhov's world are often grey. Inevitably. For he was relentlessly truthful. And he was a man of moods so dramatically portrayed that it grows easy to mistake a mood for the whole man. The doomed old professor of *A Dreary Story* is grippingly real; but he is only a part of the real Chekhov. It remains strangely perverse to bring charges of 'infatuation with death, decay, and hopelessness' against a character who went so resolutely to Sakhalín even when dangerously ill, and dreamed of going to the Manchurian front even when almost dying; who so tirelessly planted, built, conducted censuses, and fought epidemics; who could sympathize not only with weaklings like Konstantin, Vanya, Mme Ranevsky, but also with more active figures like Astrov, Tusenbach, Lopákhin—men certainly not resigned merely to 'beat their heads against stones'. Few writers have less deserved than the humane Chekhov to be taxed with 'the slumber of a brute'.

Even the admiring Gorky seems to me exaggerated when he says that 'Chekhov walks the earth like a doctor in a hospital: there are many patients there, but no medicines; besides, the doctor is not sure that medicines are any use'. For Chekhov's dreams about man's future may appear to some, on the contrary, at times too sanguine.

Equally dismal, though somewhat different, is the verdict of Melchior de Vogüé—'Ses peintures, incomparablement moins sombres et moins violentes que celles de Gogol, nous laissent pourtant une impression d'inhumanité plus navrante.'[1] Yet many will ask with wonder how it is possible to tax Chekhov, of all men, with 'inhumanity'. De Vogüé imagines him saying to his public— 'Vous aspirez tous, comme mes héros, à sortir du même marécage;

---

[1] 'His paintings of life, though incomparably less sombre and less violent than Gogol's, yet leave an impression of inhumanity that is more heart-rending still.'

je vais vous replonger avec eux durant quelques heures; et je vous prouverai qu'il est impossible de s'en dépêtrer.'[1]

But Chekhov, I imagine, would have rightly denied that creative writers can 'prove' anything. And he repeatedly satirized the very type of character that thus wallows in Sloughs of Despond.

Less extreme and unreasonable is Prince Mirsky's interpretation of both Chekhov and the great Russian novelists who preceded him: 'People are not good or bad; they are only more or less unhappy and deserving of sympathy—this may be taken as the formula of all the Russian novelists from Turgenev to Chekhov.' Yet it may still be doubted if this over-simple formula can really cover Tolstoy, or Dostoievsky, or Chekhov himself, with his uncompromising condemnation of feeble intellectuals—'I have no faith in our intelligentsia, hypocritical, false, hysterical, ill-bred, lazy. . . . I see salvation in a few people living their own private lives, scattered throughout Russia' (22/2/1899).

At the opposite pole stand those critics whom we have seen interpreting *The Seagull* as pure comedy; *Uncle Vanya* and *The Three Sisters* as cheery recalls to hopeful labour; and *The Cherry Orchard* as a light-hearted liquidation of idle exploiters. What is one to make of such total contradictions?

The truth seems to me that those are far too narrow who discuss Chekhov's view of life as if he had only *one* view of it—as if his active and sensitive mind could be thus rammed into a pigeon-hole, or pinned like a butterfly. Most men vary from day to day, even from hour to hour. Chekhov, whose plays so often concerned themselves less with action than with mood, was himself a man of widely differing moods.

There was, for example, the gay Chekhov who in younger years had poured out comic stories and farces; who could revel in light-hearted practical jokes—as when he audaciously handed from his carriage to a Moscow policeman a large paper-wrapped watermelon, then shouted back, as he drove on—'It's a bomb!'; or mischievously assured a town-bred authoress that his white-and-

---

[1] 'You all aspire, like my heroes, to escape from the same morass; for a few hours I am going to plunge you back in it; and I shall prove to you that to get clear of it is impossible.'

coffee-coloured pigeons were the result of crossing common pigeons with his coffee-coloured cat. (This the victim believed and repeated, to the measureless amusement of her hearers.) Chekhov had, in fine, what in one of his stories[1] he wisely calls 'that intelligent, good sort of frivolity only found in good-natured, light-hearted people with brains'. Almost to his last breath he jested still. He was, thank Heaven, no owl.

About his own work he could write to Lydia Avílov: 'You deplore that my heroes are sad and sombre. Alas, it is not my fault! It happens to me involuntarily; when I write, it does not seem to me that my writing is sombre; anyway, while writing, I am always in a good humour.'

And again, to Tikhonov, in 1902: 'You tell me that people cry at my plays. But that was not why I wrote them. It is Alexeyev[2] who made my characters into cry-babies. Also I wanted to say honestly to people—"Take a look at yourselves, and see how bad and dreary are your lives." The important thing is for people to realize *that*; for, when they do, they will most certainly[3] create another, better life for themselves. I shall not live to see it, but I know that it will be quite different, quite unlike our present life. And so long as the different life does not exist, I shall go on saying to people again and again, "Please understand that your lives are bad and dreary."

'What is there to cry about in this?'

An author could hardly express himself more clearly. And yet beside the cheerful Chekhov, there did exist also another Chekhov, with a temperament much more sombre.

Suvórin remarked that Chekhov's two great interests, when travelling abroad, were circuses and cemeteries. An epigram, doubtless; with the usual over-simplification of epigrams? But not, one may believe, wholly baseless. In 1894 Chekhov himself could write

---

[1] *The Examining Magistrate.*

[2] Stanislavsky.

[3] 'Most certainly' seems excessively optimistic. But I do not see how this statement by Chekhov himself, with its quite explicit statement of purpose, can be reconciled with Mr Francis Fergusson's view of Chekhov as 'predicting nothing', and having no 'thesis'; in contrast to Ibsen's moral earnestness. (*The Idea of a Theater*, 1939.) Mr Fergusson is writing of *The Cherry Orchard* (1904). But there seems no reason to suppose that *The Cherry Orchard* differs in this respect from Chekhov's other mature dramas.

to his sister from Milan: 'I have been . . . on the shores of the Adriatic, where I found beautiful rain and deep ennui. I have been to Fiume, Trieste, Venice. It only remains to go on to Genoa, where there are numbers of boats and a magnificent cemetery.' And when he finally settled at Yalta he did not mind choosing a site where, beside his garden, stretched an ancient Tartar burial-ground, green, silent, desolate, with its forgotten graves.

Again, during the early nineties, when sheltering from the rain with a friend, in a grain-drying kiln, Chekhov remarked that someone should write a vaudeville about a pair of lovers so sheltering. The man would propose, and be accepted; then, as they emerged into the returning sunshine, he would drop dead from heart-failure. 'Why, it's like that in life. Don't things happen so? We joke, laugh, and suddenly—flop! the end!' Here too, one might be listening to the very voice of Thomas Hardy, with his precisely similar sense of 'life's little ironies'. But few will consider such conceptions remarkable for cheerfulness. Indeed we are definitely told that Chekhov had moods of melancholia and misanthropy.

*   *   *

In May 1889 he wrote to Suvórin from the country: 'Nature is an excellent sedative. She pacifies; that is, she makes man indifferent. And in this world it is indispensable to be indifferent. Only indifferent characters are capable of seeing things clearly, capable of being just, and working—this, of course, applies only to people who are honourable and intelligent; egoists and imbeciles are indifferent as it is.'[1]

How can we reconcile this praise of 'indifference' with Chekhov's equal, but inconsistent praise, elsewhere, of strong feelings; of love; of having 'a fighting-cock of one's own'?

Here lies, I think, the central difficulty—but also the real key to understanding him. Imagine a man who loves some fickle, faithless woman. When the loved one is unfaithful, callous, or cruel, the anguish grows intolerable. The only cure is to cease caring at all. The only armour becomes, precisely—'indifference'. But then the loved one smiles and is kind again. The victim responds. Eagerly he flings aside his armour of indifference; for that armour is cold,

[1] Compare p. 35, for more of this key-passage of self-revelation.

killing, isolating as the shell that defends the tortoise. With indifference how can there be any joy or happiness? But again the glad moment passes. Again he is hurt and tortured. And again he clutches at his nonchalance. Once more happiness seems mere illusion; better to rest content with calm, with stoicism, with imperturbability.

So the eternal alternation goes on. The pendulum has to oscillate, till the clock finally stops. Such, I believe, was the constant conflict felt by Chekhov (as by many another) in his dealings with life—that fickle, heartless, beautiful, bewitching jade.

Only from this point of view, I believe, can Chekhov's apparent contradictions be really understood; but, seen so, they become very humanly understandable. Take some specific passages in his own work. There is, for example, his Siberian story *In Exile* (1892, after the Sakhalín journey). Here on the one hand there is the old ferry-man Semyon, called 'Canny', who endures his hard lot with a Buddhistic, Stoic 'indifference'—'Thank God, I want nothing. God give everyone such a life!' 'If you want to be happy, says I, the chief thing is to want nothing.' (The same philosophy as Chebutykin's in *The Three Sisters*—that 'nothing matters'.) And so old Semyon sneers sardonically at the poor gentleman, Vassily Sergeyitch, who is tortured as by devils with his anguished love for a faithless wife and a consumptive daughter. Yet against this indifference another voice in Chekhov cries angry protest through the mouth of another character, the young Tatar: 'God created man to be alive, and to have joy, and grief, and sorrow; but you want nothing, so you are not alive, you are stone, clay! A stone wants nothing, and you want nothing. You are a stone, and God does not love you; but He loves the gentleman.'

The story ends with the ferrymen lying down for the night in their hut, while from the drifting snow outside comes a howling like a dog's—the young Tatar's inconsolable despair. ' "He'll get u-used to it!" said Semyon, and at once fell asleep.' Yet one cannot doubt Chekhov's sympathy with the young Tatar's revulsion against this callousness that resolves never to care.

Compare, too, the reflection of the old Professor in *A Dreary Story*, when he hears by telegram of his daughter's marriage to an undesirable: 'I am dismayed, not by what Liza and Gnekker have done, but by the *indifference* with which I hear of their marriage. They say philosophers and the truly wise are indifferent. It is false: indifference is the paralysis of the soul; it is premature death.'[1]

And yet at other times Chekhov not only praised such indifference—often he gave the impression of himself possessing it. Even at thirty-two he could confess to Suvórin (8/4/1892), in a mood as melancholy as his own Ivánov: 'However strange it may seem, I crossed the thirty limit long ago, and feel already the approach of forty. I have grown old in soul as well as in body. Somehow I have become stupidly indifferent to everything on earth, and the beginning of this indifference for some reason coincided with my journey abroad.' (In 1891 he visited Austria, Italy, and France.) 'I rise from bed and go to bed with the feeling that my interest in life is dried up.' Similarly Leeka Mizinov, when deserted by Potapenko, wrote to Chekhov in 1894: 'Still, I don't think you will cast a stone at me. It seems to me that you were always indifferent to people, and their weaknesses and shortcomings.' In reply Chekhov protested that he was *not* 'indifferent to people'. None the less one still feels that this *was* the breastplate that he kept always ready to hand, for moments when life became too unbearably cruel.

And so it grows strangely revealing how often, with Chekhov, this word 'indifference' recurs, like the refrain in a poem, or the tolling of a bell. It comes again in letters to him from Olga Knipper after their marriage: 'Sometimes I feel you do not want me. . . . You can bear anything in silence. . . . You look on everyday life with complete *indifference*.' 'It isn't because you are cold or *indifferent* by

---

[1] One may recall La Fontaine's Scythian philosopher who, having learnt in Greece the art of pruning, went home and misled his countrymen to mangle their trees—a parable of the Stoic who overdoes emotional repression.

> Ils ôtent à nos coeurs le principal ressort;
> Ils font cesser de vivre avant que l'on soit mort.

> Such folk would take away the heart's mainspring,
> And, before death, leave life a lifeless thing.

It seems, in fine, one of life's most difficult problems to keep the mean between being too hard and too soft, between feeling too little and feeling too much. So, I believe, Chekhov particularly found.

nature, but because there is something in you that does not let you regard the phenomena of everyday life as of any consequence.' One begins to understand why Chekhov so admired the Stoic Marcus Aurelius.

He was full of vitality; yet mortally ill. He was sociable; yet lonely and aloof. He was a warm-hearted lover; yet, as Lydia Avílov and Olga Knipper found to their bewilderment, somehow inscrutably withdrawn. He was a detached and objective scientist; yet also an artist full of sensitiveness and sympathy. He had the eager energy of the West; yet also the fatalistic quietism of the East, of the Buddhist to whom all is Maya—illusion. Like many a thoughtful and sensitive Chinese of the past, he veers between the active, public-spirited wisdom of Confucius, and the detached, disillusioned wisdom of Lao-tse.

In the last letter from him quoted by Lydia Avílov come the lines—'Above all, keep cheerful, and don't take life too seriously; very likely, it is much more simple. And, anyway, does the life we do not know deserve all the tormenting thoughts which corrode our Russian brains?' What exactly did he mean? She puzzled over it a hundred times. Life 'much more simple'? How? For the very simple and sufficient reason, I suspect, that all, in the end, is but 'vanity of vanities'. 'Sottise, sottise, toutes choses sottise.'

Consequently the terminations of Chekhov's tales and plays are often bleak. At times he seems to feel that life becomes endurable only as a curious spectacle; and yet, again and again, gentleness and affection and conscience keep breaking in.

It is the same endless inward conflict as recurs in a moving poem by his French contemporary, Henri de Régnier (1864-1936):

> Le vrai sage est celui qui fonde sur le sable,
> Sachant que tout est vain dans le temps éternel
> Et que même l'amour est aussi peu durable
> Que le souffle du vent et la couleur du ciel.
>
> C'est ainsi qu'il se fait, devant l'homme et les choses,
> Ce visage tranquille, *indifférent* et beau,
> Qui regarde fleurir et s'effeuiller les roses
> Comme éclate, s'empourpre ou s'éteint un flambeau.

And yet the poet revolts against this stoic indifference as too icily aloof—

> Mais j'aime mieux laisser l'angoisse qui m'oppresse
> Emplir mon cœur plaintif et mon esprit troublé,
> Et pleurer de regret, d'attente, et de détresse,
> Et d'un obscur tourment que rien n'a consolé;
>
> Car ni le pur parfum des roses sur le sable,
> Ni la douceur du vent, ni la beauté du ciel,
> N'apaise mon désir avide et misérable
> Que tout ne soit pas vain dans le temps éternel.[1]

If, then, one had taxed Chekhov with the inconsistency between his stress on 'indifference' and his opposite stress on work, duty, and a 'fighting-cock of one's own', I suppose he might have answered, smiling—'Inconsistent? Yes. That is to say, human. (And we Russians live half-way between Asian quietism and the activity of Europe.) But perhaps it is not quite so inconsistent as it looks. For the one is a short-term, the other a long-term view. In a hundred years it is likely that all our cares and labours will matter not one pin. That teaches us resigned indifference. But if one thought like this all the time—every hour of the day—it would paralyse. So one's short-term view should enjoin activity, just as strongly as

---

[1]   The *true* sage takes the sand for his foundation,
Knowing all is vain, as eternity goes by—
That even love is frail in its duration
As the wind's breath, or colours in the sky.

Noble, *indifferent*, calm, his face reposes,
Watching both things and men, day after day;
Watching the flowering, fading, of the roses,
As a torch flames, grows crimson, dies away. . . .

Yet I would rather this anguish I go bearing
Should fill me, heart and soul, with dread and pain;
Rather would weep—regretting, hoping, caring—
With grief obscure that nothing cures again.

For, in that sand, no fragrant consolation
Of rose—no wind's caress—no coloured sky
Can calm my anguished longing's aspiration
That *all* be not vain, as eternity goes by.

one's long-term view enjoins resignation. The dog that worries a stick is not worried by his fleas. So he takes a stick for a rabbit. He may wish the stick were a real rabbit. Perhaps he may even find a real rabbit. Anyway one cannot have all one wants. But a wise dog realizes at intervals that the stick may be after all, only a stick; he does not let the stick begin to worry *him*. He can drop it with *indifference*.

'So with our human occupations. They may not matter much in a hundred years; yet some good may possibly come of our toiling. And so, as the Bible says, "whatsoever thy hand findeth to do, do it with thy might; for there is no work, nor device, nor knowledge, nor wisdom in the grave, whither thou goest". So spoke Ecclesiastes the Preacher, though he too had proclaimed, the very moment before, that all was vanity.'

Thus I imagine Chekhov answering; though perhaps I do him wrong.[1]

Anyway, instead of debating whether he was optimist or pessimist, it seems simpler and saner to recognize that in his work circuses and cemeteries do both lie side by side. The cemeteries do not stop the circuses; but neither can the circuses hide the cemeteries. Chekhov's mirth is often full of melancholy; his melancholy of mirth.

The melancholy Grimaldi was himself a clown. And, like Heine, Chekhov found to the end a consolation in ironic humour. Far better than whining and whimpering. But when the general public feels in his work, whatever critics may say, a heart-rending sadness, I doubt if the general public is far wrong. More than one of Chekhov's best plays could be sub-titled 'An Elegy in a Country House'.

'Perhaps I know best,' said Nietzsche, 'why only Man laughs; he suffers so profoundly that he was forced to invent laughter.' The aphorism may itself be a little forced. But the laughter of *The Cherry Orchard* does not seem to me very gay; surprisingly brave and buoyant though it may be for the laughter of a dying man.

---

[1] Cf. Montherlant (*Notebook XXI*): 'At all times the surface of my life has been agitated by passions, while my inner self has been as calm as the depths of the sea during a storm. Both should be experienced at once—attachment and detachment.' But easier said than done.

One should, however, perhaps add that Chekhov probably did not find his own view of life so gloomy as others like Tolstoy found it. For Chekhov was used to it. An Eskimo may find quite tolerable a temperature that sets European teeth a-chatter.

At times, for all his energy, Chekhov could calmly accept a complete scepticism. 'For fellows who write,' he says to Suvórin (30/5/1888), 'especially for artists, it is time to confess that one can make nothing of this world, as once Socrates confessed, and Voltaire also. The mob thinks it knows.' He could resign himself to see no supernatural purpose in life. 'You ask what is life?' he wrote to Olga Knipper, ten weeks before he died. 'That is just the same as asking what is a carrot. A carrot is a carrot, and nothing more is known about it.' To those who share Chekhov's view this seems the harsh but inescapable truth—bleak, yet also bracing. They have grown used to this attitude, and feel not the least need to tear their hair about it. After all, even if life did have a purpose, it might not be a purpose one much liked. But to a Tolstoy, whose life was an agonized search for life's purpose and meaning, such a conception must seem intolerable and inspissated gloom.

Further, the pleasure of artistic creation can cover a multitude of sorrows. There is an illuminating passage in a letter from the second Mrs Hardy to Sydney Cockerell about her husband: 'He is now—this afternoon—writing a poem with great spirit; always a sign of well-being with him. Needless to say, it is an intensely dismal poem.' Similarly Chekhov described himself to Lydia Avílov as writing in good humour about his most depressing characters. But this is very far from making it possible to call such writers optimists. Typical, perhaps, that though Chekhov laughed often, his laugh was almost inaudible.

One smiles at reading how Mounet-Sully, reproached for taking *Le Misanthrope* too tragically—for, after all, Molière himself called it 'a comedy'—replied 'Molière se trompait'. But one is almost driven, at moments when Chekhov tries to minimize the pervading sadness in his plays, to repeat—'Chekhov se trompait'.

Like his Dr Astrov, in the last desolate act of *Uncle Vanya*, 'he whistles'. If one could sum up a character so many-sided, it might be in the two simple words—'gay pessimist'. Indeed Korolenko said much the same of Chekhov long ago—'allegro malinconico'.[1] But the melancholy was not always gay; and I believe it went deeper than the gaiety.

Indeed, Chekhov may remind one of that tribute paid by a master of French tragi-comedy, Alfred de Musset, to his great predecessor, Molière—another gay pessimist and melancholy humorist.

> Cette mâle gaîté, si triste et si profonde,
> Que, lorsqu'on vient d'en rire, on devrait en pleurer.

> That virile mirth that is yet so sad, so deep,
> After our laughter, it should make us weep.

Might not the same, indeed, often be said of Shakespeare himself?

*   *   *

In some ways, as we have seen, Chekhov recalls that other great liberal, individualist, and dramatist—Ibsen. Tolstoy had condemned *The Seagull* for being like Ibsen—mere verbiage, leading nowhere. For Tolstoy had come to dismiss as futile, or worse, all literature that was not a pillar of flame leading through life's wilderness (though, in fact, such tendentious writing proves often only a column of drifting, blinding smoke). But Chekhov himself remained curiously ambivalent towards his Norwegian rival. He thought Ibsen not *simple* enough. He was bored by *The Wild Duck*—'Ibsen does not know life'. *Ghosts* he called 'a rotten play'. And when the Moscow Art Theatre was acting *Hedda Gabler*, Chekhov often stayed behind in the company's dressing-rooms after the curtain had risen for the next act; but when the actors mistook this for disapproval of their performance, Chekhov burst out—'Listen, Ibsen is no dramatist.'

[1] 'Merry melancholiac.' (So too Pushkin had said of Gogol.) It should be added that 'pessimist'—that label so disliked by Chekhov, Hardy, and Housman, all three—remains a term of abominable vagueness. 'Pessimism' is absurdly defined by the *Oxford Dictionary* as 'the doctrine that this world is the worst possible'. But who in his senses ever held such a doctrine? The most barren-witted devilkin could obviously imagine a thousand ways in which the world could be tormented still worse—for instance, if we all always had streaming colds. Surely it would be more practical to define 'pessimism' simply as 'a sombre view of life'.

Yet he could also (1903) make plans far away in Yalta for seeing a Moscow performance of *Pillars of Society*; and could write to Vishnevsky (7/11/03), 'You know Ibsen is my favourite author.'

Such contradictions one is again driven to explain by changeful moods. It might be argued that Chekhov felt Ibsen to be in some ways, as a thinker, too like himself. For writers are often less jealous (consciously or unconsciously), and more admiring, of fellow-writers totally unlike themselves—as, for example, Milton admired Euripides; or Kipling, Jane Austen. But this explanation seems not wholly convincing. Chekhov seems unusually free from jealousy, even unconscious. And though Ibsen and Chekhov did share a number of beliefs—in individualism,[1] in sincerity, in the loathsomeness of all tyranny, in freedom for women, in the heinousness of callously killing the love-life in another's heart—yet technically they remained poles apart. Ibsen would, no doubt, have approved Chekhov's theoretical stress on relevance—that one should not describe a gun hanging on the wall, in a story's first chapter, unless it is going later to be used. But in practice Chekhov's standards of relevance seem far less rigid; Ibsen would probably have thought *The Cherry Orchard* much too much of a chaos. And indeed one must admit that a succession of *Cherry Orchards* would risk becoming a real wilderness.

An easier explanation might be simply that younger writers are naturally irked and irritated by the great of the generation before them, and so are apt to hammer impatiently on their doors—as Knut Hamsun did on Ibsen's.

No matter, Chekhov and Ibsen were both men of good will, who fought on the side of light against darkness. One may not share that wistful Utopianism with which Chekhov's characters sometimes console themselves for the drabness of today. For, as Huxley once put it, 'It is not clear what compensation the Eohippus gets for his sorrows in the fact that some millions of years afterwards one

[1] Cf. Chekhov's letter to his brother Alexander who had upset their parents in 1882 by running off and living with a Moscow writer's wife: 'What do you care what some bigot thinks of your private life? . . . The whole point of life consists in making a protest without asking for pity. Every man has a right to live with whom he likes, and how he likes.' 'Making a protest without asking for pity' is the very essence of Ibsen.

of his descendants wins the Derby.' Indeed a prescient Eohippus would have had far more grounds for going melancholy-mad, could he have foreseen the horrors to be inflicted by man on his enslaved posterity in peace and war. But though one may believe that the Devil is likely to be immortal—or at least to last as long as the race of mortals—it still remains to strike one's blow on the side of light. One may not believe in the existence of the New Jerusalem; there is only too little doubt about the existence of barbarians, and the menace of their triumph. *There*, at all events, is a cause worth while. 'À bas les barbares!' Under that banner both Ibsen and Chekhov fought to the end.

For me, Ibsen remains the finer dramatist. That Master Builder's plays seem better built; more decisive and incisive; sharper in focus, and clearer in atmosphere. Through them blows a keener, cleaner, and more bracing air, like the sea-winds of Hardanger and Sogn. But this remains a matter of individual temperament. The Chekhov I love and admire is, above all, the Chekhov of the letters and stories—so wide and deep in their knowledge of mankind, and also in their human sympathy. To read them is to measure the depths of degradation—in many respects—that have overtaken Russia, and indeed much of the Western world also, in the half-century since Chekhov died.

Yet there is also the unquestionable fact that, when 1960 brought the centenary of Chekhov's birth, it brought, too, an astonishing flood of tributes and appreciations, from Russia and from the West alike. It has even been suggested that today 'his popularity surpasses that of Dostoievsky, Tolstoy, and other giants of Russian literature'.[1] Such a statement will leave many amazed. Chekhov above Tolstoy and Dostoievsky! It would have astounded Chekhov himself. The statement may be exaggerated. None the less it remains striking that it could be seriously made.

All that is truest and most typical in the mature Chekhov seems to me symbolized in those last hours at Badenweiler in the Black

---

[1] *Anton Čechov, Some Essays*; edited by T. Eekman (Leiden, 1960). In the same year Ilya Erenburg stated that in the U.S.S.R. there had been published some fifty million copies of his works. Such figures are very vague; but clearly Chekhov's public has become immense.

Forest. On the one hand, the champagne, the gaiety, the irony, the humour, the humanity, the courage, the laughing vision of the dinnerless rich in their luxury-hotels. Here lives, even in dying, the humorous Chekhov whom some superficial critics pretend to be the only one. But there is also the ice on the chest, the distant cannon and carnage of Far Eastern battlefields; the fluttering of the huge black moth in the after-silence; the unutterable solitude of that which lay waiting for its solitary grave. Here looms Chekhov's tragic side, to which even laughter, love, and courage are but a vain answer in the end—and yet, of all answers, the finest and least vain.[1]

---

[1] The two sides of Chekhov come out vividly in his best portraits, which reveal both the doctor and the artist, in the penetrating, humorous, melancholy eyes, the sensitive, yet stoic mouth.

PART II

John Millington Synge

'Wisdom keeps school out-of-doors.'

LIFE

John Millington Synge, born in 1871 at Rathfarnham near Dublin, was the son of a Protestant barrister, who died the following year.

An ancestor named Millington, a canon or precentor of the Chapel Royal, is said to have *sung* so sweetly before Henry VIII that the delighted monarch told him he should call himself 'Synge'. Whatever the truth of this quaint tradition, the name well befitted a dramatist whose dialogue has never, I think, been surpassed in lilting melody.

Ironically enough, the ancestry of this anti-clerical poet included other clerics also—Edward, Archbishop of Tuam in the days of Swift, and no fewer than four bishops; among them that Bishop of Elphin traditionally supposed to have refused ordination to Oliver Goldsmith, because the candidate presented himself in unclerical red breeches.

A further paradox is that Synge, though he became an Irish Nationalist, sprang (like Parnell) from the Anglo-Irish Protestant ascendancy—from a family that once owned Glanmore Castle, and a great estate in Wicklow.

His mother's stock was evangelical; so that the boy grew up in the sombre shadow of Sin and Hell, until at sixteen or seventeen, after reading Darwin, he rebelled against this maternal creed, with much mental conflict of his own, and to his mother's lasting distress. Further conflict came from his violent revulsion against the ruthlessness with which his brother Edward, now a land-agent, evicted a tenant on his aunt's estate near Glanmore. The real 'troubles' in Ireland were not yet; but already the shadows of their coming fell across Synge's youth.

A delicate child, who had to exchange school for a private tutor, he developed two special interests of his own—natural history and music. And indeed no drama was to be fuller than his of both the music of language, and the beauty of nature—the Irish beauty of one of the loveliest, and still least spoiled, among the countries of the earth.

From 1888 to 1892 Synge was at Trinity, Dublin. Like Goldsmith, he was no model scholar. Music attracted him far more; and also his now awakened passion for the Irish past. 'Soon after I had relinquished the Kingdom of God,' he wrote, 'I began to take a real interest in the Kingdom of Ireland. My patriotism went round from a vigorous and unreasoning loyalty[1] to a temperate nationalism, and everything Irish became sacred.'

In 1893, after taking a pass degree at Trinity, Synge went off to pursue his music in Germany; but grew sadly convinced that he had neither nerve enough to play before audiences, nor talent enough to make an effective composer. He felt, he says, innately less musical than the Germans. So in 1895 he turned from Germany and music to Paris and literature.

In Paris he lodged with a male cook, who also fabricated toothpowder, while the cook's wife made ladies' hats. But his Parisian life was not easy (Synge was now subsisting on £40 a year).[2] Often he had to stay in bed to keep warm; and, he said, the servant warned him against eating the meat served by his landlady, because it was really meat for cats.

He attended lectures at the Sorbonne; taught English; and wrote (not, as yet, very well). He also paid, in 1896, a brief visit to Italy. But he discovered his true vocation only when Yeats, meeting him in Paris (December, 1896), told him to leave busying himself with Racine and criticism. Instead, he should go to the Aran Islands (which Yeats had recently visited); live with their peasants; and set himself to express a side of human life hitherto unuttered and unknown.[3]

---

[1] Presumably to Anglo-Irish dominance.

[2] Gerard Fay (*The Abbey Theatre*, 1958, p. 61) states, without giving any source, that Synge then had 'something between four and five hundred pounds a year'. But a letter of Synge's mother in 1897 says he had 'nearly £40'; and even in 1908, after inheriting £1500 from her (which he expected, at 5 per cent. to yield £75), Synge estimated his future income at only £110. (See D. H. Greene, *Synge*, p. 295.)

[3] In a very different way that other, very different offshoot of the sophisticated nineties, A. E. Housman, likewise turned aside to the simplicities of a rustic world. But Housman remained an aloof lyric poet, who felt for nature rather than for rustics, and never got outside his own complex, sombre personality.

In May, 1898, Synge went to Aran. Oddly enough, an uncle of his had been there half a century before, as Aran's first Protestant missionary. But the seed sowed by the Rev. Alexander Synge had fallen on stony ground. For a time, indeed, he succeeded in stopping the islanders playing ball on Sunday. But, despite this momentary triumph, today, it seems, the Protestant church on Inishmore lies deserted, and not a single Protestant remains.

For the dramatist, however, things turned out differently. Aran was the making of Synge, even more than Cumberland was the making of Wordsworth (who early became one of Synge's favourite poets). Both writers found themselves only when they turned from the dusty and corrupted turmoil of cities, to 'huts where poor men lie'. But the Aran Islanders, isolated in the waste Atlantic, were far poorer than the rustics of Wordsworth's Lakes. Their lives were far wilder and more desolate; their imaginations far more primitive and untamed; and their language far stranger and more startling than anything spoken by what a medieval Irish poet disdainfully calls 'the creeping Saxon'. Wordsworth's faith about the native virtue in the speech of common men, often unconvincing in Britain (though justified at times by the rustics of Scott or Hardy), seems far more valid among the peaks and seas of Kerry, Clare, or Connemara; just as Irish skies have a magic and a mystery rarely seen above East Anglia. And so, whereas Wordsworth was too often duped by his own theory to dull his verse into drab or leaden prose, Synge learnt in Wicklow and Aran a kind of prose far more poetic than much so-called poetry. In the West particularly, where the English and Irish tongues had lived for generations side by side, the resulting blend of seventeenth-century English with the syntax of the Gael had bred something still stranger and more picturesque than the speech of eastern Ireland, where Gaelic died out far earlier.

To Aran Synge went five times in all, once in each year from 1898 to 1902. It consists of three rocky, wind-scourged islands, twenty-eight miles west-south-west of Galway. To westward swirls the limitless Atlantic; to eastward lie the limestone cliffs of Clare; to northward, the stony desolation of Connemara, with its Twelve Pins rising from a loch-starred wilderness. Fully to understand Synge's plays it is vital to read also his two descriptive works—

The Aran Islands and *In Wicklow and West Kerry*. Aran gave him suggestions for the plots of *In the Shadow of the Glen*, *Riders to the Sea*, and *The Playboy of the Western World*; Wicklow provided the scene for *The Shadow of the Glen*, and the source for *The Tinker's Wedding*. Synge indeed did not so much invent an imaginary world as remould to perfection matter drawn from real life.[1]

But it was not merely stories that Synge found in the Irish countryside. There he found also his lilting, imaginative style; his whimsical characters; his comic, yet tragic, earthy, yet unearthly, atmosphere. Ignorance or prejudice may dismiss Synge's peasants as no less unreal and artificial than the swains of conventional pastoral, contemptuously snorted at by Johnson. That is wrong. How completely wrong, can best be seen by considering a few of the glimpses of real life recorded by him in *The Aran Islands* and *Wicklow and West Kerry*.

For example, there is the typically 'Irish' thinking of that old rustic who said to Synge on Inishmaan: 'A man who is not afraid of the sea will soon be drownded, for he will be going out on a day he shouldn't. But *we* do be afraid of the sea, and we do only be drownded now and again.' Quaintly comic, in its logic; yet poignantly tragic, also, in the years of grim experience behind.

Equally 'Irish' is the confutation, by an old net-mender at Kilronan on Inishmore, of a boastful fellow-sailor who claimed to have learnt Greek at school.

> I asked him could he read a Greek book with all his talk of it.
> 'I can so,' said he.
> 'We'll see that,' said I.
> Then I got the Irish book out of my chest, and I gave it into his hand.
> 'Read that to me,' said I, 'if you know Greek.'
> He took it, and he looked at it this way, and that way, and not a bit of him could make it out.
> 'Bedad, I've forgotten my Greek,' said he.
> 'You're telling a lie,' said I.
> 'I'm not,' said he, 'it's the divil a bit I can read it.'
> Then I took the book back into my hand, and said to him—'It's the

[1] Six years before Synge's coming to Aran, Emily Lawless had already depicted its life in a novel that now seems forgotten—*Grania* (1892); a simple, sincere book, but without the pressure and intensity of Synge.

sorra a word of Greek you ever knew in your life, for there's not a word of Greek in that book, and not a bit of it you knew.'

The point here lies not merely in the whimsicality of proving that a man does not know Greek by proving that he does not know Irish; for, though odd, the proof remains sound enough. But this old net-mender is also, in his way, a born dramatist; it is his natural gift for dialogue, and gesture, that brings this snatch of grotesque comedy so vividly to life.

Here in the remote West there survived, too, a world where grown men still kept the engaging simplicity of children. When Synge showed on Blasket Island a photograph of himself in the Luxembourg Gardens at Paris, with statues in the background, he heard a man whisper in Irish to one of the girls: 'Look at that! In those countries they do have naked people standing about in their skins.' And again, when the Roman Catholic curate on Aran asked the dramatist whether he had read his Bible that Sunday morning, and the dramatist owned he had not, 'Well, begob, Mr Synge,' smiled the cleric, 'if you ever go to Heaven, you'll have a great laugh at us.' No pious pretence that religious exercises are pleasant. One buys Heaven as one buys a horse; and the laugh is against one, if another fellow buys his horse cheaper.

Such a view may seem cynical. But it is not so much cynicism as simple directness. These people still enjoy, also, that gift of wide-eyed wonder which the simple may share with child or poet. A girl of fifteen talked to Synge of a town on the mainland. 'Ah,' said she, 'it's a queer place; I wouldn't choose to live in it. It's a queer place, and indeed I don't know the place that isn't.' And again: 'Father —— is gone; he was a kind man but a queer man. Priests is queer people, and I don't know who isn't.'

And because their minds were thus unstaled and uncrowded, they enjoyed a vitality and imagination that could strike out phrases as bright as new pennies; where the city-dwellers of the modern world too often thumb only a drab coinage of words outworn and defaced; and its academic writers too often weave only pretentious cats'-cradles of tangled, faded verbiage.

There is, for example, the benediction bestowed on Synge over a lifted glass of whisky—'And now here's to your good health, and may you live till they make you a coffin out of a gooseberry bush, or till you die in childbed!'[1]

[1] Some English readers may suspect Synge of embroidering. But many other sources could confirm this delightful vivacity of the Irish mind. Take, for example, a few phrases from P. W. Joyce's *English as we speak it in Ireland* (1910)—(of a thin man) 'he could kiss a goat between the horns'; (of a willing one) 'you could lead him with a halter of snow'; (of an indifferent one) 'neither glad nor sorry, like a dog at his father's wake'; (of a liar) 'he would swear a coal-porter was a canary'; (of a buxom dame) 'a fine doorful of a woman'; (of a good razor) "twould shave a mouse asleep'; (of a bad marksman) 'he would not hit a hole in a ladder'. One may be 'cross as a bag of cats'; 'lively as a bag of fleas'; 'proud as a white-washed pig'. Or, asked to do a job better left to the servants, one may retort—'Ay indeed!—keep a dog and bark myself!'

Stephen Gwynn, again, records a description of a dusty road—'There was dust on ut the day after the Flood'; and the outcry of a harried cook—'There isn't water enough in the house to baptize a fairy, and me with the potatoes to put down for dinner!' Or, reported by Lily Yeats, there is the disgusted comment of a priest after confessing a convent—'it was like being eaten alive by ducks' (with reference, presumably, to the miserable little peccadilloes of these simple, loquacious, up-looking women); or, from Lady Gregory, the plea of a gardener reproached for leaving weeds in the drive—'Ah sure, wouldn't it be a quare battle there wouldn't be some soldiers left from!' And for climax, though more literary, there is the curse in James Stephens on a barmaid refusing to give a glass of beer—

> May she marry a ghost and bear him a kitten, and may
> The High King of Glory permit her to get the mange!

Even old Irish legends show already this boundless extravagance of fancy. The Ultonian heroes return from war so heated that their cold baths boil over; the spear of Lugh so thirsts for blood that its point must be kept submerged in poppy-juice; the leech of Conor can diagnose a man's sickness by the mere look of the smoke from the house where he lies; behind Cuchulain's chariot, the turves and blocks thrown up by his horses' hoofs are 'like flocks of dark birds pouring over a vast plain'.

Such flights of fantasy make the Greek imagination seem far more sober, even at its most romantic. In Homer the old dog Argus, lying lice-covered on a midden, recognizes Odysseus, just wags his tail, and dies. But in the thirteenth-century *Irish Odyssey* Argus has been preserved by Penelope with 'gruel of long life', and has become a rainbow-coloured hound—'Two shining white sides it has, and a light purple back, and a jet-black belly, and a greenish tail.' The creature is brought in on a chain by four men; but, when it heard Ulysses' voice, 'it dragged the four men on their backs all through the house behind it'. Again, when Ulysses pierces the Cyclops' eye, he is almost drowned 'by the broad and large loch of water which burst out of it'.

Or there is the account, much more picturesque than credible, given by an old Wicklow man of his voyagings to America—'I've been through perils enough to slay nations, and the people here think I should be rotten with gold, but they're better off the way they are. For five years I was a ship's smith, and never saw dry land, and I in all the danger and peril of the Atlantic Ocean.'

Or again, no less full of pathos than of humour, there is the old woman Synge met near Glen Macanass in Wicklow. Like a prudent mother, she had found a schoolmaster to come across the bog and give her Michael extra schooling. One evening she listened to the pair. 'And what do you think my son was after doing? He'd made a sum of how many times a wheel on a cart would turn round between the bridge below and the Post Office in Dublin. Would you believe that!' And so, thinking such enormous feats of intellect quite sufficient, she paid off the master. 'And, God bless you, avourneen, Michael got a fine job after on the railroad.'

This good woman recognized also the merits of Synge himself. 'Ah, God bless you, avourneen, *you*'ve no pride. Didn't I hear you yesterday, and you talking to my pig below in the field as if it was your brother? And a nice clean pig it is too, the crathur.' (For a moment one has an unexpected glimpse of Synge, like Shaw's Father Keegan in *John Bull's Other Island* with his grasshopper, conversing familiarly with the beasts of the field; and of that simpler, kindlier world, known also to St Francis, where no chasm has yet yawned between man and his humbler brethren who share with him, for all his pride, the mystery of birth and love and death.)

But, as usual, with such comedy was intertwined tragedy also. A year or two later this old woman lost her husband, dead of 'influence'; and had only one son left to help her harsh struggle to live. 'The poor old man is after dying on me,' she said, 'and he was great company. There is only one son left me now, and we do be killed working. Ah, avourneen, the poor do have great stratagems to keep in their little cabins at all.'

Like other Arcadias, indeed, this Irish one was by no means all Arcadian. With its simplicity went, also, brutishness—a joy in dog-fights or scurrilous flytings, a callousness that tied poor donkeys' heads painfully to their legs, or made the women quite ruthless in plucking geese and ducks alive. An old man led Synge down the road to show him proudly how far off they could hear him yelling, 'the time he had a pain in his head'. And a young man said to Synge in the train, of the bitter partings of emigrants to America from those who had so little hope ever to see them again: 'Ah, we do have great sport every Friday and Saturday, seeing the old women howling in the stations.'

There seems, indeed, in the Irish temper, as in Irish fairy-tales and legends, a certain streak of cruelty; though, remembering the bull-baitings and bear-baitings, the cock-fights and gloveless bruisers of our own ancestors, it may not be for the English to talk much.[1] Certainly Synge's Irish, with this simple charm of the uncivilized, combined also the aggressiveness and pugnacity of the savage. In Kerry he saw horse-races on the sands that recall the close of his own *Playboy*; but the ensuing battle, though delightful in his description, must have been, as a reality, less enchanting.

'There was great sport after you left,' a man said to me in the cottage this evening. 'They were all beating and cutting each other on the shore of the sea. Four men fought together in one place till the tide came up on them, and was like to drown them; but the priest waded out up to his middle and drove them asunder. Another man was left for dead on the road outside the lodges, and some gentleman found him and had him carried to his home, and got the doctor to put plasters on his head. There was a red-headed fellow had his finger bitten through, and the postman was destroyed for ever.'

'He should be,' said the man of the house, 'for Michael Patch broke the seat of his car[2] into three halves on his head.'

'It was this was the cause of it all,' said Danny-boy: 'they brought in porter east and west from the two towns you know of, and the two porters didn't agree together, and it's for that the people went raging at the fall of night.'

How much of Synge's own drama consists precisely in this!—in 'people raging at the fall of night'—raging, or laughing, or both at once. The last scene of *The Playboy* seems no longer so unreal.

Such coloured vividness of speech reminds me always of a

---

[1] I must add that as a traveller I have found no race kinder or more hospitable than the Irish.

[2] i.e. jaunting-car.

passage in Hardy—' "More know Tom Fool"—what rambling old canticle is it you say, hostler?' inquired the milkman, lifting his ear. 'Let's have it again—*a good saying well spit out is a Christmas fire to my withered heart.*'

But Synge's peasants, though not more humorous—or tragic— than Hardy's, have imaginations more untamed, and a rhythm of speech more poetic, than will easily be found in the quieter beauty of the English countryside.

It has not, I think, been superfluous to dwell thus at length on the Ireland that Synge discovered. For there Synge discovered himself; as he would never have done in Paris.

He has been accused of romanticizing his peasants, as Goldsmith, or Sterne, or Wordsworth, or Tolstoy at times were tempted to do. But, like Crabbe, Hardy, or Pirandello (in his stories), he seems to me to hold a very honest balance. He may make us laugh at postmen being 'destroyed for ever'; he may delight our ears with the poetic wooings of Christy Mahon; but he does not whitewash the darker shadows. He had no shrinking from reality. Describing a man of extraordinary ugliness and wit on the South Island in Aran, he adds: 'These strange men with receding foreheads, high cheek-bones, and ungovernable eyes, seem to represent some old type found on those few acres at the extreme border of Europe, where it is only in wild jests and laughter that they can express their loneliness and desolation.' Ugliness and wit, laughter and desolation—both sides of the truth are there.

Our civilization grows yearly cleaner, richer, healthier; but its people tend more and more to be over-populated, overcrowded, over-organized, with colourless thoughts and speech, colourless work, and a colourless leisure, which is largely given over to the gibberings and gesticulations of infinite shadows on infinite screens. After gaining so much, men are yet today in danger of losing their living selves. Nor do I see any hope of betterment except in an emptier, simpler world, with plenty of unspoilt nature and, as I have said elsewhere, an aristocracy of human beings, a proletariat of machines, that possess no senses or feelings to kill. Synge's peasants, poor, superstitious, often wretched, often brutal, had still not lost imagination, individuality, character.

Yet Synge was himself keenly and bitterly aware that this fragment of an older world must, in a few years, likewise disappear for ever. 'The thought,' he wrote at the end of his first visit, 'that this island will gradually yield to the ruthlessness of "progress" is as the certainty that decaying age is moving always nearer to the cheeks it is your ecstasy to kiss. How much of Ireland was formerly like this, and how much of Ireland is today Anglicized and brutalized!'

So too Masefield (who read the manuscript of *The Aran Islands* for his publisher), while warmly praising it, added: 'I am afraid its publication will send scores of tweeded beasts to the islands, but that cannot be helped.' Alas, it cannot. How well one knows those 'tweeded beasts'! Soon, in their motorized armies, they will have carried havoc throughout the earth.

In 1901, after his third visit to Aran, Synge began work on a play never completed and quite unlike his published dramas. For it was about people of his own class—principally, a young Irish writer, called home from Paris by his uncle's illness, and his cousin, a nun, who has been nursing the uncle. The anti-clerical Synge ended his drama by making the hero persuade the heroine to leave her nunnery, and become his bride.

He could hardly have expected anyone in Catholic Ireland to produce, or tolerate, a play whose hero perverts and marries a nun, and replies to her appeal to believe in God: 'I will believe in millions of them, but I have no doubt they care as little for us as we care for the sorrows of an ant-hill.' But in this plot Synge may have embodied an element of private wish-fulfilment. For he had long vainly wooed a girl, Cherry Matheson, brought up as a Plymouth Sister, who rejected him, at least in part, for his religion, or lack of it; just as Christina Rossetti rejected Collinson and Cayley, or as Rose La Touche rejected Ruskin.

Synge's play does not seem, from D. H. Greene's description of it, to have shown much merit. But it did show one redeeming feature—its peasant characters, with their peasant speech. There was even an anticipation of the last words of Maurya in *Riders to the Sea*—'I'm destroyed crying: but what good is in it? We must be satisfied and what man at all can be living for ever?' That, indeed, is an echo of actual words once written to Synge by an islander of Aran.[1]

Now the one thing that struck Yeats and Lady Gregory, when Synge showed them his play, was this peasant element. Therefore they told him to stick to peasants. They were right. Like Scott, Dickens, or Hardy, so Synge also was to gain his really vital successes, not with characters drawn from the educated classes, but with the language, the lives, the personalities of the poor.

*   *   *

The rest of Synge's life is mainly the history of the six plays that he wrote, and of the storms that several of them raised among his countrymen. A chronological table will be quickest and clearest.

1902-3   *Riders to the Sea* (performed 1904).[2]
           In the Shadow of the Glen (performed 1903).
1902-4   *The Well of the Saints* (performed 1905; with a first-night audience of two dozen).
1904   Synge becomes, with Yeats and Lady Gregory, one of the directing triumvirate of the new Abbey Theatre.
1905-6   *The Playboy of the Western World* (performed 1907).
1906   *The Tinker's Wedding* finished (it had been begun in 1902-3; and was published in 1907).
1908-9   *Deirdre* (published and performed 1910).
           (Four comedies, two tragedies; but three of the comedies have also their tragic undertones.)
24/3/09 Synge dies.

Apart from his creative work, there is little more to record in Synge's brief life. In 1906 he fell in love with the actress Molly Allgood, 'Máire O'Neill' (1886-1952). She was the daughter of a working-man; had served in a Dublin store; and, in 1906, was only twenty—that is, fifteen years younger than the poet.

It was not a love whose course ran smooth. Not only was Molly Allgood a Roman Catholic. Not only was she much younger; so

---

[1] p. 184.
[2] In a letter of 12/12/07 Synge says he wrote *Riders to the Sea* before *In the Shadow of the Glen* (*J. M. Synge: Catalogue of an Exhibition*, Dublin, 1959, p. 34).

that Synge suffered like his own King Conchubor with the girlish Deirdre. Like Molière, Synge found also that love in a green-room was bedevilled by jealousy. Further, as with Rossetti and Lizzie Siddal, there lay between the lovers a certain gulf of class and education; and, as with Keats and Fanny Brawne, there was not only jealousy, but the shadow of fatal malady, which denied the lover the marriage he had dreamed of.

Little wonder that quarrels between the two were not rare; that Synge's letters to his beloved were often bitter; that the private comments she scribbled on them (merely to relieve her own feelings) were often bitter also—'idiotic', 'appalling', 'I don't care if I never heard from you or saw you again, so there!'[1] However, these unspoken retorts may only have been momentary tantrums. One cannot judge. For the unhappy girl seems to have become frantic when Synge's death visibly approached; and vainly tried to get priests to say a mass for the doomed heretic. Yet one doubts whether, even had he lived, she was the woman to make him happy.

Synge suffered both from asthma and from a malady called Hodgkin's disease—still mysterious, though studied as long ago as 1832 by Dr Thomas Hodgkin (1798-1866). It caused lumps to form in his neck, which were operated on in 1897 and 1907; but in 1908 a tumour formed in his side, for which surgery could do nothing. In March 1909 Synge died in a Dublin hospital, aged only thirty-eight.

His tragedy, *Deirdre*, was still unfinished; his betrothed still unwed; his real success still unwon. And to the very last life mocked him. For the dying man was moved into a room whence his beloved Wicklow Mountains should for a last time be visible. But when his bed was put there, it proved too low; so that he could not see again those hills to which his heart had been lifted up so long. He passed into the Valley of the Shadow without even that farewell glimpse of the Shadow of the Glen.

---

[1] Lennox Robinson describes her as both beautiful and gifted—excellent as Nora Burke in *The Shadow of the Glen*, and still more so as Pegeen in *The Playboy*. But she was also, he adds, 'a bit of a divil', who vowed before a summer theatre-tour in England to return with three engagement-rings—and did!

In 1912 she married. But the marriage failed, and she returned to acting in 1916 (E. Coxhead, *Lady Gregory*, p. 146).

Synge seems to have been a curious mixture of sensitiveness and determination, gentleness and inflexibility. His face was like a bull-dog's, with a heavy, immensely resolute, chin. There is something primitive about the thick moustache,[1] and the bull-neck (though that seems partly due to his disease). Indeed his face has been thought curiously like some portraits of that most detested figure in all Irish history—Oliver Cromwell. It is only in the distant, tragic eyes that one glimpses the poet. Even the voice of this master of verbal melody was hoarse, quick, and often hard to follow.

George Moore, no doubt with his usual picturesque exaggeration, has portrayed Synge as a man of 'large impassive face' and 'of such rough and uncultivated aspect as if he had come out of Derrinrush'. Masefield, more reliable, describes him in company—with 'a dark, grave face', saying little, revealing little, but listening and watching intently. Ear, eye, brain, and heart were vividly awake; but he did not give tongue. Indeed he disliked brilliant and showy persons; he was puzzled in London by clever youths from Oxford—'That's a queer way to talk. I wonder what makes them talk like that. I suppose they're always stewing over dead things.' But though Synge talked little, he had read much—in English, French, German, Italian, even Irish and Hebrew. Rather unexpectedly, he had a special love for Racine. But above all he studied life. 'He would,' says Masefield, 'have watched a political or religious riot with gravity, with pleasure in the spectacle, and malice for the folly.' Very much what one may imagine of Shakespeare; very much what Browning imagined of his poet in 'How It Strikes a Contemporary'—

> He took such cognizance of men and things,
> If any beat a horse, you felt he saw;
> If any cursed a woman, he took note.

Yet under Synge's reticence, behind his humour, lay moods of profound melancholy—as when, on his twenty-fifth birthday, he wrote a poem wondering whether his next twenty-five years would

---

[1] And, one might add, the densely clustering hair. But after Synge's operation in December 1897, his mother describes him as wearing a wig. Whether this was permanent, I do not know.

be as bad as the last twenty-five had been. Alas, the years fate had still in store for him numbered only thirteen.

And under his quiet shyness lay also a strength, impassive but far from passive, which could be provoked into obstinacy—even pugnacity. When bigots railed at *The Well of the Saints*, as they had railed at *The Shadow of the Glen*, his reaction was not to cower, but to counter-attack—'Very well, the next play I write I will make sure *will* annoy them.' The next play was *The Playboy*. It did.

The producer of *The Playboy*, W. G. Fay, rightly foresaw what trouble it would rouse; but no pleas or persuasions of his could make Synge tone down its audacities. And when, during the actual performance, people howled and shook fists at him, sitting in the auditorium, Synge's dry comment was merely—'We shall have to establish a Society for the Preservation of Irish Humour.'

Again, Fay has recalled how, when he was walking one night with Synge in one of the roughest quarters of Dublin, they heard screams from a tumble-down, shuttered shop. In spite of the danger, in such a slum, of bringing a whole mob on their backs, Synge insisted on knocking. No answer. They forced the door and rescued a woman and her baby from some brute's violence. The man showed fight. But Synge punched him under the chin and marched him off to hand over to the police: then, relenting, let him go.

It is a typically Irish conclusion to this episode that next day, going down the same street, Fay saw the man and woman sitting and laughing together at their door, while their infant played happily at their feet. Readers of *The Aran Islands* may recall there too the same reckless enjoyment of quarrels and abuse, such as also delighted medieval Scots in the 'flytings' of poets like Kennedy or Dunbar.

But though Synge had himself an amused relish for such picturesqueness of tongue, he had, like Chekhov, no taste at all for taking part personally in political or religious flytings and fanaticisms. He became, indeed, a Nationalist. And he did not much like England or the English. As he came round from the anaesthetic after one of his operations, his first audible words were 'Damn the bloody Anglo-Saxon language that a man can't swear in without being vulgar!'[1] (Which is largely true, today at least—in marked contrast with Synge's Irish.) Yet, though a Nationalist, Synge steadily refused to become a partisan, or to mix the ephemeral squabblings of politics with the enduring things of art. It would, of course, be foolish to say poets should *never* deal with politics. From Solon of Athens, and Theognis of Megara, to Wordsworth and Victor Hugo, poets have sometimes dealt, if not always very effectively, at least eloquently, with affairs of state. All the same, for writers, politics remain dangerous. Further, they are hopelessly transient—dust that rises up and is lightly laid again.

Yeats has told how, when urged to write, for once, a political play, Synge outlined in 1903 a drama about the Irish rebellion of '98[2], where a Catholic woman and a Protestant took refuge from English and rebels in the same cave; and at once started quarrelling over Henry VIII and Queen Elizabeth with such fury, that finally one of them quitted their refuge and risked ravishment rather than endure any longer the odious company of the other.

It appears, however, from D. H. Greene, that here Yeats is a little misleading. In Synge's scenario, the two women did indeed quarrel. But in the end the Protestant helped to save the wounded son of the Catholic from the English. This version is clearly less farcical, and more human.

In any case, Synge's level-headed irony and humanity were far from common in the Ireland of his day. One cannot blame an oppressed people for embittered memories; but those who cultivate too long memories are liable to get tangled and strangled in them. The Irish have now utilized the energy of the River Shannon; but there is another river whose force they remained too long incapable of using—Lethe, the River of Forgetfulness. Long, even, after Eire had become a free state, in the mid-thirties, I can remember seeing walls in Western Ireland daubed with vast letters in whitewash that coupled the names of Cosgrave and Cromwell, or proclaimed

[1] Cf. Max Beerbohm on *The Shadow of the Glen* in 1904—'it illustrates a very odd thing about the Irish people—their utter incapacity to be vulgar'. (I am not sure, however, that this view is wholly free from the romantic enchantment of distance.)

[2] I am not quite clear whether Yeats meant 1798 or 1598. Henry VIII and Elizabeth seem remote from 1798. Yet Irish memories are tenacious.

'Ireland was a nation when England was a bloody pup'. And telegraph-poles in a Sligo village were plastered with posters whose green paint adjured the passer-by to 'Remember 1169'.[1] (For the Saxon, who does *not* remember 1169, and remembers even 1066 largely as a joke, it must be explained that 1169 is associated with the English invasion under Strongbow.) But though one cannot wholly blame this obsessive violence so common in Irish memories, one need not admire it. There seems much more to be said for the calmer balance of Synge; who apparently took the very sane view that it would be wicked folly to shed blood for Irish freedom, while there remained a reasonable hope of winning it bloodlessly from the spread of socialism in England. Unfortunately for mankind, revolutionaries seldom regard patience as a virtue.[2]

In fine, Synge's was not the kind of writing that the jargon of today calls 'engagé' or 'committed' (as if literature were some sort of crime). He was a free intelligence, like Goethe, Ibsen, or Chekhov, well aware that 'movements' are best left to mobs; and that majorities, as they grow 'compact', usually grow, also, dense.

As he was resolute in facing the world, so also this quiet man was resolute in facing his work. He revised, like so many good writers, indefatigably. His successive drafts were lettered A, B, C, D, and so on. The earlier of these versions might grow progressively longer; the later, progressively shorter. And he would rewrite a dozen times. Naturalness, as Anatole France wisely said, is what you add *last*; which is why it is so seldom attained. What, for example, could seem to flow with more spontaneous ease and liveliness than *The Well of the Saints*? Yet Synge describes himself as struggling with it 'in agony and horror'.[3]

In many ways Synge and Yeats, though often fellow-combatants in the same cause, remained curiously opposite. Synge was shy,

[1] Compare the affectionate comment of an Irish peasant-woman on Bertrand Russell's daughter, aged five—'She's a bonny girl, *in spite of Cromwell*.'

[2] More recently, however, I have seemed to notice in Ireland itself a tendency to regard the 'troubles', or the 'crossness', of forty years ago as unfortunate follies best forgotten.

[3] Letter to Frank Fay, quoted in Gerard Fay, *The Abbey Theatre*, 1958, p. 77.

reticent, and withdrawn, where Yeats consciously and conscientiously acted a poet's part. The one watched life's drama, while the other dramatized himself. Synge (like Tennyson and Hardy) scrutinized nature and peasant with a steady, microscopic intentness: Yeats, in youth at least, saw the world through an opalescent mist. It was typical that he urged Synge to omit from his book on the Aran Islands all mention of their names, or of Galway—let them just be places somewhere in Western Ireland. That would add a more magic mystery. But Synge rightly refused. He was writing of real islands—not of some Fata Morgana in faery seas, of some land east of the sun and west of the moon.

Similarly, while Yeats was fascinated by magic, theosophy, and the supernatural, Synge preferred irony. He deeply admired Anatole France, whom our tipsier age often sees fit to belittle. He mixed with earthy peasants, where Yeats went in quest of Celtic twilight, lands of heart's desire, shadowy waters, fairies, and mystic figures from the legendary past. Even when Synge wrote, like Yeats and 'A. E.' (George Russell), a play on Deirdre, he chose to give her the lilting speech of the Connemara countryside, where the fare might be miserably plain, yet the talk ran high.

Hence those two ironic stanzas to which Synge was provoked by the supernaturalism of 'A. E.'—like the glare of an angry match in the mists of the Celtic twilight.

> Adieu, sweet Angus, Maeve, and Fand,
> Ye plumed yet skinny Shee,
> That poets walked with, hand in hand,
> To learn their ecstasy.
>
> We'll stretch in Red Dan Sally's ditch,
> And drink in Tubber fair,
> Or poach with Red Dan Philly's bitch
> The badger and the hare.[1]

[1] Synge's poems (now fully assembled in his *Collected Works*, ed. R. Skelton, Vol. I, 1962) seem to me much less remarkable than his plays. They are sometimes melodious, sometimes vivid, sometimes intense—particularly two bitter stanzas, provoked apparently by a broken love-affair (1896-7?), where he curses his life, his work, and the whole world—

> Cold, joyless will I live, though clean,
> Nor, by my marriage, mould for earth

No doubt exasperation here led Synge into exaggeration. One may suspect that this professed love of ditches and drunkenness was really as Platonic as Housman's. However, it is inevitable that the tough-minded should be irritated by the tender-minded; just as the tender-minded are shocked by the tough. In practice, I think, Synge adopted the wisest answer—a balance between the two extremes, with a certain leaning to the tougher side. Magic in literature, by all means; but literature about magic easily grows childish. Leprechauns or banshees may exist. They cannot be disproved. They are not impossible. But they seem highly improbable. 'If there are men with tails,' said Johnson, 'catch an *homo caudatus*.' Till then, those with any judgement, reserve it. Yeats himself, especially in later life, could at times become bitterly realistic. He seems to me far better so than when he over-indulged in leprechauntings.

It was characteristic, therefore, that Synge, who belonged, like Goldsmith, to the more realistic type of Irishman should dislike such fantasies of Yeats as *The Shadowy Waters*; but feel strongly drawn to the robust earthiness of Rabelais, the stinging realism of François Villon.

> Young lives to see what I have seen,
> To curse, as I have cursed, their birth.

But Synge remains, I think, no less markedly inferior to Yeats as lyric poet than he is superior as playwright.

THE PLAYS

In the Shadow of the Glen
(written 1902-3, performed 1903)

> 'Take the road!
> April's sweet face grows never older;
> How light my heart, when again my shoulder
> Lifts the load!'

Here Synge's source is to be found in his own book, *The Aran Islands*. The story was told him on his first visit there (1898) by old Pat Dirane:

One day I was travelling on foot from Galway to Dublin, and the darkness came upon me and I ten miles from the nearest town I was wanting to pass the night in. Then a hard rain began to fall and I was tired walking, so when I saw a sort of a house with no roof on it up against the road, I got in, the way the walls would give me shelter.

As I was looking round I saw a light in some trees two perches off, and thinking any sort of a house would be better than where I was, I got over a wall and went up to the house to look in at the window.

I saw a dead man laid on a table, and candles lighted, and a woman watching him. I was frightened when I saw him, but it was raining hard, and I said to myself, if he was dead he couldn't hurt me. Then I knocked on the door and the woman came and opened it.

'Good evening, ma'am,' says I.

'Good evening kindly, stranger,' says she. 'Come in out of the rain.'

Then she took me in and told me her husband was after dying on her, and she was watching him that night.

'But it's thirsty you'll be, stranger,' says she. 'Come into the parlour.'

Then she took me into the parlour—and it was a fine clean house—and she put a cup, with a saucer under it, on the table before me with fine sugar and bread.

When I'd had a cup of tea I went back into the kitchen where the dead man was lying, and she gave me a fine new pipe off the table with a drop of spirits.

'Stranger,' says she, 'would you be afeard to be alone with himself?'

'Not a bit in the world, ma'am,' says I; 'he that's dead can do no hurt.'

Then she said she wanted to go over and tell the neighbours the way her husband was after dying on her, and she went out and locked the door behind her.

I smoked one pipe, and I leaned out and took another off the table. I was smoking it with my hand on the back of my chair—the way you are yourself this minute, God bless you—and I looking on the dead man, when he opened his eyes as wide as myself and looked at me.

'Don't be afeard, stranger,' said the dead man; 'I'm not dead at all in the world. Come here and help me up and I'll tell you all about it.'

Well, I went up and took the sheet off of him, and I saw that he had a fine clean shirt on his body, and fine flannel drawers.

He sat up then, and says he—'I've got a bad wife, stranger, and I let on to be dead the way I'd catch her goings on.'

Then he got two fine sticks he had to keep down his wife, and he put them at each side of his body, and he laid himself out again as if he was dead.

In half an hour his wife came back, and a young man along with her. Well, she gave him his tea, and she told him he was tired, and he would do right to go and lie down in the bedroom.

The young man went in and the woman sat down to watch by the dead man. A while after, she got up and 'Stranger,' says she, 'I'm going in to get the candle out of the room; I'm thinking the young man will be asleep by this time.' She went into the bedroom, but the divil a bit of her came back.

Then the dead man got up, and he took one stick, and he gave the other to myself. We went in and we saw them lying together with her head on his arm.

The dead man hit him a blow with the stick so that the blood out of him leapt up and hit the gallery.

That is my story.

Why 'the gallery'? There are no galleries in Irish cottages. It has been taken, rather fancifully, as a sign of Mediterranean origin. Anyway, this is a world-old and world-wide type of story. Strindberg would have loved its misogyny; which recalls, of course, that tale of The Widow of Ephesus[1] used by Chapman for his play, *The Widow's Tears* (published 1612).

The widow of Ephesus, it may be remembered, was so inconsolable for her husband's death that she took up her abode inside his mausoleum. Outside, there happened to be posted a soldier, guard-

[1] Told in the *Satyricon* (111-12) of Petronius Arbiter (d. A.D. 66).

ing the bodies of certain crucified malefactors. But soldiers can make themselves agreeable; *this* soldier became so busy consoling the widow, that one of the bodies he had to guard was stolen away. The soldier was in a panic—he would be crucified himself; but the now happily consoled widow resourcefully provided her dear departed husband's corpse as a substitute. If there exists a more cynical story, I do not know it.

Even remote China (for misogyny seems co-extensive with mankind) has a similar tale.

Chuang Tzu saw a young woman fanning a grave; she explained that her husband had begged her not to remarry, at least, till the earth on his grave was dry. Chuang Tzu obligingly helped her with the drying. A certain Chiang Shing told his wife this story; and when she gaped at it, added: 'There is nothing to be surprised at; it's the way of the world.' At this the wife was angry. Then Chiang Shing died. Shortly after, there arrived a youth called Wang Sun who said he had hoped to become the dead sage's disciple. He took up his abode with the widow to study. After a fortnight she inquired if he were married; then sent an old servant to propose he should wed herself. In reply the young Wang Sun led her to her husband's grave, and revealed himself as her dead husband. For shame, the widow hanged herself.[1]

But it was foolish of irate patriots to accuse Synge of digging up the tale of the Ephesian Widow from decadent paganism in order to besmirch the immaculate greenness of Holy Ireland. For Synge's source was Pat Dirane on Aran; and Pat, in his turn, was merely retailing a widespread folk-tale about a jealous husband shamming dead of which no less than four Irish versions have been recorded in Galway.[2] Further, there is a considerable difference between

---

[1] Cf. Voltaire, *Zadig*, ch. 2, where the young widow Cosrou swears to watch by her husband's grave while the waters of a neighbouring brook shall keep their course beside it. ' "Eh bien!" dit Zadig, "voilà une femme estimable qui aimait véritablement son mari!" ' (' "Well," said Zadig, "here is an estimable woman, who really loved her husband." ') But, two days later 'elle faisait détourner le ruisseau' ('she was having the brook diverted').

[2] Cf. Molière, *Le Malade Imaginaire*, III, xviii, where Argan exposes by shamming dead the falsity of his wife Béline; and Voltaire, *Zadig*, ch. 2, where Zadig plays the same trick on his wife Azora. Similarly in Chapman's play.

Petronius' tale of a really dead husband quickly forgotten by his widow, and the tale of a husband merely pretending to be dead, in order to trap his wife.

Problem—to turn this somewhat crude folk-story into a play. Audiences desire *some* character, or characters, that they can sympathize with; and I own that I sympathize with their desire. Now the old husband's trick, even if provoked, is hardly very sympathetic. Synge therefore transfers our sympathy to the young wife—another Nora who, like her namesake in Ibsen, walks out of house and home to liberty; though in this case, instead of marching out, she is driven out.

It would have been possible to make us feel for her lover too; as we are made to feel for Tristram, in his passion for Iseult, against the treacherous King Mark. But Synge took the more original step of presenting the lover as a contemptible oaf; and raising the fourth character, the tramp, from a mere narrator, who assists the husband, to something like the play's hero, and the champion of its heroine.

However, as usual in Synge, it is not so much the plot that really matters; it is not the ideas that matter; it is not even the characters that matter most; it is the style—the spell of the language.

Anglo-Irish like Synge's owes part of its peculiarities to Gaelic syntax. At the beginning of the nineteenth century Ireland numbered something over five million inhabitants. Four million of them, it is said, *usually* spoke Irish; two million of them spoke *only* Irish.

Here are some examples of the way Gaelic syntax imposes itself on English speech in Irish mouths.[1]

1. Use of Present Participle.
    'I'm thinking.'
    'Wasn't I telling you?'
    'Let you be making yourself easy.'
2. Use of 'have'.
    'With a tongue on her *has* the crows and seabirds scattered.'
    'To *have* drink taken.'
3. Gaelic word-order likes its verbs first. Hence—
    'It is to Derry we went yesterday.'
    'It's cold he is.'

[1] See A. G. von Hamel, *On Anglo-Irish Syntax* in *Engl. Studien*, XLV (1912), 272-92.

4. Questions: direct form retained in indirect speech.
   'Do you think could she be the widow Casey?'
   'Wait till you see is he the lad I think.'
5. Imperative in 2nd person with 'let'.
   'Let you be making yourself easy.'
6. Unusual use of prepositions 'after' and 'on'.
   'He's *after* dying *on* me.'
   'My road is lost *on* me now.'
7. Use of 'and'.
   'It was raining *and* I coming home.'
   'I wouldn't lay my hand on him for the Lough Nahanagan *and* it filled with gold.'

Such things exert on an English ear a charm of strangeness. But strangeness alone would quickly pall. The magic of Irish peasant speech lies deeper—in its lilting melody, in its uninhibited, unstaled, childlike imagination. Synge learnt the secret of this; but Yeats did not. Probably, being dreamy and self-centred, Yeats (unlike Lady Gregory) lacked the patience to listen, with careful attention, how country-folk really talked. And the attempts to repeat Synge's music made by O'Casey seem to me much inferior; those by Eugene O'Neill more inferior still.

Because so much of Synge's spell lies in his language, I feel that his plays cannot be effectively discussed without quotations on a more lavish scale than would be needed with any other playwright I can think of. I shall therefore quote with unusual fullness. Those who love Synge's style, will not regret this; those who do not love his style, are unlikely to relish him anyway.

*   *   *

The scene of *The Shadow of the Glen* seems laid in Upper Glenmalure, west of Wicklow, and south of sacred Glendalough—a valley running up under the 3000-foot peak of Lugnaquilla. It is a wild night of driving rain.

In a cottage kitchen old Dan Burke lies seemingly dead, with a sheet over his body, while his young wife Nora is lighting candles to watch beside him. A knock at the door; and, as in Pat Dirane's story, the Tramp is invited in. He starts at the sight of the dead.

Tramp (*coming in slowly and going towards the bed*).   Is it departed he is?

Nora. It is, stranger. He's after dying on me, God forgive him, and there I am now with a hundred sheep beyond on the hills, and no turf drawn for the winter.

Tramp (*looking closely at the dead man*). It's a queer look is on him for a man that's dead.

Nora (*half-humorously*). He was always queer, stranger; and I suppose them that's queer and they living men will be queer bodies after.[1]

Tramp. Isn't it a great wonder you're letting him lie there, and he not tidied, or laid out itself?

Nora (*coming to the bed*). I was afeard, stranger, for he put a black curse on me this morning if I'd touch his body the time he'd die sudden, or let anyone touch it except his sister only, and it's ten miles away she lives, in the big glen over the hill.

Tramp (*looking at her and nodding slowly*). It's a queer story he wouldn't let his own wife touch him, and he dying quiet in his bed.

Nora. He was an old man, and an odd man, stranger, and it's always up on the hills he was, thinking thoughts in the dark mist . . . (*She pulls back a bit of the sheet*). Lay your hand on him now, and tell me if it's cold he is surely.

Tramp. Is it getting the curse on me you'd be, woman of the house? I wouldn't lay my hand on him for the Lough Nahanagan and it filled with gold.

Nora (*looking uneasily at the body*). Maybe cold would be no sign of death with the like of him, for he was always cold, every day since I knew him . . . and every night, stranger . . . (*she covers up his face and comes away from the bed*).

The two fall to talk of the unearthly loneliness of the nights in that mist-swept glen; and then comes the first glimmer of light on what Nora Burke's past has been.

Nora (*looking at him for a moment with curiosity*). You're saying that, stranger, as if you were easy afeard.

Tramp (*speaking mournfully*). Is it myself, lady of the house, that does be walking round in the long nights, and crossing the hills when the fog is on them, the time a little stick would seem as big as your arm, and a rabbit as big as a bay horse, and a stack of turf as big as a towering church in the city of Dublin? If myself was easy afeard, I'm telling you, it's long ago I'd have been locked into the Richmond Asylum, or maybe have run up into the back hills with nothing on me but an old

---

[1] Compare the Aran girl's remarks about life's queernesses, quoted on p. 153 above.

shirt, and been eaten by the crows the like of Patch Darcy—the Lord have mercy on him—in the year that's gone.

Nora (*with interest*). You knew Darcy?

Tramp. Wasn't I the last one heard his living voice in the whole world?

Nora. There were great stories of what was heard at that time, but would anyone believe the things they do be saying in the glen?

Tramp. It was no lie, lady of the house . . . I was passing below on a dark night the like of this night, and the sheep were lying under the ditch and every one of them coughing and choking like an old man, with the great rain and the fog. Then I heard a thing talking—queer talk, you wouldn't believe it at all, and you out of your dreams—and 'Merciful God,' says I, 'if I begin hearing the like of that voice out of the thick mist, I'm destroyed surely.' Then I run and I run till I was below in Rathvanna. I got drunk that night, I got drunk in the morning, and drunk the day after—I was coming from the races beyond—and the third day they found Darcy. . . . Then I knew it was himself I was after hearing, and I wasn't afeard any more.

Nora (*speaking sorrowfully and slowly*). God spare Darcy; he'd always look in here and he passing up or passing down, and it's very lonesome I was after him a long while (*she looks over at the bed and lowers her voice, speaking very slowly*), and then I got happy again—if it's ever happy we are, stranger—for I got used to being lonesome.

Clear enough that Patch Darcy has been one of those on whom Nora looked over-fondly in the past.

Then she asks the Tramp if he will stay while she goes to tell a neighbour of her man's death.

Tramp (*moving uneasily*). Maybe if you'd a piece of a grey thread and a sharp needle—there's great safety in a needle, lady of the house—I'd be putting a little stitch here and there in my old coat, the time I'll be praying for his soul, and it going up naked to the saints of God.

Nora (*takes a needle and thread from the front of her dress and gives it to him*). There's the needle, stranger, and I'm thinking you won't be lonesome, and you used to the back hills, for isn't a dead man itself more company than to be sitting alone, and hearing the winds crying, and you not knowing on what thing your mind would stay?

She goes. Then, as in the tale, the old husband sits up and explains—'it's a long time I'm keeping that stick, for I've a bad wife in the house'. He lies down again, and Nora returns with the tall, naïve young herdsman, Michael Dara—who is, however, not too naïve to see that the widowed Nora would be a remunerative match. In the talk of the two one can already hear the squalid wrangles that would soon come between them, once they were wed—Michael thinking always of money (or jealousy); Nora, of love.

Michael (*looking at her with a queer look*). I heard tell this day, Nora Burke, that it was on the path below Patch Darcy would be passing up and passing down, and I heard them say he'd never pass it night or morning without speaking with yourself.

Nora (*in a low voice*). It was no lie you heard, Michael Dara.

Michael. I'm thinking it's a power of men you're after knowing if it's in a lonesome place you live itself.

Nora (*giving him his tea*). It's in a lonesome place you do have to be talking with some one, and looking for some one, in the evening of the day, and if it's a power of men I'm after knowing they were fine men, for I was a hard child to please, and a hard girl to please (*she looks at him a little sternly*), and it's a hard woman I am to please this day, Michael Dara, and it's no lie I'm telling you.

Michael (*looking over to see that the tramp is asleep, and then pointing to the dead man*). Was it a hard woman to please you were when you took himself for your man?

Nora. What way would I live, and I an old woman, if I didn't marry?[1] man with a bit of a farm, and cows on it, and sheep on the back hills a

Michael (*considering*). That's true, Nora, and maybe it's no fool you were, for there's good grazing on it, if it is a lonesome place, and I'm thinking it's a good sum he's left behind.

Nora (*taking the stocking with the money from her pocket, and putting it on the table*). I do be thinking in the long nights it was a big fool I was that time, Michael Dara; for what good is a bit of a farm with cows on it, and sheep on the back hills, when you do be sitting looking out from a door the like of that door, and seeing nothing but the mists rolling down the bog, and the mists again and they rolling up the bog, and hearing nothing but the wind crying out in the bits of broken trees were left from the great storm, and the streams roaring with the rain?

Already their temperaments pull different ways. For, like Synge's Deirdre, his Nora is obsessed with the relentless stride of time, the escapeless advance of age. She is a type perilous to marry, prone to long always for one more radiant romance before the grey years

---

[1] There seems to have been often a good deal of calculation about the Irish marriages of Synge's day. See p. 179.

arrive, when all romances lie behind—the kind of woman who follows star after star, and ends in ditches. There may be a time in youth for *Wanderjahre*; but there comes also a time for such venturesome wanderings to have an end—a time to find, and keep, values more lasting.

But so strong proves Nora's horror of the passing years that she begins to doubt whether she cares even to marry Michael at all.

Michael. . . . We'd do right to wait now till himself will be quiet awhile in the Seven Churches,[1] and then you'll marry me in the chapel of Rathvanna, and I'll bring the sheep up on the bit of a hill you have on the back mountain, and we won't have anything we'd be afeard to let our minds on when the mist is down.

Nora (*pouring him out some whisky*). Why would I marry you, Mike Dara? You'll be getting old and I'll be getting old, and in a little while, I'm telling you, you'll be sitting up in your bed—the way himself was sitting—with a shake in your face, and your teeth falling, and the white hair sticking out round you like an old bush where sheep do be leaping a gap.

> *Dan Burke sits up noiselessly from under the sheet, with his hand to his face. His white hair is sticking out round his head. Nora goes on slowly without hearing him.*

It's a pitiful thing to be getting old, but it's a queer[2] thing surely. It's a queer[2] thing to see an old man sitting up there in his bed with no teeth in him, and a rough word in his mouth, and his chin the way it would take the bark from the edge of an oak board you'd have building a door. . . . God forgive me, Michael Dara, we'll all be getting old, but it's a queer[2] thing surely.

Then suddenly the corpse sneezes. Consternation—as the old man jumps from bed, cudgel in hand.

Dan. You'll walk out now from that door, Nora Burke; and it's not tomorrow, or the next day, or any day of your life, that you'll put in your foot through it again.

Tramp (*standing up*). It's a hard thing you're saying for an old man, master of the house; and what would the like of her do if you put her out on the roads?

---

[1] Of Glendalough.
[2] More echoes of the Aran girl on p. 153?

Dan. Let her walk round the like of Peggy Cavanagh below, and be begging money at the cross-roads, or selling songs to the men. (*To Nora*) Walk out now, Nora Burke, and it's soon you'll be getting old with that life, I'm telling you; it's soon *your* teeth will be falling and *your* head'll be the like of a bush where sheep do be leaping a gap.

He pauses: Nora looks round at Michael.

Then her lover makes a remark that is stupefying in its caddish callousness.

Michael (*timidly*).   There's a fine Union below in Rathdrum.

Dan.   The like of her would never go there. . . . It's lonesome roads she'll be going and hiding herself away till the end will come, and they find her stretched like a dead sheep with the frost on her, or the big spiders maybe, and they putting their webs on her, in the butt of a ditch.

Derisively Dan Burke suggests that the Tramp should take Nora; and, at once, the Tramp takes *him* at his word.

Tramp (*going over to Nora*).   We'll be going now, lady of the house; the rain is falling, but the air is kind, and maybe it'll be a grand morning, by the grace of God.

Nora.   What good is a grand morning when I'm destroyed surely, and I going out to get my death walking the roads?

Tramp.   You'll not be getting your death with myself, lady of the house, and I knowing all the ways a man can put food in his mouth. . . . We'll be going now, I'm telling you, and the time you'll be feeling the cold, and the frost, and the great rain, and the sun again, and the south wind blowing in the glens, you'll not be sitting up on a wet ditch, the way you're after sitting in this place, making yourself old with looking on each day, and it passing you by. You'll be saying one time, 'It's a grand evening, by the grace of God,' and another time, 'It's a wild night, God help us; but it'll pass, surely.'[1]

---

[1] In case any readers find the Tramp's next (and final) speech about the pleasure of listening to the birds—herons, grouse, owls, larks, thrushes—a trait too sophisticated and aesthetic, one may compare a passage in *Twenty years a-growing* (1933) by the Blasket-islander Maurice O'Sullivan (p. 218): 'It was a fine evening. I was sitting on a rock overlooking the sea. There was a light breeze from the east, frost on the ground, hooded crows flying across the fields with a caw-caw, thrushes, blackbirds, and starlings singing sweetly in the meadows; and if you turned your eyes seaward, herring-gulls and black-backed gulls diving into the water and a sea-raven among them pursuing small

Nora gathers a few possessions in her shawl. Life with a tramp is no gay prospect. 'But you've a fine bit of *talk*, stranger, and it's with yourself I'll go.'

And so, by a crowning stroke of irony, the crabbed old husband is left drinking with his own wife's old lover.

Dan (*throwing away his stick*). I was thinking to strike you, Michael Dara; but you're a quiet man, God help you, and I don't mind you at all.

It should be realized that the Tramp, who in the play's source had been merely the eye-witness, but here takes the more active part of carrying away the heroine, has become for Synge, though less romantic than Scott's young Lochinvar, still a symbol of rebellious romance.

In later years Synge used often to end his love-letters to Molly Allgood with the signature 'Your Old Tramp'.[1] Like Chekhov, he loved an actress; but like Chekhov he remained, essentially, a lonely heart. 'Gregarious animals are imbecile,' Synge wrote once in his notebook, 'and solitary animals noble. The flea is also a nobler being than the ant. . . . All nations with a talent for political life are individually stupid, while the French are delightful. The intellectual superiority of the classes comes first of all from their privacy. The poor are always in flocks.'

This play fills only twenty-six pages. Yet, as the Chinese say, 'the thought goes on'. With all real literature that should be so—'the thought goes on'.

The piece has also an excellent Aristotelian *peripeteia*.[2] Nora planned to share her husband's farm with her lover; instead, she is

---

ish.' One should not assume that country-folk are necessarily indifferent (apart from gifted exceptions like Burns or Clare) to the spell of natural beauty. (See also many passages in Peig Sayers, *An Old Woman's Reflections*, 1962; for example (p. 130): 'Very often I'd throw myself back in the green heather, resting. It wasn't for bone-laziness I'd do it, but for the beauty of the hills and the rumble of the waves that would be grieving down from me, in dark caves where the seals of the sea lived.')

[1] Cf. Alexey Tolstoy on Gorky's sympathy for such outcasts—'Gorky became the teacher, and his tramp the hero, of the times'.

[2] Situation where a person plans something, and the exact opposite ensues.

turned adrift on the road herself, and leaves her lover drinking affably in her husband's company.

'Unreal!' some may protest. Surely a husband, even in the Wicklow of 1900, could not just pitch his wife out of doors like this? Surely she could have claimed alimony? And what a life, in spite of fine talk, to become the doxy of a tramp!

But Irish peasants are not lawyers. And as for ladies going off with tramps, let us remember Browning's Duchess, who fled from her hated domesticity to the gypsies; a tale which in its turn is based on the old ballad of *The Gypsy Laddie*:

> What care I for my house and my land?
> What care I for my money, O?
> What care I for my new-wedded lord?
> I'm off with the raggle-taggle gipsies, O!
>
> What care I for a goose-feather bed,
> With the sheet turn'd down so bravely, O?
> For tonight I shall sleep in a cold open field,
> Along with the raggle-taggle gipsies, O!

Which, in its turn, is based on a story of Johnny Faa the gipsy and the Countess of Cassilis.

Thousands of years have passed since our ancestors first turned from nomads to tillers of the fields; a drastic and fiercely contested revolution, which has left its primeval trace in the tragic Bible tale of Abel the shepherd and Cain the tiller of the soil. But the nomad impulse can still sometimes reawaken in us—as in the Wandering Scholars of the Middle Ages; in the gypsies of George Borrow; or in the Jolly Beggars of Burns, so much more crudely Hogarthian than these figures of Synge.

I do not say that the play's conclusion is very moral—Tolstoy would have denounced it; nor that it is very realistic—one cannot imagine the most romantic of tramps having much of a future for Nora. I vividly remember some Irish tramps I saw in Cahirciveen; they would have looked more romantic with a little soap. The piece remains a mixture of hard realism and dreaming fantasy. Yet under the spell of that entrancing style I have no difficulty in suspending any scepticism I might incline to feel. For an hour I live transported to a wholly different world; and that suffices.

As so often, the critics of the day made themselves ridiculous. The play was denounced by angry Irish patriots as a monstrous slander on Irish womanhood. 'For its length,' growled one bright-green purist, 'one of the nastiest little plays I have ever seen.' How inconceivable that an Irish wife should prove faithless, just like a French or English one! 'There are,' it was protested (such is the fatuity of fanatics), '*no* loveless marriages in Ireland.'[1]

Actually, there were, and are, a good many loveless marriages— perhaps exceptionally many—in a country where men have long been particularly prone to postpone marriage, so that even between thirty and thirty-five two-thirds of them remain bachelors. Hence a good many girls in the Irish countryside tend, it appears, to marry not so much for the sake of love as, simply, for the sake of marriage —like Nora Burke in the play.[2]

But in spite of all this *The Shadow of the Glen* was dismissed as 'a crude version, pretending to be Irish, of the famous or infamous story of the Widow of Ephesus'; or as 'an evil compound of Ibsen and Boucicault'.[3] Arthur Griffith in the *United Irishman* was particularly tiresome. But James Connolly and Maud Gonne also took, in the same weekly, the tedious line that Irish playwrights were in duty bound to paint Ireland as the Isle of Saints, and nothing else. Indeed Maud Gonne, beautiful goose, with two others walked out of the performance in protest. These patriots wanted art national-ized—poets in uniform. Unfortunately, little good literature has ever come from propaganda-ministries. 'Patriotism is not enough.'

This prim prudery is not less odd when one reflects that the original ruin of Ireland in the English conquest by Strongbow was supposed to have come from a faithless Irish wife—that Irish Helen, Dervorgilla, carried off from the lord of Breffni by the King of

[1] Cf. p. 174.
[2] See *The Vanishing Irish*, ed. John A. O'Brien (1954), with its strange picture both of reluctance to marry and of arranged marriages; for example the story of the bridegroom complaining to his father at the wedding: 'You didn't tell me she was lame.'—'Get along with you! Sure it's not for racing you want her!' According to C. Weygandt (*Irish Plays and Players*, p. 226) this type of marriage was usual up to 1880. Compare the Irish proverb—'It is unlucky to marry for love.'
[3] 1822-90; a once famous Irish dramatist, who wrote or adapted some 40 plays.

Leinster; or that one of the most famous of all Irish legends was the tale of Finn's Queen, Grania, and her flight with Diarmaid; or that Tristram's beloved Iseult was Iseult of *Ireland*.[1]

And yet what use in arguing with the cant of bigots, whose 'patriotism', though it would be too strong to call it, in Johnson's phrase, 'the last refuge of a scoundrel', was often the mere mouthing of hysteria?

At the play's first production, W. G. Fay was asked to reserve seats for a party which included George Wyndham, then Irish Secretary. So Fay raked out a few armchairs for them; but unfortunately the chair sat in by Wyndham was upholstered in *red*. Hence more howls in the Irish press, about providing English tyrants with chairs coloured (crowning touch) in 'England's cruel red'. Any nation that has not got over the feverish teethings of nationalism seems as little to be depended on as a dog that has not had distemper.

It is perhaps worth mentioning that a Belfast writer, Harry Morrow, wrote a skit on *The Shadow of the Glen* called *The Mist that does be on the Bog* (produced 1909); in which a young actress and her aunt, seeking local colour in W. Ireland, encounter a poet disguised as a peasant and bound on the same quest. Actress and poet, naturally, fall in love. Perhaps the pair were actually meant for Synge and the actress Máire O'Neill (Molly Allgood), to whom he was betrothed not long before his early death.

[1] And then, only a few years before, there had been the great Parnell himself, the lover of another man's wife. True, Kitty O'Shea was English; but her husband and her lover were not.

Riders to the Sea
(written 1902-3, performed 1904)

> 'What is a woman that you forsake her,
> And the hearth-fire and the home-acre,
> To go with the old grey widow-maker?'
>
> KIPLING

The simplest of one-act tragedies. If *The Shadow of the Glen* presents a peasant Helen, *Riders to the Sea* pictures a peasant Hecuba. Its scene is evidently the Aran Islands; its source is largely an actual funeral that Synge once watched there, of a young man lost at sea.

The old Maurya had six sons and two daughters. The pitiless Atlantic has already taken her husband and four of her sons. A fifth son, Michael, is lately missing, and assuredly drowned also. Bartley, the sixth, alone remains.

The elder daughter Cathleen is spinning; her younger sister Nora enters with a shirt and a stocking taken off a drowned body on the coast of Donegal, and now brought south by a priest. Even while the sisters talk in hushed voices, the pitiless sea-wind flings wide their half-shut cottage door; as if, yet again, death walked the room.

Cathleen asks Nora if the young priest would stop Bartley going with the horses to Galway fair, on this day of dangerously rising wind.

Nora. 'I won't stop him,' says he, 'but let you not be afraid. Herself does be saying prayers half through the night, and the Almighty God won't leave her destitute,' says he, 'with no son living.'

That piece of faith is to be ironically belied.

The girls, not daring to examine the drowned man's clothes while their old mother is about, hide them in the turf-loft. Then old Maurya herself appears, desperately hoping that her last son will not sail. He enters, resolved to go. In vain she tries to hold him back.

Maurya. That wind is raising the sea, and there was a star up against the moon, and it rising in the night. If it was a hundred horses, or a thousand horses, you had itself, what is the price of a thousand horses against a son where there is one son only? . . .

Bartley (*getting his purse and tobacco*).   I'll have half an hour to go down, and you'll see me coming again in two days, or in three days, or may be in four days if the wind is bad.

Maurya (*turning round to the fire, and putting her shawl over her head*) Isn't it a hard and cruel man won't hear a word from an old woman, and she holding him from the sea?

Cathleen.   It's the life of a young man to be going on the sea, and who would listen to an old woman with one thing and she saying it over?

It is an ancient and eternal story—ancient as the Hecuba that wails to Hector not to go forth against Achilles beneath the battlements of Ilios.

> But after him Hector's mother, upon the other side,
> Wept, and unbared her bosom, and lifted her breast, and cried,
> Wailing with wingéd words: 'My son revere this breast—
> Pity me, Hector! If ever it lulled thy tears to rest,
> Dear one, bear *that* in remembrance, and face thine enemy
> *Behind* our rampart—stand not forth, so recklessly,
> To brave him! For, if he slay thee, child of my womb, dear son,
> Then never shall I, nor the wife whom thou hast wooed and won
> With many a gift, bewail thee, laid on thy death-bed—nay,
> The Argive hounds shall tear thee, by their galleys, far away.'[1]

All in vain. 'Men must work, and women must weep.' On Aran also. The young Bartley goes; blessing the household, but without his mother's blessing.

Cathleen.   Why wouldn't you give him your blessing and he looking round in the door? Isn't it sorrow enough is on everyone in this house without your sending him out with an unlucky word behind him, and a hard word in his ear?

So Cathleen persuades the old woman to hurry after Bartley, by a short cut, and give him the new-baked bread he has forgotten; and, with it, her blessing. Maurya hobbles out; and now, freed from her presence, the two young girls examine the drowned man's

[1] *Iliad*, XXII, 79-89.

clothes. At first they are uncertain; but suddenly, with a cry, Nora identifies a stocking, by the dropped stitches that she remembers knitting.

Maurya totters back, with the bread still in her hand. For, as Bartley rode down on the red mare, with the grey pony following, on the grey pony's back she saw riding the wraith of her other son Michael. No less surely, then, Bartley too is doomed.

And now, like a Greek chorus, a troop of old women enters; crossing themselves, then kneeling down, with red petticoats over their heads, just as Synge had seen the women of Aran at the burying of their dead. Bartley has been pushed by the pony into the harbour, and drowned.

Maurya (raising her head and speaking as if she did not see the people around her). They're all gone now, and there isn't anything more the sea can do to me. . . . I'll have no call now to be up crying and praying when the wind breaks from the south, and you can hear the surf is in the east, and the surf is in the west, making a great stir with the two noises, and they hitting one on the other. I'll have no call now to be going down and getting Holy Water in the dark nights after Samhain,[1] and I won't care what way the sea is when the other women will be keening. . . . It's a great rest I'll have now, and great sleeping in the long nights after Samhain, if it's only a bit of wet flour we do have to eat, and maybe a fish that would be stinking. . . . Michael has a clean burial in the far north, by the grace of the Almighty God. Bartley will have a fine coffin out of the white boards, and a deep grave surely. What more can we want than that? No man at all can be living for ever, and we must be satisfied.

'No man at all can be living for ever, and we must be satisfied.'

> 'Therefore, my friend, die also. What help lamenting now?
> Even Patroclus died, that was better far than thou.'[2]

The one is the voice of a poor fisher-wife on the extreme verge of Europe; the other the voice of the most glorious of Homer's heroes, three thousand years ago. But the burden is the same—the consolation, such as it is, the same. Small comfort, and bitter; yet

---

[1] All Hallows' Day, Nov. 1 (pronounced 'Sowin').
[2] *Iliad,* XXI, 106-7.

true. When all the philosophies and all the creeds have vainly agonized to find something more, this hard bedrock of truth alone abides.

That bitter comfort Lucretius caught up and echoed from Homer; and two thousand years later Matthew Arnold and Housman in English repeated the same stoic platitude once uttered by Greece and Rome. For, however trite, it still is true:

> 'Tis sure much finer fellows
> Have fared much worse before.

As already mentioned, that final sentence of old Maurya's was not Synge's invention. He was merely adapting the words of an Aran islander. In 1902 Martin McDonough, with whom Synge had made friends on Inishmaan, wrote that his brother's wife had died in childbed. 'It happened that my brother's wife, Shawneen,[1] died. And she was visiting the last Sunday in December, and now isn't it a sad story to tell? But at the same time we have to be satisfied, because a person cannot live always. But Shawneen is good, but he is very lonely. But if he is, he has to be satisfied.'[2] The simple words of a simple man; but it is the simplest things that can cut deepest. That sentence Synge had first put in a peasant's mouth in his abortive play about the young man who wedded the nun[3]; here it finds its final place on the lips of Maurya.

It is not only in Ireland that the simple have sometimes this gift of telling style. I remember, many years ago, asking the hut-keeper on the Faulhorn, opposite the Jungfrau, whether he were not anxious for his small daughter toddling about with precipices on every side. But he merely answered: 'Man *muss nicht* Angst haben.' ('One *must not* be afraid.') That too seemed strangely Homeric.

Riders to the Sea has been variously judged. In 1904 some Irish papers called it 'morbid', 'ghastly', 'hideous in its realism', 'quite

---

[1] i.e., apparently, 'Shawneen's'—that brother being *John* McDonough.

[2] D. H. Greene, *Synge*, p. 105. Cf. the Blasket-islander Tomás Ó Crohan: 'It was imprinted on my mind that there was no cure for these things but to meet them with endurance as best I could, and I kept trying to get through a while more of life—one year good and two that turned out ill.' (*The Islandman*, published in Irish, 1929; translated by R. Flower, 1951: p. 197.)

[3] See p. 158.

unfit for the stage'. Since then it has been hailed by Irish and even by English critics as the greatest tragedy of modern times. Surely—especially if one remembers Ibsen—a little enthusiastic? George Moore, in *Vale*, has left an amusingly malicious account of Synge reading the play—'Yeats, who did not wish to have any misunderstanding on the subject, cried "Sophocles" across the table, and, fearing he was not impressive enough, he said: "No, Aeschylus".'[1] George Moore is an unreliable witness; but at least in some quarters the kind of exaggeration he mocks here has not been wholly imaginary.

Moore himself dismissed the play as 'an experiment in language rather than a work of art'—'a painful rather than a dramatic story'. But some will find this disparagement as excessive as the praise attributed to Yeats.

Similarly Joyce objected that *Riders to the Sea* was a tragic poem rather than a tragedy. But need it matter much what one calls it? Joyce objected that it was not Aristotelian. I do not know why; nor care in the least whether it is 'Aristotelian' or not. Joyce also objected that the catastrophe was due, not to the sea, but to the pony which pushed Bartley into it. But this seems a little captious. None the less, later on in Trieste, Joyce translated the play into Italian. And he had Maurya's last speeches by heart.

Riders to the Sea may indeed be more of a poem than a play—but so is some early Greek tragedy. It may seem less drama than dirge—yet in its simple sincerity it remains a deeply moving dirge. No doubt its plot is slight—an old woman, who has already lost her husband and four sons, now finds that she has lost also the two sons that alone were left. Yet there is an effective truth to nature in the way she takes it. 'The day Michael was drowned you could hear her crying out from this to the spring well'; but now with the loss of her last and youngest, instead of rising to a climax of despair, she sinks numbly into a desolate resignation. Even torture has limits—a point where the nerves can agonize no more. One recalls the story of that criminal being broken on the wheel who

---

[1] Yeats himself, however, records telling Synge that he preferred *The Shadow of the Glen*, because *Riders to the Sea*, with all its nobility, was 'too passive in suffering', like Arnold's *Empedocles*. (*Essays*, 1924, p. 417.)

stupefied the bystanders by suddenly bursting into laughter—because, he explained, after the first few bones had been broken, he found his nerves so deadened as hardly to suffer at all. One recalls, too, how David wept and wailed while his child by Bathsheba was sick; but put away that vain anguish when the child at last had died.

Yet it seems to me a little strange to rank *Riders to the Sea* above Synge's larger and completer plays. Not only is its plot a little thin; it is also a little hurried. In only twenty-two pages the death of the fifth son is established, the death of the sixth is foreboded and takes place—the very moment he reaches the harbour. And the early talk of rising wind and threatening sea does become slightly irrelevant, since in the end Bartley is simply pushed into the harbour by the grey pony, and not lost in any storm at all.

In fact, there seems much more of a dramatic plot even in the one Act of *The Shadow of the Glen*; where there is a telling dramatic irony in the unexpected *dénouement* that the young wife who gives patronizing shelter to the tramp, finds herself at the end leaving her own home for ever under that tramp's protection.

Again, the characters in *Riders to the Sea* remain a little dim. It does not in itself make a character to lose one's menfolk by drowning; or to be drowned oneself.

Even the language is, for me, less coloured, vivid, and exciting than in Synge's other plays. This one is simple, sincere, moving—but I think one should praise it reasonably. So far from being 'the greatest tragedy of modern times', I do not even find it by any means the best play of Synge's.

Riders to the Sea is supposed to have been influenced also by Pierre Loti's *Pêcheur d'Islande*. Synge, it is said, thought Loti the greatest of living prose-writers; and he might naturally try to do for the seafolk of Connaught what Loti had done for the seafolk of Brittany. Certainly the resemblance seems clear enough in such a sentence of Loti's as—'Elle confondait cette mort avec d'autres. Elle en avait tant perdu, de fils.'

But Synge's main sources lie in what he had himself seen or heard of on Aran—the borrowing of one man's carefully stored up coffin-boards in order to bury another; the identification of a stranded body by its clothes; the ominous vision of a dead man riding with another soon to die. Indeed I am so heretical as to wonder if anything in the play, fine though it is, remains quite so impressively real and moving as Synge's own description in *The Aran Islands* of the burying of a young man drowned, like Bartley, at sea. So vividly he describes there the wild keening of the women in their red dresses, with red petticoats over their heads; the rude measurement of the grave with bramble switches; the mother of the dead youth seeing her own mother's skull thrown out by the grave-diggers, and sitting with it in her lap, keening over it; the mourners beating frantically with their hands on the coffin; the holy water sprinkled by an old man from a wisp of bracken.

Synge himself strolled away and talked to some fishermen near by. 'I could not help feeling,' he says, 'that I was talking with men who were under a judgement of death.' (Indeed within ten years Synge himself would be dead.) 'I knew that every one of them would be drowned in the sea in a few years and battered naked on the rocks, or would die in his own cottage and be buried with another fearful scene in the graveyard I had come from.' Compare, too, Synge's comment on all this doomed island-life, lost in the inhuman immensities of the Atlantic, as expressed in its keenings above the dead: 'In this cry of pain the inner consciousness of the people seems to lay itself bare for an instant, and to reveal the mood of beings who feel their isolation in the face of a universe that wars on them with winds and seas.'

An interesting touch is recorded in Lady Gregory's *Our Irish Theatre*. Lady Gregory got a Galway woman near Dublin to teach the play's actors how to keen. But when they went to this woman's house, she found she could not keen in her living-room. They all had to go upstairs, so that the company-secretary might lie down under a sheet, as corpse. Then at last she could do it. Again, after the London performance the pit went away keening down the street.

In the eastern Mediterranean lies a little group of islands, drenched in sun as the Arans are drenched in mist and rain. But there too the sea is pitiless: and it seems to me a small but infinitely pathetic touch that the little snow-white cottages of Myconos among the Cyclades used to be built with a special inner room where anguished wives and mothers could hide themselves away and hear no longer the howling of the storm-winds, that their menfolk might be battling with at sea.

So too poem after poem of the Greek Anthology echoes the lament of Maurya, with a beauty far more marmoreal than hers; yet not more poignant.

> I pile the chill sea-shingle with my hands above thee, sleeping,
>   A cold and breathless body, here upon the shore.
> For the last rites to rest thee no mother renders weeping;
>   These limbs that the waves have wasted, *she* shall behold no more.
> Only the lonely beaches, in their friendless desolation,
>   *They* were thy only welcome beside the Aegean Sea.
> This little sand I give thee, and many a lamentation,
>   Stranger. So bitter a bargain thy trading brought to thee.
>
> (ZONAS OF SARDIS, 1st century B.C.)

> I mourn for Polyanthus, who died new-wed, O stranger;
>   Here his young wife laid him, Aristágorē;
> The Aegean surges sank him by Scíathus in their anger,
>   And nought but bone and dust came home to her from sea.
> For that ill-fated body, as dawn was breaking through,
> Into Torōnē's haven, O friend, the fishers drew.
>
> (PHAEDIMUS, 3rd or 2nd century B.C.?)

The Tinker's Wedding
(begun 1902-3, finished 1906, published 1907)

'It is the timber of poetry that wears most surely, and there is no timber that has not strong roots among the clay and worms.'

SYNGE

This is an early work from 1902-3, later rewritten. Synge had heard from Wicklow peasants of the free unions among the tinkers, who would pair off for the year like birds[1]; also of a tinker couple who once persuaded a priest to marry them for half a sovereign and a tin can; but then pretended that their donkey had kicked the can in the night. ' "Go on now," says the priest. "It's a pair of rogues and schemers you are, and I won't wed you at all." '

In the play the tin can is not kicked by an ass, but sold by the tinker's old mother for drink. And all ends with a quarrel in which the tinkers finally ram the priest's head into a sack, until he promises not to set the police on them.

There are six MS. drafts of the piece—rather few for Synge (though many writers would think it ample).[2] But I suspect that he saw this comedy to be essentially a slighter and lighter work than his other plays, and took less trouble with it; especially as such an unedifying priest, and such unedifying behaviour to a priest, were more than anyone could possibly stage in Ireland. True, there was at one time some hope of a production in Berlin.[3] But even when done in London in 1909, the piece was hissed. It remains a not unamusing farce. It has less than Synge's usual poetry; but plenty

[1] An old woman told Lady Gregory that once she had sat on a wall at Kilkenny, watching how the tinkers at their annual rally bartered wives—'and the children went away with the women'. (H. Howarth, *The Irish Writers*, p. 10.)

[2] In its first version it had only one act.

[3] See Synge's letters to his German translator in *Yale Review*, July, 1924.

of life in its rough-and-tumble, like a Breughel picture; and the usual vivid tang in its talk.

> Wouldn't you have a little mercy on us, your reverence? Wouldn't you marry us for half a sovereign, and it a nice shiny one with a view on it of the living king's mamma?

> Let you drink it up, holy father. Let you drink it up, I'm saying, and not be letting on you wouldn't do the like of it, and you with a stack of pint bottles above reaching the sky. . . . And I'm thinking it should be great game to hear a scholar, the like of you, speaking Latin to the Saints above.

Michael (*gloomily*). If I didn't marry her, she'd be walking off to Jaunting Jim maybe at the fall of night; and it's well yourself knows there isn't the like of her for getting money and selling songs to the men.

Mary. And you're thinking it's paying gold to his reverence would make a woman stop when she's a mind to go?

Sarah (*angrily*). Let you not be destroying us with your talk when I've as good a right to a decent marriage as any speckled female does be sleeping in the black hovels above, would choke a mule.

Mary (*soothingly*). It's as good a right you have, surely, Sarah Casey, but what good will it do? Is it putting that ring on your finger will keep you from getting an aged woman and losing the fine face you have, or be easing your pains; when it's the grand ladies do be married in silk dresses, with rings of gold, that do pass any woman with their share of torment in the hour of birth, and do be paying the doctors in the city of Dublin a great price at that time, the like of what you'd pay for a good ass and a cart? (*She sits down.*)

Sarah (*puzzled*). Is that the truth?

Mary (*pleased with the point she has made*). Wouldn't any know it's the truth? Ah, it's few short years you are yet in the world, Sarah Casey, and it's little or nothing at all maybe you know about it.

Sarah (*vehement but uneasy*). What is it yourself knows of the fine ladies when they wouldn't let the like of you go near to them at all?

Mary. If you do be drinking a little sup in one town and another town, it's soon you get great knowledge and a great sight into the world. You'll see men there, and women there, sitting up on the ends of barrels in the dark night, and they making great talk would soon have the like of you, Sarah Casey, as wise as a March hare.

In his preface Synge predicted that, if Ireland lost its humour, as some of its towns seemed to be doing, it would develop a morbidity of mind like Baudelaire's. One may fully agree that Baudelaire was morbid; yet see few symptoms of Ireland's becoming much like him. However, there is more than one way of degenerating. At all events Synge's hope that Irish folk would not mind being laughed at without malice proved optimistic. One suspects, indeed, that the publication of play and preface at the end of 1907 was not unconnected with the tumults of passion roused by *The Playboy* in January of that year—as if Synge were retorting to the uproar of his Dublin audience with a defiance more determined and unrepentant than ever.

The Well of the Saints
(written 1902-4, performed 1905)

'Mens, ma bien-aimée, mens par charité. Donne-moi le songe qui colore les noirs chagrins. Mens, n'aie pas de scrupules! Tu n'ajouterais qu'une illusion à l'illusion de l'amour et la beauté.'[1]

ANATOLE FRANCE, *Le Lys Rouge*

Here Synge first passed from one-act plays to three acts. The supposed period of the action remains extremely vague, and a little odd—'Some lonely mountainous district in the east of Ireland one or more centuries ago.' For it seems hard to imagine a saintly 'wandering Friar' going about healing the blind in the Ireland of Burke or Castlereagh, at the date of the French Revolution. However—

This play has more of a general idea, though the idea is simple—the blessing of illusion. A blind man and his wife imagine themselves handsome; are horrified when, cured, they see each other; and, when blindness mercifully returns, refuse to be cured anew. In short, ignorance can be bliss—or, if only a very moderate bliss, at least less unbearable than the harsh and naked truth.

> The Land of Dreams is better far,
> Above the light of the morning star.

One may recall the bitter phrase of another great Irishman, Swift, on the pricelessness of illusion—'This is the sublime and refined point of felicity called the possession of being well deceived.' Yet Synge remains saner and less vitriolic than Swift. *He* did not die like a poisoned rat in a hole. He could smile without gnashing his teeth.

[1] 'Lie, my darling, lie out of charity! Give me the dream that will colour the blackness of my miseries. Lie!—lie without scruple. You will only be adding one illusion more to the illusions of love and beauty.'

Once more, however, the chief virtue, as usual with Synge, lies in the vivid charm of the language—its poetry and its humour.

Act I

Late Autumn

Timmy the Smith tells Martin and Mary Doul, the blind couple, that a wonder approaches (he means, of course, the miracle-working Saint).

Timmy. If I'd a mind I'd be telling you of a real wonder this day, and the way you'll be having a great joy, maybe, you're not thinking on at all.

Martin Doul (*interested*). Are they putting up a still behind in the rocks? It'd be a grand thing if I'd a sup handy the way I wouldn't be destroying myself groping up across the bogs in the rain falling.

Timmy (*still moodily*). It's not a still they're bringing, or the like of it either.

Mary Doul (*persuasively to Timmy*). Maybe they're hanging a thief, above at the bit of a tree. I'm told it's a great sight to see a man hanging by his neck; but what joy would that be to ourselves, and we not seeing it at all?

Timmy (*more pleasantly*). They're hanging no one this day, Mary Doul, and yet, with the help of God, you'll see a power hanged before you die.

The actual healing is painfully dramatic. Martin Doul is so convinced of his Mary's dazzling beauty that, when his sight is restored, he mistakes for her, first, the pretty Molly Byrne, then other young women in the crowd. But the irony grows merciless.

Martin Doul (*ecstatically*). Oh, glory be to God, I see now surely. . . . I see the walls of the church, and the green bits of ferns in them, and yourself, holy father, and the great width of the sky.

　　He runs out half-foolish with joy, and comes past Mary Doul as she scrambles to her feet, drawing a little away from her as he goes by . . . .[1]

(*Crying out joyfully*) That's Timmy, I know Timmy by the black of his head. . . . That's Mat Simon, I know Mat by the length of his legs. . . . That should be Patch Ruadh, with the gamey eyes in him, and the fiery hair. (*He sees Molly Byrne on Mary Doul's seat, and his*

---

[1] What an opportunity, even in this simple gesture, for a clever actor!

voice changes completely.) Oh, it was no lie they told me, Mary Doul. Oh, glory to God and the seven saints, I didn't die and not see you at all. . . . Hold up your head, Mary, the way I'll see it's richer I am than the great kings of the east. Hold up your head, I'm saying, for it's soon you'll be seeing me, and I not a bad one at all.

(*He touches her and she starts up.*)

Molly Byrne.   Let you keep away from me, and not be soiling my chin.

(*People laugh loudly.*)

Martin Doul (*bewildered*).   It's Molly's voice you have.

Molly Byrne.   Why wouldn't I have my own voice? Do you think I'm a ghost?

Martin Doul.   Which of you all is herself? (*He goes up to Bride.*) Is it you is Mary Doul? I'm thinking you're more the like of what they said (*peering at her*).   For you've yellow hair, and white skin, and it's the smell of my own turf is rising from your shawl.

(*He catches her shawl.*)

Bride (*pulling away her shawl*).   I'm not your wife, and let you get out of my way.

(*The people laugh again.* . . .)

People (*jeeringly*).   Try again, Martin, try again, and you'll be finding her yet.

Martin Doul (*passionately*).   Where is it you have her hidden away? Isn't it a black shame for a drove of pitiful beasts the like of you to be making game of me, and putting a fool's head on me the grand day of my life? Ah, you're thinking you're a fine lot, with your giggling, weeping eyes, a fine lot to be making game of myself and the woman I've heard called the great wonder of the west.

(*During this speech, which he gives with his back towards the church, Mary Doul has come out with her sight cured, and come down towards the right with a silly simpering smile, till she is a little behind Martin Doul.*)

Mary Doul (*when he pauses*).   Which of you is Martin Doul?

Martin Doul (*wheeling round*).   It's her voice surely.

(*They stare at each other blankly.*)

Molly Byrne (*to Martin Doul*).   Go up now and take her under the chin and be speaking the way you spoke to myself.

Martin Doul (*in a low voice, with intensity*).   If I speak now, I'll speak hard to the two of you——

Molly Byrne (*to Mary Doul*).   You're not saying a word, Mary. What is it you think of himself, with the fat legs on him, and the little neck like a ram?

Mary Doul.   I'm thinking it's a poor thing when the Lord God gives you sight and puts the like of that man in your way.

Martin Doul.   It's on your two knees you should be thanking the Lord

God you're not looking on yourself, for if it was yourself you seen you'd be running round in a short while like the old screeching mad-woman is running round in the glen.

Mary Doul (*beginning to realize herself*). If I'm not so fine as some of them said, I have my hair, and big eyes, and my white skin——

Martin Doul (*breaking out into a passionate cry*). Your hair, and your big eyes, is it? . . . I'm telling you there isn't a wisp on any grey mare on the ridge of the world isn't finer than the dirty twist on your head. There isn't two eyes in any starving sow isn't finer than the eyes you were calling blue like the sea. . . .

Mary Doul. I wouldn't rear a crumpled whelp the like of you. It's many a woman is married with finer than yourself should be praising God if she's no child, and isn't loading the earth with things would make the heavens lonesome above, and they scaring the larks, and the crows, and the angels passing in the sky.

An Aristotelian 'recognition' of the most grisly kind. With difficulty the Saint restores peace, and goes his way.

In Act II autumn has changed to winter. Martin and Mary have not only lost their pleasure in each other's imagined distinction; they have also—most unpleasant—to work, instead of begging. They have parted company. Martin spends an unwilling existence cutting wood and doing jobs for Timmy the Smith. And he is tormented by coveting the pretty Molly Byrne, whom Timmy the Smith is soon to wed.

Martin's description of his own disillusionment when he got his sight again, is a key-passage to the whole play—an epitome of all shatterings of human romance when bleak reality breaks in.

Martin Doul. A bad black day when I was roused up and found I was the like of the little children do be listening to the stories of an old woman, and do be dreaming after in the dark night that it's in grand houses of gold they are, with speckled horses to ride, and do be waking again, in a short while, and they destroyed with the cold, and the thatch dripping, maybe, and the starved ass braying in the yard?

Madly, though knowing really it is quite useless, Martin yet cannot resist courting Molly Byrne to run away with him—only to earn her mockery, and the jealous anger of both Timmy the Smith, and his wife. But now his sight begins to fail and grow dim once more.

Martin Doul. . . . Is it a storm of thunder is coming, or the last end of the world? (*He staggers towards Mary Doul, tripping slightly over tin can.*) The heavens is closing, I'm thinking, with darkness and great trouble passing in the sky. (*He reaches Mary Doul, and seizes her left arm with both his hands—with a frantic cry.*) Is it the darkness of thunder is coming, Mary Doul! Do you see me clearly with your eyes?

Mary Doul (*snatches her arm away, and hits him with empty sack across the face*). I see you a sight too clearly, and let you keep off from me now.

Molly Byrne (*clapping her hands*). That's right, Mary. That's the way to treat the like of him is after standing there at my feet and asking me to go off with him, till I'd grow an old wretched road-woman the like of yourself.

Mary Doul (*defiantly*). When the skin shrinks on your chin, Molly Byrne, there won't be the like of you for a shrunk hag in the four quarters of Ireland. . . . It's a fine pair you'd be, surely!

   (*Martin Doul is standing at back right centre, with his back to the audience.*)

Timmy (*coming over to Mary Doul*). Is it no shame you have to let on she'd ever be the like of you?

Mary Doul. It's them that's fat and flabby do be wrinkled young, and that whitish yellowy hair she has does be soon turning the like of a handful of thin grass you'd see rotting, where the wet lies, at the north of a sty. (*Turning to go out on right.*) Ah, it's a better thing to have a simple, seemly face, the like of my face, for two-score years, or fifty itself, than to be setting fools mad a short while, and then to be turning a thing would drive off the little children from your feet.

The Smith turns Martin away; and blindness veils his eyes anew. But his final rage blazes out into a pagan savagery that would not be easy to parallel.

Martin Doul (*stands a moment with his hands to his eyes*). And that's the last thing I'm to set my sight on in the life of the world—the villainy of a woman and the bloody strength of a man. Oh, God, pity a poor blind fellow, the way I am this day with no strength in me to do hurt to them at all. (*He begins groping about for a moment, then stops.*) Yet if I've no strength in me I've a voice left for my prayers, and may God blight them this day, and my own soul the same hour with them, the way I'll see them after, Molly Byrne and Timmy the smith, the two of them on a high bed, and they screeching in hell. . . . It'll be a grand thing that time to look on the two of them; and they twisting and roaring out, and twisting and roaring again, one day and the next day, and each day always and ever. It's not blind I'll be that time, and it won't be hell to me, I'm thinking, but the like of heaven itself; and it's fine care I'll be taking the Lord Almighty doesn't know.

In the third and last Act winter has changed to early spring. Mary Doul, blind again likewise, is sitting once more by the ruined church where the Saint had healed the old couple half a year ago. The blind Martin gropes his way in, talking to himself, and unaware of her presence. It seems to me a most vivid picture of the world of the blind.

Martin Doul. It's lonesome I'll be from this day, and if living people is a bad lot, yet Mary Doul, herself, and she a dirty, wrinkled-looking hag, was better maybe to be sitting along with than no one at all. I'll be getting my death now, I'm thinking, sitting alone in the cold air, hearing the night coming, and the blackbirds flying round in the briars crying to themselves, the time you'll hear one cart getting off a long way in the east, and another cart getting off a long way in the west, and a dog barking maybe, and a little wind turning the sticks.

Then he realizes that his wife is beside him again. Already the old complacent mist of illusion begins mercifully to settle anew on both. Mary muses how becoming it will be when she has white soft hair falling round her; and Martin's to match.

Martin Doul (bursting with excitement). I've this to say, Mary Doul. I'll be letting my beard grow in a short while, a beautiful, long, white, silken, streamy beard, you wouldn't see the like of in the eastern world. . . . Ah, a white beard's a grand thing on an old man, a grand thing for making the quality stop and be stretching out their hands with good silver or gold, and a beard's a thing you'll never have, so you may be holding your tongue.

Mary Doul (laughing cheerfully). Well, we're a great pair, surely, and it's great times we'll have yet, maybe, and great talking before we die.

Martin Doul. Great times from this day, with the help of the Almighty God, for a priest itself would believe the lies of an old man would have a fine white beard growing on his chin.

But now, far off, they hear tinkling the sacred bell of the Saint. They try to run and hide—quite ineffectively. The Saint enters with his following of country folk. He can cure the blind pair a second time; and his second cures have no danger of relapse. But Martin has had enough of seeing—blindness is far better.

Martin Doul. Ah, it's ourselves had finer sights. . . . I'm telling you, when we were sitting a while back hearing the birds and bees humming in every weed of the ditch, or when we'd be smelling the sweet, beautiful smell does be rising in the warm nights, when you do hear the swift flying things racing in the air, till we'd be looking up in our own minds into a grand sky, and seeing lakes, and big rivers, and fine hills for taking the plough.

Mary feels like Martin. Yet she lets herself be talked over, and kneels down before the Saint. Then Martin, desperate, dashes the can of holy water from the Saint's hand, and sends it rocketing across the stage.

Martin Doul. Let you walk on now with your worn feet, and your welted knees, and your fasting, holy ways have left you with a big head on you and a thin pitiful arm. (*The Saint looks at him for a moment severely, then turns away and picks up his can. He pulls Mary Doul up.*) For if it's a right some of you have to be working and sweating the like of Timmy the smith, and a right some of you have to be fasting and praying and talking holy talk the like of yourself, I'm thinking it's a good right ourselves have to be sitting blind, hearing a soft wind turning round the little leaves of the spring and feeling the sun, and we not tormenting our souls with the sight of the gray days, and the holy men, and the dirty feet is trampling the world.

It is worth comparing Keyserling, *The Travel-diary of a Philosopher* (1919); 'I was blind once after an operation on my eyes, and I must say this time belongs to the richest in my life; it was so rich that I felt an unmistakable impoverishment when the sight of my eyes returned to me.' And of course the general idea of the piece recalls the 'life-lie' which makes existence tolerable for the broken creatures in Ibsen's *Wild Duck*.

The Well of the Saints has been called Synge's most perfect play. Such was the view of Lennox Robinson. An excellent play it is. But *The Playboy* and *Deirdre* impress me still more. And some would add also *Riders to the Sea*. George Moore's comment, 'a great play, more remarkable than any original play produced in England during our time', seems to illustrate only George Moore's passion for hyperbole.[1]

---

[1] Cf. his other less exaggerated remark—'it was not until Synge wrote *The Well of the Saints* that I began to feel that a man of genius had been born unto Ireland'.

Critics less partial, on the other hand, have objected that an Irish peasant would never have knocked holy water from a Saint's hand. But who can trust such dogmatic 'never's? 'Never' is a terrible, an enormous word. One may recall, for example, Gerald, Earl of Kildare, who burnt Cashel Cathedral in 1495, and pleaded to Henry VII, in excuse, that 'he thought the archbishop was inside'. This frankness is said to have found such favour with King Henry that he reappointed the Earl as Lord Deputy. At all events this priggish objection to Synge's play would not occur to any non-Irish reader; it is on a level with the objection to *The Shadow of the Glen*, that no Irish wife could ever be unfaithful.

It has also been argued that Martin Doul on receiving his sight would not be able at once to identify colours—the 'green bits of ferns', the 'fiery hair' of Patch Ruadh. But though such a colour-sense would be impossible for a man born blind, what earthly reason is there to suppose Martin blind from birth? None that I know. Why should he not have *gone* blind like Milton? Mary Doul says she went blind in her seventh year; Martin's loss of sight could easily have been much more recent.

People have also bothered about sources. They have dragged up the restoration of an old husband's sight in Chaucer's tale of January and May. But that seems extremely remote. A friend of Synge, O'Donoghue, said Synge got his root-idea from Clemenceau's one-act play *Le Voile du Bonheur* (1901).

Maurice Bourgeois found a closer parallel in a story from Lord Lytton's *Pilgrims of the Rhine*, 'The Maid of Malines'. A blind young man, Armand, is saved from a bolting horse by a young woman, Lucille Tisseur. She has a beautiful voice, but is disfigured by smallpox. She gets a doctor to cure Armand's blindness. Cured, he mistakes the beautiful Julie for Lucille, as Martin Doul mistakes Molly Byrne for Mary. Armand weds Julie; but loses his sight again in Egypt, fighting the English, and marries in the end the faithful Lucille.

Synge told Yeats he had never even read Lytton's tale. Memory can be deceptive in such matters. But I see no reason to suppose so here. Synge said his source was an old French farce, though he had forgotten the name of it. Presumably, as suggested by D. H. Greene, he meant *La Moralité de l'Aveugle et du Boiteux* (1496) by André or Andrieu de la Vigne (*c.* 1457-1527). In this a blind beggar carries a crippled one about on his back; finally, when both are unwillingly healed by the holy relics of St Martin, though the blind man is happy, the cripple is furious at losing his easy life on another's shoulders.[1]

Indeed Lea in his *History of the Inquisition* quotes from a twelfth-century chronicle a tale of two cripples really taking flight when, in 887, St Martin's relics were brought from Auxerre to Tours, to escape the Danes. The pair did not wish to be robbed of their easy livelihood; but despite themselves they were healed.

Still this indebtedness even to de la Vigne seems extremely trivial. Not much of the water of life is found by such source-hunting. It does not matter what springs fed *The Well of the Saints*. Synge's play, with its winged imagination and golden utterance, is still as lively as a yellow-billed blackbird in a spring apple-tree; though it also contains passages as bitter and savage as anything he ever wrote.

---

[1] Cf. Yeats's *The Cat and the Moon*, p. 333. It is hard, however, to see any sense in the suggestion that Synge was also influenced by a tale in Patrick Kennedy's *Bardic Stories of Ireland* (1875), 'The Blind Nun'—a flabby pietistic anecdote about a Kildare nun who had her sight briefly restored by St Brigid, but felt no wish to retain it because it distracted her from God.

The Playboy of the Western World
(written 1905-6, performed 1905)

'But surely you were something better
Than innocent!'

SWINBURNE

For the ordinary reader *The Playboy* is the essential Synge—it has outshone the rest of his works put together. Professional critics have sometimes judged otherwise. One cannot say the professional critics are 'wrong'. In the aesthetic preferences of educated and intelligent persons I believe there is not, and cannot be, *any* right or wrong. But here I share the common reader's view.

As with *The Well of the Saints*, the play's essential theme is romance—the romance of illusion, but also the illusiveness of romance. For though the blind may see marvellous visions, though the simple may thrill at the thought of splendid sins, and devilries magnificently daredevil, actual reality is apt to prove much less delightful. Distance may lend enchantment; but the magic perishes with proximity; just as 'the pride, pomp, circumstance of glorious war' can shrivel with the sight—and stench—of dead men wizened and stark upon a battlefield.

So here. These Mayo peasants, rebellious, anarchic and, after centuries of oppression, bitter against all government, gape at first with admiration at a rustic young Oedipus who *tells* how he has dared kill his wicked old father; but when they actually *see* him hit the old man with a spade, it becomes quite another thing. They are revolted. 'There's a great gap,' cries Pegeen, 'between a gallous story and a dirty deed.'

Yet romantic illusion can also have results extremely real. Christy Mahon, shy, simple lad, finding himself suddenly hero-worshipped, grows thereby transformed into something, if not

201

heroic, at least thrice as bold and confident as he ever was before. His sudden triumphs in the country-sports may seem a little incredible; but the change in his character is not.

There are teachers who believe they can make their pupils geniuses by telling them what geniuses they *are*. Optimistic. Yet it is surprising what results praise and self-confidence can sometimes bring. Perhaps the best teaching must tread the tight-rope between, on the one hand, facile praise that is worthless and misleading and, at the opposite extreme, a discouraging taciturnity. One should, I believe, never praise dishonestly: but one should never miss an opportunity for honest praise. 'Praise youth, and it will prosper.'[1] And here in *The Playboy* it is as if the dramatist himself grew infected with the intoxication of his hero. Never before had even Synge achieved such vivid 'bravery of speech'.

His starting point was a story heard on his first visit to Aran (1898). A Connaught man killed his father with a spade, and was hid in a hole by Aran relatives. A reward was offered for his arrest; and he could hear the boots of policemen crunching overhead. But the islanders succeeded in smuggling the fugitive away to the United States.

When Yeats landed in the Aran Islands, the oldest man on Inishmaan said 'very slowly and solemnly': 'If the gentleman has done a crime, we'll hide him. There was a gentleman that killed his father, and I had him in my own home six months till he got away to America.' And Yeats describes how behind the solemnity of this speech there was a mischievous glint in the old man's eyes—'as the eyes must have shone in that Trinity College branch of the Gaelic League which began every meeting with prayers for the death of an old Fellow of College who disliked their movement'.[2]

There was also the case of a man called Lynchehaun (whom Synge actually mentioned by name in an early draft of this play). This person, after assaulting a woman on Achill Island, was also hidden from the police, by peasant-women, and got away to America.

[1] Maurice O'Sullivan, *Twenty years a-growing*.
[2] Denis Brogan had also a story of a man in his village who was called 'Bagdad', because he had fired his shotgun at a parent too dilatory in dying. (Gerard Fay, *The Abbey Theatre*, 1958, p. 119.)

This hostility of the countryfolk to the law was common enough in Western Ireland, where the arm of justice was associated with the hated English oppressor.[1] But still more, Synge thought, these primitive souls regarded crime as simply a sudden madness, which a man's own conscience would punish enough in the end, without need for police or magistrates.

Ironically enough, however, when *The Playboy* came to be performed, this lawless hero of a Nationalist poet had to be protected from the Irish audience by England's cruel police. For not even the plot of *The Playboy* was to prove so fantastic a farce as its stage-history. Originally I had meant to discuss the play before discussing its reception; but the play itself may mean more to the reader if he first realizes its extraordinary effect on its earliest Irish audiences.[2]

From the outset, William Fay foresaw trouble; but the trouble he foresaw was nothing to what actually came. Fay had a shrewd theory about drama in general, that anger and savagery on the stage are infectious, and risk provoking a mood of anger and savagery in the audience also. So he and his brother begged Synge at least to make Pegeen a decent, likeable country-girl; and to cut out that final scene where she so brutally lassoes her own lover, and burns his leg with a glowing turf. But here the gentle Synge remained inflexible. Only a few specially dangerous phrases would he cut.

On the opening night (a Saturday) the audience, though quiet through the first two Acts, burst into hisses and cat-calls half-way through Act III at the words 'all bloody fools'[3]; and when it came

---

[1] Cf. Douglas Hyde:

> 'It is with the people I was,
>   It is not with the law I was;
> But they took me in my sleep,
>   On the side of Cnoc-na-Feigh;
>   And so
> To-morrow they will hang me.'

[2] Accounts of what happened vary considerably about details; but the general outline is clear enough.

[3] '*Christy*. And to think I'm long years hearing women talking that talk, to all bloody fools.'

to the mention of the unmentionable word 'shift'[1]—'a drift of chosen females standing in their shifts itself'—the howls rose to pandemonium. Fighting, it is said, broke out in the stalls, and it looked as if the stage would be stormed. Indeed the call-boy seized an axe from the boiler-room, and swore by all the saints to decapitate the first man across the footlights.

On the Monday night a riot was deliberately organized; some forty youths in front of the pit shouted, stamped, and blew trumpets; most of the piece had to be played in dumb-show. And night after night these tumults continued, despite the police, and the padding of the floor with felt to deaden the stamping.

On the last (Saturday) evening, it is reported, there were five hundred police keeping order in the theatre and its neighbourhood —police lining the walls, police sitting in a row along the centre of the pit. To crown the farce, these pillars of the law found it impossible to keep their impassive dignity through the humours of Synge's dialogue, and finally collapsed with laughter at Michael Flaherty's speech—'the peelers in this place is decent, drouthy poor fellows wouldn't touch a cur dog'. But for weeks afterwards the Abbey had audiences so scanty that Willie Fay would invite them to gather forward in the stalls. Not till a couple of months later, in March, did Lady Gregory's *Rising of the Moon* do something to appease the patriots.

There is a further account by George Moore in *Vale*, derived from the Irish dramatist, Edward Martyn, who was present. After the passage about 'shifts' the crowded pit kept shouting 'Lower the bloody curtain, and give us something we bloody well want'—a pleasing slogan, if true, for men shocked by crude language. Martyn, a devout Catholic, was himself pained by the play's irreverence. He disapproved, indeed, of rowdily interrupting performances; 'but,' he said, 'Yeats shouldn't have called in the police.[2] A Nationalist should never call for the police.' Asked by George Moore whether, by parity of logic, he would refuse to call the police even if his own house were burgled, Martyn took refuge in casuist-

---

[1] Seven pages from the end.
[2] It was not Yeats, but apparently Lady Gregory, who really first summoned the police.

ical distinctions between the rights of property and the rights of free speech. Such distinctions seem to me spider-webs.

Synge himself sat with a white face through the tumult. But the tension did serious harm to his health; as the failure of *The Seagull* to the health of Chekhov. Ibsen perhaps was tougher; but he watched from a greater distance the rage aroused by *Ghosts*.

Lady Gregory took a more active part than Synge, herself calling in the police (though she seems afterwards to have asked them to withdraw), and getting a nephew at Trinity, Dublin, to bring some fellow-undergraduates as supporters of the play. Unfortunately these young men still further inflamed political passions by singing 'God save the King'.[1]

Reactions outside the theatre were equally grotesque. William Boyle withdrew his three plays from the Abbey. Arthur Griffith denounced it as an anti-Irish institution, financed by English gold. *The Playboy*, he thundered, was 'a vile and inhuman story told in the foulest language we have ever listened to from a public platform'. (Which suggests that Arthur Griffith must have passed his life in surroundings singularly pure.) And the *Freeman's Journal* echoed: 'The hideous caricature would be slanderous of a Kaffir kraal.'

Among the maunderings of the press appeared also a letter signed 'A Girl from the West', lamenting that 'Miss Allgood ... is forced to use a word indicating an essential item of female attire which the lady would probably never utter in ordinary circumstances even to herself.' Did Irish ladies, one begins to wonder, when they bought the things in shops, do it in dumb-show? Such prim cant only demonstrates anew how admirably true to life was Ibsen's *Enemy of the People*.

Yeats was away lecturing in Scotland, as the guest of Sir Herbert Grierson, when Lady Gregory wired news of the disturbances. At

---

[1] Actually, though she battled so bravely for it both in Ireland and in America, Lady Gregory wrote to her nephew Hugh Lane, 'If you knew how I hate *Playboy*!' Her moral code was less unconventional than Synge's. But all the more credit to her courageous fight for the piece, and for the freedom of the stage; and all the harder on her that she should have been boycotted for it even at Coole, with the local council forbidding schoolchildren to go to her house, or even to take cakes or presents from her. (W. S. Blunt, *Diaries*, 1/6/07.)

once he rushed back to Dublin, and showed himself at his best by refusing to yield an inch to the rabble, and holding a public debate in the theatre on the Monday after the last performance. Synge was ill and absent; but Yeats, in full evening-dress, together with his father, defended the play to an audience of workmen, students, and citizens, who now cheered, now howled him down. Mary Colum, who was present as a girl-student, has written—'I never witnessed a human being fight as Yeats fought that night, nor knew another with so many weapons in his armoury.' That was brave. It reveals Yeats at his finest.

The American tour of the Abbey Players four years later, in 1911-12, let loose fresh frenzies. By now Synge was cold in Mount Jerome cemetery; but the Irish-American press still gabbled with hysteria. 'The Playboy must be squelched,' wrote The Gaelic American, 'and a lesson taught to Mr Yeats and his fellow-agents in England.' And again—'we pledge ourselves as one man to drive the vile thing from the stage . . . and we ask the aid in this work of every decent Irish man and woman and of the Catholic Church, whose doctrines and devotional practices are held up to scorn and ridicule in Synge's monstrosity.'

At the New York performance there were showers of potatoes and vegetables, followed by cubic capsules of asafoetida, a resinous gum with a strong stench of garlic. (Art and science combined!) However, police dealt with the roughs; and Theodore Roosevelt both went to the theatre and published in his paper a warm tribute to the play. In Philadelphia arrest-warrants were issued for the company, under a bye-law forbidding 'immoral and indecent plays'; which had been enacted for the benefit of Sarah Bernhardt on her visit of 1910.

In Chicago the City Council vainly directed the Mayor to ban the play; the Mayor, however, 'instead of finding anything immoral . . . found the whole thing was wonderfully stupid'. In Chicago also, Lady Gregory received a letter illustrated with pistol, coffin, hammer, and nails, beginning:

'Lady Gregory . . . ha, ha. Foster-mother of the funny play boy.

this is to console you from the dread that may fill your grizzly breast after you have read the contents of this note. *Your fate is sealed.* never again shall you gase (*sic*) on the barren hilltops of Connemara

Your doom is sealed'

But Lady Gregory, judging from the drawing of the pistol that the author knew little of firearms, calmly ignored him. And despite these patriotic audacities the American tour became an artistic and financial triumph. Today, so one hears, Dubliners applaud *The Playboy* as an Irish classic, that does honour to the Eire which produced it.

Why did people make such idiots of themselves? The reasons seem partly religious, partly prudish, partly political.

First, the religious. God, the Virgin, and the Saints fill the mouths of Synge's characters; but it did not take much penetration to see that they held small place in the mind of Synge himself. He used these holy names for their picturesqueness. And picturesque they are. The plays would lose without them. Still, in fairness, one must grant that they might not unnaturally offend pious Catholics. The robust faith of the Middle Ages might not have turned a hair; but modern faith is often more sensitive.

So one can understand the attitude of some critics; though one may not much sympathize with it. For, after all, the work of orthodox writers like T. S. Eliot or Graham Greene is often equally distasteful to honest sceptics; but sceptics have usually more sense than to protest. Men are born to disagree; and they should not be so touchy. The most credulous and the most incredulous both have a right, within reason, to freedom of speech. By 'a right' I mean merely that free speech seems to work better than bigoted suppression, for the happiness and well-being of civilized people.

Objections to *The Playboy* on grounds of morality appear far more foolish. Some persons, for example, were shocked at Pegeen and Christy being left alone in the house all night.[1] But since no harm came of it, this feature should have pleased rather than displeased the moralists. Such pedantries remain tiresomely Victorian.

[1] This appears to have brought the uproar to a climax on Monday, Jan. 28. (Gerard Fay, *The Abbey Theatre*, p. 115.)

Then there was the hullabaloo about the word 'bloody'—on which comment is today superfluous; and the far worse hullabaloo about the word 'shift'. Lady Gregory asked the theatre charwoman what *she* thought. The charwoman replied that she would not mention such a thing at all, if she could help it; but if she did, she hoped she would always say 'chemise', even though alone by herself. After which, descending to the stage, and encountering the stage-carpenter, 'Isn't Mr Synge,' cried the worthy woman, 'a bloody old snot to write such a play!' Such, remarked Synge in telling the story, was 'Dublin delicacy!' The taboos of the respectable can certainly be peculiar. So a hundred and fifty years before, another great Irishman, Oliver Goldsmith, had his *Good-Natured Man* hissed in London for being 'low'.

The best answer to all this nonsense was a witty poem, produced, it seems, by A. E.'s woman secretary, Susan Mitchell—*The Blushes of Ireland*.

> You're quite too dense to understand
>   The chill—the thrill—of modest loathing
> With which one hears on Irish land
>   Of underclothing. . . .
>
> Allusions to a flannel shirt
>   (Young man, remember this, I urge 'ee)
> Afflict with agonizing hurt
>   Our patriot clergy. . . .
>
> And look, sir, do not sh-ft your scenes—
>   There's scandal aided and abetted.
> Let them, now virtue intervenes,
>   Be chemisetted.

In such matters there can be no logical line. Conventions about language are aesthetic rather than ethical; matters of refinement or crudity, rather than of morals. Our tendency today is perhaps towards excessive crudity. But one should not become a pernickety fool. Things must have names, and names are for use; it is merely that *certain* words have crude overtones. And there are certain drawbacks, I think, to being crude. But crude, for me, Synge never is.

The English language, one may add, perhaps raises this question of crudity more than some others, because English has a kind of double-talk. Often we have on the one hand, words of Saxon origin (which are sometimes gross in tone); and, on the other, alternative terms derived from French, or Latin, or Greek (which sound more civilized). Thus 'stomach' comes from French and Latin; 'belly' (like 'bellows'), from the conquered Saxon. 'Entrails' originates from French, Latin, and Greek; 'guts' from the Saxon churl. This double descent has had interesting psychological effects. It may have aided English hypocrisy; but it has also, I think, helped to keep English a language more sensitive and less thick-ankled than, say, German.

So far as the real morality of *The Playboy* is concerned, it is worth remembering the young doctor who told Synge he could hardly refrain from jumping on a seat and pointing out the virtuous brawlers in the audience whom he himself was treating for venereal disease.

Similarly Synge himself had written in 1904 to his friend Stephen Mackenna (the translator of Plotinus) after the rage produced by *The Shadow of the Glen*: 'I have as you know perambulated a good deal of Ireland in my thirty (years) and if I were (to) tell, which Heaven forbid, all the sex horrors I have seen I could a tale unfold that would wither up your blood. . . . I think squeamishness is a disease, and that Ireland will gain if Irish writers deal manfully, directly and decently with the entire reality of life.'

So Ibsen had done in Norway; and so, too, Ibsen had been reviled. Truth goes with a scratched face.[1]

But the silliest objections of all to *The Playboy* were political. During the last 150 years nationalism, unfortunately for the world, has become an endemic mania. No sooner does one oppressed race get free than it starts oppressing others. Ireland, having got rid of English domination, was eager to dominate Ulster. India, having got liberty from the British, proceeded to deny it to Kashmir. Such experiences do not make it easier to be patient with the outcries of frenzied nationalists. Synge was *not* patient with them; and he had to pay heavily.

[1] It was stated in 1956 that the 'Free' State government censorship still bans 1000 books a year. (H. Howarth, *The Irish Writers*, 1958.)

In a way, indeed, *The Playboy* was prophetic. It satirizes that human tendency to romanticize crime and violence which now fills our screens with revolver-shots and punches on the jaw, our shelves with crime and horror novels. Unfortunately within a few years of Synge's death that kind of romanticism was to fill Ireland itself with blood and butchery. The 'troubles' are now a faded memory; but those who died in them remain dead—lives wasted on futilities. It is even possible that *The Playboy* aroused such rancour in its audiences partly because they dimly felt in it an implied criticism of their own ideals of patriotic violence. Could Pegeen be an insidious parody of Cathleen ni Houlihan?

'Those who accuse Synge of some base motive,' wrote Yeats in 1909,[1] 'are the great-grandchildren of those Dublin men who accused Smith O'Brien of being paid by the Government to fail. It is of such as these Goethe thought when he said, "The Irish always seem to me like a pack of hounds dragging down some noble stag".'

At all events the play's reception remains an ugly and outstanding instance of mob-hysteria. Men in masses are largely loathsome; though, as individuals, sometimes superb. Well might Danton cry, after seeing human nature naked in the French Revolution, 'I am sick of men'—'Je suis soûl des hommes'. One should never surrender one's individualism. Masses are asses.

The first act of *The Playboy* opens in a rough pot-house at the north-west corner of Mayo in Connaught—if one sees Ireland as shaped somewhat like an infant turning its back on bloody England, with Ulster for its head, then Mayo is the top of the short arm it stretches out westward towards America.

Pegeen, daughter of the publican Michael James Flaherty, is writing the orders for her trousseau from Castlebar. Then enters the timid oaf she is to marry, Shawn Keogh; followed a little later by her father and two of his friends, Philly Cullen and Jimmy Farrell, who are off, the three of them, to a night's hard drinking at a dead woman's wake. The question arises whether Shawn shall stay to keep company with Pegeen, left alone in the empty house; but the

<hr />

[1] *Estrangement* (1926), p. 26.

owlish Shawn is terrified of such impropriety—what on earth *would* Father Reilly say?

But now, from the autumn dusk outside, there slinks in a slight, timid, mud-stained figure—Christy Mahon. A most insignificant-looking vagrant. All the greater the thrill that shudders through the company at a hint that he is running from the police. What kind of exciting criminal can this be? Has he stolen? Or been evicted from his land, and lifted his arm against the oppressor?

Philly. Did you strike golden guineas out of solder, young fellow, or shilling coins itself?

Christy. I did not, mister, not sixpence nor a farthing coin.

Jimmy. Did you marry three wives maybe? I'm told there's a sprinkling have done that among the holy Luthers of the preaching north.

Christy (shyly). I never married with one, let alone with a couple or three.

Philly. Maybe he went fighting for the Boers, the like of the man beyond, was judged to be hanged, quartered, and drawn.[1] Were you off east, young fellow, fighting bloody wars for Kruger and the freedom of the Boers?

Christy. I never left my own parish till Tuesday was a week.

Pegeen (coming from counter). He's done nothing, so. (*To Christy*) If you didn't commit murder or a bad, nasty thing; or false coining, or robbery, or butchery, or the like of them, there isn't anything that would be worth your troubling for to run from now. You did nothing at all.

Christy (his feelings hurt). That's an unkindly thing to be saying to a poor orphaned traveller, has a prison behind him, and hanging before, and hell's gap gaping below.

Pegeen (with a sign to the men to be quiet). You're only saying it. You did nothing at all. A soft lad the like of you wouldn't slit the windpipe of a screeching sow.

Christy (offended). You're not speaking the truth.

Pegeen (in mock rage). Not speaking the truth, is it? Would you have me knock the head of you with the butt of the broom?

Christy (twisting round on her with a sharp cry of horror). Don't strike me. I killed my poor father, Tuesday was a week, for doing the like of that.

---

[1] In the phrase 'drawn, hanged, and quartered', 'drawn' means dragged to the place of execution on a hurdle or the like; in the phrase 'hanged, drawn, and quartered', 'drawn' means 'disembowelled', as with a fowl. But Philly of course contrives to use 'drawn' in a way that makes it a meaningless absurdity.

Pegeen (with blank amazement). Is it killed your father?

Christy (subsiding). With the help of God I did, surely, and that the Holy Immaculate Mother may intercede for his soul.

Philly (retreating with Jimmy). There's a daring fellow.

Jimmy. Oh, glory be to God!

Michael (with great respect). That was a hanging crime, mister honey. You should have had a good reason for doing the like of that.

Christy (in a very reasonable tone). He was a dirty man, God forgive him, and he getting old and crusty, the way I couldn't put up with him at all.

Pegeen. And you shot him dead?

Christy (shaking his head). I never used weapons. I've no licence, and I'm a law-fearing man.

Michael. It was with a hilted knife maybe? I'm told, in the big world, it's bloody knives they use.

Christy (loudly, scandalized). Do you take me for a slaughter-boy?

This daredevil stranger is surely the very lad to look after Pegeen; who has already been clamouring for a pot-boy to help her in the pothouse.

Jimmy (jumps up). Now, by the Grace of God, herself will be safe this night, with a man killed his father holding danger from the door, and let you come on, Michael James, or they'll have the best stuff drunk at the wake.

Naturally poor Shawn becomes at once as greenly jealous as he dares. No use. Pegeen bundles him out. But while she and Christy are more and more enjoying their solitude together, there comes a knock at the door. It is a neighbour, the Widow Quin, brought along by the anxiously jealous Shawn to lure this dangerous rival away to her own house. At once she heaps Christy with her blandishments; much to the jealous fury of Pegeen.

Pegeen. . . . Walk on from this, for I'll not have him tormented, and he destroyed travelling since Tuesday was a week.

Widow Quin (peaceably). We'll be walking surely when his supper's done, and you'll find we're great company, young fellow, when it's of the like of you and me you'd hear the penny poets singing in an August fair.

Christy (innocently). Did you kill your father?

Pegeen (contemptuously). She did not. She hit himself[1] with a worn pick, and the rusted poison did corrode his blood the way he never

_____
[1] i.e. her husband.

overed it, and died after. That was a sneaky kind of murder did win small glory with the boys itself.

Widow Quin (*with good humour*).   If it didn't, maybe all knows a widow woman has buried her children and destroyed her man is a wiser comrade for a young lad than a girl, the like of you, who'd go helter-skeltering after any man would let you a wink upon the road.

Pegeen (*breaking out into wild rage*).   And you'll say that, Widow Quin, and you gasping with the rage you had racing the hill beyond to look on his face.

Widow Quin (*laughing derisively*).   Me, is it? Well, Father Reilly has cuteness to divide you now. (*She pulls Christy up.*) There's great temptation in a man did slay his da, and we'd best be going, young fellow; so rise up and come with me.

Pegeen (*seizing his arm*).   He'll not stir. He's pot-boy in this place, and I'll not have him stolen off and kidnapped while himself's abroad.

Widow Quin.   It'd be a crazy pot-boy'd lodge him in the shebeen where he works by day, so you'd have a right to come on, young fellow, till you see my little houseen, a perch off on the rising hill.

Pegeen.   Wait till morning, Christy Mahon. Wait till you lay eyes on her leaky thatch is growing more pasture for her buck goat that her square of fields, and she without a tramp itself to keep in order her place at all.

Widow Quin.   When you see me contriving in my little gardens, Christy Mahon, you'll swear the Lord God formed me to be living lone, and that there isn't my match in Mayo for thatching, or mowing, or shearing a sheep.

Pegeen (*with noisy scorn*).   It's true the Lord God formed you to contrive indeed. Doesn't the world know you reared a black ram at your own breast, so that the Lord Bishop of Connaught felt the elements of a Christian, and he eating it after in a kidney stew?

Not even this crowning flight of fancy can ruffle the Widow's good humour; but finally she is driven off; and Pegeen locks herself in her room, while the bewildered Christy settles down for the night.

Christy.   Well it's a clean bed and soft with it, and it's great luck and company I've won me in the end of time—two fine women fighting for the likes of me—till I'm thinking this night wasn't I a foolish fellow not to kill my father in the years gone by.

In Act II it is next morning. Pegeen has gone to get some goat's milk for her guest, while he cleans her boots.

But already the neighbourhood is buzzing with the fame of this glamorous adventurer. Four colleens arrive with gifts—eggs, butter, a cut of cake, and a boiled pullet, opportune victim of the curate's jaunting-car. Hard at their heels reappears the Widow Quin—the Playboy has now gathered a chorus of no less than five admirers. In answer to their questions, he again describes his killing of his father, more picturesquely than ever. The beguiling widow has already got his arm in hers, when Pegeen returns and scatters her rivals to the winds. Sternly she warns Christy of the dangers of chattering 'with a pack of wild girls the like of them do be walking abroad with the peelers, talking whispers at the fall of night'. And then comes a touch of that Irish ruthlessness of which Pegeen will show a good deal more before the end.

Christy (*with terror*).   And you're thinking they'd tell?
Pegeen (*with mock sympathy*).   Who knows, God help you?
Christy (*loudly*).   What joy would they have to bring hanging to the likes of me?
Pegeen.   It's queer joys they have, and who knows the thing they'd do, if it'd make the green stones cry itself to think of you swaying and swiggling at the butt of a rope, and you with a fine, stout neck, God bless you! the way you'd be a half an hour, in great anguish, getting your death.

It takes Christy a deal of coaxing flattery before he can calm her angry jealousy. Then Shawn Keogh reappears, with the Widow Quin; both equally interested in detaching Christy from Pegeen. Shawn turns to bribery. Having decoyed Pegeen from the room, he offers Christy half of a ticket to the Western States, together with his new hat, his new coat, his breeches, and his blessing to boot, if only his rival will decamp. And the Widow suggests that at least Christy should try wearing these fine clothes for the country-sports that day. He goes out to put them on; and in his absence the Widow asks the desperate Shawn what he will give *her* if she rids him of this dangerous rival.

Widow Quin.   Aye. Would you give me the red cow you have and the mountainy ram, and the right of way across your rye path, and a load of dung at Michaelmas, and turbary[1] upon the western hill?

[1] The right to cut turf or peat.

Shawn (*radiant with hope*). I would, surely, and I'd give you the wedding ring I have, and the loan of a new suit, the way you'd have him decent on the wedding-day. I'd give you two kids for your dinner, and a gallon of poteen, and I'd call the piper on the long car to your wedding from Crossmolina or from Ballina. I'd give you . . .

Widow Quin. That'll do, so, and let you whisht, for he's coming now again.

Then poor Shawn goes out to measure the racecourse on the sands.

But hardly has Christy returned, gorgeous in his new finery, than to his horror his dead father enters, with a bandaged head. Christy darts behind a door. The Widow sends the old man chasing off on a false scent; and Christy in his turn begs her to help him, despite this unlooked-for disaster, in winning Pegeen.

Widow Quin (*looks at him for a moment*). If I aid you, will you swear to give me a right of way I want, and a mountainy ram, and a load of dung at Michaelmas, the time that you'll be master here?

Christy. I will, by the elements and stars of night.

Widow Quin. Then we'll not say a word of the old fellow, the way Pegeen won't know your story till the end of time.

High diplomacy—rather like Bismarck's reinsurance alliance with Russia, when Germany was already allied with Austria.

In Act III Christy, inspired by his new self-confidence, has carried all before him at the races—a very similar festivity to that which Synge described watching on the Kerry coast.[1] The Playboy has won as prizes some bagpipes, and a fiddle, and a blackthorn stick, as well as the admiration of the whole countryside. And now, intoxicated with triumph, he turns in earnest, the moment he is alone with her, to woo Pegeen. This brings the poetic climax of the whole audacious play.

Christy (*looking at her with delight*). I'll have great times if I win the crowning prize I'm seeking now, and that's your promise that you'll wed me in a fortnight, when our banns is called.

Pegeen (*backing away from him*). You've right daring to go ask me that, when all knows you'll be starting to some girl in your own townland, when your father's rotten in four months, or five.

[1] p. 156.

Christy (*indignantly*). Starting from you, is it? (*He follows her.*) I will not, then, and when the airs is warming, in four months or five, it's then yourself and me should be pacing Neifin[1] in the dews of night, the times sweet smells do be rising, and you'd see a little, shiny new moon, maybe, sinking on the hills.

Pegeen (*looking at him playfully*). And it's that kind of a poacher's love you'd make, Christy Mahon, on the sides of Neifin, when the night is down?

Christy. It's little you'll think if my love's a poacher's, or an earl's itself, when you'll feel my two hands stretched around you, and I squeezing kisses on your puckered lips, till I'd feel a kind of pity for the Lord God is all ages sitting lonesome in His golden chair.

Pegeen. That'll be right fun, Christy Mahon, and any girl would walk her heart out before she'd meet a young man was your like for eloquence, or talk at all.

Christy (*encouraged*). Let you wait, to hear me talking, till we're astray in Erris,[2] when Good Friday's by, drinking a sup from a well, and making mighty kisses with our wetted mouths, or gaming in a gap of sunshine, with yourself stretched back unto your necklace, in the flowers of the earth.

Pegeen (*in a low voice, moved by his tone*). I'd be nice so, is it?

Christy (*with rapture*). If the mitred bishops seen you that time, they'd be the like of the holy prophets, I'm thinking, do be straining the bars of Paradise to lay eyes on the Lady Helen of Troy, and she abroad, pacing back and forward, with a nosegay in her golden shawl.[3]

Pegeen (*with real tenderness*). And what is it I have, Christy Mahon, to make me fitting entertainment for the like of you, that has such poet's talking, and such bravery of heart?

Did Irish peasants ever talk quite like that? I do not know. I have doubts. But then did Scottish kings ever talk like Macbeth; or Africans like Othello?

---

[1] Nephin (2646 ft.), 10 miles N. of Castlebar.

[2] The barony of Erris, 'as lonely a region as Ireland can show', lies W. of Ballycastle.

[3] This introduction of Greek Helen might be criticized as too literary for a Munster peasant. Yet the blind peasant-poet Raftery (d. about 1840) likewise loved such blendings of the classical with the Gaelic. 'I am death that has hidden hundreds: Hannibal, Pompey, Julius Caesar; I was in the way with Queen Helen. I made Hector fall, that conquered the Greeks, and Conchubar that was king of Ireland.' 'She beats Deirdre in the beauty of her voice; or I might say Helen, Queen of the Greeks, she for whose sake hundreds died at Troy.'

Now Pegeen's father, the pothouse-keeper, reels home drunken from his all-night wake, with eloquence of a more forcible kind.

Michael (*to Christy*).   The blessing of God and the holy angels on your head, young fellow. I hear tell you're after winning all in the sports below; and wasn't it a shame I didn't bear you along with me to Kate Cassidy's wake, a fine, stout lad, the like of you, for you'd never see the match of it for flows of drink, the way when we sunk her bones at noonday in her narrow grave, there were five men, aye, and six men, stretched out retching speechless on the holy stones.

Then his daughter breaks it to him that she wants to marry Christy instead of Shawn.

Michael (*loudly, with horror*).   You'd be making him a son to me, and he wet and crusted with his father's blood?

Pegeen.   Aye. Wouldn't it be a bitter thing for a girl to go marrying the like of Shaneen, and he a middling kind of a scarecrow, with no savagery or fine words in him at all?

Michael (*gasping and sinking on a chair*).   Oh, aren't you a heathen daughter to go shaking the fat of my heart, and I swamped and drownded with the weight of drink! . . . Have you not a word to aid me, Shaneen? Are you not jealous at all?

Shaneen (*in great misery*).   I'd be afeard to be jealous of a man did slay his da. . . .

Pegeen (*playfully*).   And you think you're a likely beau to go straying along with, the shiny Sundays of the opening year, when its sooner on a bullock's liver you'd put a poor girl thinking than on the lily or the rose?

Shawn.   And have you no mind of my weight of passion, and the holy dispensation, and the drift[1] of heifers I'm giving, and the golden ring?

Pegeen.   I'm thinking you're too fine for the like of me, Shawn Keogh of Killakeen, and let you go off till you'd find a radiant lady with droves of bullocks on the plains of Meath, and herself bedizened in the diamond jewelleries of Pharaoh's ma.

Indeed the wretched Shawn makes so poor a show that even Pegeen's father turns against such a poltroon.

Michael (*to Christy*).   It's many would be in dread to bring your like into their house for to end them, maybe, with a sudden end; but I'm a decent man of Ireland, and I'd liefer face the grave untimely and I

---

[1] 'Drove.'

seeing a score of grandsons growing up little gallant swearers by the name of God, than go peopling my bedside with puny weeds the like of what you'd breed, I'm thinking, out of Shaneen Keogh. (*He joins their hands.*)

But now Christy's own father, having picked up the trail again, rushes in, knocks his son down, and begins to beat him. With a fickle shift of all their sympathies, Pegeen and the crowd burst into jeers at this impostor who had so impudently claimed to be a parricide—'an ugly liar was playing off the hero and the fright of men'. Goaded to desperation by lost love and tarnished glory, Christy in his turn picks up a loy (a kind of spade), chases his father through the door, and strikes him down in turn. This time the crowd think the old man is really killed. But not even that can regain Christy their capricious sympathy. Things seen are sometimes mightier than things heard; but sometimes they look uglier. An old man struck down by his son with a spade is not particularly pretty. So the villagers come bursting in to secure Christy with a noosed rope. And since some of them are too drunk, and Shawn too cowardly, to drop the noose over his head, it is left to Pegeen herself to do it; like Brutus stabbing Caesar, or the Nurse slipping the strait-jacket on to the Captain in Strindberg's *Father*.

There is a violent struggle, as Christy hooks his legs fast round the table, and bites Shawn in the calf. In vain. Pegeen has blown a peat to redness, and burns Christy's own leg to make him let go. But now Christy's father comes crawling in once more. The crowd flee in terror from this ghastly, bleeding spectre. The old man sets his son at liberty; and the hopeful pair go tramping off together side by side.

Mahon (*grimly, loosening Christy*). My son and myself will be going our own way, and we'll have great times from this out telling stories of the villainy of Mayo, and the fools is here. (*To Christy, who is freed.*) Come on now. . . .

Christy. Ten thousand blessings upon all that's here, for you've turned me a likely gaffer in the end of all, the way I'll go romancing through a romping lifetime from this hour to the dawning of the judgment day.

But the last word is Pegeen's cry of regret, as she boxes Shawn's ears—'Quit my sight! Oh, my grief, I've lost him surely. I've lost the only Playboy of the Western World.'[1]

It is interesting that Synge originally planned the resurrection of old Mahon to occur at the very door of the chapel where Christy was to wed Pegeen.[2] But in the end it seemed better to keep the unity of place (scene-shifting was difficult for the Abbey Theatre).

Similarly the play was originally planned to begin in the ploughed field where Christy struck down his father. But, again, the tiny Abbey stage would have found it difficult to render that 'wide, windy corner of high distant hills'. And it would have meant another change of scene. As Ibsen also found, the unities have solid advantages.

In the original scheme, too, after Act I in the potato-field, and Act II in a pothouse where Christy boastfully related his parricide three times over, in Act III Christy was elected county councillor, made a speech from a table, proudly recording his murder yet again, and was just telling how he split his father's head, when the old father himself walked disgusted out of the meeting—'You're a bloody liar, that's what you are.' In the end Christy slunk away, exposed and derided, while a ballad-singer, who had already immortalized his deed in verse, strolled off to exploit this master-piece in other parts of the country, where the sorry truth was not yet known.

Clearly all this is vastly improved in the play's present form; not only by adopting the unities, but also by replacing Christy's prosaic

---

[1] Dr Walter Starkie (*Pirandello*, 2nd ed. 1937, p. 13) has pointed out a distant but not uninteresting parallel to the central paradox of *The Playboy* in Chiarelli's *La Maschera e Il Volto* (*The Mask and The Face*), written in 1914. A husband, Paolo, avers to his friends that he would kill his wife, Savina, if he found her unfaithful. Soon after he does find her unfaithful; feels he must, at least in appearance, live up to his protestations; and so, while pretending to have killed his wife, sends her secretly away. He is tried for murder, and acquitted amid general admiration for his resolute character, like that showered on Christy Mahon. A body thought to be Savina's is found in a lake, and given an elaborate funeral. But Savina has returned, veiled, to her husband; at the funeral, her lover recognizes her; and so, to avoid new prosecution, for contempt of court, Paolo and his wife flee. 'As long as they thought I had killed my wife, they left me at liberty; now, when they find I have *not* killed her, they will put me in prison.'

[2] Compare *Jane Eyre.*

election as a county councillor with his romantic love and loss of Pegeen. Strange how simple brain-work and revision have sometimes made silk purses out of what were, to begin with, the most unpromising of sows' ears.

Revision in plenty there was with *The Playboy*. Act I reached draft 'G'; Act II got as far as 'I'; Act III as 'K'. But it was labour well spent. And it seems to me another great improvement that, in Synge's final version, Christy Mahon no longer creeps out crestfallen, but departs exultant at having found himself 'a likely gaffer in the end of all, the way I'll go romancing through a romping lifetime to the dawning of the judgment day'.

This is comic enough; but there is also the note of tragedy in Pegeen's final cry for the love she has wantonly thrown away.

The Playboy remains in many ways a farce, full of exaggerations and improbabilities. But so is Voltaire's *Candide*, or Titania's infatuation with Bottom, or the adventures of Falstaff. Beneath lies the bitter truth that human romanticism can often become grotesque. To idolize a young man for killing his father may be fantastic; but is it any more fantastic than the incorrigible tendency of the human race through history to idolize men for killing millions of sons and fathers—like Alexander or Caesar, Charles XII, Napoleon, or Stalin? Murder one man and you are hanged; murder millions, and you are deified. Gallows or apotheosis—it is merely a question of quantity.

But, quite apart from its moral satire, the play lives by its *diablerie*, its ironic humour, its glory of imaginative language—now lovely, now ludicrous. Who indeed would have conceived it possible to stand the *Oedipus* of Sophocles on its head, and write a play about a man cast out into ignominious exile, not, this time, for having killed his father, but for *not* having killed him?[1]

---

[1] In *Conversations with Kafka* Gustav Janouch records a curious comment by that writer: 'The revolt of the son against the father is one of the primeval themes of literature, and an even older problem in the world. Dramas and tragedies are written about it, yet in reality it is material for comedy. The Irishman Synge was right in realizing this. In his play *The Playboy of the Western World* the son is an adolescent exhibitionist who boasts of having murdered his father. Then along comes the old man and turns the young conqueror of paternal authority into a figure of fun.'

To call *The Playboy*, as George Moore did, 'the most significant play of the last two hundred years' seems typical George Moore extravagance. But the play remains extraordinary fun; perhaps even better—unless it is quite superbly acted—to read than to see. For its greatest quality is literary—its eloquence.

As literature, *The Playboy* remains a miraculous example of the power of style. If the drama were translated into Cockney or Lancashire, and set in Whitechapel or Wigan, as the glorification of a teddy-boy, it would become, for me, absolutely loathsome. But, as it is, the smell of stale poteen in it is blown away by the winds off the Atlantic; the ugliness of the real facts is lost in the unconscious humour of a primitive simplicity, in the lilt of an imaginative poetry as different from our urban vulgarity as the clouds of Connemara from the smog of our abominable industrialism, drifting across its grimy deserts of brick-and-mortar. Synge's own preface to *The Playboy* puts all this admirably; and should never be forgotten by all who care for style. In one paragraph Synge says, I think, far more of value about poetic language than Wordsworth and Coleridge together, in their dozens of muddled pages; and says it in prose vastly more vivid than theirs.

In writing *The Playboy of the Western World*, as in my other plays, I have used one or two words only that I have not heard among the country people of Ireland, or spoken in my own nursery before I could read the newspapers. . . . Anyone who has lived in real intimacy with the Irish peasantry will know that the wildest sayings and ideas in this play are tame indeed, compared with the fancies one may hear in any little hillside cabin in Geesala, or Carraroe, or Dingle Bay.[1] All art is a collaboration; and there is little doubt that in the happy ages of literature, striking and beautiful phrases were as ready to the story-teller's or the playwright's

---

Such rather hasty dogmatisms of Kafka's are apt to be treated by his devotees as pieces of oracular profundity. But why should revolts of the younger generation be comic rather than tragic? Does not all depend on treatment? Is there much comic about *Oedipus, Lear, Père Goriot, Fathers and Sons, The Master Builder*; or such real-life tragedies as that of King Henry II? Indeed Kafka's own life was lastingly darkened by the shadow of paternal authority. Conceivably he pretended this theme was essentially comic just in order to forget how tragic it had really proved for himself.

[1] This may leave most readers a little sceptical. Synge was surely too modest.

hand, as the rich cloaks and dresses of his time. It is probable that when the Elizabethan dramatist took his ink-horn and sat down to his work he used many phrases that he had just heard, as he sat at dinner, from his mother or his children. . . . When I was writing *The Shadow of the Glen*, some years ago, I got more aid than any learning could have given me from a chink in the floor of the old Wicklow house[1] where I was staying, that let me hear what was being said by the servant girls in the kitchen. . . . In the modern literature of towns, however, richness is found only in sonnets, or prose poems, or in one or two elaborate books that are far away from the profound and common interests of life. One has, on one side, Mallarmé and Huysmans producing this literature; and on the other, Ibsen and Zola dealing with the reality of life in joyless and pallid words. . . . In a good play every speech should be as fully flavoured as a nut or apple, and such speeches cannot be written by anyone who works among people who have shut their lips on poetry. In Ireland, for a few years more, we have a popular imagination that is fiery, and magnificent, and tender; so that those of us who wish to write start with a chance that is not given to writers in places where the spring-time of the local life has been forgotten, and the harvest is a memory only, and the straw has been turned into bricks.[2]

All that is terribly true—truer than even Synge could know. How true, can be fully seen only now, as we look back, after another fifty years of city-sprawl, cheap newspapers, and radio vulgarization.

But, of course, it would be extremely unjust to Synge to take him too much at his word and imagine that he just went round Ireland with a notebook, recording good phrases and pasting them together

---

[1] Tomrilands House, Co. Wicklow.

[2] Here, in illustration of what Synge says about the popular imagination, are some phrases from Tomás Ó Crohan, *The Islandman* (published in Irish, 1929; translated by R. Flower, 1951): 'a heavy mist descended, so that you couldn't see to put your finger in your eye'—(of a man elated) 'he could have trodden on a shell-less egg without breaking it'—'she went on to explain the whole affair to us, like a woman reciting a litany, till she had the whole lot of us as tame as a cat.' Still livelier is Maurice O'Sullivan (*Twenty years a-growing*, translated by Moya Llewelyn Davies and George Thomson, 1933)—'at sparrows' chirp'—'the blackness and blindness of the night'—'I gave my heels to the road'—'Great God of Virtues, I cried, where am I?'—'I put a listening ear on myself'—'after three weeks of drilling I swear by the book my bones were sore from my little toe to the roots of my hair'—'but the old women who come in to you have great mouths on them for gossip'—'when I heard her say "dear" I started up like a cat you would call to its milk.'

Both men lived on the Blaskets, off Kerry. (Compare p. 154, note.)

into plays. The life and lilt of his diction were also the product of endless pains. David Greene[1] has excellently illustrated the superiority of Synge's afterthoughts, from the opening lines of *The Playboy* where Pegeen writes her order to Castlebar. In the first draft this ran, dully enough: 'Two dozens of Power's Whiskey. Three barrels of porter, two bottles of hops. To be sent by Timmy Farrel's creel-cart on the evening of the coming fair to Mister Michael James Flaherty.' How stuffy and boring!

Then Synge realized that it would be much more lively and attractive for his heroine to be writing, not merely of prosaic whisky and porter, but of her own bridal trousseau. So, after various further changes, the final version became: 'Six yards of stuff for to make a yellow gown. A pair of lace boots with lengthy heels on them and brassy eyes. A hat is suited for a wedding-day. A fine tooth comb. To be sent with three barrels of porter in Jimmy Farrel's creel cart on the evening of the coming fair to Mister Michael James Flaherty.'

The dawn of romance; but, alas, a false dawn.

Nor again was it by any means at one stroke that Christy's famous sentence about the holy prophets in Paradise and the Lady Helen of Troy attained its final imaginativeness and melody.

Like Shakespeare, Synge triumphs first and foremost by his magic style; secondly by his characters. Our generation mass-produces books in wagon-loads on Shakespeare's ideas. One need not go to the opposite extreme of Shaw and Tolstoy, in treating Shakespeare's ideas as mainly stupid or wicked. But I continue to believe Shakespeare's ideas to be really of minor importance compared with his verbal enchantments. Shakespeare was far more musician than thinker. As a thinker he seems often perfunctory, sometimes foolish. Prospero remains childish beside Montaigne or Bacon; but Prospero is an enchanter, and they are not. So with Synge.

George Moore, hearing of the Abbey Theatre riots, wired for a copy of *The Playboy*. He was, he says (being an ardent realist), convinced by its very first words—Pegeen's orders for her trousseau from Castlebar—that Ireland had here, at last, produced a masterpiece. 'Never,' he says, 'was there such a picture of peasant life in a

[1] *Journal of English and Germanic Philology*, xlvi (1947), 199 ff.

few lines.' Enthusiastic; but there is perhaps something in it. Moore would, indeed, have liked certain changes, to keep the note of comedy, in Act III. But Synge replied that he had already written this third act thirteen times. He would not write it a fourteenth.

In the end Moore came to think him right. Moore's comments on the second run of the play are also interesting. In the original production Christy Mahon had been played by Willie Fay, who was a little man, too weedy, seedy, and forlorn to fit the part. The second production succeeded better because Christy was now acted by a more attractive youth—as is obviously essential. A Playboy should be a Playboy, even if absurd—one who *can* 'go romancing through a romping lifetime'. No doubt, Christy enters as a pitiable figure; but it is absolutely essential that he should flower into a vital one. Dramatists are terribly at the mercy of unperceptive actors and producers.

Deirdre of the Sorrows
(written 1908-9, performed 1910)

> 'Had not God
> Turned upside-down the happiness of Troy,
> We should have lain forgot, instead of giving
> Songs to the poets of the after-time.'
>
> EURIPIDES, *The Trojan Women*

> 'After great fire
> Great frost
> Comes following. . . .
>
> By Grainne
> Of high Ben Gulbain in the North,
> Was Diarmuid lost.
>
> The strong sons of Uisneac,
> Who never submitted,
> They fell by Deirdre.'
>
> JAMES STEPHENS

This tragedy was unfinished, after more than fifteen drafts, when Synge died. He had probably put into the heart of the ageing Conchubor, in love with the young Deirdre, some of the anguish of his own love for the young actress, Molly Allgood. Like Conchubor, he was never to win the girl he had sought so long, and guarded so anxiously. But there is said to be no truth in Yeats's picturesque story (though he claimed to have it from Molly Allgood herself) that she acted some scenes in the dying poet's hospital room, to help his last efforts at finishing the play.

Deirdre is a straight tragedy, on one of the famous love-legends of the world. Synge's main source seems to have been a version by an eighteenth-century Irish poet, first printed in 1898, and apparently translated into English by Synge himself during his first visit, that year, to Aran.

His chief change seems to lie in making Naisi and Deirdre return from Alban to Ulster and the treacherous trap laid for them by King Conchubor, not (as in the source) because they are the king's passive dupes, but because both lovers dread the passing of the years,[1] the coming of white hair, the fading of their love. This makes at least a more active and tragic motivation. One may compare the lovers in Ibsen's *Love's Comedy* who prefer to break their romance altogether rather than see it fade.

Hitherto Synge had not ventured into the past except, very vaguely, in *The Well of the Saints*, which is simply dated 'One or more centuries ago'. And some rough notes written by him in early 1908, when planning a play on some Irish saint, perhaps St Kevin, take a rather pessimistic view both of poetic drama and of historic drama.

The moment the sense of historical truth awoke in Europe historical fiction became impossible. . . . Now it is impossible to use our own language or feelings with perfect sincerity for personages we know to have been different from ourselves. Hence historical fiction insincere. . . .

The real world is mostly unpoetical; fiction even in poetry is not totally sincere, hence failure of modern poetry. This is to be taken with all reserve—there is always the poet's dream which makes itself a sort of world where it is kept a dream. Is this possible on the stage? I think not. Maeterlinck, *Pelléas and Mélisande*? Is the drama as a beautiful thing a lost art? The drama of swords is. Few of us except soldiers have seen swords in use; to drag them out on the stage is babyish. . . . For the present the only possible beauty in drama is peasant drama. For the future we must await the making of life beautiful again before we can have beautiful drama. You cannot gather grapes of chimney-pots.

Here Synge is questioning two different things—first, the possibility of writing poetic plays in an unpoetic age; second, the possibility of writing imaginative works about the past.

That poetic drama has become extremely difficult, seems obvious. The fifty years since Synge wrote have produced little to confute

---

[1] A thought that haunted Synge, whose own years were to be so few. Compare the passages from *The Shadow of the Glen* and *The Well of the Saints* quoted on pp. 175, 195, 196.

him. Still Ibsen, Strindberg, and Synge himself had at least succeeded in producing plays where life is transfigured at intervals—sometimes for long intervals—by the light of poetry.

It seems also true that, the more we acquire a sense of history, the more difficult it becomes to write historic fiction or drama. There is the paradoxical contradiction that in some ways human nature seems never to change; in others, to change constantly. We may feel that we vividly understand characters as old as Chaucer, as Homer even; and yet even successive generations often find each other incomprehensible. The modern young tend to feel quite alien to the poetry of 1914, even to the poetry of the thirties; we cannot even conceive the mentality of Victorian ladies who thought it 'excessively improper' to travel by train, where one might have to sit opposite a complete stranger; and the men chronicled by Gregory of Tours or Ailred of Rievaulx appear as remote in their notions and emotions as if they had landed from another planet. How then, it may be argued, can we hope really to portray characters at any distance from us in the mists of time? Imagination, no doubt, can sometimes do wonders. Happy intuition might conceivably grasp with some correctness even the mind of a caveman. But it would remain a guess. We could never know whether it *was* correct.

To this a cynic might answer: 'Why this fuss about understanding the past, when we do not really understand even our contemporaries, even ourselves? Why this bother about historic truth, when the ordinary reader or playgoer rarely cares a rap about historic truth, provided he is entertained?'

There may be truth in this. Much historical fiction or drama may be only pleasant dreams, alluring shadows, far from any reality that ever existed. But Synge's scrupulously truthful mind was clearly bothered by the problem. Part of the difficulty he avoided by taking a subject not historic, but legendary and remote, like those of Greek tragedy. There remained that other standing difficulty in re-creating the past—the language. For if too archaic, it estranges; if too modern, it jars. The only safe compromise seems a style neither obtrusively ancient nor obtrusively up to date.

For *Deirdre* Synge adopted this compromise in an unusual form. He used a diction based—though often heightened and distanced—

on that of his own peasant plays. There were precedents—Lady Gregory had employed the dialect of her Kiltartan countryside for retelling the heroic legends of Ireland, or for translating Molière; Yeats and Moore had a similar idea in collaborating on a tragedy about Diarmuid and Grania.

It is an experiment in style that could hardly be often repeated without seeming too artificial; yet here, for the nonce, I think it succeeds. Synge's *Deirdre* seems much more vividly alive than the parallel plays by Yeats and by A. E. And it avoids almost wholly that colloquial modern vulgarity too often shed by writers like Shaw over the figures of the past like Jeanne d'Arc; and too often thought piquant by modern translators of the classics.

In Homer, so far from princes talking like swineherds, swineherds talk like princes. He composed, I imagine, for aristocratic ears. Yet Homer's Princess Nausicaa does go to wash the family-linen without losing one jot of her dignity. This worried the eighteenth century: but it delights us. And just as it seems perfectly right in that primitive world for Nausicaa to wash clothes like a country girl, so here it seems perfectly right for Deirdre to talk like one. The style of Synge's tragedy remains intimate enough for sympathy, yet remote enough to keep his characters strange, with that mysterious, essential strangeness of a past for ever gone.

The old legend is grimly simple. Deirdre of the Sorrows was doomed, as foretold by Cathbad the Druid, to bring ruin on Ulster and on the three sons of Usna—Naisi, Ainnle, and Ardan. None the less the High King, Conchubor (whose supposed date is about the time of Christ), had the young Deirdre bred up to be his bride. But from this loveless match she fled with Naisi and his two brothers to Alban (Scotland). After seven years Conchubor lured them all back by false promises, and treacherously slaughtered the sons of Usna. Then Deirdre killed herself above her dead lover. It is one of those tragedies that tell of a doom that cannot be averted—that is accepted—that is even invited. A tragedy also, of the hopeless love of age for youth, which turns away, despite all consequences, to a lover that is young (as Henry VIII found to his cost with Katherine Howard).

Act I begins in the house of Lavarcham, Deirdre's nurse. The

High King comes to visit his betrothed; but the girl, wild, tameless creature, is out in the thunderous twilight, wandering alone high up the hills. The King falls listlessly to examining her workbox.

Lavarcham (*sinking into sadness again*).   I'm in dread so they were right she'd bring destruction on the world, for it's a poor thing when you see a settled man putting the love he has for a young child, and the love he has for a full woman, on a girl the like of her; and it's a poor thing, Conchubor, to see a High King, the way you are this day, prying after her needles and numbering her lines of thread.

Already it grows apparent that this royal lover is far too much of a father—is courting not so much a bride as a disaster.

Deirdre enters with a bag of nuts and a bundle of twigs, indifferent as a squirrel to all the claims and splendours of royalty. She stands aghast when the king tells her that within two days or three she must become his queen. Conchubor goes out into the storm; then, with a sudden passionate whim, Deirdre bids her nurse take forth from chest and coffer the royal splendours that are to be hers.

Deirdre.   . . . Lay out your mats and hangings where I can stand this night and look about me. Lay out the skins of the rams of Connaught and of the goats of the west. I will not be a child, or plaything; I'll put on my robes that are the richest, for I will not be brought down to Emain as Cuchulain brings his horse to the yoke, or Conall Cearneach puts his shield upon his arm; and maybe from this day I will turn the men of Ireland like a wind blowing on the heath.

Suddenly Naisi and his brothers knock at the door for shelter—not by mere chance. For they had already encountered Deirdre on the hills, not knowing her, nor her destiny. Frankly and fearlessly, the girl tempts Naisi to carry her away.

Deirdre (*sitting in the high chair in the centre*).   Come to this stool, Naisi (*pointing to the stool*). If it's low itself the High King would sooner be on it this night than on the throne of Emain Macha. . . . You must not go, Naisi, and leave me to the High King, a man is ageing in his dun, with his crowds round him, and his silver and gold. (*More quickly*) I will not live to be shut up in Emain, and wouldn't we do well paying, Naisi, with silence and a near death? (*She stands up and walks away from him.*) I'm a long while in the woods with my own self, and I'm in little dread of death, and it earned with riches would make the sun red with envy, and he going up the heavens; and the moon pale and lonesome, and she wasting away. (*She comes to him and puts her hands on his shoulders.*) Isn't it a small thing is foretold about the ruin of ourselves, Naisi, when all men have age coming and great ruin in the end?

When Act II opens in Alban, seven years have gone. Now Lavarcham comes by sea to the tent of Deirdre and Naisi, with urgent warning that the High King has sent Fergus to lure the exiles home. At all costs Deirdre must make Naisi refuse the treacherous summons. But Deirdre, oppressed by her sense of fate, her dread of gnawing time which makes, in the end, all love decay, grows too numb to resist the inevitable. (One may recall, in the *Volsunga Saga*, the treacherous invitation of King Atli to the Niblungs; which they too accept with open eyes.)

Deirdre. I've dread going or staying, Lavarcham. It's lonesome this place, having happiness like ours, till I'm asking each day will this day match yesterday, and will tomorrow take a good place beside the same day in the year that's gone, and wondering all times is it a game worth playing, living on until you're dried and old, and our joy is gone for ever.

Lavarcham. If it's that ails you, I tell you there's little hurt getting old, though young girls and poets do be storming at the shapes of age. . . . Take my word and stop Naisi, and the day'll come you'll have more joy having the senses of an old woman and you with your little grandsons shrieking round you, than I'd have this night putting on the red mouth and the white arms you have, to go walking lonesome byeways with a gamey king.

One has always to remember that, like Rossetti's *King's Tragedy* about James I of Scotland, Synge's *Deirdre* was written by a man soon himself to die; and who doubless knew, or at least foreboded, that coming death. To deepen that bitterness of death, Synge was betrothed to the very actress who was to be his Deirdre on the stage—and, as it proved, in reality also. In the play's third act there is an open grave; that open grave must often have seemed to gape by the bedside of the doomed dramatist.

Now Fergus enters, a noble dupe, the High King's decoy, loaded with the lying parchments, seals, and promises that remain as current in the statecraft of the twentieth century as of the first. Coldly he reminds the homesick Naisi that no love endures, not even love for a Deirdre.

Fergus. . . . Listen now to what I'm saying. You'd do well to come back to men and women are your match and comrades, and not be lingering until the day that you'll grow weary, and hurt Deirdre showing her the hardness will grow up within your eyes. . . . You're here years and plenty to know it's truth I'm saying.

(*Deirdre comes out of tent with a horn of wine, she catches the beginning of Naisi's speech and stops with stony wonder.*)

Naisi (*very thoughtfully*). I'll not tell you a lie. There have been days a while past when I've been throwing a line for salmon or watching for the run of hares, that I've a dread upon me a day'd come I'd weary of her voice (*very slowly*) and Deirdre'd see I'd wearied.

Fergus (*sympathetic but triumphant*). I knew it, Naisi. . . . And, take my word, Deirdre's seen your dread and she'll have no peace from this out in the woods.

Naisi (*with confidence*). She's not seen it . . . Deirdre's no thought of getting old or wearied; it's that puts wonder in her ways, and she with spirits would keep bravery and laughter in a town with plague.

(*Deirdre drops the horn of wine and crouches down where she is.*)

From that instant her choice is taken—though it will mean destruction for them all. Very well—let them go back to Ulster, and die.

Deirdre. There's no place to stay always. . . . It's a long time we've had, pressing the lips together, going up and down, resting in our arms, Naisi, walking with the smell of June in the tops of the grasses, and listening to the birds in the branches that are highest. . . . It's a long time we've had, but the end has come, surely. . . . There's no safe place, Naisi, on the ridge of the world. . . . And it's in the quiet woods I've seen them digging our grave, throwing out the clay on leaves are bright and withered . . . and isn't it a better thing to be following on to a near death, than to be bending the head down and dragging with the feet, and seeing one day a blight showing upon love where it is sweet and tender? . . . There are as many ways to wither love as there are stars in a night of Samhain; but there is no way to keep life, or love with it, a short space only. . . . We're seven years without roughness or growing weary; seven years so sweet and shining, the gods would be hard set to give us seven days the like of them.

Act III opens in a shabby tent prepared for the exiles' welcome, outside the High King's palace at Emain. Once more Lavarcham tries to save Deirdre, by pretending to Conchubor that the beauty of his beloved has grown blowzed and withered with years of exile in the woods of Alban. But in vain. And now behind the tent's hangings Deirdre discovers an open, new-dug grave[1]; and in the shadows of the trees gather the warriors of Ulster. From outside comes the cry of Naisi's brothers as the steel trap closes on them. In vain Deirdre begs her lover not to leave her alone; but Naisi flings her off. Bitter words pass between them, for the first time, and the last. Then Naisi rushes out to fall. And above the three dead brothers, Deirdre speaks her last farewell.

Deirdre (*in a high and quiet tone*).   I have put away sorrow like a shoe that is worn out and muddy, for it is I have had a life that will be envied by great companies. It was not by a low birth I made kings uneasy, and they sitting in the halls of Emain. It was not a low thing to be chosen by Conchubor, who was wise, and Naisi had no match for bravery. It is not a small thing to be rid of grey hairs, and the loosening of the teeth. (*With a sort of triumph.*) It was the choice of lives we had in the clear woods, and in the grave we're safe, surely. . . . It's a pitiful thing to be talking out when your ears are shut to me. It's a pitiful thing, Conchubor, you have done this night in Emain; yet a thing will be a joy and triumph to the ends of life and time.
   (*She presses the knife into her heart and sinks into the grave.*)

'A pitiful thing . . . yet a thing will be a joy and triumph to the ends of life and time.'

That, surely, is often the keyword of tragedy itself—the sense that men and women remain finer than the blind forces that crush them into clay—so far finer, that the spectators watch their sorrows with a sense, not only of grief, but also of pride and triumph and exaltation in what human beings can be. I do not say that this is a truer formula for tragedy than Aristotle's famous 'purgation'. Both are true, in different aspects. Yet purgation seems no very poetic metaphor for describing poetry.

---

[1] It is said that Padraic Colum questioned the introduction of this grave on the stage; and that Synge replied that he had been close to death in hospital—'the grave was a reality to him, and it was the reality in the tragedy he was writing'.

Deirdre is, to me, a play with first-rate passages rather than a first-rate play. In fairness one must always remember that the piece was left unfinished; and unfinished at times, it feels. At moments the plot creaks; and, of the characters, perhaps only Deirdre herself and Conchubor are fully alive. None the less, there remain superb passages. Synge's tragedy is not, like *Macbeth*, a great crashing waterfall of doom; rather it is like a single jet of water from a mountain crag—cold and clear, with the bitter bleakness of the misty hills.

The style too seems at times half-finished—in such phrases as 'Conchubor'll be *in a blue stew* this night and herself abroad', or 'There's things a King can't have, Conchubor, and if you go *rampaging* this night you'll be *apt to win* nothing but death for many, and a *sloppy face of trouble* on your own self before the day will come'. But such lapses into the prosaic or the vulgar as 'blue stew', 'rampaging', 'apt to win', 'sloppy face of trouble' are exceptional, and might very possibly have been revised away. Blemishes of this kind are noticeably absent from the last pages of the piece, which remain among its best. Indeed, I do not know any poetic tragedy of the twentieth century with a style as satisfying, or an end as fine.

In one way Synge's *Deirdre* has a significance which its author can hardly have meant, but which seems there none the less. The Playboy of the Western World, though his heart is sore for Pegeen, still goes gaily off at the end to 'romance through a romping life-time'. No doubt that life-time will be full of hard knocks as well as romps. But all the same. . . . In contrast, Deirdre goes open-eyed to a self-sought doom. The peasant cries a buoyant 'Yes' to life; the princess, a tragic 'No'. In the eyes of the thorough-going pessimist, no doubt, who thinks death better than life, Deirdre's lot may still seem preferable, and her choice right. She has enjoyed her happy girlhood, her seven happy years in Alban; she has escaped the ignominies of old age. But most of us are, rightly or wrongly, not quite such pessimists. We may feel that the tragedy of Deirdre is yet one more tragedy of *hubris*. For she has rebelled against that law of life—Ibsen's 'Law of Change'—which says 'All things must pass; age must give place to youth; generation, to generation.' Surely some will find far wiser the warning of the old Lavarcham—'Take my word and stop Naisi, and the day'll come you'll have more joy having the senses of an old woman and you with your little grandsons shrieking round you, than I'd have this night putting on the red mouth and the white arms you have, to go walking lonesome byways with a gamey king.'

Deirdre, in short, is guilty of *hubris* against the most powerful of all gods, whose name is Time. Shakespeare perhaps was wiser—'Ripeness is all.' To Deirdre there apply very cogently those words of Macduff in *Macbeth*—'He has no children'. Had Deirdre borne children, she would not have been so hag-ridden by the thought that Naisi would come to care less for her; and the danger of his caring less for her would have lessened likewise. This, too, is one of the laws of life; which those who break, may break themselves. Whether Synge would have agreed I do not know. Yet he did put that wise speech in Lavarcham's mouth.[1] At all events, such seems to me the conclusion from the contrast that leaps up if you set *The Playboy of the Western World* and *Deirdre of the Sorrows* side by side. But both are excellent; the peasant lights up the princess, the princess the peasant.

If one asks what Synge himself really thought, perhaps the answer is that he was wise enough to see both points of view—both

---

[1] Mr Alan Price in his interesting *Synge and Anglo-Irish Drama* takes a much poorer view of Lavarcham. He talks of 'the flaw in her case', of her mingling of 'heroism, cowardice and pathos'. 'Lavarcham's existence is proof that life, once youth and love are gone, is nightmare, yet she clings to it.' 'She asserts, against all evidence and instinct, . . . that life may be tolerable if one comes to terms with it.'

All this seems a little romantic. What 'instinct' denies that one may come to tolerable terms with life? Whatever the elderly may lack, it is seldom the 'instinct' of self-preservation. And plenty of grandparents would passionately agree with Lavarcham. Indeed, if all mankind took Deirdre's view that one should die the moment passion passes its crowning rapture, the human race would long have disappeared, and Deirdre herself never have been born. Better so? Who can say? But there seems no evidence that such was the conclusion of Synge.

I doubt if he meant to take sides. He was intelligent enough to be fair to both. Lavarcham, like many a Greek chorus, puts the view of ordinary humanity and common sense. What she says, *is* true for many—though not, perhaps, for Deirdre. Lavarcham is the voice of Realism against Romance. Why, then, dub her coward and fool?

Synge in 1906 (from the pastel by James Paterson)

Yeats about 1902 (aged
about thirty-seven)

Yeats broadcasting

common sense like Lavarcham's and the opposite protest of Landor, which Landor's own tragic old age so bitterly exemplified:

> Is it not better at an early hour
>> In its calm cell to rest the weary head,
> While birds are singing, and while blooms the bower
>> Than sit the fire out and go starved to bed?

Better, certainly, to be extinguished once for all than to smoulder on like a dying log, whose feebly wavering smoke brings only tears to the eyes, but no warmth to the heart.

Most of Synge's work is a curious example of that often artificial and ridiculous, yet often admirable form, the pastoral.[1] For pastoral, Johnson felt limitless contempt. Yet when Johnson died, there was an odd, gaunt, dreamy boy at Hawkshead school who was to show once more that pastoral could become, not only one of the most artificial and precious forms, but also one of the most genuine and sincere—William Wordsworth. And in Edinburgh, on the threshold of a drab lawyer's office, stood a lame lad of seventeen whose Scottish rustics were to become immortal, while his gentlemen and ladies remained, always, a little sawdusty—Walter Scott. And in Ayrshire there was just starting to farm a youth of twenty-five, Robert Burns, whose rustic poetry in dialect was to endure, while his politer Anglicized verse fell still-born. Johnson himself lived long enough to recognize the sturdy worth of yet another pastoral-writer, George Crabbe from Aldeburgh. And Crabbe was still to be followed in this field by writers as lasting as Tennyson and Arnold, George Sand, George Eliot, and Thomas Hardy. Pastoral is not always to be despised.

From the time when big cities, such as Alexandria, first began, it was natural that some minds, like Theocritus with whom pastoral starts, should long for a return to Nature, to the open spaces, to simplicity. For it is human to see at last the value of things now lost. And as long as there is country to go back to—which may not be very long now—that impulse seems likely to recur. For big cities remain fundamentally abominable—cancers of mankind. In this

---

[1] The note of traditional pastoral is particularly clear in the surviving fragments of Synge's verse drama, *The Vernal Play* (1902).

pastoral tradition, so often moribund, yet so tenacious of life, Synge takes his place; and he belongs to the genuine side of it. For pastoral comes fully alive only in the hands of men who really know what they are talking about—who have lived in the rural world—not merely (like some Renaissance and eighteenth-century poets) gone to picnic there.[1]

Synge was himself no Playboy; as Irish writers not seldom have been, as Shaw, and even Yeats, tended at times to be—men talking through masks. Synge, like Chekhov, was more reticent and often, I feel, more deeply sincere. He has been condemned by Forrest Reid because 'his sympathies lay too exclusively with what is exceptional'. That seems to me the sort of dreary language fit for a business-manager, anxious to recruit for his corporation only 'well-rounded men', good mixers, full of 'togetherness'; and terrified lest a human individual, with a mind and personality of his own, should somehow slip into the ants' nest. Forrest Reid talks of Synge's 'intense, hard, narrow, bizarre talent'. To call Synge 'hard' seems to me unfair; but 'intense' he certainly could be. No doubt the field he covered in six plays, and thirty-eight years of life, was 'narrow' beside the range of Shakespeare, Scott, or Balzac. But it appears as pointless, and thankless, to bring this charge of narrowness against Synge as to bring it against Keats or Burns.

Fault has also been found with Synge because he left no school, no successful disciples. But why should it be a fault in a writer to stand lonely and unique? It is a schoolmasterly sort of criticism that judges poets by the number or success of their pupils. This, indeed, became a foible of that great inspector of schools, Matthew Arnold. He was constantly worrying whether writers were good *models*. So Milton in our day has had visited on his head the sins of his eighteenth-century children—as if even Homer and Shakespeare had not given rise to deplorable imitators. Synge's worth is not a whit less because he remains a figure of solitude.

Synge had no pretensions as a philosopher. He was a humorous pessimist. His plots seem slight—a pair of tinkers who try to get

---

[1] It is interesting, however, that Synge—so Yeats told Francis Bickley—had come by the date of *Deirdre* to say he was sick of Irish stage-peasants, and was thinking of a play about Dublin slums (a foreshadowing of Sean O'Casey).

married, and fail; an old woman who loses her sons at sea; a peasant's wife who runs off with a tramp; two old people who are cured of blindness, and dislike it; a lad who claims to have killed his father, and finds he has not; an elderly king who sees his betrothed elope with a youth, and brings them both to their deaths. Even Synge's characters, though vividly alive, do not leave the stage to inhabit our imaginations as eternal types, like Antigone, Hamlet, Falstaff, or Rebecca West. They simply possess vitality, and are true to their own selves; as their author was to his. Perhaps Synge's greatest achievements were that he found a new corner of the world to write of; took the trouble to know thoroughly what he wrote of; and worded his writing in a style both new and bewitching. Indeed I do not know any dramatist whose success depends quite so pre-eminently on the magic of his style. It is fifty years since I first heard the language of Synge in a paper read by a master to a literary society at school. It was instant intoxication. And from that day to this, its enchantment has never failed or staled.

Synge may be narrow; he may be minor. But there are certain minor writers—such as Sappho, or Beddoes—who remain, none the less, unique.[1] There are certain combinations of qualities to be found in them alone. If you miss such writers, you will go to your grave having missed something, a certain kind of savour, that you will find nowhere else. So it is a pity to go through life without ever tasting Synge, who so admirably deserved his name—that name which the melodious voice of an ancestor had won, according to the story, from Henry Tudor four centuries before.

[1] There is interest in the judgements of Raleigh (who, like the Johnson he admired, was refreshingly unacademic): 'There's a man called Synge, a dramatist, who's a jewel. Speaks Irish. Very unlike Yeats; much more *to* him' (1905). And again, in 1920: 'If you want to read a great living English author, read Thomas Hardy, if you want to read an author of twenty times Bernard Shaw's imagination, who combines truth and imagination in dealing with Ireland, read J. M. Synge.'

PART III

William Butler Yeats

'All is bot gaistis and elriche fantasies,
Of brouneis and bogillis full this buke.'

GAVIN DOUGLAS

'Be not so desolate
Because thy dreams have flown
And the hall of the heart is empty
And silent as stone,
As age left by children
Sad and alone.

Those delicate children,
Thy dreams, still endure:
All pure and lovely things
Wend to the Pure.
Sigh not: unto the fold
Their way was sure.'

A. E.

INTRODUCTION

'And they said one to another, Behold, this dreamer cometh.'

Genesis, xxxvii, 19

In Shaw's excellent play, *John Bull's Other Island* (written 1904)—so much more genuine than a lot of his later work—occurs one of the truest, yet most romantic passages, which this mocking realist ever wrote.

Larry Doyle, the hard-headed Irishman, is arguing in London with that well-meaning Liberal optimist, that beef-witted John Bull, Tom Broadbent. And what Doyle here says of Ireland vividly applies both to some characters in Synge (another realistic Irishman) and, even more, to that highly romantic Irishman, Yeats himself.

Doyle. Rosscullen! oh, good Lord, Rosscullen! The dullness! the hopelessness! the ignorance! the bigotry!

Broadbent. The usual thing in this country, Larry. Just the same here.

Doyle. No, no: the climate is different. Here, if the life is dull, you can be dull too, and no great harm done. But your wits can't thicken in that soft moist air, on those white springy roads, in those misty rushes and brown bogs, on those hillsides of granite rocks and magenta heather. You've no such colours in the sky, no such lure in the distances, no such sadness in the evenings. Oh, the dreaming! the dreaming! the torturing, heartscalding, never satisfying dreaming, dreaming, dreaming! No debauchery that ever coarsened and brutalized an Englishman can take the worth and usefulness out of him like that dreaming. An Irishman's imagination never lets him alone, never convinces him, never satisfies him; but it makes him that he can't face reality nor deal with it nor handle it nor conquer it. . . . If you want to interest him in Ireland you've got to call the unfortunate island Kathleen ni Hoolihan[1] and pretend she's a little old woman. It saves thinking. It saves working. It saves everything except imagination, imagination, imagination. . . .

It is a piece of eloquence that has long clung in my memory.

[1] Was Shaw perhaps thinking in particular of Yeats's play so named, produced two years before, in 1902?

Exaggerated? No doubt—for when did Shaw refrain from exaggerations?[1] One may also smile a little at Larry Doyle's rhetorical passion for the Ciceronian artifice of constantly saying things in triplets— 'Oh, the dreaming! the dreaming! the torturing, heartscalding, never satisfying dreaming, dreaming, dreaming!' 'It saves thinking. It saves working. It saves everything except imagination, imagination, imagination.'

All the same the passage may well impress anyone who has read Irish history, or walked Irish hills, where the clouds off the Atlantic build skies castled with shapes and colours of a forlorn, magic melancholy that English heavens seldom see. And it gives a very living picture of one side of Yeats.

Of course Yeats might justly have retorted that on occasion he had 'handled reality' most effectively (for example, the troubles of the Irish theatre); and that his life-work was uncommonly full of 'worth and usefulness'. He could also have riposted that Shaw himself, with his jaunty, prosaic brilliance, would have been all the better for a little more sense of poetry and dream. Indeed, Yeats once had an amusing dream-vision of Shaw as a clicking, shiny sewing-machine—'but the incredible thing was that the machine smiled, smiled perpetually'. Similarly Yeats detested Shaw's *Arms and the Man*—'it seemed to me inorganic, logical straightness and not the crooked road of life, and I stood aghast before its energy'. (Yeats associated the crooked with intuition, which he loved, and straightness with logic, which he hated.) Yet one may wonder whether life's road must always be 'crooked'; and must admit that, whatever its 'straightness', Shaw's play marched, as efficiently as a Roman legion along a Roman way, to a more decisive conquest of the stage than any drama ever written by Yeats; simply because it contained, not dreams, but vividly real characters, a vigorously amusing plot, witty dialogue, and some very true ideas.

[1] Such as the prediction in his preface that, once the Irish were free, 'the Catholic laity will make as short work of sacerdotal tyranny in Ireland as it has done in France and Italy. . . . Home Rule will herald the day when the Vatican will go the way of Dublin Castle.' After forty years, not much sign of that! On the other hand the Rosscullens of today are, it appears, still being bought up and 'developed'; though now by Germans—not by Mr Tom Broadbent, but by Herr Thomas Breitbogen.

In fine, the two men were temperamental opposites. Yeats, the follower of Blake, could have little in common with Shaw the follower of Marx. True, they both admired William Morris. But that great man was like a mountain; they could admire him from opposite sides. Both also admired Synge. But when, in 1905, Yeats generously praised Synge's way of writing, one notes with amusement how (as so often with critics) it is qualities much more his own that Yeats finds and praises in the style of Synge. 'It perfectly fits the drifting emotion, the dreaminess, the vague yet measureless desire, for which he would create a dramatic form. It blurs definition, clear edges, everything that comes from the will, it turns imagination from all that is of the present, like a gold background in a religious picture, and it strengthens in every emotion whatever comes to it from far off, from brooding memory and dangerous hope.' But is Synge really like that? Do not his plays succeed, on the contrary, because they are so full, also, of emotions that were *not* 'drifting'; of desires that were *not* 'vague'; of edges that were *not* 'blurred'; of imaginations that were *not* 'far off'? For Synge, enchanting dream and harsh reality were alike essential—the warp and woof of his web. His twofold vision could see both the lady Helen in Paradise, and the dead tramp-woman spun over by the big spiders in the ditch; both 'the grand houses of gold', and 'the starved ass braying in the yard'.[1]

Yeats himself, however, seems often just such a visionary as he here describes; like the King of Ireland's son in that poem by Nora Hopper which would run in his head for hours—

> All the way to Tir na n'Og are many roads that run,
> But the darkest road is trodden by the King of Ireland's son.
> The world wears on to sundown, and love is lost and won,
> But he recks not of loss or gain, the King of Ireland's son,
> He follows on for ever, when all your chase is done,
> He follows after shadows—the King of Ireland's son.

[1] In his useful edition (1961) of *Riders to the Sea* and *In the Shadow of the Glen* (pp. 15-16) T. R. Henn, I find, makes exactly the same point—that Yeats's criticism was here perhaps 'over-poetical'; and that Synge can be, also, 'violent and brutal' (as, indeed, the later Yeats sometimes came to be).

Indeed, far from denying this dreaminess, Yeats repeatedly proclaimed it in his own enchanting verse—

> But I, being poor, have only my dreams,
> I have spread my dreams under your feet,
> Tread softly because you tread on my dreams.

> The death of friends, or death
> Of every brilliant eye
> That made a catch in the breath—
> Seem but the clouds of the sky
> When the horizon fades;
> Or a bird's sleepy cry
> Among the deepening shades.

> All would be well
> Could we but mix ourselves into a dream,
> And get into their world that to the sense
> Is shadow, and not linger wretchedly
> Among substantial things; for it is dreams
> That lift us to the flowing, changing world
> That the heart longs for.

> The dreams the drowsy gods
> Breathe on the burnished mirror of the world
> And then smooth out with ivory hands and sigh.

> What happiness
> Can lovers have that know their happiness
> Must end at the dumb stone? But where we build
> Our sudden palaces in the still air,
> Pleasure itself can bring no weariness,
> Nor can time waste the cheek, nor is there foot
> That has grown weary of the whirling dance.

> Fair are poppies on the brow;
> Dream, dream, for this is also sooth.

How bewitchingly beautiful is much of this dreamery! And yet, perhaps, how dangerous! True, without dreams a man may decline into a mechanical Philistine, and his world into a desert of dust and ashes; and yet a man who is all dreams may grow a drug-fiend, and his world a vista of mirage. Dreams can lend life's prose the magic poetry of moonlight; but 'moonshine', not without reason, has also become only another name for deceptive nonsense.

Yeats was a creature of the moon, rather than of the sun. George Russell (A. E.), when teaching Yeats to draw with pastels, found that his pupil, sketching a wood in a July noon, had transformed it into a wood by moonlight. Even as a boy in London Yeats was moved to call his toy yacht, modelled on one called 'The Sunbeam', by the more appropriate name of 'Moonbeam' instead.

This fundamental quality in him may be illustrated by contrasting a typical poem of his with an English one, and a French.

It is an ancient gambit, when a lady threatens to be cruel, to retaliate by threatening her with the cruelty of Time. Greek poets had done it; Catullus and Horace had done it; then our own Wyatt took up the theme in what is for me the most moving of all his poems.

> My lute, awake! Perform the last
> Labour that I and thou shall waste,
>   And end that I have now begun;
> For when this song is sung and past,
>   My lute, be still, for I have done. . . .

> Perchance thee lie, withered and old
> The winter nights that are so cold,
>   Plaining in vain unto the moon:
> Thy wishes then dare not be told;
>   Care then who list! for I have done.

That, with its simple directness, its rare purity of style, moves me more than any Metaphysical ingenuities. It pierces the darkness with the sweetness of lute-strings and the bitterness of a lonely anger.

Then came Ronsard, with perhaps the most magnificent of all his sonnets; which, after Wyatt's bitter serenade, rises like the rounded gold of an autumnal moon.

Quand vous serez bien vieille, au soir, à la chandelle,
Assise auprès du feu, devidant et filant,
Direz chantant mes vers, en vous esmerveillant:
Ronsard me celebroit du temps que j'estois belle.
 Lors vous n'aurez servante oyant telle nouvelle,
Desja sous le labeur à demy sommeillant,
Qui au bruit de 'Ronsard' ne s'aille resveillant,
Benissant vostre nom de louange immortelle.
 Je seray sous la terre et, fantaume sans os,
Par les ombres Myrtheux je prendray mon repos:
Vous serez au fouyer une vieille accroupie,
 Regrettant mon amour, et vostre fier desdain.
Vivez, si m'en croyez, n'attendez à demain:
Cueillez dès aujourd'huy les roses de la vie.

 When you are old, and in the candle's rays
You wind your thread, by the fire, at eventide,
Singing my songs, you will say with a wondering pride,
'Ronsard so praised me in my beauty's days.'
 Then never a maid whose tired head nods and sways
Drowsily over her labour at your side,
But at the word 'Ronsard', will open wide
Her eyes, and bless your name's immortal praise.
 I shall be under earth, faint phantom strayed
To rest at last amid the myrtle-shade;
You, huddled by your fireside, old and grey,
 Regretting my lost love and your proud scorn.
Believe me! Live! Wait not tomorrow's morn,
Gather the roses of your youth today!

Wyatt's poem runs to forty lines, albeit short ones; Ronsard's to only fourteen. Yet how much more Ronsard compresses into the Sonnet's narrow room!—the double vision of the white-haired Helen in candle-light beside her fire among her nodding maids, and of his own wraith among the shadowy myrtles of the netherworld; the trumpet-call 'Ronsard' in the fourth line, and its fainter echo in the seventh; the dignity of this voice, less embittered than Wyatt's, not dwelling on the physical ignominies of old age, but on the pity of mortal transience, the immortal splendour of great art. No wonder it has become one of the great poems of the world.

 Yeats in his turn adapted Ronsard. He was not fluent in French; but his beloved Maud Gonne had many links with France, and was indeed called 'the Irish Jeanne d'Arc'. But with Yeats, as one might expect, all becomes changed to the remoteness of misty mountain-top and dreaming stars.

> When you are old and grey and full of sleep
> And nodding by the fire, take down this book,
> And slowly read, and dream of the soft look
> Your eyes had once, and of their shadows deep;
>
> How many loved your moments of glad grace,
> And loved your beauty with false love or true;
> But one man loved the *pilgrim* soul in you,
> And loved the *sorrows* of your changing face.
>
> And bending down beside the glowing bars,
> Murmur, a little sadly, how love fled
> And paced upon the mountains overhead,
> And hid his face amid a crowd of stars.

All three poems are superb. But it is characteristic that, where Wyatt's mistress moans bitterly awake in her cold and lonely bed, and Ronsard's Hélène sings, proudly awake among her drowsing maids, the mistress of Yeats herself grows drowsy, as she 'slowly reads' alone beside her fire. The ladies of Wyatt and Ronsard are stung by frank and bitter physical regret; but Yeats bids his beloved 'dream'—a little complacently—of her own past beauty, and 'murmur, *a little sadly*, how love fled'; while the poet himself, a little too complacently, suggests that, of all her lovers, he alone loved her soul. And, besides her soul, in typically Irish fashion he loves her sorrows. No less typically, his whole poem and his love end above the clouds, in the vagueness of the infinite stars.

Whichever piece one happens to prefer, Wyatt and Ronsard seem to me here more clear-cut, more *dramatic*. Wyatt's lines (as often) speak with a directness recalling stage-dialogue; Ronsard dramatizes before us a whole scene, with white-haired mistress and drowsy maids who awake with theatrical suddenness. But Yeats has preferred an enchanted twilight where the tall and lovely phantom of Maud Gonne rises for a moment blurred with silvery mist.

It is interesting to find the same dream-worship in a letter from the poet's father (21/12/14):

The chief thing to know and never forget is that art is dreamland and that the moment a poet meddles with ethics and the moral uplift of thinking scientifically, he leaves dreamland, loses all his music and ceases to be a poet. Meredith is musical while he stays in dreamland—Browning also. . . . Shakespeare never quitted his dreams. . . . We all live when at our best, that is when we are most ourselves, in dreamland. A man with his wife or child and loving them, a man in grief and yielding to it, girls and boys dancing together, children at play—it is all dreams, dreams, dreams.

(Which seems a little extravagant.)

Seven years later, however, another letter from J. B. Yeats to his son (30/6/21) strikes a curiously opposite note, as if the old man had now come to realize the need for a corrective:

When is your poetry at its best? I challenge all the critics if it is not best when its (*sic*) wild spirit of your imagination is wedded to concrete fact. Had you stayed with me and not left me for Lady Gregory, and her friends and associations, you would have loved and adored concrete life for which as I know you have a real affection. What would have resulted? Realistic and poetical plays—poetry in closest and most intimate union with the positive realities and complexities of life. . . . Not idea but the game of life should have been your preoccupation, as it was Shakespeare's and the old English writers', notably the kinglike Fielding. The moment you touch however lightly on concrete fact, how alert you are! and how attentive we your readers become!

Very sound advice; especially for drama. For dream-lyrics have more chance of succeeding than dream-plays. And yet what earthly use in adjuring Yeats, of all people, to write like 'the kinglike Fielding'? As well urge a night-hawk to acquire the kingly qualities of a bull. For Yeats was a poet through and through: whereas Fielding could say 'I should have honoured and loved Homer more had he written a true history of his own times in humble prose'. It is true that in his later verse, as he 'withered into the truth' and took to 'walking naked', Yeats did often become harsher and harder, clearer and more direct—as when, towards the fall of night, the day's clouds clear from some mountain-land. But though Yeats's later verse grows sometimes more dramatic, it may be doubted whether his dramas do. For his ideas still remained mystic and fantastic. But even if his twenty-six plays have held the stage less successfully than the six of Synge, whom he so generously and bravely championed, one may still feel drawn to explore the illuminating contrasts between this fascinating pair; and even if Yeats's plays may seem far less interesting, it may still be interesting to inquire exactly why.

LIFE AND PERSONALITY

> 'An inspiration caught from dubious hues
> Filled him, and mystic wrynesses he chased;
> For they lead further than the single-faced,
> Wave subtler promise when desire pursues.
> The moon of cloud discoloured was his Muse,
> His pipe the reed of the old moaning waste.
> Love was to him with anguish fast enlaced,
> And Beauty where she walked blood-shot the dews.'
>
> MEREDITH, *A Later Alexandrian*

Yeats was born near Dublin in 1865. His grandfather had been a strictly orthodox clergyman of the Church of Ireland. But his father, J. B. Yeats, became a sceptic and a painter; while his mother, Susan Pollexfen, felt less at home in the drawing-rooms of Dublin, or London, than exchanging ghost and fairy tales with fisherwives in Sligo kitchens (who may well, indeed, have been far more amusing). Yeats himself shared both his father's interest in painting and his mother's preference for the world of reverie and gramarye; wandering as a boy among Sligo caves, or burying himself, later, in a thicket on the promontory of Howth. 'That thicket,' he afterwards wrote to Katherine Tynan (31/1/1899), 'gave me my first thought of what a long poem should be. I thought of it as a region into which one should wander from the cares of life. The characters were to be no more real than the shadows that people the Howth thicket.' Such shadowiness, indeed, was always to be the trouble with his characters.

In 1884-6, when he was between nineteen and twenty-one, Yeats studied art in Dublin. Not only was his father a painter; his brother Jack was also to become one. But Yeats himself hated the French impressionists; and felt much more sympathy with his fellow art-student, George Russell, better known as 'A E.' (1867-1935), who depicted spirits lost in a misty atmosphere like that of Corot.

Even at eighteen—the age when Rossetti wrote *The Blessed Damozel*—Yeats had already discovered one side at least of his characteristic style.

I've built a dreaming palace
With stones from out the old
And singing days, within their graves
Now lying calm and cold.

Of the dreamland marble
Are all the silent walls
That grimly stand, a phantom band,
About the phantom halls.

In 1885, with Russell and others, he founded the Dublin Hermetic Society. ('Hermetic' means 'occult', from 'Hermes Trismegistus'— 'Hermes thrice greatest'; the Greek Hermes being identified with the Egyptian God Thoth, patron of occultism and alchemy.) The young mystics dabbled in theosophy and the wisdom of the East; they were lectured to by the Brahmin theosophist Mohini Chatterjee; and Yeats, rebellious against orthodox religion, yet abominating science, propounded to the Society the principle that 'whatever the great poets had affirmed in their finest moments was the nearest we could come to an authoritative religion, and that their mythology, their spirits of water and wind, were but literal truth'.

To the profane this dogma may seem a little curious. For, apart from the difficulty of agreeing who, precisely, *are* 'the great poets', and which are 'their finest moments', 'great poets' constantly disagree among themselves. How reconcile, for example, the bitter scepticism of Lucretius, or Leopardi, with the faith and piety of Dante, or Milton?

But Yeats, having lost the religion of his childhood, craved a religion of his own. He was, by temperament, violently averse from that 'negative capability' of Keats, which resigned itself *not* to know the unknowable.

Yeats's other great interest in these youthful years was Irish Nationalism. Here he came under the influence of that Fenian son of a Tipperary shopkeeper, John O'Leary (1830-1907), who had been sentenced in 1865 to twenty years' imprisonment, as editor of the Fenian journal, *The Irish People*. After a period in Portland Prison, and further years in Parisian exile, O'Leary returned to Ireland in 1885, sceptical about Parliamentary agitation for Home

Rule, but convinced that Ireland's future depended largely on re-discovering her past—her history, her poetry, her folklore. 'From O'Leary's conversation,' said Yeats, 'and from the Irish books he lent or gave me, has come all I have set my hand to since.' Yet here, as often, Yeats overstated. For he was swayed not only by O'Leary's nationalism, but also by an occultism on which O'Leary frowned. 'If,' Yeats wrote to him in 1892, 'I had not made magic my constant study, I could not have written a single word of my Blake book, nor would *The Countess Cathleen* ever have come to exist.' One might indeed say, for short, that the Muse of Yeats was daughter of Cuchulain by the Witch of Endor.

In 1887 Yeats's family moved back to London, where as a boy he had passed unhappy years at school. But now he came in personal contact with the English aesthetes and the English nineties. His early poetry was often pre-Raphaelite. He owed a good deal to Pater and Rossetti. William Morris once said in the Strand to the young author of *The Wanderings of Oisin*—'You write *my* kind of poetry.' And he met other literary personalities such as Wilde, Beardsley, Henley, Lionel Johnson, Ernest Dowson, John David-son, Arthur Symons. But he remained busy also with the world of the unseen. In 1887 he joined the theosophist lodge of a plump, peasant-like Russian lady, the famous Mme Blavatsky; though, only two years before, the Society for Psychical Research had sent out an investigator to examine her activities in India, and two of her disgruntled servants there had given evidence far from favourable to her integrity. In 1890 she made Yeats regretfully resign from the theosophist lodge (he seems to have been too anxious to make occult experiments). However, a little earlier that year, he had already joined a more secret and magical body, *The Hermetic Students of the Golden Dawn*.

Meanwhile, in 1889, he had met and fallen in love with that strange beauty, Maud Gonne; who seems from her own auto-biography to have been a person of immense courage, great generosity, quick wits, but not much sense—indeed, at times, a disastrous fanatic. With her, Yeats dreamed of founding yet another mystical order, which should establish a new religion for Ireland, and set up a 'Castle of Heroes' in an empty fortress, Castle Rock, on an island of Lough Key, twenty miles south of Sligo. But Maud Gonne was incorrigibly political and activist: Yeats was not. In 1903 she married (with unhappy results) a man of action, Major John MacBride, newly returned from fighting for the Boers in the Transvaal,[1] and destined to be shot after the Easter Rising of 1916. Yeats got her letter announcing this marriage, just before he was to give a lecture, in February, 1903. He duly lectured; but in a trance so complete that afterwards he could not recall a single word said.

As he wrote in his bitterness (though he did not publish it)—

> My love is angry that of late
> I cry all base blood down,
> As though she had not taught me hate
> By kisses to a clown.

And yet to read even thirty pages of Maud Gonne's autobiography makes one doubt whether Yeats had ever the ghostliest chance of winning or of keeping her. He was a poetic somnambulist; she, a political Valkyrie. It was like a swan sighing for a falcon. At all events, in her memoirs,[2] her references to 'Willie' seem both scanty and chill. His poetry has immortalized her as a figure of bewitching, heroic beauty; yet also as one who bartered her priceless gifts for 'an old bellows full of angry wind'.

But, lest details grow confusing, at this point it may be best to summarize the career of Yeats, both past and future, in chronological form. For its main landmarks are his published works.

1865 Yeats born near Dublin.

---

[1] Cf. *The Playboy of the Western World*, 'Were you off east, young fellow, fighting bloody wars for Kruger and the freedom of the Boers?'

[2] Maud Gonne Macbride, *A Servant of the Queen* (1938). Her article on Yeats in Stephen Gwynn's memorial volume on him (*Scattering Branches*, 1940) is warmer and kinder. But one still feels that, though often close, they were lastingly incompatible.

Yeats, on his side, in *Dramatis Personae* (1935) could refer to his past passion as 'a miserable love affair'; and add with a touch of cold disillusion— 'My devotion might as well have been offered to an image in a milliner's window, or to a statue in a museum, but romantic doctrine had reached its extreme development.'

1887 His family moves to London.

He meets English literary figures like L. Johnson, Henley, Morris; also Mme Blavatsky.

1889 *The Wanderings of Oisin* (poetry).

1891 Irish Literary Society founded in London.

1892 National Literary Society founded in Dublin.

The Countess Cathleen (play).

1893 The Gaelic League founded by Douglas Hyde and others.

The Celtic Twilight. Edition of Blake.

1894 *The Land of Heart's Desire* produced in London.

1895 *Poems*.

1896 Yeats meets Lady Gregory (1859-1932) at Coole in Galway; and Synge in Paris.

1899 Foundation of Irish Literary Theatre.

The Countess Cathleen produced (with police protection).

The Wind among the Reeds (poetry).

1900 *The Shadowy Waters* (play).

1902 Irish National Theatre Society founded.

Cathleen ni Houlihan produced (April), with Maud Gonne herself in the title-part.

The Pot of Broth produced (October).

1903 Maud Gonne marries MacBride (separation in 1905).

Ideas of Good and Evil.

The Hour Glass produced (March).

1904 Foundation of Abbey Theatre, Dublin.

The King's Threshold produced (October).

On Baile's Strand produced (December).

1906 Yeats's *Deirdre* produced (November).

1907 The *Playboy* riots. Yeats hurries back from Scotland to oppose; and shows himself in this emergency at his finest— both fearless and practical.

1908 *The Golden Helmet* produced (March).

1909 *Poems, 2nd Series.*

1910 *The Green Helmet and Other Poems.*

(He was now forty-five; and up to this time, so Yeats said in the Senate (11/3/27), his books never earned him so much as £4 a week.)

1911 Possibility of succeeding Dowden as Professor of English Literature at Trinity, Dublin.[1]

1914 *Responsibilities* (poetry).

1916 The Easter Rising. MacBride executed.

1917 Yeats proposes to Maud Gonne (on condition that she should give up politics); then to her adopted niece Iseult; then to the English Miss Hyde-Lees, whom he married. His wife begins automatic writing.
The Wild Swans at Coole (poetry).

1919 Move to Ballylee Tower.
The Player Queen produced (December).

1921 *Four Plays for Dancers.*

1922 *Later Poems.*

1922-8 Member of the Irish Senate.

1923 Nobel Prize (which, some feel, should have gone first to Hardy).

1924 *Essays.* Interest in Fascism.

1925 *A Vision.* Yeats opposes in the Irish Senate a resolution against divorce.
Oedipus at Colonus produced (September).

1926 *Oedipus the King* produced (December).

1928 *The Tower* (poetry).

1930 *The Words upon the Window-Pane* produced (November).

1931 *The Cat and the Moon* produced (September).
The Dreaming of the Bones produced (December).

1932 *Words for Music Perhaps* (poetry).

1933 *The Winding Stair* (poetry).
Interest in the Fascist Blue-Shirts of O'Duffy.

1934 Rejuvenated by Steinach operation.
The Resurrection and *The King of the Great Clock Tower* produced (July).

---

[1] There is a typical Irish directness about Mahaffy's view of the job. When the poet referred to the bad sight which debarred him from much reading, the old man (says Yeats) replied: 'It has been of great value to this University having Professor Dowden associated with it, because he has a reputation as a scholar; but he has been teaching here for 30 years and hasn't done a pennyworth of good to anybody. *Literature is not a subject for tuition.*' (So William Morris likewise thought.)

1935 *A Full Moon in March* (play).
1937 Later version of *A Vision*.
1938 *The Herne's Egg* (play).
　　 Purgatory produced (August).
1939 *The Death of Cuchulain* (play).
　　 Yeats's own death at Cap Martin, near Monaco.
1940 *Last Poems.*
1948 Brought home to Drumcliff churchyard, near Sligo.

THE MAGICIAN

'Nam isti qui linguam avium intellegunt
Plusque ex alieno iecore sapiunt quam ex suo
Magis audiendum quam auscultandum censeo.'[1]

PACUVIUS (220-130 B.C.)

Externally Yeats's career was not specially eventful; but it was the
career of a very strange person in a very strange world of his own.
Plenty of other poets and dramatists since the Romantic Revival
have treated of magic and the supernatural. But for Yeats these
things were much more than picturesque fictions. He believed in
them. How much, is much disputed (clearly his moods varied);
but often with intensity. His own art seemed often a part of this
magic; the poet in him could become a sort of shaman; just as in an
earlier world ᾠδή or *carmen* could mean both 'song' and 'spell';
vates, both 'poet' and 'seer'. In this fantastic world a modern sceptic
feels at times as if he had wandered out of the twentieth century into
the twelfth.

So bizarre, for example, seems that moon-faced, cigarette-rolling
Mme Blavatsky—'an old Russian savage' she called herself—
mysterious with wisdom derived from Mahatmas in far-off Tibet;
in whose mystic circle tumult might arise (so Yeats amusedly
reports) because a ponderous materialist accidentally sat down on
the astral body of a young Indian, which chanced to be reclining on
the sofa beside its owner; or Yeats himself, with his fellow-adepts,
might try the extreme necromantic feat of raising the ghost of a
flower (just as Sir Thomas Browne speaks of raising up in the bed
of Cleopatra the ghost of a rose).

Queerer still was the Order of the Golden Dawn, presided over
by a certain 'MacGregor Mathers' who in the Théâtre Bodinière at
Paris celebrated masses to the Goddess Isis; and would play chess-
foursomes with his wife, Yeats, and a spirit—Mathers shading his

[1]   'Men that can understand the speech of birds,
And learn more from a beast's heart than their own—
Such should be rather heard than hearkened to.'

257

eyes and gazing intently at an empty chair, before making his phantom-partner's moves. Mrs Mathers, most incongruously, was the sister of Bergson. The philosopher, indeed, remained obdurately sceptical; though, Mathers complained, 'I have shown him all that magic can do.' But this sister was herself a witch. Because Maud Gonne, who was likewise an initiate of the Golden Dawn, remembered from her childhood an apparition of a woman in grey, Yeats, suspecting this to be an evil spirit, got Mrs Mathers to make a symbol for him, on the assumption that this spectre was an inhabitant of the fifth element. By this means the spirit would be made visible, and disarmed of its maleficence. The spirit obligingly became visible; and turned out to be a part of Maud Gonne's own personality that had split off when, ages before, she had been a priestess in Tyre, and had been influenced by a certain priest to utter a false oracle.

The chief personages of the Golden Dawn adorned themselves with sonorous Latin titles. That of Yeats, for example, was 'Demon est Deus Inversus' (' A Demon is Inverted God'); that of Mathers— 'Deo Duce Comite Ferro' ('With God for Guide and Sword for Comrade'). But Mathers, unfortunately, could become as peremptory as his title.

According to Yeats, he grew bored with ladies seeking his spiritual advice. And when one of them complained that at night decayed corpses tried to get into her bed, Mathers rebuffed the poor woman with the scathing comment—'Very bad taste on both sides.' Indeed he grew so masterful that in 1900 the Golden Dawn revolted, with Yeats prominent among the rebels, and expelled him. The great wizard is said to have finally perished during World War I, vanquished in a psychic duel by a former disciple, the infamous Aleister Crowley, once undergraduate of Trinity, Cambridge, and later notorious for the unmentionable procedures he was reputed to practise in a palace at Sicilian Cefalù.

In our age of science when even the magic moon, alas, has become a target for fireworks, and might any evening rise upon us branded with red hammer-and-sickle, the ordinary reader may be moved by all this merely to smile. But to Yeats (as, even now, to some of his devouter disciples) the occult seemed of transcendent and permanent importance—in his own words to O'Leary (1892), 'a study which I decided deliberately four or five years ago to make, next to my poetry, the more important pursuit of my life'. And without taking account of it one cannot fully grasp his poetry or his plays.

The reasons for his strange faith lay partly in his period. In the late nineteenth century, particularly in France, as once in declining Greece and Rome, there was a strong revival of occultists and sorcerers. Like bats, wizards seem particularly active both in the dusk before a religion rises, and in the twilight of its decline. Another famous instance is Strindberg, concocting gold, and tormented by magicians, in Paris bedrooms of the nineties. Occultism, indeed, persists vigorously even in our own century of science. It has been asserted that in the United States today less money is spent on astronomy than on astrology; and we all know how Hitler employed horoscopes (luckily for us) to improve his strategy.

With Yeats, however, there was the further influence of his own childhood surroundings, in a land of ghosts and fairies. His story *John Sherman* tells of a Sligo garden where the gardener used to see a former owner in the shape of a rabbit; and of a Sligo street-corner that no child would pass at night for fear of the phantom that haunted it, in the shape of a soldier without a head. Typical, too, is Yeats's comment on some relatives, the Middletons—'They let their houses decay and the glass fall from the windows of their greenhouses, but one among them at any rate had the second sight.' Doubtless a full compensation; though the cynical may feel that, amid all this domestic decay, even the second sight might perhaps have been usefully supplemented by a little foresight also.

No wonder, then, that to the end of his days Yeats was fascinated by the supernatural. At Coole Park both he and the housemaid encountered female phantoms Elizabethanly attired in tall hats and ruffs.[1] His uncle's old servant was constantly seeing fairies or angels.

---

[1] Lady Gregory, on the other hand, could wander there night and day and 'never see anything worse than herself'. Nor presumably did that complete antithesis of Yeats, Anthony Trollope, who (incongruous thought!) had stayed at Coole Park with Sir William Gregory; for to Kate Field the bluff novelist wrote: 'I should like of all things to see a ghost, and if one would come and have it out with me on the square I think it would add vastly to my

Even in the Abbey Theatre at Dublin during performances of Yeats's *Oedipus* there were heard the barkings of a spectral hound. The actors thought it simply the ghost of a dog that had been accidently starved to death in summer when the theatre was shut. But Yeats himself inclined to connect this phantom beast with a chorus in Sophocles' play, which says (as translated by Yeats)—

'Nor may the hundred-headed dog give tongue.'[1]

The ghost of a dog that never even existed would be a ghost indeed. But, Yeats observed, 'poems seem to disturb the spirits'; and he added: 'you will see that I am still of the opinion that only two topics can be of the least interest to a serious and studious mind—sex and the dead'. (Which seems a little exclusive.)

In 1902 he wrote that 'my alchemist' (apparently an Oxfordshire clergyman) 'has just made what he hopes is the Elixir of Life. If the rabbits on whom he is trying it survive, we are all to drink a noggin full—at least all of us whose longevity he feels he could honestly encourage'. Later, despite his hate of science, Yeats was to try the more scientific Steinach. But Old Age, alas, still laughs at our nostrums.

Again, in 1914, the poet travelled with Maud Gonne all the way to Mirebeau, near Poitiers, to investigate an oleograph of the Sacred Heart, which had, it was said, begun to bleed. And at a Hampstead séance he was accosted by the spirit of Leo Africanus (a Moroccan traveller of the early sixteenth century), who announced that he was Yeats's attendant spirit. Yeats, said the spirit, must write to him; then he would dictate an answer.

Even in the most practical matters, the spirit-world was carefully consulted. Thus in 1913 a young woman who had been intermittently the poet's mistress since 1909, wired that she was with

---

interest in life. . . . But when tables rap and boards write, and dead young women come and tickle my knee under a big table, I find the manifestation to be unworthy of the previous grand ceremony of death.'

[1] Actually the Greek (*Oedipus at Colonus*, 1568-9) merely invokes 'Hell's goddesses' (the Erinyes) 'and the shape of that unconquered hound'. Nothing is said about asking it not to 'give tongue'; nor about its having a hundred heads. (Cerberus was normally content with a mere three.)

child. The matter was referred to a medium, who peremptorily replied—'Deception!' Which, indeed, proved true.

Later, in 1920, when Yeats needed a throat-operation, he was inclined to have it in London, though his wife urged Dublin. But the London surgeon turned out to have moved; the maid at his former house gave a wrong address; and Yeats mysteriously failed to find him in the telephone-book. 'Being a superstitious man,' he says, he began to think that 'the finger of providence was in it.' So his wife consulted the stars. The stars pronounced that London would be death; but they were as favourable as possible to Dublin— 'Venus, with all her ribbons floating, poised upon the mid-heaven!' So Dr Oliver Gogarty duly operated on Yeats in Dublin; and with success.

In 1922 when Yeats became a Senator, his first action on being sworn in was again to consult the stars; which predicted rising trouble for the Free State in the next six years, but personal safety for himself. Fortunately the stars told truth about himself, and lied about the Free State. But it all seems as strange as those generals of early Rome who let their strategy be governed by the capricious appetites of sacred chickens.

As might be expected, in this field all argument was vain. Walking with a friend, Dr Sturm, Yeats heard a whistle. 'Some boy,' said the Doctor. 'Not at all, Sturm, not at all. I was just on the point of revealing to you a magical formula which would enable you to remember your past incarnations, when your daemon gave that whistle to warn me not to do so. It would be dangerous for you to know.'

Again, in Sturm's house there were steps at night on the stairs. 'Do you hear the daemons now?' 'I do not, Yeats, it is the maid going to bed.' The Doctor then called up the stairs—'Is that you, Mary?'—'Yes, Sir, good night!'—'There are your daemons!' 'Do not be deceived,' replied the poet. 'Remember that daemons may take *any* shape.' (Conceivably at this point humour was breaking in? I cannot say.)

Confucius seems to me wiser, when he refused to bother himself about the other world while he knew so little of this; or to puzzle himself about spirits while he knew so little of living men.

But perhaps the most picturesque incident of all is Yeats's reported explanation, to Gosse and Gilbert Murray, of why he had dropped a certain acquaintance. 'As he paced the room, he was followed by a small green elephant. And then I knew he was a very *wicked* man.'

Supposing this story to be true, Yeats might have replied that he did not mean that he really believed (as A. E. might have) a small trunked mammal unknown to science to be literally trotting across his carpet; but simply that all is only appearance; and that his intuition of the man's bad character had symbolized and dramatized itself, for him, in the guise of this seeming astral body. But though intuitions are often valuable—often, indeed, they are the source of the most scientific hypotheses—they seem highly dangerous and unreliable guides unless most critically checked. In theory, Yeats might have agreed; but in practice he did not, I think, sufficiently dissect his little green elephants.

Such oddities might be written off, like Johnson's obsessive compulsions to touch posts, or twitch off ladies' shoes, as merely the stray aberrations of genius. But there is a difference. Johnson's eccentricities have not affected his literary work; no one would even guess their existence from his virile discussions of Shakespeare, or the Three Unities, or his poets' lives. But Yeats's writings are constantly haunted, and moulded, by his occultism; and in the light —or shadow—of it they must be read. He built up for himself an extraordinary fabric of mythological theology, collected from the most various sources—such as Cornelius Agrippa, Blake, Blavatsky, Boehme, Buddhism, Druidism, Hinduism, the Kabbala, the Neo-Platonists, Rosicrucianism, spiritualism, Swedenborg, and the Upanishads. At moments, indeed, one is reminded of that strange character in *The Forest Lovers* of Maurice Hewlett—Spiridion; who sits in his lonely castle, while his enemies approach to kill him, and by reading and crystal-gazing seeks the one true God. (Perhaps, he thinks, one had best create one's own Deity; since it would be unjust of Him to have revealed Himself to any one race, leaving all the rest in ignorance.) ' "Here," said Spiridion, standing in his nightshirt before the shelf of images, "here are images of Christ on the Cross, of Mahound (made by a Maltese Jew), of Diana of the Ephesians, and Jupiter Ammon. Here, too, are Thammuz wrought in jade, and a cat-faced woman sitting in a chair. All are gods, and any one of them may be very God. Before which shall I kneel? For to one I will as surely kneel as I shall surely die."

'Prosper flushed red with annoyance. "Brother," said he, "thou art a greater fool than I thought possible. Die how you will." '

In the age of Zola and Naturalism, Yeats, like Strindberg, remained what one may call 'a supernaturalist'. His dramatic kingdom remains for the most part 'not of this world'. And this tendency will be found to increase markedly in the plays of his last twenty years.

IDEAS

'Et je vis l'ombre d'un esprit
Qui traçait l'ombre d'un système
Avec l'ombre de l'ombre même.'[1]

SCARRON

Yeats's system is chiefly expounded in *A Vision* (1925; much revised later edition, 1937; reprint, 1962), a most curious philosophy of history.[2]

Sources of Information

1. 1925 edition: *Speculum Angelorum et Hominorum* (*sic*),[3] by Giraldus (Cracow, 1594). But this work seems merely a whimsical invention by Yeats, like the supposed utterances of 'Michael Robartes' and 'Owen Aherne'.

2. 1937 edition: automatic writings of the poet's wife soon after their marriage in 1917; later replaced by her sleep-talking. Both forms of revelation, we are told, came from spirits, 'the Communicators', or 'Instructors'; with occasional Puckish interferences by other spirits, 'the Frustrators'. One may wonder if the poet's wife was not telepathically playing back to him his own subconscious fantasies. It may also be noted that, like Socrates, he heard sometimes an admonitory voice; which the rationalist might suppose an auditory self-hallucination.

Doctrines

'Touchynge the eighte and twenty mansions
That longen to the moone, and swich folye.'

CHAUCER

[1]   'And I saw the shadow of a ghost—
A system's shadow there it drew
With the shadow that a shadow threw.'

[2] At times its complexities seem to trip the author himself; as when he says (*A Vision*, 1937, p. 179)—'Phase 1 and phase 28 are not human incarnations.' For consistency seems to require, rather, 'Phase 1 and phase 15'.

[3] Or, under the portrait of Giraldus, 'Homenorum' (for 'Hominum'). Yeats was a wayward Latinist.

The destinies both of individual souls, and of mankind pass through recurrent cycles, corresponding to—symbolized by—the 28 phases of the moon. (It may be suspected that Yeats was often less concerned with any objective truth than with the aesthetic satisfaction of thus schematizing experience in visual, symbolic patterns.)

(a) *The Individual Soul*

(i) Souls pass from phase to phase by reincarnation. (Apparently Yeats believed in reincarnation, but not in transmigration; that is, souls pass through a series of *human* bodies, but not also through the bodies of *beasts*.)

(ii) The recurrent cycles of destiny have, like the moon, 28 phases; ranging from extreme 'objectivity' at phase 1 (corresponding to new moon) to extreme 'subjectivity' at phase 15 (corresponding to full moon). In other words, the bright part of the moon symbolizes 'subjectivity'; the dark part, 'objectivity'. From phase 1 to phase 15, therefore, the 'subjective' element waxes, like the moon; from phase 15 to phase 1 the process is reversed.[1]

Further, since no human being can be one hundred per cent. 'subjective' or 'objective', no reincarnations can take place at phase 1 (when the moon is wholly dark) or at phase 15 (when the moon is quite full). This leaves 26 phases for reincarnation.

With 'objectivity', which concentrates on external things, Yeats associated reason, morality—and space (presumably because an external world must take up space); with subjectivity he linked emotion, the aesthetic—and time.

Further, being himself so subjective, he formed the agreeable view that objective natures are ugly; whence the unpleasing appearance of reformers, philanthropists, politicians, and scientists.

[1] Yeats's highly visual mind chose to illustrate this by a diagram of two interpenetrating cones laid horizontally, with the apex of each touching the centre of the other's base—one cone representing 'objectivity'; the other 'subjectivity'. These cones he also called 'gyres'; a 'gyre' being a conical spiral, a vortex. The objective element moves, one might say, like a fly walking in narrowing spirals from its cone's base to the apex, while the subjective element moves like another fly walking in widening spirals from its cone's apex to the base; and then *vice versa*. As one goes from minimum to maximum, so the other goes from maximum to minimum.

(iii) This picture of the soul's progress is complicated by what Yeats calls the 'Four Faculties'—(1) 'Will or normal ego'; (2) 'Mask' —the 'Will's' object of desire, or moral ideal; (3) 'Creative Mind', or thought; (4) 'Body of Fate', the 'external' conditions it perceives. These four vary from phase to phase, and so make up the individual's character in that phase. Further, both 'Mask' and 'Creative Mind' may take a 'true' or 'false' form. That is to say, the Will, for example, may pursue the right or the wrong anti-self or Mask.

But those who wish further details of these complexities should turn to the original.

(iv) Yeats then describes the various human types characteristic of each phase of reincarnation. For example, phase 24. '*Will*—the end of ambition. *Mask* (from phase 10). *True*—Self-reliance. *False* —Isolation. *Creative Mind* (from phase 6). *True*—Humanitarianism through constructive emotion. *False*—Authority. *Body of Fate* (from phase 20)—Objective action.

'Morality, grown passive and pompous, dwindles to unmeaning forms and formulas. . . . All is sacrificed to this code; moral strength reaches its climax, the rage of phase 10 to destroy all that trammels the being from without is now all self-surrender.

'Examples: Queen Victoria, Galsworthy, Lady Gregory.'[1]

(v) In the intervals between reincarnations the soul dreams over again its emotional experiences; until at last it can contemplate these with detached and dispassionate calm.

(vi) It is not clear how many times souls pass through the cycle of reincarnations. Of phase 8 we are told 'the being is often born up to four times at this one phase, it is said, before the *antithetical tincture*[2] attains its mastery'.

Again, of phases 8 and 22 we hear, 'to these two phases, perhaps

---

[1] A somewhat incongruous trinity? Similarly as specimens typical of phase 22 we are given Flaubert, Herbert Spencer, Swedenborg, Dostoievsky, and Darwin; and as typical of phase 7, Borrow, Dumas père, Carlyle, and James Macpherson. (Though one may well wonder how much there is in common between Dumas and Carlyle, or between Dostoievsky and Darwin.) Again one reads with some surprise that 'in Keats, in some ways a perfect type, intellectual curiosity is at its weakest'. Surely Keats would have vehemently disagreed.

[2] The essence of 'objectivity'.

to all phases, the being may return up to four times, my instructors say, before it can pass on'.

How souls begin is not stated; nor is it clear exactly what happens to them when they 'pass on' out of the cyclic Wheel. It is no use trying to be clear about points that Yeats himself left completely obscure.

(b) *World History*

(i) There seem to be cycles within cycles. 'A Great Wheel of 28 incarnations is considered to take, if no failure compels repetition of a phase, some 2,000 odd years'; and 12 of these make 'a single great cone of some 26,000 years'. (Compare the 'Eternal Recurrence' of Nietzsche and others.)

Again, the periods 2000 B.C. to 1 B.C. and A.D. 1 to A.D. 2000 form each an entire wheel; and each of these contains two smaller wheels of 1000 years.

Here are a few examples of cyclic recurrences and correspondences:

The Greek era began with Leda and the swan[1]; the Christian, with Mary and the dove.

The flowering of Attic art with Phidias and the fall of Persia (fifth century B.C.) are matched a thousand years later by the flowering of Byzantine art and the fall of Rome; and a thousand years later still by the flowering of Renaissance art and the fall of Byzantium.

---

[1] Yeats says an *unhatched* egg of Leda's hung in a temple at Sparta. But his source Pausanias (c. A.D. 150; III, 16, 2) actually says it was '*that* (famous) egg which Leda laid', implying that she laid only one egg, and this was it; and that it was *not* unhatched, for Leda's offspring must have come out of it. This, presumably, was only the egg-shell. (There are very various accounts of Leda's performances. For example, some authors say she laid one egg; others, that she laid two. Some say that Helen came out of the one egg; others, that it produced the twins, Castor and Pollux, as well; others, that the twins came from a second egg.)

Yeats, however, was led to play with the fantasy that Leda laid *three* eggs; from one came Castor and Clytemnestra; from another, Helen and Pollux; and the third, having passed from Sparta to Byzantium, from Byzantium to Harun Al-Rashid, was bought from an old man in a green turban by Michael Robartes. This egg, still miraculously unaddled, he and Owen Aherne were to leave in a hole in the desert to be hatched by the sun; with fateful consequences to follow for the world. (*Stories of Michael Robartes*, 1931, p. 19 ff.; *A Vision*, 1937, pp. 50-1.)

With Christianity triumphs 'objectivity', self-denial, service.

The break-up of Charlemagne's empire (ninth century A.D.) corresponds to the break-up of Alexander's (late fourth century B.C.).

In 1005-1180 appear the Arthurian legends and Romanesque architecture, corresponding to the Homeric period 2000 years before.[1]

The decline of Christian faith in the later fifteenth century (did it really decline?) corresponds to the decline of Greek religion in the fifth century B.C.

In modern times 'objectivity' returns. (Modern science corresponds to the medieval schoolmen!) And our cycle now darkens towards its close, with the shadows of authoritarian rule and totalitarian states; till a new cycle shall begin.

All this world-history seems rather fanciful. If some transcendental series of cycles really governed the destinies of mankind, one would expect it to govern them everywhere on earth. If, for example, the climax of Byzantine civilization is to be associated with Phases 12-15 of the moon, why was that same period marked in Western Europe by little but barbarism? And what of events at that date in Asia, Africa, America? By pouncing on arbitrary items now here, now there, it becomes, surely, a little too easy to find mystic correspondences. And to parallel, for instance, Leda and the swan with Mary and the dove is so audacious that one half suspects an impish desire to exasperate the Catholic Church. Yeats, indeed, seems a little too much obsessed by the amours of women either with birds (Leda's swan, the Great Herne) or with unicorns (animals usually of blameless reputation). Even a lampoon of his on George Moore had to suggest that Moore was a decayed Don Juan now rejected by the Muse, and so reduced to begetting his novels on *geese*.

Again, what of prehistory and evolution? We are only told—'The Great Wheel revolved innumerable times before the beast changed into man and many times before man tilled the ground.' But are we, then, to picture even trilobites, pterodactyls, and dinosaurs alternating between 'objectivity' and 'subjectivity'? Yeats adds: 'Perhaps

[1] Yeats could have added here the first Crusades, to match the Trojan War.

the hunting age gave way to agriculture when our present revolution brought round Phase 4 or 5.' But surely this change from hunting to agriculture must have taken place in different parts of the world at widely differing epochs?

Again, Egypt and Mesopotamia in the third millennium B.C. must have been approaching the end of their cycle, as we of ours. Therefore one would expect to find parallels between Ancient Egypt, or Sumeria, and the modern age. But they are not obvious.

Compared with such strange historicism, even Spengler and Toynbee seem sober. Indeed much of *A Vision* appears hardly more sensible than the mystic significances assigned by some to the measurements of the Great Pyramid. Why, then, did Yeats devote enormous time and labour to building this temple in the clouds, this fantasy of a ceaselessly recurrent universe, that to most minds would seem the ghastliest of merry-go-rounds?

Firstly, it would seem, because he loathed contemporary science, as ugly and prosaic. 'Deprived by Huxley and Tyndall, whom I detested, of the simple-minded religion of my childhood, I had made a new religion.'

Secondly, he loved, like Sir Thomas Browne, the intrinsic romance of mystery. He loved, too, the romance of being himself a revealer of mysteries, a hierophant. Hence his early zest for the elaborate rituals of the Golden Dawn.

Thirdly, he was by temperament self-centred, isolated, aloof; and therefore wished to construct a private religion of his own, made to his own measure; not to accept from others a religion ready made. The lost creed of his childhood may have been a 'simple-minded' Christianity; but to that the adult Yeats had no wish to return. Further, disliking the masses, the mob, the common man, he preferred to belong to some small esoteric group, like the Golden Dawn. Again, there may be truth in Orwell's suggestion that Yeats's aristocratic conservatism welcomed this nightmare of a world-history revolving in endless cycles, just because it made nonsense of that optimistic faith in 'Progress' which has been contemptuously called 'une doctrine de Belges'.

Fourthly, he was by temperament a rebel. Therefore he found much in Christianity repulsive. His sympathies were with the defiant old Oisin, rather than with St Patrick. He did not want a religion of meekness; for he was proud. He did not want a religion of love; for he also felt, and prized, a good deal of hate. He did not want self-denial, but self-realization; not duties, but liberties. And so he stressed the view that Christ was 'objective', while he himself, like the men he most admired, remained 'subjective'—resolute to be, and develop, himself. He was like the aloof white heron of his *Calvary*, for whom Christ did *not* die.

Fifthly, his intense love of life grew only fiercer and more insistent as he felt the relentless approaches of age. And so, though he adopted the eastern idea of reincarnation, this was much less because he wanted to escape from 'the Wheel'—a prospect for which he showed very tepid enthusiasm—than because he liked to dream of living again and again—'forgetting and returning, life after life, like an insect in the roots of the grass'; and liked to dream, too, of perhaps winning in later lives the loves he had missed in this; or of enjoying in discarnate intervals those wilder ecstasies and completer unions described by Swedenborg, which blazed like a conflagration as soul melted wholly into soul.[1]

Sixthly, Yeats wanted a symbolic mythology as background and framework for his writing. Even a false philosophy can provide a poet's work with a frame of unity. Greek mythology had already been ransacked by writers through thousands of years for its stories, symbols, images. Celtic mythology, though less rich, continued to serve Yeats himself; but, unfortunately, it too was dead. Christian legend moved him less. Even his *Countess Cathleen* had to be enlivened with demons and man-faced birds; just as medieval churches swarmed with grotesque heads and monstrous gargoyles. And so Yeats—like Blake, but perhaps more successfully—turned to fabricate a poetic mythology of his own. 'I wished for a system of thought that would leave my imagination free to create as it chose and yet make all that it created, or could create, part of one history, and that the soul's.'[2]

Hardy, in contrast, was content with personifications frankly

---

[1] Cf. the hints given to Adam by Raphael in *Paradise Lost* (viii, 618-29), which caused the angel to blush 'celestial rosy red, love's proper hue'.

[2] *A Vision* (1925), p. xi.

admitted to be fancies and fictions; such as the Spirits, Ironic or Pitiful, of *The Dynasts*. But Yeats, who cared little for Hardy,[1] would have thought these too cold and unmysterious. Ibsen, again, put poetry into life's prose by a simpler symbolism, such as his wild duck. But Yeats detested Ibsen,[2] and would have insisted on making the Wild Duck, at the very least, a man-faced bird. Indeed Yeats himself reminds one at moments of the Ekdals seeking their 'life-lie' in the shadows of their mysterious bird-haunted attic.

Often, however, Yeats's symbols seem to have become more important to him in themselves than for what they symbolized. Symbolism for symbolism's sake.

> And yet when all is said
> It was the dream itself enchanted me. . . .
> Players and painted stage took all my love,
> And not those things that they were emblems of.[3]

So Spenser too may at times have felt among the tangling allegories of his *Faerie Queene*.

*   *   *

How far did Yeats really believe his own bizarre mythology? A much disputed question. 'Nobody,' says Hone, 'ever felt certain about Yeats's faith in the occult.' Did he really believe, or was it just a playing with fantastic images?

His friend Sturge Moore, for example, according to Ursula Bridges,[4] took the view 'that although he was always stirred in his imagination by the paraphernalia of mysticism, and strongly attracted by the attendant thrill of conspiracy, yet he remained at heart a sceptic'.[5]

---

[1] Compare his remark that reviewers praised Hardy's poems 'because they know nothing about poetry: they like Hardy because he has not technique, they feel he is still a novelist'.

[2] Compare his remark about 'that horrible generation that in childhood sucked Ibsen from Archer's hygienic bottle'.

[3] 'The Circus Animals' Desertion'.

[4] Introduction to *W. B. Yeats and Sturge Moore, Their Correspondence* (which, as one might expect, does not show the poet very competent as a controversialist).

[5] Cf. Yeats himself in *Estrangement* (written 1909, published 1926): 'All thinkers are alike in that they approach the truth full of hesitation and doubt. . . . A great lady is as simple as a good poet . . . both are full of uncertainty

On the other hand, Yeats himself could write of the doctrine in *A Vision* that, after four or five years' reading of metaphysics, 'my conviction of the truth of it all has grown also' (13/9/29). And again, to Olivia Shakespear (9/3/33): 'Europe belongs to Dante and the witches' sabbath, not to Newton.' For Yeats (as for Blake) Newton's apple was, indeed, deadlier than Eve's; and when it fell, the world fell with it. He had none of that balanced sanity with which Chekhov saw the need for *both* art *and* science side by side.

Even action, in such a case, is not a complete test of belief (for one may 'see the better, yet choose the worse'); still it is often a good indication. When a man allows 'Venus with all her ribbons floating' to decide whether he shall have a serious operation in London or in Dublin, it seems clear that he must believe a good deal in astrology. And when a poet, despite serious eye-defects (like Tennyson's), yet devotes vast reading and labour to writing and rewriting *A Vision*, it becomes unlikely that it was all always just an intellectual game; especially when his other serious works continually allude to it and depend on it.

And yet. . . . There still persists an impression that in this matter Yeats veered and varied a good deal according to his moods. The spirits themselves, he says, had frankly announced—'We have come to give you metaphors for poetry'. No less frankly, Yeats's introduction to the *Vision* of 1937 confesses that, though sometimes swept away by it, he had come to regard his chronological system, his phases of sun and moon, as 'stylistic arrangements of experience, like the cubes in the drawings of Wyndham Lewis'. At times, in short, the whole thing became merely 'a wild parable'.

In general, one comes to feel that Yeats was like Shaw's picture of the typical Irishman, with *two* eyes in his head, *two* different kinds of vision—that, often, 'part of me looked on, mischievous and mocking'.[1]

---

about everything but themselves, about everything that can be changed, about all that they merely think.' Montaigne himself could not have put it more sceptically. But Yeats was a chameleon.

[1] Cf. *Reveries* (1916), p. xxi, of being carried off by fairies: 'I did not believe with my intellect that you could be carried away body and soul, but I believed with my emotions and the belief of the country people made that easy.' It is as if Yeats's beliefs were often only 'suspended disbelief'.

Yeats's revelations would, I think, have drawn from Chekhov only an ironic smile; from Pirandello, a bitter laugh; from Synge, the same exasperation as he felt for A.E.'s mystic dallyings with the 'plumed, yet skinny Shee'. But one must take one's poets as they come. Had one of their characteristics been absent, one cannot know what other characteristics, more valuable and desirable, might have disappeared as well.

On the other hand, when devoted critics try to elevate Yeats into a profound thinker and sage, then it seems time to pause. The affable familiar ghosts,

> which nightly gulled him with intelligence,

appear often to have been singularly blind guides. The trouble with spirits, indeed, is that though they may manage well enough without bodies, they seem to suffer badly from lack of brains. Their communications are often so futile or fatuous, so trivial or tawdry. At all events, whatever the cause, it is not always easy to swallow Yeats's judgements on the real world.

There was, for example, his dalliance (though less disastrous than his friend, Ezra Pound's) with Fascism—with the black shirts of Mussolini, the blue shirts of O'Duffy. Shaw and Pirandello, indeed, had similar lapses. Yet perhaps Shaw did it from paradoxical perversity; Pirandello, because he was sceptically cynical; but Yeats, for the opposite reason—because he was often too passionately credulous. As late as 1934 (*Wheels and Butterflies*) he could ask whether 'D'Annunzio and his terrible drill at Fiume' (1919-20) might not prove 'as symbolic as Shelley'! (He would doubtless have felt full sympathy with d'Annunzio's gloomy phrase about 'the grey flood of democratic mud'.) And in 1937 when Professor Bose asked him for a message to India (with its Hindu-Moslem troubles), Yeats replied: 'Let 100,000 men of one side meet the other. That is my message to India, insistence on the antinomy'. Then he strode across the room, unsheathed the ancient Samurai sword given him by a Japanese admirer, and shouted 'Conflict, more conflict!'[1]

[1] So Hone, *Yeats*, p. 459. The meaning is, presumably, 'Let 100,000 men from one side meet 100,000 from the other.' If one considers the ghastly death-

In 1938 Yeats's *On the Boiler* led him into still fiercer pugnacities. Already, Hitler stood menacing at the gates of the West: but the thoughts of Yeats were far away (yet in some ways all too similar). If the growth of general welfare, he wrote, 'enables everybody without effort to procure all necessities of life and so remove the last check upon the multiplication of the uneducatable masses, it will become the duty of the educated classes to seize and control one or more of those necessities. The drilled and docile masses may submit, but a prolonged civil war seems more likely, with the victory of the skilful, riding their machines as did the feudal knights their armoured horses. . . . The danger is that there will be no war, that the skilled will attempt nothing, that the European civilization, like those older civilizations that saw the triumph of their gangrel stocks, will accept decay.'

Now it may be perfectly true (though men dare not face it) that the world is, in the long run, more imperilled today by excessive babies than by atomic bombs; and that in the short run the domination of comfortable masses, pampered by science, may indeed bring a threat of cultural barbarism. But it remains a little surprising that a man so sensitive and so generous, who had lived through the anguish of the First World War, of the Irish Civil War, of the Black-and-Tans, with the menace of a Second World War already looming to eastward, should yet have toyed with fantasies about educated Lancelots and Galahads redeeming the world by riding around in armoured vehicles to put the populace in their places.

Equally startling, in a different field, were Yeats's views on education. In 1931 he expressed the wish (in an imaginary letter to a schoolmaster) that his own son should learn Greek; but not one word of Latin. For Latin, he said, had destroyed both Milton, and the French seventeenth century, and the Anglo-Irish eighteenth. Nor should the boy learn one word, either, of geography, or of

---

roll ten years later (1947), when India gained her independence, such 'antinomies' may seem a little costly in terms of human suffering.

But Yeats belonged to a generation that could still believe in the beneficence of wars. 'I think,' he had written in 1910 ('J. M. Synge and Ireland'), 'that all noble things are the result of warfare; great nations and classes, of warfare in the visible world, great poetry and philosophy of invisible warfare, the division of a mind within itself.'

history (for history, Shakespeare and Dumas were enough).[1] Nor should he be taught science—'he can get all he wants in the news-paper, and in any case it is no job for a gentleman'.

On the other hand, his son must do all the mathematics his capacity admitted, because 'I know that Bertrand Russell must, seeing that he is such a featherhead, be wrong about everything, but as I have no mathematics I cannot prove it. I do not want my son to be as helpless'. But perhaps it was hardly for a man who thought Bertrand Russell refutable by school-mathematics, to talk about 'featherheads'.

It becomes clear enough that Yeats was irritated past endurance by the dry light of that sceptical type of intelligence found in Cambridge figures like Bertrand Russell or George Moore (the philosopher). 'Damn Bertrand Russell!' he could say to John Sparrow. 'He's a proletarian. He has a wicked and vulgar spirit.' Yet 'proletarian' seems an odd term to choose, whatever Bertrand Russell's shortcomings, for a scion of the noble house of Russell and the ducal line of Bedford. And it was surely a little topsy-turvy

---

[1] The consequences of this light-hearted notion of history (a little strange in one so concerned with its supposed cycles and recurrences) can be seen in Yeats's denunciation of Flecker's *Hassan*. 'We know Harun al Raschid,' wrote Yeats, 'through *The Arabian Nights* alone, and there he is the greatest of all traditional images of generosity and magnanimity. . . . Considered as history, *Hassan* is a forgery, as literature an impertinence, for it makes him put two such lovers to death with every horror of cruelty. One feels that its nightmare-ridden author longed to make Galahad lecherous, Lancelot a coward, and Adam impotent.' (A curious echo of Tennyson on Vivien's slanders of Arthur's court.)

Now it is unfortunately true that Flecker's *Hassan*, despite some fine poetry and humour, shows also an unpleasant streak of sadism. But, firstly, it seems wild to say that we know Harun al-Raschid *only* from *The Arabian Nights*. *The Arabian Nights* are no more history than Malory or Tasso. The main original authority on Harun (763-809) appears to be Ibn al Athir (c. 1225, summarizing earlier writers).

Secondly, had Yeats even dipped into an encyclopedia, he would have found his idealized Caliph, despite some great qualities, described in terms that go far to justify Flecker—'the most merciless and blood-thirsty ferocity' —'unreasoning and ferocious cruelty'—'his nature contained, and long absolute power permitted to develop, an evil element of savagery, by which almost as much as by his splendours, he is remembered'. Harun was, indeed, not only the exterminator of the fallen Barmecides, but also, it seems, the murderer of a too jealously loved sister.

to write to Sturge Moore (26/6/26): 'Part of the trouble is that your brother, like the ecclesiastics, does not examine evidence, because he is satisfied with faith or thinks evidence is impossible, and another part is that your brother has that English University habit which made it possible for the edition of the *Cambridge Ancient History*[1] to ignore India and China and that keeps all English Universities entirely ignorant of the arts.' Whatever the truth about English Universities and the arts, this picture of Moore the philosopher as an ecclesiastically-minded obscurantist, refusing to examine evidence is, for anyone who knew him, the wildest of travesties.

Obviously Yeats was one of the many anti-rationalists of our distracted century.[2] Still let it be remembered that he also wrote those two lines of terrible truth—

> We had fed the heart on fantasies,
> The heart's grown brutal from the fare.

It was indeed 'fantasies' that gave us two world wars, and the Easter-Rising, and Auschwitz and Dachau and the labour-camps of Russia, and other evils untold. But however often that is pointed out, the anti-rationalists refuse to see.

Yet one is half disarmed when, near his end, to Dorothy Wellesley's question whether he had any solution for the world's insistent ills, the old poet answers: 'O my dear, I have no solution, none.' Were the lips of the spirits, formerly so confident, sealed at last? It recalls that fragment of Housman—

> The old deceived diviner
> Awakes in hell to find
> The web of doom spun finer
> Than any mortal mind.

But at least this belated avowal was honest—and tragic.

[1] The *Cambridge Ancient History* is concerned primarily with countries bordering on the Mediterranean; but it does *not* always ignore India; and the six fat volumes of the *Cambridge History of India* (1922-32) were already in course of publication.

[2] Compare an early letter (1887?) on his dislike for George Eliot: 'She is too reasonable. I hate reasonable people, the activity of their brains sucks up all the blood out of their hearts. I was once afraid of turning out reasonable myself. The only business of the head in this world is to bow a ceaseless obeisance to the heart.' (A difficult gesture, one might have thought.)

In fine, what Goethe said (with much exaggeration) of Byron, seems to me sometimes applicable to Yeats—'as soon as he reflects, he is a child'. Some of his criticism was acute; much of his prose, splendid in its eloquence and music; he was, above all, a remarkable poet; but I simply cannot see in him a remarkable prophet.

And yet—such is the bewildering complexity of human character —there remains another side. The best painted portrait can only give one side of a man; but biography, like sculpture, must try to see all round. As a corrective to fantasies like *A Vision*, the reader should turn to *The Senate Speeches of W. B. Yeats*.[1] Often the hard sense of these is equalled only by their courage. Yeats's speeches may not always have been very politic or diplomatic; they may sometimes have produced more fury than converts; but on perilous themes like censorship, birth-control,[2] divorce,[3] he could be bitingly

[1] Edited by D. A. Pearce, 1961.

[2] 'If those men of science are right who say that in a hundred years the population will overtake the food supply, it' (the Church) 'will doubtless direct the married to live side by side and yet refrain from one another, a test it has not imposed upon monk and nun, and if they do not obey—well, Swift's "Modest Proposal" remains, and that, at any rate, would make love self-supporting.' (Draft for speech, from *Spectator*, 29/9/28.)

[3] Yeats protested (11/6/25) against enforcing the Catholic marriage-code on the non-Catholic minority. (A Father Peter Finlay had written that it was even more a matter of justice to do so than for the English to ban suttee in India; since divorce was worse even than being burnt alive.) Yeats urged that indissoluble marriage always meant increased adultery. And he audaciously reminded the puritans of certain conspicuous monuments in Dublin. 'The monuments are on the whole encouraging. I am thinking of O'Connell, Parnell, and Nelson. We never had any trouble about O'Connell. It was said about O'Connell, in his own day, that you could not throw a stick over a workhouse wall without hitting one of his children, but he believed in the indissolubility of marriage, and when he died his heart was very properly preserved in Rome. I am not quite sure whether it was in a bronze or marble urn, but it is there, and I have no doubt the art of that urn was as bad as the other art of the period. We had a good deal of trouble about Parnell when he married a woman who became Mrs Parnell.' *The Chairman* (*Lord Glenavy*). 'Do you not think we might leave the dead alone?' *Yeats*. 'I am passing on. I would hate to leave the dead alone. . . . In the opinion of every Irish Protestant gentleman in this country he did what was essential as a man of honour. Now you are going to make that essential act impossible.' Many men in those years had been murdered for saying less. (Colonel Moore, George Moore's brother, then turned the proceedings into high comedy by solemnly protesting: 'He quotes the poet Milton as an authority. I do not know whether the poet Milton ever wrote on divorce.')

realistic. Further, this visionary poet could yet strike practical colleagues as a man who might have made a shrewd banker, or an admirable lawyer; this dreamer who could seem, at times, to have in his bonnet all the bees of Innisfree, might yet at other moments show the sardonic penetration of a Swift. No use asking which aspect of him was the true one. Both were.

No doubt this paradoxical view of Yeats as the strangest blend of sense and nonsense, veracity and absurdity, insight and intoxication, may be indignantly contested by many of his devouter admirers.[1] But, in the long run, the best friends of a man's fame are not his blind idolaters. In the last century writers like Shelley and Browning, Carlyle and Meredith, Tennyson and Arnold were often extolled not only as the gifted Romantics they were, but also as sages and oracles which they were not. But because they were overpraised then, they are disparaged now. 'Tell Mat,' said Tennyson, 'not to write any more of those prose things like *Literature and Dogma*, but to give us something like his *Thyrsis* or *The Forsaken Merman*.' Here Tennyson was surely right; yet he himself made the same mistake, allowing his poetry to be blurred with less excellent philosophizing. However, men of high character when they feel a call to prophesy, cannot but follow it—even if, sometimes, it leads them into a wilderness.

Yeats, then, may be judged by some both ego-centric and eccentric. And both qualities seem to me important reasons to explain why he failed to become a major dramatist.

[1] In particular, Mr F. A. C. Wilson, whose patient research into Yeats's sources and meanings seems to me admirable, has put very clearly one of the crucial points at issue (*Yeats's Iconography*, 1960, p. 20): 'He believed easily (*and there is no especial virtue in believing only with difficulty*).'
Is that really so certain?
When one counts the cost in human misery, through the ages, of too facile belief in military glory, or in territorial conquests, or in religious persecution; of too facile belief that heaven can be pleased by human sacrifice, or torture, of too facile belief in the superstitions and prejudices of compact majorities—then one may see rather more point in that ancient verse of Epicharmus: 'Still be sober, still be doubting. Such the sinews of the mind.' Men seem to me wildly and dangerously extravagant, not only in the quality, but also in the quantity, of their beliefs. There may, therefore, I suspect, be quite a lot of virtue in 'believing only with difficulty'. And so, at times, Yeats said himself (Compare p. 271.)

'Ego-centric' need not mean 'egoistic'. He was generous, loyal, disinterested, disdainful of money-making. But he remained an aristocratic, day-dreaming introvert, who gazed inward upon himself rather than on the outer world. To call him 'self-centred' is not necessarily blame. He had a self so gifted and unusual that on it his interest might very well be centred. But though lyric poets may often have been introverted (like Donne, Wordsworth, Byron, Leopardi, the Rossettis, or Baudelaire), for the writer of drama, or epic, or novel, such a temperament can become a serious hindrance. For drama, epic, and novel need the power to create characters; and that requires a more extraverted and wide-awake interest in observing the humours of humanity, in getting inside the skins of others, even of the opposite sex. In default of that, not even his marvellous blank verse, style, and imagination could turn the eccentric Beddoes into an effective playwright.

Hence few authors seem to have excelled both in lyric poetry and in drama. On the one hand Aeschylus, Sophocles, Euripides, Aristophanes, Menander, Plautus, Terence, Seneca, Racine, Goldsmith, Sheridan, Ibsen, Chekhov, Shaw, and Synge have left little—often nothing—that is outstanding in non-dramatic lyric. On the other hand, Wordsworth and Coleridge, Keats and Byron, Tennyson, Browning, and Arnold did not fare very well with drama—less well than Yeats himself. Shakespeare and Goethe, no doubt, were exceptional in this as in other ways. Another rare exception is Alfred de Musset, with his enchanting comedies. But such exceptions seem too uncommon to disprove the general rule.

Secondly, Yeats's ideas also were highly eccentric. To a lyric poet such eccentricities may be no hindrance—they may even be a help. Blake was odd. Smart was mad. The strange cosmology of Yeats with its Great Year, its gyres and pernes, its world-process alternately winding and unwinding between subjectivity and objectivity like the two spools of a typewriter-ribbon—all these things have been sources of persistent joy to a certain kind of critic. But such recondite dreamings, less near to the stage of Athens than to the mysteries of Eleusis, are not easily built into enduring drama. *The Cat and the Moon* and *The Only Jealousy of Emer* fill, together, only twenty-seven pages; to explain them, one expert has needed no less than ninety. Goldsmith would have warned the esoteric Yeats, as he warned the esoteric Gray, to 'study the people'. For it is hard to pack a theatre into an ivory tower. Hence Yeats's very natural longing, in later years, for a tiny audience like that of Strindberg's 'Intim Theater'—an élite like a secret society, very fit and very few.

It can, of course, be retorted that Parnassus is no democracy, where victory goes automatically to majorities; and that Yeats's plays are not proved minor by their lack of popularity. That is undeniable.

But it seems a little perverse to go further, like some of Yeats's more ardent advocates, and dismiss the suggestion that he was a better poet than dramatist, as merely 'trite'. To critics bursting with originality, 'trite' can, no doubt, become the equivalent of 'false'; and a 'truism' mean 'something untrue'. But a view is not really disproved by the fact that quite a number of people have held it. Whether this preference for Yeats's poetry over his plays is so 'trite', I do not know.[1] And if 'trite' it is, I care not two pins. I still believe that, though Yeats wooed the Muses of Tragedy and Comedy as persistently as he wooed Maud Gonne, yet, like her, they remained but cold to him; his true mistress, from first to last, was another—Euterpe, the Muse of Lyric. However the reader must form his own opinion. The only object of these pages is to help him to it.

---

[1] This view of Yeats, I find, was also held by H. W. Nevinson—one of the few critics with whom one would really regret to disagree.

THE PLAYS

The Countess Cathleen
(written 1889-92; revised 1895, 1901, 1911; produced 1899)

> *Mephistopheles.* Sie ist gerichtet!
> *Stimme (von oben).* Ist gerettet![1]
>
> GOETHE, *Faust*

Yeats says he drew his plot from a collection of Irish folklore in an Irish paper. Apparently the tale was based on Léo (Napoléon) Lespès, *Les Matinées de Timothée Trimm* (Coulommiers, 1865), which professed to derive it from popular legend and a ballad.

During an Irish famine, says the story, two sinister merchants appeared. Their method of famine-relief was to buy souls. Damaged ones they bought at a heavy discount; but souls in good condition—such as those of innocent young girls—fetched thumping prices.

Countess Kitty O'Connor, hearing of this diabolical traffic, sold all she had, except one castle, to save the poor from Satan. But the two demon-merchants cunningly stole her gold. Then, to redeem her people from perdition, the Countess went to the merchants and sold them her own soul; for which they very properly paid a prodigious sum. Then she died of anguish. But God, none the less, admitted her to Paradise.

Yeats thought this story 'the most impressive form of one of the supreme parables of the world'. Even Alcestis, he says, who gave her life for her husband Admētus made a sacrifice 'less overwhelming, less apparently irremediable'.

But here perhaps Yeats grows a little enthusiastic. Whatever its origin, the Irish story recalls many a picturesque medieval legend;

---

[1] *Mephistopheles.* She is condemned!
Voice (from above). Is saved!

one can imagine it retold with mischievous, yet not unsympathetic irony by the graceful pen of Anatole France. But, dramatically, the value of a plot does not depend simply on the value of the sacrifices made in it. Despite its lyric beauty, *The Countess Cathleen* may not so easily eclipse on the stage the *Alcestis* of Euripides.

One can imagine a fifth-century Athenian saying, with some astonishment: 'Yes, no doubt a touching myth. But what strange people you barbarians are, who believe in a deity that consigns myriads of souls to endless torment; and in a devil who toils endlessly to collect such evil souls! What good could *that* do him? And then you say God cheated. Should a God of Justice cheat? Alcestis may have sacrificed only her life, not her immortal soul. Yet are not the characters of Euripides far closer to ourselves; their conflicts far nearer to our own?'

Would these objections be wholly wrong? The most interesting conflicts in drama are often those *within* a character—as with Medea or Hamlet. And the *Alcestis* of Euripides, like Meredith's famous novel, is really the study of an egoist. It depicts how that egoist comes to grief and is gradually redeemed. When Admētus, King of Pherae, let his queen Alcestis die to save him, after all others had refused, he did not realize until too late what he was doing—that life preserved so basely was not worth preserving at all. He takes a first step towards his own redemption when, in reverence for hospitality, he forces himself, though heart-broken, to welcome the wandering Heracles—and finds he has entertained an angel unawares.

There are also in Euripides other scenes that give an audience what it needs—not only the poetic, but the dramatic. There is the scene of conflict between the resentful Admētus and his old father, who, not unnaturally, fails to see why *he* should be expected to die for his son's convenience. There is the scene, no less vividly human, where Heracles in his Falstaffian mood of revelry is suddenly sobered into a rescuing St George, by learning of his host's bereavement from the lips of an old servant who can endure no longer to watch the hero roystering in this house of death. And there is that final scene where Heracles returns with a veiled woman whom he pretends to have won for prize in the games; but who is really the Alcestis he has just wrested from the grip of Death Himself.

This comparison between *Alcestis* and *The Countess Cathleen*, seems to me worth making, because it illustrates so clearly the contrast between a poet, lyrical, indeed, but still more dramatic, like Euripides, and an essentially lyric poet turning to the stage, like Yeats. For most audiences, no amount of verbal music replaces breathing personalities.

In fairness to Yeats, however, it can be argued that his play was less remote from life than it may now seem. For if *Alcestis* is the nemesis of egoism, one may also see in *The Countess Cathleen*, at least at moments, the nemesis of altruism. Even a noble soul may be endangered by descending too much into the mire and blood of politics; even for an idealistic cause like the freedom of Eire. Such was the case of Maud Gonne, giving herself up to frantic political agitations, in her generous rage at evictions and famines.

> I thought my dear must her own soul destroy,
> So did fanaticism and hate enslave it.

To her, Yeats dedicated his play; for her he wrote the part of the Countess; by her he wanted it acted (as, later, she did consent to act the more patriotic part of Cathleen ni Houlihan). But this time she refused. 'Just because I loved the stage so much,' she writes, 'I had made the stern resolve never to act. I was afraid it would absorb me too much to the detriment of my work.' Actually, much of her life—defying the police, raising mobs, outwitting British agents—proved more dramatic than many stage-plays.

But though this conflict in Yeats's own life and love may be thus poetically allegorized in *The Countess Cathleen*, it remained his private tragedy. No audience could have guessed it. It takes special knowledge thus to read between the lines. And, even so, if the theme is the debasing effect of politics, the correspondences between allegory and reality remain imperfect.

The Countess may indeed sell her soul. But in *her* there is no sign of debasement. And at the end she is instantaneously redeemed. Whereas the ideas of *Alcestis* remain as dramatically lucid as the parables of the *New Testament*, or the allegory of *Pilgrim's Progress*, or the fables of La Fontaine.

SCENE I

This opens in a poor Irish cottage where the mother, Mary, is a pious peasant-woman; but Shemus Rua, the husband, and Teig the son, remain merely sordid clod-hoppers. Yet Yeats is little concerned (unlike Shakespeare or Scott, Hardy or Synge) to bring his rustics to life by any homely realism of speech; their arms may be hairy as Esau's, but their voices are still the poetic voice of Yeats.

> *First Merchant.* We know the evils of mere charity.
> *Mary.* Those scruples may befit a common time.
> I had thought there was a pushing to and fro
> At times like this, that overset the scale
> And trampled measure down.

This recalls the style of Shakespeare; but hardly the rustics of Shakespeare. And it is very different from the racy prose that tumbles from the lips of Mary Doul or the Widow Quin.

A famine is raging through the land; and evil spirits are abroad—

> At Tubber-vanach
> A woman met a man with ears spread out,
> And they moved up and down like a bat's wing. . . .

> In the bush beyond
> There are two birds—if you can call them birds—
> I could not see them rightly for the leaves.
> But they've the shape and colour of horned owls
> And I'm half certain they've a human face.

Delightful gargoyles of the demon's world, these men with wiggly batlike ears, these owls with human faces. Yeats, I suppose, would have thought such creatures quite possible to meet on an evening-walk. Why less so than little green elephants? Here, however, these devilish creatures do well; they enliven the play with their creepy presences. Often, indeed, Yeats was better with the supernatural than with the natural.

Then appear the Countess Cathleen, her old nurse Oona, and a poet, Aleel, who is hopelessly in love with the Countess. Presumably Aleel embodies Yeats himself, with his vain love for Maud Gonne.

The Countess lavishes on the poor cottagers her last remaining money—she has already given away the rest—and even leaves them her empty purse, with its clasp of silver. But the boorish Shemus is still unsatisfied. When she has gone, he calls in ravenous rage on whatever devils there may be. At once there enter two Eastern merchants (lately, no doubt, disguised as the two owls). These unroll a carpet, sit down on it, and start to lay out their piles of money. Their errand, they explain, is to act as a sort of Marketing Board to buy up souls.

Shemus and Teig are quite ready to sell whatever souls they may possess—'Why should we starve for what may be but nothing?'

But at this point, surely, an audience may be excused slight bewilderment. Are such Voltairean doubts about the soul really in character for superstitious peasants who fervently believe themselves surrounded by men with bats' ears, men without mouths, human-faced owls, and whole legions of devils?—

> They say
> They are as common as the grass, and ride
> Even upon the book in the priest's hand.

However the two demon-merchants now send out Shemus the father and Teig the son as commission-agents to advertise their pending purchases of souls. The wife Mary swoons away.

SCENE II

A Wood near the Countess's Home

Aleel makes poetic love to the Countess. Seemingly he is as unorthodox as Yeats himself. Indeed he has not even been christened; his thoughts run, rather, on Queen Maeve and the hosts of fairyland.

Shemus and Teig burst in proclaiming the mart of souls. To prevent it, the horrified Countess orders the sale of whatever property she has.

SCENE III

A Hall in the Countess's Home

Aleel has seen a fairy vision, and vainly begs the Countess, on peril of some fearful death, to flee with him to the hills. But Cathleen, refusing to forsake her duty and her people, sends him away.

> I kiss your forehead.
> And yet I send you from me.

But now the two demon-merchants have broken into her castle in their owl-shapes, and stolen all her charitable gold. Then the Countess, in despair at the sight of these suffering peasants whom she can no longer redeem, resolves on her supreme sacrifice.

Scene IV

(This seems a little superfluous)

Peasants pass, talking greedily of the demon-gold. The two merchants follow. Then Aleel, singing a Yeats lyric of typically entrancing music.

> Impetuous heart, be still, be still,
> Your sorrowful love can never be told,
> Cover it up with a lonely tune.
> He who could bind all things to His will
> Has covered the door of the infinite fold
> With the pale stars and the wandering moon.

Scene V

The Cottage of Scene I

Mary, the peasant-wife, has died of starvation; her body is laid out on the bed; the two Merchants are busy opening their soul-mart; and here the play suddenly quickens to a much more dramatic humanity.

The peasants crowd in. A middle-aged man asks three hundred crowns for his soul. But the demon-merchants possess embarrassing dossiers about everybody's private life. They find the man has been contemplating robbery. So his soul can fetch only a mere two hundred.

Then a woman. Her record reveals she has meditated adultery. She is worth only fifty crowns; or at most a hundred.

The love-crazed poet Aleel offers his soul for nothing. But the Merchants refuse it even as a gift—'We cannot take your soul, for it is hers.' A vivid touch; even if not perhaps very orthodox. And as they will shortly take even the Countess's own soul, it does not seem very logical either.

Next an old woman who was always safely ugly, is valued at the high price of a thousand crowns. 'God bless you, sir!' she says; then screams that God's name, as she uttered it, stabbed through her like a flame. At this the other sellers grow terrified, and try to back out.

The Countess enters and for her own soul she demands no less than half a million crowns.

Second Merchant. Sign with this quill.
It was a feather growing on the cock
That crowed when Peter dared deny his Master,
And all who use it have great honour in Hell.

Another pleasing touch; though at the time some imbeciles took these four lines for an attack on the Pope!

Then the Countess distributes the gold among the poor, goes out, is brought back, and dies.[1]

Aleel sees a vision of angels and devils battling in mid-air. Darkness descends. Armed angels appear. Aleel grips hold of one and conjures him to tell of Cathleen's fate.

The Angel. The light beats down; the gates of pearl are wide
And she is passing to the floor of peace,
And Mary of the seven times wounded heart
Has kissed her lips, and the long blessed hair
Has fallen on her face. The Light of Lights
Looks always on the motive, not the deed,
The Shadow of Shadows on the deed alone.
(*Aleel releases the Angel and kneels.*)
Oona.[2] Tell them who walk upon the floor of peace

---

[1] In old age Yeats said that, were he to create this situation again, he would have made the Countess, as soon as she had signed her own damnation, burst into laughter and blaspheme. More tragic, perhaps? Yet one may doubt whether it would be dramatically satisfying for a character to change so abruptly into its complete opposite—as easily imagine Shakespeare's Imogen suddenly talking like Doll Tearsheet! It would be convincing only if one supposed the Countess to go mad; like Ophelia.

[2] Cathleen's old nurse.

That I would die and go to her I love;
The years like great black oxen tread the world,
And God the herdsman goads them on behind
And I am broken by their passing feet.

This ending, with a metrical simplicity that recalls some early Elizabethans, seems absolutely typical of Yeats's lyric gift. These trampling years, in the shapes of great black oxen, are superb. But relevant? Might it not have shown more sense of drama to conclude with that final summing-up in the lines before?

The Light of Lights
Looks always on the motive, not the deed,
The Shadow of Shadows on the deed alone.

As with the soul of Faust at the end of Goethe's play, the devil is cheated. Poor old devil! He has a rough deal. Burns was sorry for him—even Milton, a little. And well one may be.

It makes a pretty mystery-play. Were it a genuine piece from the Middle Ages, written by a writer really convinced of such things, it might move us more deeply. But as a product of the late nineteenth century it has, perhaps, a touch of the artificial and factitious. One finds it hard to believe that the Countess's sacrifice, with its deliberate echo of the Christian doctrine of the Atonement, could really be a mortal sin, or seriously imperil her generous soul.

However nineteenth-century Ireland still retained plenty of medieval bigotry. And so in 1899 this play, like Synge's *Playboy* eight years later, raised raving howls of superstition. The orthodox felt outraged at Shemus trampling on the holy shrine that fell from its niche, and at the demons' blasphemies—as if it were not precisely the business of demons to blaspheme! And patriots screeched at the notion that *Irish* peasants, however poor and ignorant, could conceivably sink to sell their souls. Was not Ireland the Isle of Saints? How could any Irish heart dream of such a thing? (It must, however, in fairness be owned that most of Yeats's Irish peasants in this play were an unflatteringly squalid lot, without the imaginative gaiety and charm of Synge's.)

Again, the devout were indignant that the Countess should sell her soul and yet get off—a still more surprising objection. None the less a Cardinal condemned the play—without reading it; and there was such an outcry in the press, and in a pamphlet entitled *Souls for Gold*, which incited the audience to riot, that a score or so of police were required in the theatre, to let the Countess sell her soul in peace.

Yeats himself, in a speech of 1899, described his play as 'purely symbolic'.[1] The two demons,' he said, 'are the world, and the gold is simply the pride of the eye, and the peasants we have in our hearts, and the Countess Cathleen is simply a soul or human spirit which perpetually makes the sacrifice she made, which perpetually gives itself into captivity for the service of all good causes, and in the end wins peace, because every high motive is in the substance peace.'

Eloquent; but perhaps a trifle facile? Yeats was a little inclined to assume that a beautiful idea, or even a beautiful sentence, *must* be true. Is it the fact, in this world at least, that 'high motives' must always bring peace? Did not the noble Brutus die calling virtue a mere name? And the great Pope Gregory VII pass away in 1085 with the embittered conclusion—'I have loved justice and hated iniquity, *therefore* I die in exile?' Indeed, there is even that mysterious last cry of despair from the lips of the Crucified.

The Countess Cathleen may or may not be Yeats's best play; but it seems the best known. Which again suggests that his true field was not drama, but lyric. Yeats came to feel that his lyricism led him into too effeminate dreaming; and hoped drama might bring out his manlier side. Yet the remedy seems doubtful. In this play, and others, he remains a dreamer still. *The Countess Cathleen* makes a striking contrast to Synge's *Well of the Saints*, with its very different saintliness, its far livelier peasantry, its tougher-minded irony (like Pirandello's) about the blessedness of being well deceived.

[1] Perhaps 'allegoric' would express it better. Cf. *Estrangement* (written 1909; published 1926): 'my "Countess Cathleen" for instance was once the moral question, may a soul sacrifice itself for a good end?'

*　　　　*　　　　*

The Land of Heart's Desire (1894)

> 'Come away, O human child!
> To the waters and the wild
> With a faery, hand in hand,
> For the world's more full of weeping
> than you can understand.'
>
> YEATS, 'The Stolen Child'

This was later called by Yeats, rather severely, 'a vague sentimental trifle' (though a half-crown edition in 1925 sold 10,000 copies). It was first produced in London in 1894 as a curtain-raiser—a most incongruous one—for Shaw's *Arms and the Man*.

George Moore—as so often, a little malicious; yet, as so often, irresistibly lively—has very divertingly described this occasion. 'It amused me to remember the amazement with which I watched Yeats marching round the dress circle after the performance of his little one-act play. . . . His play neither pleased nor displeased; it struck me as an inoffensive trifle, but himself had provoked a violent antipathy as he strode to and forth at the back of the dress circle, a long black cloak drooping from his shoulders, a soft black sombrero on his head, a voluminous black silk tie flowing from his collar, loose black trousers dragging untidily over his long, heavy feet— a man of such excessive appearance that I could not do otherwise— could I?—than to mistake him for an Irish parody of the poetry that I had seen all my life strutting its rhythmic way in the alleys of the Luxembourg Gardens, preening its rhymes by the fountains, excessive in habit and gait.' A highly dramatic dramatist; though one must always distrust the imaginatively derisive mind of George Moore. St Patrick may have banished all other venomous things from Ireland; but he seems to have failed with Irish tongues.

The Land of Heart's Desire presents in one act the stealing away of a young wife by the fairies. In a cottage-room, wearing the dress 'of some remote period', are gathered an old farmer, Maurteen Bruin, his wife Bridget, his son Shawn, his son's wife Mary, and an old priest. It is May Eve, when fairies are most dangerous, and fondest of kidnapping mortals.

Mary, the young bride, is deep in an old book about Fairyland—

> Where nobody gets old and godly and grave,
> Where nobody gets old and crafty and wise,
> Where nobody gets old and bitter of tongue.[1]

But Mary's mother-in-law, Bridget, who belongs to the tribe, not of Mary, but of Martha, *is* bitter of tongue, and rebukes the young woman's dreamy indolence.

At old Bridget's bidding Mary hangs on the door-post a branch of quicken, or rowan, wood, which should persuade the fairies to send good luck. But at once a green-clad fairy child, emerging from the wood that is visible through the open door at the back, snatches the quicken-branch away. (Quicken-wood, it appears, is rather a broken reed.)

Then a little old green-clad woman comes with a cup—Mary offers her milk. A little old man makes signs that he wants fire for his pipe—Mary offers him a glowing peat.

Now it is fatal for a household on May Eve to give milk and fire to the 'good people', as the faeries are euphemistically called; for that puts the house in their power for a whole year to come. But Mary is stung by her mother-in-law's reproaches to defiance—

> Come, faeries, take me out of this dull house!
> Let me have all the freedom I have lost;
> Work when I will and idle when I will!
> Faeries, come take me out of this dull world.

She genuinely loves her adoring young husband. But she has been driven to tempt Providence. And the harm is done. There comes the voice of the fairy-child, singing at the door a lyric that sums up the whole theme of the play; and may perhaps outlive it.

[1] From at least as early as *The Wanderings of Oisin* (1889) Yeats seems haunted by a horror of old age; which only deepened into fury when he himself reached it. One senses, too, all through this play a sympathy with the world of Faery rather than with orthodox Christianity. One cannot, indeed, blame the Church for regarding Yeats with suspicion, even from very early days.

The wind blows out of the gates of the day.
The wind blows over the lonely of heart,
And the lonely of heart is withered away.
While the faeries dance in a place apart,
Shaking their milk-white feet in a ring,
Tossing their milk-white arms in the air;
For they hear the wind laugh and murmur and sing
Of a land where even the old are fair,
And even the wise are merry of tongue;
But I heard a reed of Coolaney say,
'When the wind has laughed and murmured and sung,
The lonely of heart is withered away!'

The old father brings the fairy-child into the house. They treat it to milk and honey and bread. It is just about to dance when it suddenly shrieks at the crucifix on the wall—'What is that ugly thing on the black cross?'

The old priest—whom one might have expected to be much less compliant, and much less unsuspicious—then removes the crucifix into the next room.

> We must be tender to all budding things,
> Our Maker let no thought of Calvary
> Trouble the morning stars in their first song.

Now the fairy-child can freely sing and dance. And when the priest asks her how old she is, she answers:

> I'll soon put on my womanhood and marry
> The spirits of wood and water, but who can tell
> When I was born for the first time? I think[1]
> I am much older than the eagle cock
> That blinks and blinks on Ballygawley Hill,
> And he is the oldest thing under the moon.

Terrified, the old couple cower behind the priest. But the priest,

---

[1] This line has its orthodox ten syllables; but its feet seem strangely lame. It may well be that Yeats relied less on metrical theory than on intuition and an exquisite ear; like that other verbal musician, Walter de la Mare, who once said to me in his simple way—'Do you understand all this about prosody?' The intuitions of genius are worth stacks of theory; but intuitions can sometimes stumble. (Compare Yeats, *Reveries*, 1916, XVI: 'My lines but seldom scanned, for I could not understand the prosody in the books.')

having rashly removed the crucifix, is himself powerless. The child puts her arms round Mary.

> You shall go with me, newly married bride,
> And gaze upon a merrier multitude. . . .
> Where beauty has no ebb, decay no flood,
> But joy is wisdom, Time an endless song.
> I kiss you and the world begins to fade.

Hypnotized, the young wife is torn between love for her husband and desire to go. She dies, and the child vanishes, while dim in the outer world towards the forest, there glimmer strange figures in a dance, 'and it may be a white bird' (I suppose, Mary's soul), and many voices sing their chant of final triumph—the twelve lines already sung by the child in the middle of the play.[1]

> The wind blows out of the gates of day,
> The wind blows over the lonely of heart,
> And the lonely of heart is withered away. . . .

The angels saved Countess Cathleen; but the old priest could not save Mary.

As the reader may already have guessed, Mary, like the Countess Cathleen, seems suggested by the hopeless love of Yeats for Maud Gonne, whose heart was likewise set on the impossible and the impracticable, on things fantastic as any fairyland. Her quarrel with him, he felt, had been due to her longing for what he calls 'some impossible life, some unwearying land like that of the heroine of my play'. Ideals, indeed, can prove dangerous idols, and have probably cost more blood and tears than all the idolatry in history. Once again, a touch of biography brings us far closer to the poet's inward thought.

Later, Yeats himself took a dislike to this piece. In 1904 he wrote to Russell (A. E.) that he now found in it, as in some of his lyrics of that date, 'an exaggeration of sentiment and sentimental beauty which I have come to think unmanly . . . a womanish introspection . . . let us have no emotions, however absurd, in which there is not an athletic joy.'

[1] p. 292.

However, after many revisions, in 1912 it played, he said, 'well enough to give me pleasure'.

*   *   *

Cathleen ni Houlihan
(written with Lady Gregory, 1902)[1]

> 'Life, to be sure, is nothing much to lose;
> But young men think it is, and we were young.'
>
> HOUSMAN

This became Yeats's most popular play, because it descended to nationalist propaganda;[2] being really *The Land of Heart's Desire* reset to a patriotic tune. For, this time, instead of a young bride witched from home by a fairy-child, a young bridegroom is lured away by a supernatural old woman, Cathleen ni Houlihan, the spirit of Ireland herself.

And here yet again there rises the tall, pale phantom of Maud Gonne, who was likewise witched from Yeats's arms by the call of patriotic ardours. Indeed the part of Cathleen ni Houlihan was first acted, very impressively, by Maud Gonne herself.

This time blank verse is replaced by prose—but a rather leaden prose compared with Synge's, or indeed with the vibrantly musical prose of Yeats's own best criticism. If it was mainly Lady Gregory's, she was not at her best.

---

[1] The play seems to have been based on a dream of Yeats about a cottage with firelight, talk of a marriage, and the entry of an old woman in a long cloak. But it appears that most of the actual dialogue was Lady Gregory's; 'in a word, that he thought of it and she wrote it; and this is the assertion made to me by the Gregory family, who had many times heard it from her own lips'. (E. Coxhead, *Lady Gregory*, p. 68.)

According to Yeats, *The Unicorn from the Stars* was likewise really hers, except for its plot and chief character. She also contributed dialogue to *The Pot of Broth*; and helped with the construction of some poetic plays, especially *The King's Threshold* and *Deirdre*.

[2] It was also translated into an Irish version (acted 1946).

294

The scene is a cottage near Killala in Mayo during 1798. For those unfamiliar with Irish history it should be explained that 1798 was a year of abortive risings. In particular (as Lady Gregory's old Irish nurse could herself remember) the French general Humbert landed at Killala; succeeded for a short time in occupying Ballina and Castlebar; then was hurled back to the Atlantic.

Michael Gillane is to be married tomorrow. Michael's old father admires the lad's wedding-clothes; and Michael's old mother reminds her husband that *he* had nothing so fine to wed her in. Then from the window there is seen a mysterious old woman, passing down the road.

There follows a good deal of desultory talk about dowries and land; then the same mysterious old woman reappears. Admitted to the house, she tells how far she has travelled, but how restless, still, is her heart. For she has had many troubles. 'My land that was taken from me . . . my four beautiful green fields.' (Of course, the four provinces of Ireland.)

Then she begins singing, at first half to herself, then louder, about men that have died for love of her, from yellow-haired Donough, hanged at Galway, to Brian that died at Clontarf. (Brian Boru fell fighting the Norsemen at Clontarf, near Dublin—fifty-two years before Harold fell at Hastings—in 1014. As usual, the Irish have long memories.)

The old woman refuses food, drink, or money. But she casts her Ancient-Mariner spell on Michael, saying that it is men's help she needs. 'It is a hard service they take that help me. Many that are red-cheeked now will be pale-cheeked, many that have been free to walk the hills and the bogs and the rushes will be sent to walk hard streets in far countries . . . many a child will be born and there will be no father at its christening to give it a name.'
Then she goes out saying—

> They shall be remembered for ever,
> They shall be alive for ever,
> They shall be speaking for ever,
> The people shall hear them for ever.

This is, of course, the consecrated phraseology on such occasions.

Sixty years ago it rang less hollow, in a world not yet bled white with wars, and nauseated with propaganda. It would be unjust to blame men of the past for sharing the illusions of their day. And yet, one feels, a clearer, wider mind, like Goethe's for instance, would not have written those lines. Nor would Synge have written them. For, to anyone who thinks, it has long been all too clear that such 'eternal' remembrance of the fallen is conventional cant. The whole thing can become as bitterly ironic as Verlaine dropping his mistress's dead greenfinch through a grating into the cellars of the Pantheon.

Most of my fellow-undergraduates at Trinity in 1914, most of the officers and many of the men I served with on the Somme, have now been dust for half a century. And already many of them are no more 'remembered' than if they had never been born. It is sometimes necessary to die for one's country; but at least one might be spared all this humbug about immortal remembrance. Much good it would be anyway! People should be left to do their job without being mocked with bogus bonuses of undying memory. One name in many millions, one episode in tens of thousands, may be recalled for a few centuries; deformed, at that, by the usual falsifications of tradition, or of what is called 'history'. The Stream of Lethe is as inescapable as the River of Death. It flows a little more slowly. That is all.

However, at this point in the play there rises an uproar from without—'The French are landing at Killala!'[1] Michael breaks away from his poor bride's arms to follow the voice of the old woman, Cathleen ni Houlihan. The aged father lays his hand on his younger boy's arm—'Did you see an old woman going down the path?' And the boy answers: 'I did not, but I saw a young girl, and she had the walk of a queen.' Curtain.

Nationalism has become so much a blighting infatuation of our century that it grows hard to feel hot enthusiasm about nationalist plays. No doubt national independence is important. It is natural, and human, for a people to prefer misgoverning itself, even to being

---

[1] Here, says Stephen Gwynn (who saw the production in which Maud Gonne acted), 'such a thrill went through the audience as I have never known in any other theatre'.

well governed by others. But patriotism is not enough; national independence is not enough—it is only the beginning, not the end; the bottom rung of the ladder, not the top. And liberty has too often turned sour as soon as won, for it to be easy now to stomach raptures on the subject. Suppose the French *had* conquered—would Napoleon have proved kinder to Catholic Ireland than to Catholic Spain?

No doubt, it is often evil when stronger states dominate weaker ones. Not only does it turn the oppressors into damnable brutes; it turns the oppressed into damnable bores. I remember a dreary evening in the thirties at the Gate Theatre, Dublin, with a tiresome young man beating his too naked chest while twaddling interminably about 'the Gael' and 'the Gall'—that is, the Irish and the strangers, the English. What tedium! Would that the Irish had been given Home Rule half a century sooner!—as they might have been but for the prudes and prigs who howled down Parnell. But when one thinks of some of the uses to which Dark Rosaleen has put her Home Rule—such as banning books by the thousand, or objecting even to *The Lady of Shalott* being read in schools because Tennyson is 'a poet of Revolt'—Tennyson!—why, then it grows a little hard to cheer quite so madly for Cathleen ni Houlihan. The Irish have their independence. The better for them; and the better for us. But, thanks to human beastliness and folly, the price was tragically extravagant.

The wiser Synge reasoned that, with patience and a Socialist government in England, Irish freedom would one day come bloodlessly. Today Irish graveyards are filled with heroic dust, Irish fields with the blackened skeletons of noble houses, which were alike sacrificed to a natural, yet needless fanaticism; and some Irishmen I have talked to regretted as bitterly as anyone that hideous, futile waste.

Inevitably, however, in 1902 *Cathleen ni Houlihan* won paroxysms of applause. And on some its effect was lasting. A leading member of the Irish Republican Brotherhood told Donald Pearce that though till then he had 'never had a political thought', he took to politics the day after seeing the first performance. Others, however, even then were affected differently. James Joyce (aged twenty) and his brother Stanislaus looked only with cold eyes on what seemed to them, already, dramatic and political clap-trap.

*   *   *

The Pot of Broth (written with Lady Gregory, 1902)
This is a light-hearted farce, recalling that ancient dream of the philosopher's stone. A sly tramp fools an old cottager and his middle-aged wife into believing that a common stone has magic powers of producing soup, wine, or poteen; and thereby walks off triumphant with a chicken and a bottle of whisky in exchange for his pebble.

A slight affair (though it acquires a certain unconscious irony when one thinks of Yeats's own hopeful occultism); however, like some of Chekhov's farces, it proved highly popular on the stage.

*   *   *

The King's Threshold
(first version, 1903, produced 1904; second version, 1906; third, 1921)

> 'I have no spirit of skill with equal fingers
> At sign to sharpen or to slacken strings;
> I keep no time of song with gold-perched singers
> And chirp of linnets on the wrists of kings.'
> SWINBURNE

King Guaire, at Gort in Galway, prompted by his jealous bishops, soldiers, and law-makers, has denied the traditional place at his council-board to his chief poet Seanchan (Shanahan). At this the outraged Seanchan undertakes a hunger-strike. In 1903 hunger-strikes, all too familiar now, were hardly known; though the militants of the movement for women's suffrage were soon to make full use of this form of resistance. But in ancient Ireland there had been a tradition of fasting against the mighty when they did evil. For example, in the sixth century King Dermot arrested the murderer of a royal officer, though the murderer was protected by St Ruadan. Then the clergy fasted against the King, with the malediction 'Desolate be Tara!' And desolate it remains to this day—a low rise crowned with ancient mounds, south of the fatal beauty of the Boyne.

So now Seanchan fasts on the palace-steps. In vain he is dissuaded by the King, and by his pupils, and by the Mayor of his town, Kinvara, and by his own old servant, the King's Chamberlain, and by the two young Princesses, and by Seanchan's own betrothed. In vain the King himself brings in the bard's pupils with halters round their necks, ready to be hanged. Seanchan dies defiant; and his pupils bear him to his mountain-grave.[1]

> *Youngest Pupil.* O silver trumpets, be you lifted up
> And cry to the great race that is to come.
> Long-throated swans upon the waves of time,
> Sing loudly. For beyond the wall of the world
> That race may hear our music and awake.

But the Oldest Pupil is less hopeful—he signs to the musicians to lower their trumpets.

> Not what it leaves behind it in the light
> But what it carries with it to the dark
> Exalts the soul; nor song nor trumpet-blast
> Can call up races from the worsening world
> To mend the wrong and mar the solitude
> Of the great shade we follow to the tomb.

Originally the play seems to have been meant as a kind of 'Defence of Poetry', or 'Declaration of Independence', provoked by bigoted attacks in press and pulpit against the Abbey Theatre. But the ordinary reader today, not knowing that, may excusably find

[1] In the first two versions it was from *dining* at the King's table that Seanchan was excluded—a somewhat trivial ground for suicide; and in these earlier versions Seanchan did not actually die—he triumphed, for the King gave way. But in October, 1920, Terence MacSwiney, Lord Mayor of Cork and himself a poet, died after 74 days of hunger-strike in Brixton prison. The play's third version was acted in 1921. (See H. M. Black's interesting article on *The King's Threshold* in *Philological Quarterly*, XXXIV, 1955.)

the plot somewhat fantastical. Why, he may ask, should poets be seated at King's council-tables? Why should a Poet Laureate expect a place in the House of Lords? Men of the pen have often shown small aptitude for governing kingdoms. And why should they even wish to? They have better things to do. There are, no doubt, precedents for poets in public office, like Sophocles or Lamartine; but Sophocles and Lamartine do not seem to have succeeded very well.

True, the play is in a sense prophetic. In 1922-8 Yeats was himself to become an Irish Senator. When it was asked why a poet should hold state-office, Dr Gogarty is said to have retorted, 'If it had not been for W. B. Yeats, there would be no Irish Free State.' And Yeats's speeches in the Senate suggest that few Senators served it better.

But such exceptions do not prove the rule. The theme of *The King's Threshold* remains, as the bard's Oldest Pupil says, somewhat unreal.

> And though I all but weep to think of it,
> The hunger of the crane, that starves himself
> At the full moon, because he is afraid
> Of his own shadow and the glittering water,
> Seems to me little more fantastical
> Than this of yours.

The play's strongest point seems now its pure poetry; and its praise of poetry—

> I said the poets hung
> Images of the life that was in Eden
> About the child-bed of the world, that it,
> Looking upon those images, might bear
> Triumphant children. . . .
> If the Arts should perish,
> The world that lacked them would be like a woman
> That, looking on the cloven lips of a hare,
> Brings forth a hare-lipped child.

Unscientific perhaps, as regards hare-lipped children; but it might yet prove all too true of an excessively scientific world.

Note. Yeats's picture of the injured Seanchan makes a curious contrast to Irish tradition. *There* it is not kings that outrage bards, so much as bards that outrage kings, with the most impertinent and impossible extortions.

According to the *Book of Lismore*, Senchán Torpéist visited King Guaire with a whole horde of poets, minor poets, women, servants, and hounds—a hundred and fifty of each—and vexed the unfortunate monarch with fantastic demands, which honour required him to fulfil. For example, the late chief bard's widow must have a bowl of new milk, with the marrow of a wild pig's trotter; a pet cuckoo singing on a tree beside her, though it was between Christmas and Little Christmas; a full load on her back of lard from a white boar; a horse with purple mane and white feet; and a dress made from spider-webs. Similarly Senchán's daughter wanted a load of black-berries, though it was now the end of winter. Only with the help of a saintly half-brother could the king meet these preposterous claims.

In the sixth century, according to Keating (early seventeenth century), one-third of the free men of Ireland belonged to the poetic order. We hear of swarms of bards quartering themselves on chiefs and farmers from November to May; or visiting their victims with a silver pot, called by the people 'the pot of avarice', and hung by golden hooks from the spears of nine poets. In return for a panegyric the chieftain must throw gold and silver in the pot; otherwise he would be satirized. And Irish satires, it should be remembered, could raise literal blisters on the face.

Indeed the bards made themselves such a nuisance that King Aedh at a convention summoned from all Ireland proposed their expulsion; but St Columcille, himself a bard, crossed from Iona to intercede; and it was compromised that bardic numbers should at least be limited.

Seldom, it seems, have poets lived in such clover. (See Douglas Hyde, *Literary History of Ireland*, 1899, pp. 410-1, 488-90; M. Dillon, *Cycles of the Kings*, 1946, pp. 90-8.)

Yeats knew the old story; but, he says, 'revised the moral . . . to let the poet have the best of it.' He revised it with a vengeance!

*   *   *

The Shadowy Waters
(begun 1885, published 1900, produced 1904,
revised 1905-6[1])

'Her lips, her eyes, all day became to me
The shadow of a shadow utterly.'

ERNEST DOWSON

The hero, Forgael, is on a privateering voyage with his friend
Aibric. But theirs is a curious form of piracy. For, as guides, Forgael
follows certain man-headed birds—souls which emerged from the
dead of a galley which they sank. Yeats had, indeed, an excessive
passion for symbolic birds—in particular, for man-headed or man-
faced birds. These may, I imagine, go back ultimately to Egyptian
representations of the 'Ka', or soul, as a bird with human face.

The sailors have grown as sick of their long voyage as the crew
of Columbus, and would much like to kill Forgael. But they fear
him, and a magic harp of his.

Forgael is following his birds because, in the words of his friend
Aibric—

> They are to bring you to unheard-of passion,
> To some strange love the world knows nothing of,

---

[1] In dealing with this much-revised drama I have followed the version in
Collected Plays. The earliest form is dreamier, vaguer, more obscurely
symbolic. There, for example, Dectora sees scurrying across the waters a
hornless deer pursued by a red-eared hound (i.e. man's desire of the woman
chasing the woman's desire for the desire of the man—but how should an
audience grasp that?). The version of 1906 attempted to redress the balance
with touches of cruder realism from the crew—

> I am so lecherous with abstinence
> I'd give the profit of nine voyages
> For that red Moll that had but the one eye.

But this seems a little too like putting the Wife of Bath arm in arm with
Dante's Beatrice. See T. Parkinson, 'W. B. Yeats: a poet's stagecraft', in
ELH (Baltimore) XVII (1950).

> Some Ever-living woman as you think,
> One that can cast no shadow, being unearthly.

It is the same sort of dream-world as Oisin found with his Niamh. The more rational Aibric suggests that it would be better to content oneself with earthier and less fantastic loves. But Forgael cannot. For, he says, the ordinary lover of ordinary women—

> Loves in brief longing and deceiving hope
> And bodily tenderness, and finds that even
> The bed of love, that in the imagination
> Had seemed to be the giver of all peace,
> Is no more than a wine-cup in the tasting,
> And as soon finished.

One may question whether human love is always quite so poor and so ephemeral. But Forgael is of the type that wants better bread than was ever made of wheat.

At length amid the misty seas, he and his men encounter a ship fragrant with spices; on board is a king kissing a queen. Aibric and the sailors storm this strange vessel, kill its king, and bring back his queen, Dectora, as their prize.

Meanwhile Forgael has spent the time calling to his man-headed birds (five of them now), which have appeared overhead—souls from the slain on the captured ship.

Dectora, the captured queen, demands from him the death of the sailors that have killed her husband. Forgael addresses her in words of mysterious love. But this she meets with defiance—

> There's nothing in the world that's worth a fear.

Curiously enough, almost these very words begin Maud Gonne's *Autobiography*. Her soldier father once said to her—'You must never be afraid of anything, even of death.' It seems possible that Yeats had heard her repeat this saying.

Dectora now makes as if she would jump overboard. Then she tries to raise the crew against Forgael.

> Nine swords with handles of rhinoceros horn
> To him that strikes him first.

A curious bribe.

But Forgael plays his enchanted harp. (The play might perhaps exert more magic if it employed less.) Bewitched, the crew return to the captured ship, to hold a funeral-wake over the slain king.

Dectora too is bewitched. She lowers the sword she had seized from Aibric; she loosens her hair; she lays her crown on the deck. It now seems to her, at moments, that her husband died a thousand years ago; at moments, that Forgael is himself her husband. She has become infatuated with him. (One can well imagine how Yeats might play passionately with the vain dream that one day Maud Gonne might at last look on him with just such enchanted eyes.)

But Forgael hears the crying of the birds—

> Can you not hear their cry?—
> 'There is a country at the end of the world
> Where no child's born but to outlive the moon.'

Presumably this land is the land of death. But Aibric and the sailors have no desire for any such sombre destination. Forgael suggests to Dectora that she too should leave him. But she refuses, flinging back to Aibric his sword, so that he may sever the hawser holding the two vessels side by side.

> We are alone for ever, and I laugh,
> Forgael, because you cannot put me from you.
> The mist has covered the heavens, and you and I
> Shall be alone for ever.

Then the magic harp takes fire, and Forgael winds about him Dectora's long hair.

> Beloved, having dragged the net about us,
> And knitted mesh to mesh, we grow immortal;
> And that old harp awakens of itself
> To cry aloud to the grey birds, and dreams,
> That have had dreams for father, live in us.

Dreams, dreams, dreams! Horace, or Chaucer, or Villon would have thought it all unspeakably odd. But the central idea becomes a little clearer if one recalls that the French symbolist, Villiers de l'Isle-Adam (1838-89), wrote a Rosicrucian play *Axel* (1885) about two lovers, both magicians, who die together rather than spoil by consummation their perfect passion. And Yeats had apparently seen *Axel* performed in Paris in 1894.

But, whatever its sources, *The Shadowy Waters* seems to me somewhat maundering. I find it a relief to recall by contrast a passage in my friend Marie Mauron's *Mont-Paon*, where a bored village-mayor in Provence, weary with waiting for peasant-voters who refuse to turn up, beguiles his tedium by scanning the *faits divers* in the local newspaper.

'The desperate pair, fastened together by the young man's red woollen belt, had promised each other marriage. Unable to unite their lot in this life, they shared death together in the bosom of the waters.' Well may they say (remarked the mayor) that there are in the world three dozen sorts of imbeciles! A famous idea, to drown oneself, in winter, when it's so simple to elope!

Better this clear sun and laughter of Provence, this realistic gaiety of the Latin mind, than an excess of Celtic mists. How much saner and more human than Yeats's Forgael is Homer's Odysseus when he refuses, on the contrary, to abandon his mortal Penelope even for the immortal radiance of Calypso; even though, with her love, she offered him that immortality which Forgael so desperately seeks.

> Dread Goddess, be not angry. Well it is known to me
> That less in loveliness the wise Penelope
> Is than thyself, and meaner in stature to behold—
> For mortal is she; but thou, a Goddess that grows not old.
> Yet, even so, day after day, I crave and yearn
> For the sight of home again, and the day of my return.
> And if some God shall break me, far out on the wine-dark wave,
> Why, then, my heart must bear it, with the patience of the brave.
> Many a toil and trouble, by sea, in fields of war,
> I have endured. This also I will bear, as those I bore.[1]

One can quite well understand that devoted lovers should sometimes find it better to perish together because they cannot live together; like Antony and Cleopatra. But to indulge in the morbid pleasure of a *Liebestod*, just because love at the end of ten years must

---

[1] *Odyssey*, V, 215-24; *Greek Poetry for Everyman*, pp. 119-20.

differ from love at the end of ten days, seems more than a little mad. As well kill oneself today because one will be dead in a hundred years' time.

However, other poets not so wise as Homer have likewise played with this idea of preferring death to decay, or an immediate end to a slow decline. There are, for example, the hero and heroine of Ibsen's *Love's Comedy*, who kill their romance rather than expose it to decline. There is Synge's Deirdre who prefers to go back and perish with Naisi in Ireland rather than see his passion for her perish (which does not, however, show much consideration for Naisi's two brothers, who had to perish too). But I doubt if, in this respect, real human lovers often do what the poets are so fond of dreaming. Ibsen himself married. Yeats himself turned away, at last, from Maud Gonne (who would probably have made him miserable) to an English wife who seems to have made him happy. Trees may wish they could grow up to the sky: but they resign themselves to reality. Trees are not rockets; and, after all, how horrible if they were!

Synge himself deeply disliked this play; and George Moore's comment is also interesting. 'The intellect,' he wrote, 'outlives the heart, and the heart of Yeats seemed to me to have died ten years ago; the last of it probably went into the composition of *The Countess Cathleen*.' I do not think that the heart of Yeats had really died. But it may well be that shadows had come too much to over-shadow his whole mind and imagination. He seems here beginning, like his own Cuchulain, to battle in vain delusion against the waves of the sea of life itself.

Cuchulain may be highly poetic: Mrs Partington is less so.

*   *   *

The Hour-Glass
(written 1902, produced 1903)

> 'Ah, Faustus,
> Now hast thou but one bare hour to live,
> And then thou must be damn'd perpetually.'
>
> MARLOWE

This is another morality play, with a certain naïve and archaic charm; though Wilfrid Blunt found it, when performed, 'a terrible infliction'. 'What Yeats can mean by putting such thin stuff on the stage I can't imagine.'

A Wise Man has taught his disciples and neighbours to disbelieve in God. But suddenly an Angel appears, and tells him he will die as soon as the last grain of sand has fallen through the hour-glass now standing on his desk. And then, of course, the Wise Man will go to Hell—unless he can find, within the hour, some soul that still believes. But the Wise Man can find not a single one. For he has converted everybody to his own unbelief. Only Teigue the fool has kept his faith; and Teigue will not speak.

With his last breath the Wise Man cries—

> It is enough, I know what fixed the station
> Of star and cloud.
> And knowing all, I cry
> That whatso God has willed
> On the instant be fulfilled
> Though that be my damnation.

This passion for being damned seems a little unreal. Lack of imagination, perhaps. Then the Wise Man dies. The Angel reappears with a golden casket. Teigue the Fool catches the white butterfly of the soul, just fluttered from the dead man's lips, and puts it in the box—'He has gone through his pains, and you will open the lid in the Garden of Paradise.' Like the Countess Cathleen, the Wise Man is saved at the last minute of the last hour; and saved by something of a cheat.

The piece seems itself a butterfly, which it would be harsh to break on any ruthless wheel of logic. Yet Yeats can hardly have supposed that if the Wise Man honestly believed his error (supposing it *was* an error), he thereby merited Hell. Nor is it very obvious, on the other hand, why his fortunate failure to convince a fool should merit heaven. But I suppose it might be answered—'All this is part of life's mystery.' The Fool stands for that intuition, that wisdom of babes and sucklings, which is wiser (sometimes) than the wisdom of this world.

*   *   *

On Baile's Strand
(produced 1904)

This retells a legend of the death of Cuchulain, the Irish Achilles. Cuchulain was son of Dectire, half-sister of Conchubar, King of Ulster, by the sun-god Lugh, who begot Cuchulain by dropping, in the form of a may-fly, into Dectire's wine at her wedding-feast, when she married an Ulster chieftain.

Cuchulain in his youth went off to Alba (Scotland), where he warred with the Amazon princess Scathach and her rival-queen Aoife (Eefa). These viragoes seem curiously like Greek Amazons. One wonders if they recall some prehistoric struggle between matriarchy and patriarchy; like the *Eumenides* of Aeschylus.

At all events Cuchulain conquered Aoife, just as Heracles, Theseus, and Achilles all conquered their Amazon queens; and Aoife bore Cuchulain a son. But Cuchulain went back to Ireland and wedded Emer. Then the jealous Aoife bred up her son Conlaoch (Conla) to become the slayer of his sire. In due course, the lad arrived at Dundealgan (now Dundalk), the home of Cuchulain; forced a duel on his unwilling, unknowing father; and was killed. Dying, the young hero revealed himself. And the frenzy of

Cuchulain was such that, to prevent him from destroying the men of Ulster, Cathbad the Druid bewitched him; so that his hallucination mistook the sea-waves for advancing warriors. With these Cuchulain battled till he died; vainly, and literally, 'taking arms against a sea of troubles'.

This of course recalls Sohrab and Rustum, and the many other legends of sons battling with fathers or killing them, like Oedipus; stories that, on Freudian theory, embody the Oedipus-complex itself. In any case this strife of sire and son is familiar enough in the human as in the animal world, with its bulls, or cocks, or robins. The younger generations, alike of men and beasts, are apt to knock ruthlessly at the door.

Yeats's play contains a quasi-chorus of singing women; and also a kind of second chorus, or anti-masque, consisting of a Blind Man and a Fool, who provide a macabre sort of comic relief, with their rags and grotesquely moulded masks. Indeed Yeats came to acquire a passion for masks; partly, perhaps because he grew drawn to the idea that each man in life should have his own mask; and partly because his own strength did not lie in creating lifelike individuals.

The piece opens with a dialogue between Fool and Blind Man who have been cooking behind the scenes a stolen hen. The Blind Man reveals that Conchubar is going to impose an oath of allegiance on Cuchulain; and, further, that a red-haired youth from Aoife's country has landed to kill the hero. The Blind Man hints that, having himself been in Aoife's country before he lost his sight, he knows this youth to be Aoife's own son, bred up by her to kill Cuchulain. And the Blind Man also throws out mysterious hints as to who the young man's father is.

Then there enter Cuchulain, a dark man a little over forty, and the much older Conchubar; wrangling, rather like Homer's Achilles and Agamemnon, because Conchubar wishes to impose on the imperious Cuchulain an oath of allegiance. Fool and Blind Man spoke prose; but the two kings use blank verse. They drift into a rather rambling discussion on the advantages and drawbacks of having sons. Taxed with scorning the princesses of Ireland, Cuchulain admits that he would soonest have had a child by the proud, warlike Aoife of Scotland.

And here, as usual with Yeats, though this time after a rather long delay, there breaks in some real poetry.

> Ah! Conchubar, had you seen her
> With that high, laughing, turbulent head of hers
> Thrown backward, and the bowstring at her ear,
> Or sitting at the fire with those grave eyes
> Full of good counsel as it were with wine,
> Or when love ran through all the lineaments
> Of her wild body—although she had no child,
> None other had all beauty, queen or lover,
> Or was so fitted to give birth to kings.

And yet, replies Conchubar, she now hates you. And Cuchulain answers (Yeats was curiously, perhaps morbidly, obsessed, like Strindberg, with the hatred that can be intermixed with love)—

> No wonder in that, no wonder at all in that.
> I never have known love but as a kiss
> In the mid-battle, and a difficult truce
> Of oil and water, candles and dark night,
> Hillside and hollow, the hot-footed sun
> And the cold, sliding, slippery-footed moon—
> A brief forgiveness between opposites
> That have been hatreds for three times the age
> Of this long-'stablished ground.

But if that was all Cuchulain had known, he had been unlucky. Yeats still seems haunted by his obsession with Maud Gonne.

Again Conchubar presses the oath of allegiance on Cuchulain, who refuses—'I will no more of it.' Yet a moment later (with that dream-like inconsequence which makes, and mars, so many of Yeats's characters) Cuchulain acquiesces, when the other princes of Ulster demand it—

> I'll take what oath you will.

The oath is duly taken—with much rather tedious ritual and stuff about

> miracle-working juice
> That is made out of the grease
> Of the ungoverned unicorn.

One wearies of Yeats's herds of unicorns—let alone their grease.

Now enters Cuchulain's unknown son, to challenge him. But Cuchulain, sensing the red-haired lad's likeness to his mother Aoife, is reluctant; and seeks to make friends with this young stranger. Then, however—most unconvincingly—Cuchulain lets himself be persuaded that he has been bewitched into this groundless fondness, and rushes out to fight.

Three women sing a choric dirge of foreboding. Then squalid realism returns, with the Fool and Blind Man quarrelling because the Blind Man has stealthily eaten up the stolen hen.

Cuchulain re-enters victorious, with blood upon his sword. Then the Blind Man reveals to him that he has killed his own son. Yet why he did not reveal this vital fact before, remains obscure. Timidity? Indifference? Malice?

Here, however, comes an effective moment—

Blind Man.　　Somebody is trembling, Fool! The bench is shaking. Why are you trembling? Is Cuchulain going to hurt us? It was not I who told you, Cuchulain.

Fool.　　It is Cuchulain trembling. It is Cuchulain who is shaking the bench.

Yet a moment later, I feel, the effect is destroyed.

Cuchulain.　　'Twas they that did it, the pale windy people.[1]
　　　　　　　　Where? where? where? My sword against the thunder!
　　　　　　　　But no, for they have always been my friends;
　　　　　　　　And though they love to blow a smoking coal
　　　　　　　　Till it's all flame, the wars they blow aflame
　　　　　　　　Are full of glory, and heart-uplifting pride,
　　　　　　　　And not like this. The wars they love awaken
　　　　　　　　Old fingers and the sleepy strings of harps.
　　　　　　　　Who did it then? Are you afraid? Speak out!

What ranting bluster! No grief, no love, no pity for the son he has just killed—only the pompous fury of an egotist who finds himself hoaxed and fooled. Arnold managed very differently those passionate last words that pass between Rustum and the dying Sohrab.

[1] The Sidhe, the fairies.

Fierce man, bethink thee, for an only son!
What will that grief, what will that vengeance be?

In Cuchulain there is much vengeance, but too little grief. It seems to me typical of that lack of simple, compassionate humanity which is so often the fatal flaw of Yeats's plays (though not, at its best, of his poetry).

Then, realizing that it was Conchubar who drove him on, Cuchulain rushes out to kill the High King. But, bewitched, he mistakes the white wave-crests for the King's crown; and plunges battling into the sea.

Fool. The waves have mastered him.
Blind Man. There will be nobody in the houses. Come this way; come quickly! The ovens will be full. We will put our hands into the ovens.

The trouble with this play, I feel, is that there is again not a single character who wakens sympathy. Far better the old legend in its original form. Yeats's drama seems in this respect also the exact opposite of Arnold; whose poem is, on the contrary, so vastly superior to its own source, the fantastic Persian epic of Firdausi. For though the source of Arnold's poem was Persian, its spirit comes straight from the Greek—from the noble, compassionate fatalism of Homer.

> Quick! quick! for number'd are my sands of life,
> And swift; for like the lightning to this field
> I came, and like the wind I go away—
> Sudden, and swift, and like a passing wind.
> But it was writ in Heaven that this should be.

All such preferences must remain merely subjective. But Arnold's ending, with the calm onflow of Oxus towards Polar Star and Aral Sea, seems to me far more satisfying than masked beggars plundering ovens.

Yeats, however, hating his time and its tendencies, is haunted, here too, by the survival of the meanest when the noblest fall.[1] By

---

[1] Compare p. 339 (*Purgatory*); p. 340 (*The Death of Cuchulain*); and such poems as *The Old Age of Queen Maeve*:

temperament he was an aristocrat, with a dislike of the populace which was later to lead him dangerously far on the greasy road towards Fascism.

More important, there seems to me lacking in Yeats's play—as in most of his plays—one vital tragic quality which is intense in Arnold, as in Arnold's master, Homer—the quality of pity. Cuchulain appears to claim not so much our sympathy and compassion as merely our admiration. But thus to demand admiration can be dangerous; it may provoke refusal. About it there clings something a little harsh and arrogant. With Sohrab and Rustum it was other-wise.

*   *   *

Deirdre
(begun 1904, finished and produced 1906, revised 1922)

'But Melanippus and Comaetho I count as beyond the reach of calamity; since, for man, love fulfilled is the one thing worth buying with life itself.'

PAUSANIAS, VII, 19

Here the inevitable comparison with the parallel tragedy by Synge is of particular interest, for the light it throws on both writers, whichever one may prefer.[1]

> She had been beautiful in that old way
> That's all but gone; for the proud heart is gone,
> And the fool heart of the counting-house fears all
> But soft beauty and indolent desire.

[1] There is also a *Deirdre* in three acts by George Russell (A.E.). But this seems to me a watery affair. Here Lavarcham, instead of being Deirdre's old nurse, becomes a Druidess. (Synge's nurse was far more real.) There is also too much blind fate, too much Druid magic, too little human passion and conflict. Naisi, again, returns to Ulster simply because of pride and home-sickness. There is not that other, gnawing sense of the transience of all life, all love, which makes Synge's play so tragic.

The *Deirdre* of Yeats has only a single act, corresponding to the last of Synge's three. And not only is the *Deirdre* of Yeats more like a Greek play in thus keeping the unities by beginning the story near its end; it also contains a chorus, consisting of three comely, middle-aged women-musicians. The piece opens with a sort of Euripidean prologue by two of these musicians, explaining the plot's previous events. And, in general, the whole drama, with the stiff, cold, marmoreal dignity of its blank verse, remains as remote, stylized, and archaic as a group of ancient statues.

The prologue is Euripidean in its baldness.

> *First Musician.* I have a story right, my wanderers,
> That has so mixed with fable in our songs
> That all seems fabulous.

Already this iteration of 'fable' and 'fabulous' seems to toss away disdainfully any idea of realism. Contrast the naturalistic opening of Synge:

> *Old Woman.* She hasn't come yet, is it, and it falling to the night?
> *Lavarcham.* She has not. . . . It's dark with the clouds coming from the west and south.

Yeats's musicians tell how the ageing King Conchubar found in a hillside house the child Deirdre, with an old witch to nurse her (witchcraft again); loved her; planned to wed her; then lost her seven years since, when she fled with Naoise, son of Usna.

Yet the tragic end of Deirdre and Naoise loses much by this omission of their love's beginning; just as *Romeo and Juliet* would suffer if Shakespeare had given us only that final, fatal night in the churchyard of Verona. Synge, one may feel, managed more wisely in showing us both the wild charm of his girlish Deirdre and, in contrast, the tragic Deirdre of the close. It takes a rare dramatic mastery to make the Unities worth the heavy price they often cost.

Now enters Fergus, a sort of old Polonius, who imagines he has persuaded Conchubar to grant the fugitives forgiveness. Trusting to that, they have just returned to Ulster. But the First Musician remains suspicious of the King's good faith. Can Deirdre and her lover have grown tired of life?

Fergus and the First Musician argue the point; a little tediously, since most of the audience already know the simple answer—that Conchubar is falsity itself.

Then dark-faced warriors in barbaric dress pass the window. Why these swarthy Libyan barbarians should be imported into Ireland by a King with many famous warriors of his own, one fails to see. Fergus, indeed, suggests—

> They may have brought him Libyan dragon-skin
> Or the ivory of the fierce unicorn.

Not very plausible. And more unicorns! Synge preferred the simple poetry of human passion to whole studs of unicorns, whole acres of dragon-skin. The contrast between him and Yeats is not wholly unlike that between the homely Wordsworth and the romantic Coleridge; of whom it has been said, with pardonable exaggeration, that he would have turned even Wordsworth's leech-gatherer into a collector of humming-birds. But in drama at least, it may be well to be less exotic. Indeed one is tempted to see a self-portrait of one side of Yeats himself, in the words here spoken by Fergus—

> Your wild thought
> Fed on extravagant poetry, and lit
> By such a dazzle of old fabulous tales
> That common things are lost, and all that's strange
> Is true because 'twere pity if it were not.

The Musicians now sing a brief choric ode while Fergus re-enters with Naoise and Deirdre. And the two last lines of this song are moving in their simpler truth—

> What is all our praise to them
> That have one another's eyes?

Naoise wonders that Conchubar should have sent no welcome. Yet he represses his suspicions.

> I have his word and I must take that word,
> Or prove myself unworthy of my nurture
> Under a great man's roof.

Surely a most curious doctrine?—as if the words of kings had not been, from the very dawn of history, things that honest men might very well distrust; and that prudent men have constantly distrusted. Whoever dreamed that the psalmist demeaned himself by crying 'Put not your trust in princes'? And since when has it become 'unworthy' to face such simple facts?

Then Naoise sees on a side-table a chessboard—

> It is the board
> Where Lugaidh Redstripe and that wife of his
> Who had a seamew's body half the year,
> Played at the chess upon the night they died . . .
> If the tale's true,
> When it was plain that they had been betrayed,
> They moved the men and waited for the end
> As it were bedtime.

No doubt Yeats was delighted to be able to drag in this good lady who wore gull's feathers half the year—what a find! But surely, in a human tragedy, sea-mewing ladies interpose an abyss of remoteness—a distance that does *not* enchant; and, in that void, human sympathy grows chilled.

Naoise and Fergus go out to look for a messenger. The First Musician hints to Deirdre that the King has sewn into his bedcurtains

> strange, miracle-working wicked stones
> Men tear out of the heart and the hot brain
> Of Libyan dragons.

These will enchant Deirdre, once she is bedded there, to forget Naoise and to love the King. (Yet one may wonder why a monarch with so much magic at his disposal ever lost Deirdre at all.)

Naoise and Fergus return. Naoise still disbelieves, or pretends to disbelieve, Deirdre's suspicions of the High King. Then, to goad him into escape, she tries rousing his jealousy, and feigning that she really loves Conchubar. But escape, says Fergus, is impossible. Then appears a Dark-faced Messenger. He bids Deirdre and Fergus to sup with the King; but *not* the traitor Naoise. Fergus (who is made unconscionably stupid) pretends that so outrageous a message *must* be false. Then he goes to rally his own followers, that he may save, or at least avenge, the lovers.

Naoise bids Deirdre, since all is clearly lost, sit down and play chess with him. Then follows another choric ode; close in spirit, this time, to *The Shadowy Waters*—

> What's the merit in love-play,
> In the tumult of the limbs
>   That dies out before 'tis day,
> Heart on heart, or mouth on mouth,
>   All that mingling of our breath,
> When love-longing is but drouth
>   For the things come after death?

So persistent in Yeats were the love of the impossible, and the craving for things beyond the grave. But Deirdre cannot go on playing this cold-blooded chess. She starts up from the board, and kneels down at Naoise's feet.

> I cannot go on playing like that woman
> That had but the cold blood of the sea in her veins.
> *Naoise.*   It is your move. Take up your man again.
> *Deirdre.*   Do you remember that first night in the woods
> We lay all night on leaves, and looking up,
> When the first grey of dawn awoke the birds,
> Saw leaves above us? You thought that I still slept,
> And bending down to kiss me on the eyes,
> Found they were open. Bend and kiss me now,
> For it may be the last before our death.
> And when that's over, we'll be different;
> Imperishable things, a cloud or a fire.
> And I know nothing but this body, nothing
> But that old vehement, bewildering kiss.

Lyric beauty, as so often. Lovely, poignant! Yet how ghostly! These lovers are so fatalistic, so dreamily inert, that they patiently wait to be murdered—playing chess! Surely one of the greatest warriors of Eire, caught in such a snare, would have been using his wits and his muscles to hack a way out; not sitting to let the woman he loves be ravished, and himself killed, so unlike Synge's Naisi, in sheep-like helplessness?

Sir Lancelot showed himself much more practical, when *he* was trapped defenceless in the bower of Guinevere. Lancelot had not even his armour; none the less, he opened the door a little, so that Sir Colgrevance of Gore, 'a much man and a large', came striding in; and then Sir Lancelot smote him grovelling and 'with the help of the queen and her ladies was lightly armed in Sir Colgrevance's armour'. And then he burst out and slew Sir Agravaine and twelve of his fellows. Sir Thomas Malory may have been 'touched with war and wantonness'; but at least he was an effectual man of his hands, in refreshing contrast to this passive, nightmare impotence.

Now Conchubar himself appears for a moment, spying in at the door. Naoise rushing after him is caught in a great net, and dragged back by the Libyan guards. But one may doubt whether all this makes life easy for the play's producer. On the stage a hero netted like a fish by blackamoors will find it hard to keep much heroic dignity.

Conchubar now promises Naoise freedom, if Deirdre will become his queen. And Deirdre tries to force herself to accept. But Naoise will not have it.

> O eagle! If you were to do this thing,
> And buy my life of Conchubar with your body,
> Love's law being broken, I would stand alone
> Upon the eternal summits, and call out,
> And you could never come there, being banished.

And yet how cold seems this talk of 'eternal summits' for lovers in such a torturing dilemma!

In Morris's poem of the Hundred Years War, *The Haystack in the Floods*, a triumphant villain plays exactly the same trick of blackmail on the woman he desires—your body, or your lover's life. But in Morris the doomed lover keeps the anguished silence that in such an agony he well might keep; and as for the girl—

> She laid her hand upon her brow,
> Then gazed upon the palm, as though
> She thought her forehead bled, and —'No',
> She said, and turn'd her head away,
> As there were nothing else to say.

318

Natural, unforced, unpretending—far more human, and more moving, than rhetoric about 'eternal summits'.

In Morris's poem I can see the horror really happening; as hundreds of such horrors *have* really happened. I feel the dark, deathly chill of that sodden haystack in the floods of France. It has the very sting of life and death.

But Yeats's Deirdre only kneels to Conchubar and begs for mercy. If anyone, she pleads, is punished, it should be herself—for it was really she that wooed Naoise to love her.

> The very moment these eyes fell on him;
> I told him; I held out my hands to him;
> How could he refuse . . .
> What do I say? My hands?—No, no, my lips—
> For I had pressed my lips upon his lips—
> I swear it is not false—my breast to his.

Once again one feels that Yeats was far better as poet than as dramatist or psychologist. Surely Deirdre had less than her share of woman's wit if she could think this a good way to pacify a jealous old tyrant. His jealousy would only be maddened to redoubled rage by such a picture, in all its physical detail, of her passion for his rival. And what use in begging Conchubar to punish herself instead? His thoughts are set, not on punishing, but on possessing her; in such a brute, the lust for possession might grow only the sweeter for the thought that it would be, to her, punishment as well.

While Deirdre talks, Naoise is gagged; then taken behind a curtain, and put to the sword. At sight of the bloodstained blade Deirdre sinks into a deathly calm of despair. She pretends to resign herself. She will become Conchubar's queen—only first let her bid Naoise an eternal farewell.

> In good time,
> You'll stir me to more passion than he could . . .
> I will see him
> All blood-bedabbled and his beauty gone.
> It's better when you're beside me in your strength
> That the mind's eye should call up the soiled body,
> And not the shape I loved.

319

But, again, Deirdre seems an abysmal goose to suppose that a pretext so far-fetched, so hollow, so callously crude, could convince or persuade a jealously passionate king. Besides, since Conchubar has had sown into his bed-curtains those magic stones from the hearts and brains of Libyan dragons, which will make Deirdre intoxicated with him instead of Naoise, the need for her to see Naoise loathsomely mangled becomes, were it possible, more needless still.

> *Conchubar.*   How do I know that you have not some knife
> And go to die upon his body?
> *Deirdre.*   Have me searched,
> If you would make so little of your queen.
> It may be that I have a knife hid here
> Under my dress. Bid one of these dark slaves
> To search me for it.

Here again the dramatist does not seem to get inside the skins of his characters. Was it likely that Conchubar would have his Deirdre fumbled by black slaves? And what need, when there were already in the room three women-musicians who could quite well search her?

However most improbably, Conchubar let her go. Exactly as he suspected, she *has* a hidden knife; and kills herself above her dead lover, while the Chorus laments—

> They are gone, they are gone. Whispering were enough.
> Into the secret wilderness of their love.
> A high, grey cairn. What more is to be said?
> Eagles have gone into their cloudy bed.

Here would have been the place to stop. But the ending is further dragged out by the entrance of the ineffectual Fergus at the head of his ineffectual mob, who can do no more than bawl 'Death to Conchubar!' Conchubar, however, is not in the least perturbed.

> I have no need of weapons,
> There's not a traitor that dare stop my way.
> Howl, if you will; but I, being King, did right
> In choosing her most fitting to be Queen,
> And letting no boy lover take the sway.

Lamer ending for a tragedy it might take long to find.

No wonder Synge was not deterred by Yeats's *Deirdre* from rehandling the subject himself. And though Synge never lived to finish *his* play, even so it finishes, as it began, far better.

Lavarcham (*beside the grave*).   Deirdre is dead, and Naisi is dead; and if the oaks and stars could die for sorrow, it's a dark sky and a hard and naked earth we'd have this night in Emain.

Synge's prose seems to me here far more poetic than Yeats's verse—and far more suited to the stage, in a period when so few actors have the power to speak blank verse, and so few audiences ears to hear it. Yet it is typical of Yeats's generosity that he himself called Synge's last act 'the most poignant and noble in Irish drama'.

*   *   *

The Unicorn from the Stars
(produced 1907)

This is a rewriting (with Lady Gregory) of an earlier play, *Where There Is Nothing* (written in 1902, produced in London in 1904).[1] Yeats had once heard a strange story about a Catholic mystic known to A. E. (George Russell); and told George Moore of it. Yeats and Moore then laid a plan for collaborating to dramatize it. Next, Yeats cried off; and Moore said he would make it into a novel. Then Yeats hastily wrote the play, *Where There Is Nothing*, published it as a supplement to the paper *United Ireland*,[2] and wrote to Russell— 'Tell Moore to write his story and be hanged.'

[1] 'Though *The Unicorn* is almost altogether Lady Gregory's writing, it has far more of my spirit in it than *Where There Is Nothing* which she and I and Douglas Hyde wrote in a fortnight to keep George Moore from stealing the plot.' (Letter to A. H. Bullen, 1908.)

[2] Moore, he says, would not have dared to issue an injunction against *United Ireland*, a Nationalist paper, for fear of having his own windows broken.

In *Where There Is Nothing* a landowner, Paul Ruttledge, gives up his wealth; takes to the road with tinkers; falls ill; enters a monastery; turns to preaching wholesale destruction, including that of the church itself; and is finally murdered by a misunderstanding mob. 'Where there is nothing, there is God'—such is the theme. 'We perish into reality.'

In the first days of the world when men came freshly from God they lived as God meant them to live. . . . And as I gather these flowers to my breast, they gathered all His love into their hearts. . . .

Then men ate the fruit of the tree of knowledge. And because when they lived according to the will of God in mother-wit and natural kindness they sometimes did one another an injury, they thought it would be better to be safe than to be blessed, and they made the laws. The laws were the first sin. They were the first mouthful of the apple. We must put out the laws as I put out this candle.

And then men began to make cities and build villages, because, when they lived in the midst of the love of God, that is the changing heavens and the many-coloured fields, they were sometimes wetted by the rain, and sometimes cold and hungry, and sometimes alone from one another. They thought it would be better to be comfortable than to be blessed. We must put out the cities as I put out this candle. . . .

God made everything holy because everything that is full of life is full of His will, and everything that is beautiful is an image of His love. But man grew timid, and called some things holy, and some things unholy, because it had been hard to find his way among so much holiness. . . . And from these and from like things he built up the Church. We must destroy the Church. We must put it out as I put out this candle. . . .

The Christian . . . must so live that all things shall pass away. He will so live that he will put out the body. (*Puts out a candle.*) He will so live that he will put out the whole world. (*Puts out a candle.*) We must destroy the world. We must destroy everything that has law and number, for where there is nothing there is God.

One can imagine this rhythmic eloquence and poetic symbolism being effective on the stage; and the play's beginning shows unusual life and humour (though that may be mainly Lady Gregory's). But the rest of the piece seems thin; and its general idea might have provoked from Johnson, even at his mildest, a disdainful Fiddle-de-dee, my dear!'

One can recognize in it echoes of Rousseau, nostalgic for the primitive; and the voice of Blake with his passion for spontaneity, his rage against restraint, and law, and government, and 'priests in black gowns'.

A Freudian, I suppose, might see in all three men—Rousseau, Blake, and Yeats—an anti-rational reversion towards early child-hood; that golden age when wishes seemed all-powerful, because mothers and nurses rushed to do our will; when life's laws and rules and restraints and frustrations had hardly yet dawned on us. The Golden Age imagined for the race seems a dream-reflection of that Golden Age of the individual's infancy. A not uncommon dream. And yet—

> 'But what good came of it at last?'
> Quoth little Peterkin.

Later, Yeats himself took a dislike to *Where There Is Nothing*, and transformed it into *The Unicorn from the Stars* (with three acts instead of five). This, however, has been generally judged much inferior.

Here the mystic has become strangely transformed into a coach-builder's apprentice, in the Ireland of George IV. The lad has mystic visions of unicorns (the symbols of virginal, tireless strength) breaking the world to pieces. 'And I heard the command, "Destroy, destroy, destruction is the life-giver! destroy!" ' And so, misunder-standing his own vision, he rouses a lot of beggars and vagrants to burn and sack a great house; and is accidentally shot by a constable, after realizing, too late, that the true battle to be fought lies within the human soul.

But a lot of the dialogue seems to me undistinguished; and though Yeats as a person seems to have been by no means without wit and humour, as a writer his strength lay elsewhere. The death-scene at the play's end brought from George Moore the comment—'Poor Yeats! He's dead.' But in view of the play's history, as related above, George Moore could hardly be impartial.

*   *   *

The Green Helmet (1908-10)

This reverts to the legends of Ancient Ireland, and is a kind of heroic farce. The three Ulster heroes, Laegaire (Leary), Conall, and Cuchulain, are perpetual rivals; so are their wives and servants. Cuchulain, returned from Scotland, finds the other two heroes waiting anxiously for the Red Man, a supernatural being who two years ago offered to let them cut off his head, on condition that he should afterwards have a return blow at theirs. Conall duly cut off the Red Man's head; the Red Man picked it up, laughing, and went off; now this supernatural creature is due to return, and claim his counterblow.[1]

The Red Man arrives attended by three black, cat-headed followers. Cuchulain alone dares to kneel down and face decapitation. But he is spared by the Red Man; whose final words, in the staple metre of the piece (which is that of Morris's *Sigurd the Volsung*), reveal Yeats's ideal attitude to life at this time, in reaction (I take it) from his long, sorrowful service of Maud Gonne—

> I have not come for your hurt, I'm the Rector of this land,
> And with my spitting cat-heads, my frenzied moon-bred band,
> Age after age I sift it, and choose for its championship
> The man who hits my fancy.
>   (*He places the Helmet on Cuchulain's head.*)
>   And I choose the laughing lip
> That shall not turn from laughing, whatever rise or fall;
> The heart that grows no bitterer although betrayed by all;
> The hand that loves to scatter; the life like a gambler's throw;
> And these things I make prosper, till a day come that I know,
> When heart and mind shall darken that the weak may end the strong,
> And the long-remembering harpers have matter for their song.

But this mask of light-hearted laughter did not, I feel, really fit the face of Yeats. And the humour of the piece does not seem very amusing.

---

[1] This legend of the Red Man bears, of course, an obvious resemblance to *Sir Gawain and the Green Knight*.

*   *   *

FOUR PLAYS FOR DANCERS

In 1915 Yeats was fifty. The world of his youth had vanished in the cataclysm of a World War, with the Irish 'troubles' soon to follow. The poet must by now have realized that he was not made for a popular dramatist. Yet the drama still lured him. So he came to long for 'an unpopular theatre and an audience like a secret society—just fifty or so'. It was ironic that Yeats who had done so much to found an Irish stage for the Irish folk, should thus turn away towards an exclusive élite; while the Irish stage itself, moved, with dramatists like Synge, and soon O'Casey, in an opposite direction along the road of naturalism. But in the Noh plays of Japan, with their dreamy remoteness, their ghosts and masks and musicians, Yeats now found a model to his mind; and in 1916 he began his *Four Plays for Dancers—At the Hawk's Well, The Only Jealousy of Emer, The Dreaming of the Bones*, and *Calvary*.

To Yeats, aloof and mask-loving, it was natural that such plays should hold a special appeal; but it may also be suspected that the type of temperament which shares his taste is likely, as he thought, to remain rare. He wished to gain an effect of 'distance'; but this distance does not necessarily add much magic. Characters are largely replaced by ideas; and even the ideas seem often ghostly-thin. Yeats had called a work of his youth *The Island of Statues*; his stage now becomes almost a stage of statues, with intervals of dance—a saraband of shadows—a kind of spiritualist séance, with the playwright as a kind of hieratic, yet heretic, ritualist.[1]

---

[1] It has been suggested that masks were needed for this kind of intimate drama because the players were too close to the audience for ordinary make-up. But this seems contradicted by the stage-directions. For, though some characters are masked, some are made-up to look *as if* masked; and some, we are told, can be either. For others, again, there is no indication. Masks of the kind Yeats wanted were things of considerable elaboration; and he seems to have demanded them for certain important characters, not so much from any practical necessity as because he liked the effect.

At the Hawk's Well
(performed 1916, published 1921)

'And then the old man totters nigh,
And feebly rakes among the stones.
The mount is mute, the channel dry;
And down he lays his weary bones.'
MATTHEW ARNOLD, *The Progress of Poesy*

An old man has sat waiting fifty years (Yeats himself was now fifty) beside a magic well that flows only at rare moments (as the healing Pool of Bethesda in St John was troubled only at intervals by its angel).

He who drinks, they say,
Of that miraculous water lives for ever.

It is, however, left ambiguous how far this new life is meant as *literal* immortality, how far it signifies some revelation of the world's mystery. At all events, whenever the water flowed, the old man was cheated of it by falling asleep. And now to his dismay arrives a young rival, Cuchulain, seeking the same water of life. But the hawk-like Woman of the Sidhe,[1] entering into the woman-guardian of the well, lures the young hero away; the old man again falls asleep; and again the mystic water flows in vain. Love, war, the weakness of the flesh—all cheat man of the ultimate wisdom. And the Chorus of Three Musicians concludes that the quest is but a bitter vanity—better a quiet acceptance of the simple joys of human transience.[2]

*   *   *

The Only Jealousy of Emer
(1917, printed 1919)

This forms a sequel to *On Baile's Strand* and *The Hawk's Well*. It will be recalled that, after Cuchulain had killed his own son, he

[1] Fairies (pronounced 'Shee').
[2] For a patient elaboration of Yeats's mystical sources and meanings, see F. A. C. Wilson, *Yeats's Iconography*, pp. 27-72.

seemingly died in frenzied battle with the waves. Now his (masked) figure lies on a bed in a fisher's hut, while a similar masked figure (his ghost) wanders in the room; and beside the bed sits his wife Emer. At her summons enters his mistress Eithne Inguba. The two women cannot see Cuchulain's ghost. But Emer, suspecting the figure on the bed to be only a changeling, set there by supernatural powers, bids her rival Eithne Inguba, the beloved mistress, cry to Cuchulain's spirit to return; and then kiss the figure on the bed. Hereupon the recumbent body wakes, and declares itself to be really Bricriu of the Sidhe, the discord-maker with the withered arm. Touching Emer's eyes, he reveals to her the ghost of Cuchulain, who has been snared by the Goddess Fand, the Woman of the Sidhe—the same as lured him, long years before, away from the Hawk's Well. Only one thing, says Bricriu, can force Fand to surrender Cuchulain—that is, if Emer will renounce her own hope that, after all his infidelities, Cuchulain will come back to her own arms again. This vital secret is revealed to her by Bricriu because he is Fand's enemy. Then Fand herself appears, and lures Cuchulain's spirit to follow her. In agony, Emer cries out her desperate renunciation. At once Cuchulain himself awakens on the bed—Bricriu has vanished. Eithne Inguba returns; claims exultantly that it was *her* love that won the hero back; and falls into his arms. Poor Emer's sacrifice has been made; has succeeded; but is utterly ignored.

The Musicians chant their closing chorus; whose essence seems to lie in the lines—

> He that has loved the best
> May turn from a statue
> His too human breast.

For Fand is absolute beauty, symbolized by the full moon on her fifteenth day; and that absolute remains beyond human love.

Behind it all seems to stand, once more, that statuesque phantom of Maud Gonne, from whom Yeats had turned away at last to a wife and home.[1]

---

[1] Yeats produced also a prose version, *Fighting the Waves* (acted 1929). But I feel serious doubts when F. A. C. Wilson calls this 'Homeric'. It may or may not be true that Eithne's reunion with Cuchulain rescued from the

But some readers will feel that poor Emer is rather harshly treated by the poet, as well as by her husband; and that the piece as a whole, with all its esoteric significances, remains as ghostly, and as masked, as its ghosts.

*   *   *

The Dreaming of the Bones
(1917, printed 1919, produced 1931)

Here still reek bitterly the blood and smoke of the Easter Rising. A young Sinn Feiner, escaped from the fighting in Dublin, is on the run westwards towards Aran. Now, on the barren coast of Clare, near Corcomroe Abbey,[1] he enters through the darkness with a lantern. There meet him two ghosts, a man and a woman in heroic masks, who guide him to the Abbey. They warn him that the place is full of phantoms—in particular, the lonely phantoms of two lovers, who wander there in agelong torment and frustration; together, yet sundered by their memory of guilt—Diarmuid and Dervorgilla.[2] Their curse can be lifted only if, at last, an Irishman

---

waves owes something to Helen's reunion with Paris rescued from the battle-field, in *Iliad III* (though Mr Wilson seems wrong in saying that Helen 'comes to persuade her lover back to consciousness'; for Paris was *not* unconscious). But Yeats and Homer belong, I feel, to utterly different worlds. The creator of the dog Argus would, I feel, have shared Johnson's preference for a picture of a dog he knew, to all the allegories in creation. One might, indeed, parallel Cuchulain, turning from the goddess Fand to the human Eithne, with Odysseus, turning from the divine Circe and Calypso to the human Penelope. But a vast gulf still remains. Yeats seems to me wholly un-Homeric.

[1] Not far from Gort, Coole, and Yeats's Tower of Ballylee.

[2] According to the story, Diarmuid, or Dermot, MacMurrough, King of Leinster, carried off in 1152 Dervorgilla, wife of the one-eyed Tighernan O'Ruairc, Lord of Brefni. Driven from his kingdom fourteen years later (1166) by the injured husband, in 1167 Dermot brought the Normans into Ireland.

But the true facts are in part obscure; in part, different. (1) Dermot and Dervorgilla were not romantic young lovers, but middle-aged (42 and 44 respectively). (2) Dervorgilla's real feelings are unknown—was she carried off willingly or unwillingly? In any case, before long she either went back, or was captured and sent back, to her husband. Further, in the general nature of things the Norman conquest was probably inevitable, even though poor Dervorgilla had never been born.

will forgive them. Never, answers the young man, can those two find forgiveness. Then he realizes that these two strangers were themselves Diarmuid and Dervorgilla, as they vanish into the driving cloud, accursed still.

> I had almost yielded and forgiven it all—
> Terrible the temptation and the place!

The piece ends with a chorus from the usual Three Musicians. They sing of the bitter dreaming of those guilty lovers; but also of the red March-cocks crowing for a new dawn that banishes all spectres of the past (and, presumably, shall usher in a braver future).

As in *Purgatory*,[1] Yeats is here, apparently, expressing his genuine belief that souls must relive their earthly transgressions in purgatorial nightmare, till at last they can view them with 'calm of mind, all passion spent'. The impatient reader, weary of Yeats's too abundant private beliefs, may murmur 'why believe anything of the sort?' Still it is only fair, for these few pages, to control one's impatience, and suspend one's disbelief.

The piece is influenced, as pointed out by F. A. C. Wilson, both by Dante's Paolo and Francesca, and by the ghostly conventions of the Japanese Noh, especially *Nishikigi*.[2]

Poets are licensed to steal. The nymph Echo has often been a tenth Muse. But only on one condition—that they better what they steal. Otherwise the reader is left dissatisfied. Now *The Dreaming of the Bones* does not seem to me to better what it steals. Beside Dante's Paolo and Francesca, it shrivels.

Further, this refusal of forgiveness, which condemns the lovers still to endure the anguish they have suffered for seven hundred years, leaves a somewhat nasty taste of vindictiveness, rancour, and propaganda. Surely seven centuries might suffice, even for the over-tenacious memories of Ireland.

When Yeats thus accused her of ruining Ireland, her ghost might have accused him in reply of condemning her on inadequate evidence. True, she has been dead a long time; but a writer, I feel, should try to be just even to the dead—even to the dead of centuries ago.

[1] p. 337.

[2] *Yeats's Iconography*, p. 207 ff. (with a helpful summary of *Nishikigi*).

No doubt 'the troubles' or 'the crossness', as the Irish call them, could understandably breed a bitterness from which, in general, Yeats kept himself finely free. Still, one may contrast, and prefer, the generosity of Homer's Priam to Helen on the wall of Ilios, when the old king blames, not her, but the gods, for his country's ruin; or the generosity of Gisli Sursson in the Icelandic saga—'I blame thee not; for, once things are doomed, someone *must* speak the words that seem to bring them to pass'. So Blake felt, when he likened the Furies to 'clergymen in the pulpit, scourging sin instead of forgiving it'. And so, in finer moods, felt Yeats himself. Had he not written in 1901, of Balzac?—

He would have us understand that behind the momentary self, which acts and lives in the world, and is subject to the judgement of the world, there is that which cannot be called before any mortal Judgement seat, even though a great poet, or novelist, or philosopher be sitting upon it. Great literature has always been written in a like spirit, and is, indeed the Forgiveness of Sin, and when we find it becoming the Accusation of Sin, as in George Eliot . . . literature has begun to change into something else.

This seems (except in its unfairness to George Eliot) far truer and more generous. And Lady Gregory's *Dervorgilla* (acted 1907), with its picture of that unhappy woman's remorseful old age, seems to me likewise more generous and more genuine.

Perhaps the best quality of Yeats's play, for those who love Ireland, lies in those quieter moments when there breaks in a gust of Irish air, or the music of Irish place-names—

> before the cocks
> Of Aughanish or Bailevelehan
> Or grey Aughtmana shake their wings and cry.

> Even the sunlight can be lonely here,
> Even hot noon is lonely.

This beauty of Irish landscape is more moving than all its ghosts. Like Tennyson, Yeats was happier with landscapes than with portraits; better able to create earthly Paradises than breathing Adams or Eves. Most typical, indeed, that he should elsewhere have written—

And love is less kind than the grey twilight,
And hope is less dear than the dew of morn.

*   *   *

Calvary (1920)

To Yeats, Christianity seemed a religion of 'objectivity', in which
the individual was subdued to duties and self-denials. And though
the phases of 'objectivity' were, in the eternal cycle, just as essential
and inevitable as those of 'subjectivity', rebelliously 'subjective' this
individualist poet remained.

A main source of *Calvary* is a clever story of Wilde's, 'The Doer
of Good', in which Christ encounters a leper whom He had cured—
but the man is now a voluptuary; then a woman whom He had
forgiven, and a blind man whom He had healed—but now the
woman is a harlot, and the man in pursuit of her. Last He meets a
youth whom He had raised from the dead—but now the youth can
only weep because he is alive.

Yeats regarded lonely birds like heron, hawk, eagle, or swan as
natural symbols of the lonely subjective man, contemplating the
world in Promethean aloofness; but beasts, especially gregarious
ones, as symbols of the objective type that he liked less.[1] Accordingly the play opens with a song by its Three Musicians about a
white heron brooding alone; with the refrain—

God has not died for the white heron.

Such lonely, self-sufficient souls crave no Redeemer.[2]

Then appears a player with the mask of Christ, bearing the Cross.
Lazarus reproaches the Saviour for dragging him from the tranquil
freedom of the tomb—

[1] As so often with Yeats, this seems a little arbitrary. Plenty of birds are
gregarious. Even herons congregate in heronries, swans in swanneries (there
used to be 7000 at Abbotsbury). And there are also solitary animals; like the
cat that walks by itself, or the rogue elephant.

[2] Compare the similarly self-centred Wordsworth; who, after stating that
he sympathized, not with Unitarians, but with orthodox Christians who felt
the need to flee to a Redeemer, could yet add the startling disclaimer—'though
perhaps I do not want one for myself'.

(*H. Crabb Robinson on Books and Their Writers*, I, 87.)

that corner
Where I had thought I might lie safe for ever.[1]

Then appears Judas explaining that he betrayed Christ to vindicate his own freedom from the dominance alike of God and destiny.

It was decreed that somebody betray you—
I'd thought of that—but not that I should do it,
I the man Judas.

Can it, one wonders, be predetermined that a deed shall be done, yet not predetermined who shall do it? An odd sort of predestination. Clearly, however, for Lazarus and Judas the Saviour has come in vain; and equally in vain for the soldiers who now ironically dice for the clothes of the Crucified. These are low, common types, like the Fool and Blind Man who pursued their petty ends although Cuchulain died.

The play ends with another lyric by the Musicians—like the white heron, so the lonely sea-bird or the soaring eagle 'is content with his own savage heart'; the swan needs only another swan.

God has not appeared to the birds.

A curious anti-Christian mystery-play.[2]

[1] Lazarus appears to ignore Yeats's cycles of reincarnation.

[2] Much fuller details, sometimes perhaps a little fanciful, or irrelevant, in F. A. C. Wilson, *Yeats's Iconography*, pp. 163-203.

It is hardly surprising that Yeats was not much liked by Irish Catholicism of the kind typified by that Connaught bishop who, says Yeats, told his flock that 'they should never read stories about the degrading passion of love'. And so, as the poet records in a letter of 1928, a Mother Superior could warn her women-hearers at a Retreat 'a few years ago', that there were two men they must never know, must not even bow to in the streets—Lennox Robinson and W. B. Yeats.

For the super-orthodox, Yeats was, after all, an ex-Protestant who had further degenerated into a magician and necromancer; who had written the heretical *Countess Cathleen*; who had championed the anti-clerical blasphemies of Synge. In 1924 he was accused of conspiring with A.E. and the Head of the Education Board to destroy the Catholic faith by free education. Still worse, in 1925, he courageously opposed in the Senate a measure against divorce. Nor were matters mended by such audacities as his parallel between Leda and the Virgin Mary, or later plays like *The Herne's Egg* and *Purgatory*.

*   *   *

The Cat and the Moon
(1924, produced 1931)

A slight, odd piece. A Blind Beggar carries a Lame Beggar in search
of Saint Colman's holy well. The Saint offers each a choice—cure or
blessedness? The Blind Beggar prefers to receive his sight; the Lame
Beggar, to be blessed. The Blind Beggar sees his companion has
stolen his sheepskin; beats him; and goes. The Lame Beggar takes
the Saint on his back, and dances out.

Yeats says he 'kept in mind, while only putting the vaguest
suggestion of it into the play, that the blind man was the body, the
lame man was the soul.'[1] And in the play's lyrics Minnaloushe the
cat, whose eyes change like the changing moon, signifies man in
pursuit of his opposite.

But whatever it may signify, *The Cat and the Moon* seems to me
lame, blind, and impotent beside Synge's treatment of a vaguely
similar theme in *The Well of the Saints*.

*   *   *

The King of the Great Clock Tower
(produced 1934) and its revised form,
A Full Moon in March (1935)

A king and queen sit enthroned. A strolling poet enters. He has
heard, a year since, that the queen is the most beautiful of women;
whereas his own wife is a fat goose. And he has been singing of the
queen ever since. He has sworn to dance with her, and Aengus, god
of love, has promised he shall kiss her.

---

[1] *Wheels and Butterflies* (1934), p. 138.   F. A. C. Wilson, however, inter-
prets the blind man as the proletariat; he is ridden by the lame man who stands
for the aristocratic intellectual, preferring spiritual blessedness in 'Unity of
Being' (*Yeats's Iconography*, 152-7.)

The poet is at once decapitated, and his head brought in. The queen takes it up and dances with it like Salome. Then the severed head begins to sing, like the head of Bran in the Welsh legend, or that of Orpheus in Virgil.

> Clip and lip and long for more,
> Mortal men our abstracts are;
> *What of the hands on the Great Clock Face?*
> All those living wretches crave
> Prerogatives of the dead that have
> Sprung heroic from the grave.
> *A moment more and it tolls midnight.*

The clock strikes midnight. The queen kisses the head. The king draws his sword, but then kneels and lays it at her feet. The Attendants close the curtain (one recalls Elizabethan dumb-shows). Then the two Attendants sing an epilogue.

A Full Moon in March is a still simpler rehandling of the same theme. Here the king has disappeared. The queen remains. The strolling poet is replaced by a swineherd. The queen has promised to give herself at the March full-moon to the man who best sings his passion for her. But in the past she has killed or maimed many of her wooers. So now the swineherd is the only candidate—but all this strange suitor promises is—

> the night of love,
> An ignorant forest and the dung of swine.

The queen has his head chopped off, then sings and dances with the head in her hands.

> Child and darling, hear my song,
> Never cry I did you wrong;
> Cry that wrong came not from me
> But my virgin cruelty,
> Great my love before you came,
> Greater when I loved in shame,
> Greatest when there broke from me
> Storm of virgin cruelty.

And the swineherd's head sings in answer—

334

> I sing a song of Jack and Jill.
> Jill had murdered Jack;
> *The moon shone brightly*;
> Ran up the hill, and round the hill,
> Round the hill and back.
> *A full moon in March.*
>
> Jack had a hollow heart, for Jill
> Had hung his heart on high;
> *The moon shone brightly*;
> Had hung his heart beyond the hill,
> A-twinkle in the sky.
> *A full moon in March.*

Then the queen dances in adoration of the head and kisses it. Finally the curtain closes on her. Why, asks the 2nd Attendant, must this queen's proud feet descend so low?

> *1st Attendant.* For desecration and the lover's night.

What is the point of all this oddity? Briefly, it seems to be as follows. Some religions regard spirit as good, matter as evil. Hence their praise of asceticism, abstinence, virginity, in order to free the pure spirit from evil matter. The angels fell, from loving the daughters of men; man fell, from eating the forbidden fruit.

But other religious minds, especially heretical mystics, have refused to regard matter as thus wholly evil. Blake, for example, says 'The Messiah fell, and formed a heaven of what he stole from the abyss.' God is not only transcendent; He is also immanent. Spirit, seeking that completeness found in the union of opposites, may therefore desire the physical beauty of the material world.

So here, the spirit of the queen, though at first aloof, is won by the strolling poet, or even by the swineherd, and yields to

> desecration and the lover's night.

On the other hand, in each play the audacious lover (spirit that has thus embedded itself in matter) has to suffer in expiation a ritual death, like the slain gods of ancient religion—like Dionysus who was torn in pieces by the wicked Titans of this lower earth, though

335

Athena saved his heart; or like Attis who was punished by the Great Mother-goddess with castration, for descending below the Milky Way.

Further, Yeats associated Dionysus with John the Baptist; whom Patmore strangely thought to stand for natural love, as Christ stood for divine love. Indeed Patmore noted that Leonardo da Vinci painted St John like Dionysus, Dionysus like St John.

Hence, in both these plays, the Salome-dance with the severed head. But this motif was also linked to an Irish legend about a minstrel, Aodh, who loved Queen Dectira, and sang his love for her. Being interrupted by a battle, he promised to sing his love afterwards. At dawn the Queen sought him, and found his head hanging from a bush—singing.

Finally, there is the stress on the perfect union of lovers after death. For example, at the end of *The King of the Great Clock Tower*—

> Crossed fingers there in pleasure can
> Exceed the nuptial bed of man;
> *What of the hands on the Great Clock Face?*
> A nuptial bed exceed all that
> Boys at puberty have thought,
> Or sibyls in a frenzy sought.
> *A moment more and it tolls midnight.*[1]

'I do not doubt,' says Yeats elsewhere, of the dead, 'that they make love in that union which Swedenborg has said is of the whole body and seems from far off an incandescence.'[2]

In both plays a Freudian might see, rather, a dramatization of the Oedipus-complex; further complicated by streaks of sadism, masochism, necrophily, and also a certain 'nostalgie de la boue'— a fleshliness which in later life strangely reversed the austerity of the poet's youth. It is certainly curious how the later Yeats becomes preoccupied with decapitated heads, Belles Dames sans Merci, and the ambivalent hatred underlying love.

[1] The Great Clock Face stands for Time; the stroke of midnight is the witching hour when wonders come.
[2] Cf. p. 270.

*   *   *

The Herne's Egg (1936-7)

This piece is more esoteric still. Congal, King of Connacht, and Aedh, King of Tara, steal the eggs of the divine Great Herne, or Heron, despite the protests of his priestess Attracta. At the feast that follows, Congal, insulted by being given a hen's egg instead of a heron's, kills Aedh with a table-leg; then, with six of his men, ravishes the priestess. In retribution, he is doomed to be slain by a fool. When he meets a fool, sooner than be slain by him, Congal throws himself on a spit, as Brutus at Philippi on his sword; and is then doomed to be reborn as a donkey.

Naturally such a piece had no hope of being acted in Ireland. According to Yeats, it so upset the board of the Abbey Theatre that he withdrew it. 'An admiring member had decided that the seven ravishers of the heroine are the seven sacraments.' More detailed explanations can be found, by those interested, in Mr F. A. C. Wilson's *Yeats and Tradition*, and Giorgio Melchiori's *The Whole Mystery of Art*. But the ordinary reader may be tempted to recall Johnson's comment on Dodsley's *Cleone*—'I am afraid there is more blood than brains.'

*   *   *

Purgatory
(produced 1938)

'Aetas parentum, peior avis, tulit
Nos nequiores, mox daturos
Progeniem vitiosiorem.'[1]
HORACE

This has been called Yeats's finest play. It would be terrible if that were true.

[1] 'Our fathers' generation, baser than our grandsires,
Has bred us yet wickeder, to beget hereafter
Posterity more evil still.'

337

An old man and his son of sixteen, tramps, are standing outside a ruined, moonlit house. The old man explains that here he was born. It belonged to his mother; but (like Strindberg's Miss Julie) she was decadent and gave herself to a groom, who drank and squandered. She died in giving birth to the old man who now tells the tale. The groom, his father, neglected him; and after sixteen years, in a drunken fit, burnt down the house. And while it burnt (so the old man now confesses), he himself, then a boy of sixteen, stabbed his degraded parent to death.

As the old man speaks, he sees (though his son does not) a window supernaturally lighted up in the ruined house. He sees standing there his mother's ghost. He hears the ghostly hoof-beats of the groom his father, riding home drunk, as on that night when he was himself conceived. Then the phantom light fades out; and the old man finds the boy pilfering money from his pack. While they struggle, the old man (and, this time, the boy also) sees the ruined window light up anew. They see the ghost of the drunken groom pouring ghostly whisky into a ghostly glass. Suddenly the old man stabs his own son; just as he had once stabbed his own father. Then he explains to his unseen mother (and the audience) that he has done so to prevent this degenerate youth from perpetuating the family-heritage of corruption. (A somewhat drastic form of birth-control.)

But again the old man hears the phantom hoofs. He has murdered both his father and his son in vain—even now his mother's spirit finds no rest.

> Twice a murderer and all for nothing,
> And she must animate that dead night
> Not once but many times!
> O God,
> Release my mother's soul from its dream!
> Mankind can do no more.

Naturally this unorthodox view of Purgatory raised fresh cries of anger from pious Catholics. But Yeats replied: 'I have put nothing into the play because it seemed picturesque; I have put there my own conviction about this world and the next.' But naturally, for the orthodox, this blunt avowal could only make things even worse.

One may wonder, however, on the supposition that such crimes

produce such spectres, why there are not far more of these appari-
tions. Given the endless sins of endless ages, one might expect such
phantom pantomimes to recur nightly all over this guilty earth.

However, the play embodies both Yeats's belief that the soul
after death had to dream back in expiation its own past life, till it
could view that past with dispassionate tranquillity; and his other
melancholy conviction that we are now declining towards the
decadent end of one more historic cycle. Just as the Old Man's
mother was a degenerate from her ancestors, the Old Man has sunk
yet further, and his son further still.

> Great people lived and died in this house;
> Magistrates, colonels, members of Parliament,
> Captains and Governors, and long ago
> Men that had fought at Aughrim and the Boyne . . .
>   to kill a house
> Where great men grew up, married, died,
> I here declare a capital offence.

It may or may not be true that, apart from scientific progress and
popular welfare, ours is an age of decline. No one who reads history
can suppose that the road of civilization winds upward *all* the way.
But such a world-problem seems over-vast (though Mr Samuel
Beckett might not agree) to be carried on the shoulders of this
unpleasant pair of vagabonds. Not easy to make an impressive
Götterdämmerung out of a Twilight of Tramps. And further,
passionately sincere though Yeats was in his regret for the aristocratic civilization of the past, one may still wonder whether this
piece about a brutal old pedlar who in youth murders his father,[1]
and in age his son, is itself very civilized.

*   *   *

The Death of Cuchulain (1938-9)

Yeats's last play returns for a last time to the heroic Ireland he had
loved all his life long. Perhaps its most interesting feature is its

---

[1] Curious how Yeats seems preoccupied with the theme of parricide;
cf. his translations of Sophocles' two plays on Oedipus, and his own *Baile's
Strand*, where Cuchulain kills his own son.

prologue, which again vibrates with loathing for 'this vile age'. The Old Man who speaks it repeats his poet's demand for only a small audience—'if there are more than a hundred I won't be able to escape people who are educating themselves out of the Book Societies and the like, sciolists all, pickpockets and opinionated bitches'. No less virulent is his loathing for the modern ballet. 'I spit three times. I spit upon the dancers painted by Degas. I spit upon their short bodices, their stiff stays, their toes whereon they spin like pegtops, above all, that chambermaid face.... I spit! I spit! I spit!' But even those who sympathize, may doubt whether all this spitting against the wind is very effectual. There was more deadliness in the smile of Voltaire.

Emer, wife of Cuchulain, had sent his mistress, Eithne Inguba, to keep him, safe in her arms, from opposing Maeve's invasion of Ulster. But Cuchulain's mistress, bewitched by supernatural power, tells him just the opposite—he *shall* go 'forth to fight'. And so, hough the letter in her hand contradicts her words, Cuchulain passes to his doom.

The stage darkens for a moment. Then it lightens again to show the mortally wounded hero binding himself to a pillar, so that he may die standing, like the Emperor Vespasian. Now there enters the Blind Beggar of *On Baile's Strand*, and beheads the still living hero with a knife, for the sake of a twelve-penny reward.

Then Emer appears and performs yet another Salome-dance (Yeats had grown over-fond of these) in front of the severed head.

The piece ends with a harlot's song, to the music of a modern Irish fair, about Pearse and Connolly who died in the 1916 rising, and are still commemorated in the Dublin Post Office by a statue of Cuchulain.

The essence of the play lies in its defiance of death, by a poet soon himself to die; and in its expression of admiration, mingled with contempt, for the blended heroism and squalor, idealism and sexual crudity, of human life itself.

But if it is a question of farewells to life, one may feel that Landor in 'I strove with none', or Tennyson in *Crossing the Bar*, or Hardy in *An Ancient to Ancients*, or Yeats himself in the last section of

Under Ben Bulben, passed from the stage with an exit more dignified.

*   *   *

A word must also be said of the much-praised versions of Sophocles—*King Oedipus* (produced 1926) and *Oedipus at Colonus* (produced 1927). For Oedipus, like Lear, seems to have deeply preoccupied the imagination of the ageing Yeats.

In both plays the dialogue is rendered into prose, not very distinguished and not always accurate; the choruses into verse, which is sometimes much more alive, but often too free to be justly termed 'translation'. For example—

> In the long echoing street the laughing dancers throng,
> The bride is carried to the bridegroom's chamber through
>   torchlight and tumultuous song;
> I celebrate the silent kiss that ends short life or long.
>
> Never to have lived is best, ancient writers say;
> Never to have drawn the breath of life, never to have looked into
>   the eye of day;
> The second best's a gay goodnight and quickly turn away.

Here the original Greek says simply: 'To all alike comes at last the Deliverer, Death, when stands revealed the doom of Hades—of Him that knows not bridal, nor dance, nor song. Best, when all is counted, not to be born at all; and for him that has once seen the light, next best by far, to hasten with all speed back whence he came.'[1] Nothing in Sophocles about echoing streets, laughing dancers, torchlight, bridegroom's chambers, silent kisses, ancient writers, eyes of day, or gay goodnights. 'He is translation's thief that addeth more.'

---

[1] *Oedipus at Colonus,* 1220-9.

> One helper at the last is left for all,
> One no bride-song gladdeneth,
> Nor yet dance, nor music—Death,
> When the hour of Doom shall fall.
>
> Never to be born is best;
> Next to that, far happiest
> He that hastens from his birth,
> Fast as may be, back to earth.

Had Yeats called his work simply 'an *adaptation*', there would be no cause to complain. But 'A Version for the Modern Stage' is ambiguous. A 'version' may mean a rigorous translation,[1] like the Authorized and Revised 'Versions' of the Bible; or it may mean 'a variant form'. It seems likely that a good many Greekless readers are here misled.

Actually Yeats was attempting to produce a translation from other men's translations, without knowing Greek. A difficult task.[2]

[1] *Oxford Dictionary*, 'version—a rendering of some text . . . a translation . . . a particular form or variant of something'.

[2] Thus the last two lines of Yeats's *King Oedipus* miss the point both of the Greek passage and of the whole play—

> Call no man fortunate that is not dead,
> The dead are free from pain.

The chorus of *Oedipus at Colonus* does, indeed, lament—'All life is so *wretched*, that it is better to be dead'; but here Sophocles says something quite different— 'All life is so *fickle*, that it is rash to call anyone happy *until* he is dead, and therefore safe from that fickleness'. (For even those happiest hitherto, like Priam or Oedipus, Croesus or Polycrates, may be ruined tomorrow without a moment's warning.)

Yeats was quite honest in admitting that he was *not* learned (though some of his admirers are less honest). In the course of his life he read voraciously; but he was far from having the accurate mind or retentive memory of the pedant. He had more precious qualities. But he would certainly have made Macaulay stare. Not merely because he spelt badly when young, and worse, it appears, when old; not merely because he was capable of such solecisms as 'Cephīsus' for 'Cephīsus', 'chameliontos' for 'chamaileontos', 'hominorum' for 'hominum', *Aeneids* for *Enneads* (of Plotinus). He also went out of his way to strew his pages with recondite allusions, and then often got them wrong.

For example, The Seven Sleepers of Ephesus did *not* sleep 'when Alexander's empire past'—they were persecuted Christians, supposed to have slumbered from about A.D. 250 to A.D. 447. An 'unhatched egg' of Leda did *not* hang in a Spartan temple; Pausanias simply says '*that* egg which Leda is related to have brought forth' (presumably the egg-shell which once held Helen; see p. 267). Athene did *not* seize Achilles by the hair in battle (*Iliad*, I, 197); it was in the assembly of the Achaeans. The *Odyssey* (XI, 601-4) does *not* depict the wraith of Achilles as drawing his bow in Hades, while his real spirit was on Olympus with his wife Hebe; it was Heracles. The fragment of Archilochus, boasting that he both served the God of War and knew the Muses' art, is *not* 'all that remains of a once famous Greek poet and sea-rover'; we have whole pages of him. Swift's Latin epitaph does *not* say 'where fierce indignation can lacerate *his* heart no more'; 'ubi saeva indignatio cor ulterius lacerare nequit' is as general as Job's praises of the grave—'can lacerate *the*

I have not thought it worth while to dwell on *The Player Queen* (produced 1919), a most dismal attempt at facetiousness; nor on *The Resurrection* (1931, produced 1934), which seems to me redeemed only by a few snatches of lyric[1]; nor on *The Words upon the Window-pane* (produced 1930) which vulgarizes the tragedy of Swift by involving him with a muddy-minded medium in a spiritualist séance. Yeats repeatedly attacked Ibsen for his drab prosiness. Whatever may happen in translations, this does not strike me as fair to Ibsen's Norwegian. But in any case the worst Ibsen translation seems to me less common, and less commonplace, than the style of *The Words upon the Window-pane*.

But candour must add that all these plays have been admired by others.

---

heart no more'. Heraclitus did *not* say anything remotely like 'the Daemon is our destiny'; he said 'character governs man's destiny' ('ἦθος ἀνθρώπῳ δαίμων'—δαίμων, originally 'a presiding spirit', has here come to mean little more than 'lot', 'fortune').

In fine, Yeats showed for simple fact something of the same disdain as the Emperor Sigismund for Latin grammar. But, after all, so did that other excellent poet, but less excellent thinker, Victor Hugo.

[1] There is also supposed to be a particularly dramatic moment at the end, when the young Greek goes up to the phantom of Jesus and passes his hand over its side—'The heart of a phantom is beating! The heart of a phantom is beating! (*He screams.*)'

CONCLUSION

Yeats's solitary introversion, more deeply interested in life's mysteries than in the infinite variety of other minds, seems to me to have hampered him *dramatically* in two ways. First, it debarred him, as I have said, from sufficient observation and grasp of character. Often he remained like Tennyson's eagle on its mountain-top, 'close to the sun in lonely lands'; but not very close to humanity. Secondly, to justify his own practice, he was tempted to some rather thin dramatic theorizing.

In particular, he maintained character to be unimportant in tragedy; 'for tragedy must always be a drowning and breaking of the dykes that separate man from man', whereas 'it is upon those dykes comedy keeps house'. Less poetically put, this appears to mean that, whereas comedy plays with humours or manners observed in the real world, tragedy expresses the generalized passion of the human spirit beating against the walls of destiny, like Oedipus, or Everyman, or Cuchulain—'images that remind us of vast passions, the vagueness of past times, all the chimeras that haunt the edge of trance'. 'Tragedy is passion alone, and rejecting character, it gets form from motives, from the wandering of passion; while comedy is the clash of character. . . . A poet creates tragedy from his own soul, that soul which is alike in all men.'

Musical; but true? What is this soul 'alike in all men'? And can one doubt that *Agamemnon* and *Prometheus Bound*, *Antigone*, *Hippolytus*, and *Medea*, *Hamlet*, *Macbeth*, and *Antony and Cleopatra* do depend extremely on the vividness of great individuals? As regards Shakespeare, Yeats tried to meet the difficulty by arguing that Shakespearian tragedies were really tragi-comedies. But this seems mere evasion. If *Hamlet* and *Macbeth* are not supreme tragedies, then what is?

As a producer, Yeats appears to have been highly competent and observant, full of attention to dress and scenery, lighting and stage-business. But as a creator of serious drama, too introvert I think he remained; even though he toiled with tireless revision to make his plays more convincing.

344

He tells a typical story of an old woman who counselled a young Noh player not to observe life, or copy the harshness of aged voices, when impersonating the old; but simply to find it all in his own heart. And in this there may be truth. Much may be gained by trusting imagination, intuition, and unconscious memory. Trollope, for example, had little personal acquaintance with clergymen. But surely both actor and dramatist need *also* a keen-eyed observation of the world. 'To be a creative writer,' said Ibsen, 'is to *see*.' Nothing escaped the old Norwegian—not even the wallpaper in a room, nor the faces he watched in the mirror of his restaurant. He started from the individual; and on the individual he kept his concentration, down to the last gaiter-button.

Indeed, in judging the work of another, Yeats himself could take a more balanced view. To O'Casey he wrote, of *The Silver Tassie*: 'There is no dominating character, no dominating action, neither psychological unity nor unity of action; and your great power of the past has been the creation of some unique character who dominated all about him and was himself a main impulse in some action that filled the play from beginning to end' (20/4/28). Very true. But it contradicts Yeats's own theories. And such 'unique characters' he found it hard to create.

Yeats's plays, then, in my belief belong less to the theatre than to poetry; less to the main stream of drama than to a side-channel. They bear, not the busy traffic of the stage, but at their best, a charm of their own. However, it can always be retorted that, if a backwater carries no busy barges, yet it keeps a deeper beauty in the quiet of its water-lilies, in the colour of its kingfishers and dragon-flies.

It is also arguable that Yeats's persevering pursuit of drama benefited him as a poet, by making his verse more dramatic, less dreamy, less isolated from the world.

And yet, despite the perfection of his last lyrics, Yeats still remains a puzzling writer; not, for me, one of the few that one can unreservedly love, and admire, and make friends with—like Chekhov.

Why? It is not just that the ideas of Yeats seem sometimes foolish. Goldsmith in real life could be far more foolish. Indeed, for all his wise simplicity, Goldsmith can sometimes be foolish even on paper; yet this does not cause the same sense of slight estrangement. The trouble, I think, lies rather in one's impression of something about Yeats that is too self-centred; too artificial; too posed. Some are alienated by his questionable doctrine of 'the Mask'.

'I think,' wrote Yeats in his *Death of Synge*, 'that all happiness depends on the energy to assume the mask of some other self, that all joyous or creative life is a re-birth as something not oneself. . . . We put on a grotesque or a solemn painted face to hide us from the terrors of judgment, invent an imaginative Saturnalia where one forgets reality, a game like that of a child, where one loses the infinite pain of self-realization.'

Yet why 'hide'? Why this fear of reality, and of self-realization— the very things on which Ibsen so insisted? When Yeats asserts that 'one constantly notices in very active natures a tendency to pose', it would be more convincing to have more examples. No doubt Napoleon posed; but Wellington emphatically did not—he was as blunt as he was sharp. Or, again, there is that great-hearted character whose life, of all those he had personally known, Yeats said he would most gladly have lived—William Morris. Few men have been as 'active'; yet few felt such scorn of 'pose'. For Morris, though most un-Johnsonianly romantic, had yet a Johnsonian disdain for all pretence. Again, Yeats criticized Wordsworth because his moral sense had 'no theatrical element'. To others, precisely this may seem one of Wordsworth's most sterling merits. Surely it was not wholly in error that some of the eighteenth-century's subtlest minds so praised that stamp of character which is 'amateur du vrai, du noble, du simple, ennemi de la prétention, de l'affectation, et de tout ce qui a l'air de contrainte ou de grimace ou de vouloir briller au dépens de la justesse on du naturel'.[1]

One's 'mask', for Yeats, might be a social self, different from the real self (as often in Pirandello); or it might be a diametrically opposite self, as, for example, Morris or Landor as persons seemed

---

[1] 'Devoted to the true, the noble, and the simple, enemy to pretence, to affectation, to any semblance of constraint, any airs of artifice, any attempt to dazzle at the expense of what is natural or scrupulously true.' (Du Châtel, on Mme du Deffand.)

often the very antithesis of their writings[1]; or it might be an ideal, to which one gradually approximated. An interesting theory. But perhaps a little too like deliberately cultivated schizophrenia.

It can, indeed, be urged in partial explanation that, during the eighties and nineties, the period of *Dr Jekyll and Mr Hyde* and *The Portrait of Dorian Gray*, masks were very much the wear, and dual personalities the height of fashion.

Thus George Russell had to double himself as 'A. E.'; Magee disguised himself as 'John Eglinton'; Wilde, as 'Sebastian Melmoth'; William Sharp, as 'Fiona Macleod'—indeed it long remained uncertain whether William Sharp and Fiona Macleod were two people or one, male or female.

Oscar Wilde put the point with his usual whimsical extravagance —'The first duty in life is to assume a pose; what the second is, no one has yet found out.' (Perhaps the duty of *not* being found out?) Yet one may question whether cutting figures is a game that, in the long run, cuts much ice.

Some of Yeats's admirers, of course, passionately deny this charge of pose. But it is not so clear that the poet himself would have much objected to it. He gives a disarming account of himself as a young man at the Kildare Street Art School—'I was still very much of a child . . . sometimes walking with an artificial stride in memory of Hamlet and stopping at shop windows to look at my tie gathered into a loose sailor-knot and to regret that it could not be always blown out by the wind like Byron's tie in the picture.'

Certainly Yeats often seemed to others a poseur. Wilfrid Blunt, after dining with him and Lady Gregory in 1903, recognized his genius, but felt 'a strong touch of the charlatan'. (Which seems far too strongly put.) Shaw described him as much more like Gilbert and Sullivan's Bunthorne in *Patience* than Wilde ever was. And, again, there is George Moore's account of the young poet in London —malicious, no doubt, yet not, I suspect, totally unfounded: 'He was an instinctive mummer, a real dancing dog.' The Yeats of those

---

[1] It is curious to contrast the young Yeats dreaming 'that, having conquered bodily desire and the inclination of my mind towards women and love, I should live as Thoreau lived, seeking wisdom', with the old Yeats who became at times the outspoken poet of 'lust and rage'.

days, says Moore, 'was clothed like a Bible reader, and chanted like one in his talk. All the same I could see that among much Irish humbug there was in him a genuine love of his art, and he was more intelligent than his verses had led me to expect.' 'He is,' Moore concluded, 'the type of the literary fop, and the most complete that has ever appeared in literature.'

No doubt, with such witnesses as Shaw or Moore, one needs a whole salt-cellar of scepticism. But the more admiring L. A. G. Strong also records how, after a government assemblage of celebrities for the revival of the Tailteann Games in 1924, which Yeats attended in a tall hat, A.E. remarked with wonder on Yeats's fondness for functions which A.E. would have walked miles to avoid. But Yeats replied by quoting from Goethe: 'The poor *are*. The rich *are*, but are also permitted to *seem*'; and explained that, to cure his own youthful shyness, he had deliberately acquired 'the technique of *seeming*'. I suspect that it was this which made St John Ervine feel, after meeting Yeats, or reading him, 'as if one had been taken into a richly decorated drawing-room, when one had hoped to be taken into a green field'. And when, a few years back, I talked at Gort to an elderly lady who had passionately admired Lady Gregory, and asked her about Yeats, there again recurred that same, inevitable word—'pose'. Similarly—though I should not wish to stress so fleeting a contact—when I once saw Yeats in his old age, the impression he gave was strikingly different from the frank straightforwardness of, for example, that gallant old man, H. W. Nevinson.

Yeats, I remember, was talking (characteristically) of some mysterious green light seen off the coast of Ireland. As we then rambled on into the shadowy glades of the supernatural, I mentioned that pleasantly gruesome tale, in Procopius, of the Emperor Justinian being suddenly seen by his horrified courtiers without any face.[1] This detail Yeats caught up eagerly. Yes, he cried, here was a

---

[1] Cf. *The Countess Cathleen*:

Two nights ago, at Carrick-orus churchyard,
A herdsman met a man who had no mouth,
Nor eyes, nor ears; his face a wall of flesh.

thing recorded by a reputable historian—which sceptics yet dismissed.

Now the Procopius of the *Secret History* cannot possibly be called a reputable historian. His *Secret History* is, in fact, a work of raving scandal, solemnly setting forth the view that Justinian and Theodora were not really human beings at all, but devilish demons who assumed human shape only for the torment of mankind. Little wonder, then, that Gibbon, when dealing with Procopius, speaks of 'the venom of his malignity'.

Did Yeats really believe in faceless emperors? I suppose he thought them quite possible. Did he not know about the general unreliability of Procopius—or did he simply refuse to know about it? I cannot tell. Perhaps the second. But that evening I came to wonder whether this excellent poet was as excellent a judge of evidence; and whether he really cared much about intellectual honesty.[1]

Years after, I came on a passage about Yeats in a letter from A.E., which in many ways exactly confirmed my own impression after reading, and seeing, this strange, gifted figure.[2]

He began about the time of *The Wind among the Reeds*[3] to do two things consciously, one to create a 'style' in literature, the second to create or rather to re-create W. B. Yeats in a style which would harmonize with the literary style. People call this posing. It is really putting on a mask like his actors, Greek or Japanese, a mask over life. The actor must

---

[1] George Moore in old age I found a striking contrast. He was much more comical and less dignified; perhaps vainer, but much more spontaneous. The vanity became as disarming as a child's, when he explained that hardly any English writers (except George Moore) knew the way to tell a story. Then he read aloud from the manuscript of *Aphrodite in Aulis*; inviting comments, but (very humanly) not much liking the comments he had invited. Vain to suggest to him that Greek rhapsodes would carry their Homers in rolls, not 'quires' ('Oh, I *must* have quires'). Vain to question whether ancient Greeks would breakfast off Greek tortoises ('Oh, I dare say the tortoises would be quite nice'). However he *did* admit that it was Europa, not Proserpine, who mounted a 'gainly bull'; and that it would be better not to make the sun rise on Aulis from behind Mount Helicon (which would be due *west*).

Moore, in short, seemed perfectly natural (he could not help it); but Yeats did not.

[2] John Eglinton, *A Memoir of A.E.* (1937), pp. 110-12.

[3] 1899.

talk to the emotion on the mask, which is a fixed emotion. W. B. Y. began twenty years ago vigorously defending Wilde against the charge of being a poseur. He said it was merely living artistically, and it was the duty of everybody to have a conception of themselves, and he intended to conceive of himself. The present W. B. Y. is the result. The error in his psychology is that life creates the form, but he seems to think that the form creates life. If you have a style, he argued once with me, you will have something to say. He seems to have also thought, though he never said so, that if you make a picturesque or majestic personality of yourself in appearance, you will become as wonderful inside as outside. He has created the mask and he finds himself obliged to speak in harmony with that fixed expression of the mask, and that accounts for the lifelessness of his later talk and writing. . . . He bores me terribly now, and he was once so interesting. . . . I want life and thought, and he talks solemn platitudes under the impression that this nonsense is arcane wisdom. Any bit of pedantry a couple of hundred years old seems to him a kind of divine authority. . . . Yeats is his own coffin and memorial tablet. Why can't he be natural? Such a delightful creature he was when young! And at rare moments when he forgets himself he is still interesting as ever almost.

Here, no doubt, A.E. though patently sincere may seem to exaggerate. Few would now call Yeats's later lyrics 'lifeless'; whatever some may feel about his later plays. But it is easy to see what, in general, A.E. meant.

Other admirers of Yeats will stoutly defend his use of masks in life. I remember arguing this point with one of his best critics, for whose opinions I have great respect—Mr T. R. Henn. But here arguments are useless. It seems ultimately a matter of temperament. And one can only state one's own feeling.

How far does a love of masks and masquerading really damage a writer? Good writers in the past have sometimes adopted histrionic attitudes—Byron, Chateaubriand, Balzac, Hugo, Meredith, Shaw. And perhaps the Irish have more than most a tendency to parade—for example, Burke, and Sheridan, and even honest Goldsmith, with his misplaced craving for finery and for shining in company. But, as I grow older, and approach the point where, for me, life and literature alike will end, I feel more and more that, though honesty of mind and sincerity of temper cannot make good writers, there are no qualities more vitally important for good writers to possess.

Better than any masks seems that line of Europe's first dramatist, Aeschylus (in his *Seven against Thebes*), which made all eyes turn to where, in the Athenian audience, sat Aristides 'the Just'—

> He does not strive to *seem* the best, but *be* it.

Marcus Aurelius, again, may appear at times a solemn prig; but how excellent is his stress on living *not* like a tragic actor—ἀτραγῴδως! The writers one can really trust are those like Ibsen with his call to be *oneself*, not to seem something else; or Chekhov with his contempt for all that was not simply and straightforwardly natural. Why is Dryden, even in *All for Love*, despite his gifts, so inferior to Shakespeare? Partly, I feel, because Dryden was less sincere, more anxious to astonish. As Chekhov's Trofímov would have said, 'he flaps'.

Or again there is the vivid contrast between Yeats and Hardy. Both hated the artificialities of modern city-civilization—what Hardy called 'the hot-plate of London', where men simmer away to dust; both loved the simpler folk of Irish, or Wessex, countrysides; both longed to spiritualize the prosaic in everyday life by a sense of things more poetic, more unearthly, more mysterious. But Hardy, with his sterling honesty, would play no tricks on his intelligence. In a letter of 1901, he put the view that there was little prospect of reviving old transcendental beliefs, but that men might come to an 'Idealism of Fancy; that is, an idealism in which fancy is on longer tricked out and made to masquerade as belief, but is frankly and honestly accepted as an imaginative solace in the lack of any substantial solace to be found in life.' Like Yeats, Hardy too wrote a poetry that was haunted with ghosts—'thin elbowers'; ghosts of the woman he had loved, or of friends now dead, or even of his dog Wessex. But Hardy saw them, with sadder disillusion, as figments only, the visionary embodiments of a dreaming brain.

> I wayfared at the nadir of the sun
> Where populations meet, though seen of none;
> And millions seemed to sigh around
> As though their haunts were nigh around,
> And unknown throngs to cry around
> Of things late done.

Yet the Spirits Ironic, or the Spirits of Pity, who provide the choruses of the Dynasts do not seem the less moving or truthful for being, confessedly, mere voices and nothing more. Hardy appeals to those who, like Porson, dislike all subscriptions, but especially subscriptions to articles of belief.

To the simple grace of Athens Yeats often preferred the elaborations of Byzantium. It is only just to add that, even if he often wore a mask, behind that mask lived a genuine kindness and generosity. Perhaps his mask, like Johnson's pride, was often only 'defensive'. But in any case his better self in poetry seems to me the simpler self, that could turn back from subtle complexities like Donne's to a passionate straightforwardness like Landor's; as in 'A Prayer for my Daughter' (1919).

> In courtesy I'd have her chiefly learned,
> Hearts are not had as a gift, but hearts are earned
> By those that are not entirely beautiful;
> Yet many, that have played the fool
> For beauty's very self, has charm made wise. . . .
> May she become a flourishing hidden tree.
> That all her thoughts may like the linnet be. . . .
> Nor but in merriment begin a chase
> Nor but in merriment a quarrel.
> Oh may she live like some green laurel
> Rooted in one dear perpetual place.
> An intellectual hatred is the worst,
> So let her think opinions are accursed.
> Have I not seen the loveliest woman born
> Out of the mouth of Plenty's horn,
> Because of her opinionated mind
> Barter that horn and every good
> By quiet natures understood
> For an old bellows full of angry wind?

Clearly these last lines are yet again bitterly haunted by Maud Gonne, vainly loved, and vainly wed to another nearly twenty years before. But much in the poem might stand as a parable of the Muse of Yeats himself. Would that she too had been more awake to the cursedness of fanatical opinions; less ready to hate; less goaded by an opinionated mind! For her true gifts were passion and song.

'Merriment' needs no masks. Nothing is more simple and natural than 'linnets', or that 'green laurel Rooted in one dear perpetual place'.

Yeats, like his white heron, was really a subjective solitary. His place was among Galway streams or Connemara Bens—not on the public stage. That calls for clearer ideas,[1] more psychological insight, a more disinterested interest in the monster-haunted labyrinths of the human brain.

It is not that playwrights need always to be profound thinkers or subtle philosophers. It has been said that Napoleon thought the same as every grenadier in his army; but thought it with an intensity unparalleled. Whether that is the whole truth about Napoleon, may be doubted; but is not something of the kind true of Shakespeare? We value his thoughts, not because they are profound, but because they are so vividly incarnated in figures of flesh and blood; in language of gold and fire.

It may seem paradoxical that Yeats should not have been a better dramatist, since all his life he dramatized himself. Yet the paradox is only apparent. Self-dramatizers—such as Byron, Browning, Hugo, Swinburne—do not seem to make good dramatists; whereas real dramatists like Aeschylus, Sophocles, Euripides, Shakespeare, Racine, Molière, Ibsen, Chekhov, Synge, appear to have been, on the contrary, men who did not dress up, or flaunt before the world. They effaced themselves behind the curtain. They were busy watching their fellow-men. And it is living characters, above all, that make living plays.

Synge, for example, going his quiet, sceptical, observant way, could translate the peasants of Aran or Wicklow living to the stage; but Yeats, who spent so much of his life wrestling in public with

---

[1] My doubts whether Yeats was important as a thinker are not lessened by the endless researches into Yeats's symbolic thinking which have now become something between a minor industry and a new religious sect. We are told, for example, that in *The Wanderings of Oisin* the hero's endless battles with a dusky demon, 'hung with slime', represent the poet's relations with his father, or sexual orgasm, or both. Yet it may be wondered what real purpose is served by such speculations. They have little to do with science, being wild and unevidenced surmises; and they have even less, if less be possible, to do with art.

angels and daemons for the salvation of his own soul, found it much harder to incarnate the souls of others.

In fact, if I try to think of a really vital character in the works of Yeats, apart from the poet himself, there leaps to my mind a creature not human at all.

> Being out of heart with government
> I took a broken root to fling
> Where the proud wayward squirrel went,
> Taking delight that he could spring;
> And he, with a low whinnying sound,
> That is like laughter, sprang again
> And so to the other tree at a bound.
> Nor the tame will, nor timid brain,
> Nor heavy knitting of the brow
> Bred that fierce tooth and cleanly limb,
> And threw him up to laugh on the bough;
> No government appointed him.

Andrew Marvell has pictured his own soul as a silver-winged bird gliding into the boughs of a tree; so in that squirrel one may seem to glimpse the true soul of Yeats himself, a thing of wild grace and energy, proudly aloof and alone, not made to be caged either in government offices or box-offices; a creature, not for green-rooms, but for green forests; a spirit of magic, and mystery, and solitude.

When I went on pilgrimage to Yeats's Tower of Ballylee, I found only a desolate shell, beleaguered with nettles. Names or initials scratched by stupid vandals crowded the blue, flaking walls within. Agricultural machines and cow-dung cumbered the ground-floor. Close by at Coole Park, bureaucracy has likewise left not one stone upon another of the house which that great-hearted woman, Lady Gregory, so longed to leave to son or grandson, and where she once gathered so much Irish brilliance. Even the ghosts of Coole had lost their home—the last relic left was that one sacred tree, a copper-beech, carved with initials, as long years passed, by the hands of Synge and Shaw, Masefield and Augustus John, A.E., and Yeats. Yet perhaps better so, Yeats might have felt. Better desolation than vulgarities.

Among those shadowy woods of Coole, in all the twilit entrance-ment of an Irish June-night, there rose not a wraith, of all the spectres that Yeats once encountered there. And the kindly old Irishman who guided me, when I asked him if there still survived in that countryside any belief in fairies, simply shook a disdainfully smiling head.[1] *Sic transit.*

The gods are forgotten in Morven of the glens.

Only on the dim shimmering of Coole Lake still floated in silence the poet's swans—shapes, like him, not of drama, but of a pure, and lonely, and enchanting poetry.

Whatever his eccentricities, his seeming poses, his mystifications, Yeats remains one of the finest poets and personalities of his time—brave, generous, often shrewd, nobly disdainful of wealth or personal gain. Chekhov and Hardy would have agreed, I think, that he was better when simpler; that his more straightforward lyrics will live long after the critics who swarm in clouds about his less happy obscurities and obscurantisms have buzzed off after newer stickinesses. But as a dramatist I could never equal him to Synge. On the stage, Yeats had visions; but Synge, vision. Yet even if Yeats never perhaps created a really living character, he *was* one. His true gifts lay elsewhere.

[1] For a quite contrary view, however, see *The Middle Kingdom* (1959) by Yeats's friend D. A. Macmanus; which is full of quite recent fairy-stories.

PART IV

Luigi Pirandello

'All that remains to me is a great pity for humanity, forced to live out its allotted span upon this cruel earth.'

PIRANDELLO

'Let us treat the men and women well: treat them as if they were real: perhaps they are.'

EMERSON

LIFE

Luigi Pirandello was born in 1867, as the son of a wealthy owner of sulphur-mines, in the district of Sicilian Agrigento, the Greek Acragas, once the home of Empedocles—that ancient Paracelsus who, like Pirandello, possessed a penetrating mind, but did not always keep it clear of mystification and sophistry. The house of his birth near Porto Empedocle was strangely named, from a neighbouring grove of oaks and olives, 'the Wood of Chaos'. There was to be a good deal of chaos in the dark wood of Pirandello's life. And his theatre became a chaotic world, lit only, at fitful moments, by ironic laughter or a gleam of pity.

One may easily grow fanciful about influences of race and country. Still it is worth bearing in mind that Sicily, like Ireland, has been throughout history a land both of beauty and of misery. One of the constant battlefields of the Mediterranean, it became also a melting-pot of many races—Sicel, Greek, Carthaginian, Roman, Arab, Norman; and, century after century, its people have been ground under crushing poverty and oppression. This island of passionate violence, of tragic revenges, and of melancholia, was an appropriate home for a writer so pessimistic and disillusioned, so many-sided, and so sceptical.

'The action,' says Dr Hinkfuss in Pirandello's *Tonight We Improvise*, 'takes place in a city in the interior of Sicily, where (as you know) passions are violent, first smouldering unseen, then blazing out in fury; among those passions, and fiercest of them all— jealousy.' We may perhaps recall that the most insanely jealous of all Shakespeare's characters is Leontes King of *Sicily*.[1]

Pirandello's father, Stefano, the youngest of twenty-four sons, was a gigantic Garibaldian, masterful and violent, who married the

---

[1] By a curious coincidence Pirandello's Sicily was also, in ancient days, the home of Tisias and Gorgias, famous for an ingenious kind of rhetorical sophistry which seems likewise a weakness of the too subtle Pirandello himself.

Gorgias (c. 483-376 B.C.) was likewise an extreme sceptic, who is said to have held that nothing exists; or if anything exists, we cannot have knowledge of it; or if we have knowledge, we cannot communicate it.

gentle, diminutive Caterina Ricci Gramitto, sister of a comrade-in-arms. Stefano himself, choleric and anti-clerical, fought a number of duels; and even fired on one occasion from his window at a church-bell that was disturbing his siesta—a sacrilege only with difficulty smoothed over by a tactful priest. Naturally such a character made no easy husband. At one time, it is said, he had a love-affair with a cousin, whom he used to meet in the parlour of a convent where their aunt was abbess. The boy Luigi, the future dramatist, then aged thirteen, is supposed to have gone there; to have told his father's mistress what misery she was costing his mother; and to have spat in her face. But suddenly, below a green curtain, he glimpsed the black shoes of his hidden father. Drama, for Pirandello, began all too early.[1]

But (if the story is true) this is hardly the sort of boyish theatricals to imbue a young mind with confident health and happiness. One's own father behind a curtain! Just like old Polonius! Is *all* life merely a masquerade?

There are other tales of Pirandello's childhood no less typical in their jarring clash between young idealism and harsh reality. One Sunday, dressed in a new sailor-suit, the little Luigi met a ragged urchin and, seized by an impulse of very literal Christianity, set out to 'clothe the naked' by changing clothes with him; but only to find the sailor-suit returned at once to his home by the urchin's embarrassed mother. Christian theory, it seems, has little to do with Christian practice. Is *all* life merely a masquerade?

Again, there was a church-lottery for a wax statuette of the Madonna. The young Luigi gave his own lottery-ticket to a little pale boy who had been prevented by illness from taking part. That ticket won. But though Pirandello's own name had been clearly crossed out by him, and the other boy's name substituted, yet the name the priest read out was still—'Luigi Pirandello'. In vain he protested, in tears. His mother returned the statuette. And Pirandello never entered the church again. Is *all* life merely a masquerade?

At sixteen Pirandello began writing poetry; at eighteen he was sent to the University of Rome. Thence, having come into

[1] See F. V. Nardelli, *L'Uomo Segreto* (2nd ed. 1944), p. 69 ff.

conflict with the authorities, he passed in 1888 to the University of Bonn, to win his doctorate with a dissertation on the dialect of Agrigento. In 1890 he returned to Italy.

Before going to the University, he had been already engaged, at eighteen, to a girl of twenty-two; but this tie was broken off, and in 1894 he was married, by his parents' arrangement, to Antonietta Portulano, daughter of his father's mining partner. It throws light on the strange world these people lived in, that Antonietta's mother died in childbirth after refusing the aid of a doctor, on account of her husband's morbid jealousy. Indeed, Signor Portulano was so jealous about his daughter also, that he could only with difficulty endure her being married at all.

Between 1895 and 1899 Pirandello had two sons and a daughter. But disaster dogged him. His father's sulphur-mines were flooded; his father's fortune and his wife's dowry were lost; under the stress of this and her third childbirth, his wife's mind grew unhinged. Pirandello, almost penniless, thought of suicide—for then his father-in-law would have to support his wife and children. But, instead, he stooped to become Professor of Italian Literature in a Teachers' College for women in Rome (Instituto Superiore Femminile di Magistero); and to give Italian lessons, for a pittance, to foreigners.

But far worse was to come. From 1904 his home was made a hell by a wife now grown still more insanely jealous, if possible, than even her father had been. She was jealous of imaginary mistresses; jealous even of the imaginary world of her husband's artistic creation. A writer, she felt, gives away his soul to the world; was that not in itself a betrayal—an infidelity to her who should have possessed that soul in her own exclusive keeping?

With angelic restraint, Pirandello submitted. He gave up his friends; stayed at home; refrained even from going to productions of his own plays; and handed over all his earnings to this unfortunate woman. Deranged though she was, he refused to send her away to a sanatorium. But Signora Pirandello, noting the sympathy of her children for this most long-suffering of fathers, grew jealous of them also. Suspecting that they might poison her, she came to insist on her food being regularly tasted by her daughter first.

Pirandello's existence had become a nightmare—a truly Pirandellian nightmare. For what *was* his own real character?—was he
the honest man he seemed to himself, or the monster imagined by
this madwoman? After all, each of these opposite conceptions was to
the observer a compelling reality. Is *all* life merely a masquerade?

With the First World War his wife's mind grew still further
unhinged by anxiety for her son Stefano in the army. She now
accused her daughter Lietta of wanting to usurp control of the
household. Lietta tried to shoot herself with an old pistol; but the
bullet stuck in the barrel. Even after that, her mother would not
have her in the house. Stefano was taken prisoner; his younger
brother fell seriously ill on service. At last in 1918 the unhappy
Antonietta was released by death. Pirandello had seen more than
enough of drama, even of melodrama, by his own fireside—enough
to paralyse, or break, a weaker man. But Pirandello was brave, with
a stoicism that endured twenty years of this domestic hell. One
cannot know whether this real Inferno was worse than that inflicted
on Strindberg by his own diseased imagination; but Pirandello
stood it unbroken.

As a dramatist, he began his rise to fame during the First World
War. Eventually he wrote some forty plays—nine in one year; one
in six days; one (*Pensaci, Giacomino*) in three. Even his two most
famous dramas, *Six Characters* and *Henry IV*, are said to have been
completed within five consecutive weeks—*Six Characters* in three
weeks; *Henry IV*, in the following fortnight. A miraculous pro-
ductivity—very different from Ibsen's deliberate, methodical tempo
of one play every two years. Yet perhaps Ibsen was wiser. No soil
cropped too often can hope to escape exhaustion.[1]

In 1925 Pirandello took over the Odescalchi Theatre in Rome. He
was patronized by Mussolini. He led his company on tour through
England, France, and Germany—with great success, but with a

---

[1] Pirandello himself has stated that he would long brood over a subject,
perhaps for years; then type his works rapidly, without pause or correction.
'In my own native Sicily I have seen washerwomen give birth to a child at
the river's edge, and five minutes afterwards they were continuing their work!
Any creative work that is great should be equally facile.'

But this dogma would have made Flaubert furious. One cannot generalize.
It depends on a writer's temperament.

loss of 600,000 lire.[1] He became, with Bernard Shaw, the most famous of living playwrights. In 1934 he received the Nobel Prize.

But this year he also got into trouble with Fascism. Outwardly at least he had conformed; he had been officially approved and patronized; but now he gave offence with a rather trivial operetta, *La favola del figlio cambiato*, *The Tale of the Changeling Son*. A poor woman's beautiful infant is mysteriously replaced in his cradle by a nasty little monster; spirited away to a palace; and reared as a prince. As a young man, he is seen and claimed by his poor mother; and gladly goes back to her, leaving his crown to the idiot monster. To his protesting ministers he proclaims, in true Pirandellian fashion—

> Believe me,
> It does not matter
> Whether it is one person or another;
> The crown alone matters!
> Change his diadem of cardboard and glass beads
> For one of gold and precious stones,
> His short mantle for a royal robe,
> And the king of jest becomes a king in earnest,
> To whom you bow.
> No more is needed, only
> That you believe it. . . .
> Nothing is true,
> The truth may be anything;
> Enough, for a moment, to believe.

Naturally this suggestion that any figurehead, however doltish, will do for ruler would not much appeal to the Duce and his devotees. The piece was booed, and suppressed for 'moral incongruity'. The idea that 'nothing is true' was condemned as contrary to Fascist principles (though some may think that, in practice, it was only too much the very principle of Fascism).

Unfortunately in 1935 Pirandello is said to have mended matters

---

[1] The reader may wonder that one whose works so desolately reiterate the futility of all human effort (see, for example, p. 437), should have done anything so strenuous. But I suppose Pirandello might have answered, with a wry smile, that he too, like other men, was a bundle of differing personalities, from which it were vain to ask consistency.

by defending the invasion of Ethiopia, while on a visit to America, with the familiar retort—'What about the Red Indians?' 'Why was he a Fascist?' 'Because I am an Italian.'[1] A reply not wholly free from ambiguity. Cynicism? Weariness? Blindness? It seems hard to tell. 'I am unpolitical,' he once said, '—*apolitico*; I feel myself merely a man upon the earth.'

Next year (1936) Pirandello died. His last instructions were Spartanly, almost savagely, laconic—'Il carro, il cavallo, il cocchiere, e basta!'—'The hearse, the horse, the driver—and enough!' After all those dramatic complexities, an epilogue gauntly plain. A pauper's funeral, and no religious rites. In death at least there should be, at last, no more masquerades. The urn with his ashes was to be walled up in some rugged rock of the countryside round his native Girgenti—that parched landscape which his pen had so often quickened to life, under its half-African sun.

In the nineties, after publishing some volumes of verse, Pirandello had effectively turned to fiction. Of his novels perhaps still the best known is *Il Fu Mattia Pascal, The Late Matthias Pascal* (1904), his first great success.

Here already appears one of Pirandello's lifelong themes—the problem of individual identity. Mattia Pascal, having come into possession of a few hundred lire, takes flight from the bad wife and worse mother-in-law who torment his life, and from the rat-ridden provincial library where he earns a miserable pittance, to Monte Carlo. After winning handsomely at the gaming-table, he recrosses the Italian frontier; but reads to his astonishment in a newspaper that a drowned body near his home has been identified as himself. Here is a real chance to escape from his dreary past! So he goes underground, assumes a new name, and starts a new life, released from all his old entanglements (as perhaps Pirandello in his own miserable home-life was sometimes tempted to dream of doing).

But it proves less easy than Matthias had thought, to be born again; even in that far freer world of 1904. He fares even worse than

---

[1] J. Gassner, *Masters of the Drama* (1954), 444. Pirandello is said also to have given his Nobel Prize medal to be melted down for guns at the time of the Abyssinian War; not a very appropriate gesture, if one recalls that the name of Nobel was also linked with a prize for *peace*.

the displaced persons of today, who have no country; for he has become a fictitious phantom, with no status of any kind. He falls in love with a girl; but, without identity-papers, he dare not marry her. He is robbed; but, without identity-papers, he dare not call the police. He dare not even acquire a dog. Finally, these intolerable frustrations drive him to stage a second suicide, so that he can resurrect Mattia Pascal anew. His wife has meanwhile remarried; and he deeply relishes the revenge of reappearing to her. But he leaves the wretched woman to live on with her now illegal husband, while he resumes his own dull existence in his dull locality. Escape from oneself, as from the tentacles of society, has proved, after all, an empty dream.

The reader may feel that a more resourceful and resolute Mattia Pascal would have somehow contrived to forge himself a new identity, and grow new roots. Many a malefactor manages that in peace time; many a secret agent, in war. Yet *Il Fu Mattia Pascal* remains an original and engaging tale, already typically Pirandellian.

I Vecchi e i Giovani, *The Old and the Young* (1909), deals with the ignoble and tragic degeneration of Garibaldian heroes in the corrupt Italy and oppressed Sicily of the closing nineteenth century. Sometimes moving, it yet seems often overlong.

Uno, Nessuno e Centomila, *One, No one, and a Hundred Thousand* (begun 1910, published 1926-5), returns anew to the mystery of personality. Its hero, Vitangelo Moscarda, grows maddened by finding that his own individuality is really more like a cloud of a hundred thousand midges—all the infinite different selves that he represents to each of his fellow-creatures. He is like the demoniac among the tombs in St Mark, who 'answered, saying, My name is Legion: for we are many.' And so, of his own will, Moscarda finishes in a madhouse. For, after all, no strait-waistcoats are so horrible as the masks that sophisticated life crushes on to our faces. The only escape from it all lies in a mystic dissolution of our individual identity into a dreaming, twilit Nirvana; where, returning to natural surroundings, we can lose ourselves in a vegetative semi-sentience, such as may be enjoyed by animals and plants, exempt from man's accursed knowledge that is no knowledge, man's accursed consciousness of a self that is only a labyrinth of selves—a maze of nightmares.[1] Though too long, too pedantic, too repetitive, this extraordinary novel has at least the merit of making its reader think, and think again.

It may be doubted, however, whether Pirandello was at his best in the novel. He seems far more effective on smaller canvases. His full-length romances—and not infrequently his plays also—suffer, I think, from their lack of characters that are either big enough to win our admiration, or attractive enough to win our sympathy. Perhaps Pirandello did not care enough about the human beings he drew. They might, indeed, haunt and obsess him; they might stir his pity; but he seldom seems to love them. A writer often does well to be detached; but not *too* detached. Old-fashioned novelists at the end of their stories would carefully recount what afterwards became of the characters. This habit of theirs may seem to us inartistically artificial; but at least it proves their genuine concern for the human beings they had brought to life. In the novels of Pirandello, however, figures that have duly served his purpose often tend just to be tossed aside like puppets, in a way that some readers may find a little heartless. For example, one is given no notion what becomes of various personages in *I Vecchi e i Giovani*, or of Moscarda's wife and his partners in *Uno, Nessuno e Centomila*.

This may be partly because Pirandello's ideas, especially in his plays, are inclined to dwarf his characters; just as, in ancient Egyptian reliefs, the Pharaohs dwarf their pygmy subjects. But I believe that in novels and plays the ideas, however exalted, should be kept, like Homer's gods, in the background; and should leave the foreground, the main interest, the living sympathy, to the human personalities.

At all events Pirandello's true field was, I think, not the novel, but the drama and, still more, the short story. In this respect he resembles Chekhov; who could never complete a novel, and whose short stories, for some readers, surpass even his plays.

In his dramas likewise Pirandello's dominant idea was the mystery of human identity. He is like Peer Gynt peeling layer after layer from the wild onion, in symbolic search for the ultimate kernel of

Compare p. 435.

Luigi Pirandello: two selves

reality—and finding in the end that there is *no* kernel—nothing. Is not all life a masquerade?

Or one may recall the words of Hume, here too so far in advance of his own age—'For my part, when I enter most intimately into what I call *myself*, I always stumble on some particular perception or other, of heat or cold, light or shade, love or hatred, pain or pleasure. I never can catch *myself* at any time without a perception, and never can observe anything but the perception.' In short—

> We are such stuff
> As dreams are made on.

Again, there is the cry of Walt Whitman—

> Do I contradict myself?
> Very well then I contradict myself
> (I am large, I contain multitudes).

Or, far less complacently exultant, there is Proust, in whom, it has been well said, the human personality becomes likewise a cloud of midges. For Proust sees all men as irremediably alone. Even when A and B are lovers, there results only a ghostly masque danced by A, and B, and A's idea of B, and B's idea of A. Friendship too becomes an illusion. 'L'artiste qui renonce à une heure de travail pour une heure de causerie avec un ami sait qu'il sacrifie une réalité pour quelque chose qui n'existe pas.'[1] For social converse is 'l'erreur d'un fou qui croirait que les meubles vivent et causerait avec eux'.[2] (Though one may wonder, if these precepts were followed literally, how an artist thus confined to his cell could ever learn enough of life or human beings to depict them. Proust did, indeed, become a recluse; yet he had by no means always been one. Again, if communication between men is so impossible, why write books at all?)

At all events the essential Pirandello seems often a literary Hamlet, a dramatic Hume—a sceptical pessimist for whom truth is only

[1] 'The artist who gives up an hour's work for an hour's conversation with a friend knows that he is sacrificing a reality for something which does not exist.'

[2] 'The delusion of a lunatic who should imagine the furniture to be alive, and talk to it.'

an illusion that, for a while at least, contrives somehow to work. Personality becomes a mere mask—a dream so variable and capricious that we can know neither one another nor ourselves. All is relative.

A bleak view, with some truth, sometimes; but also, I think, with much exaggeration. For surely the world does also contain characters honest enough to wear no masks; strong enough to be consistently themselves; and *not* mere weathercocks or chameleons. Their actions and reactions *are* predictable. These are the people who never let one down; as Pirandello himself refused to let down his demented wife. Such may be rare. But they exist. And they are the salt of the earth. Indeed one may wonder if all ethics could not be summed up in the one commandment—'Thou shalt not let people down.'

THE PLAYS

Since Pirandello wrote so many plays, it seems practical to deal first with some of the most typical; and then to treat in fuller detail two of the most tragic, and the most famous—*Six Characters in Search of an Author* and *Henry IV*.

La ragione degli altri (1915)
(*The reason of others*)

'I have had my day, the child's day has to come.'
MARY EMMA DAVIDSON of Liverpool,
fatally injured in saving a child from a lorry (1930).

A married journalist, childless, falls in love with his widowed cousin, once his fiancée, and now in need of his help. They become lovers; while the journalist's wife suffers in silence, and lives on in silence with her unfaithful husband. Then the lovers tire of each other; yet the small daughter born to them still chains them together. The wife's father discovers their *liaison*. There is a crisis. The husband would like to return to his wife's arms. But his wife is a lofty, logical Pirandellian. Though she still loves her husband, for her, as for Pirandello, the innocent infant is the one that must come first. (Nor, from a social point of view, can one disagree.) So the wife, who is rich, goes to the mistress who, like the husband, is poor, and suggests that the mistress give up her child to be adopted by the wife and her husband. Confronted with this extraordinary proposal, at first the mother passionately refuses. She is, indeed, tired of her lover; but her child remains a very different matter. However, at last, seeing that the child's future is at stake—that it will otherwise be condemned to a life of hardship and poverty—she makes the sacrifice and gives it up.

A rational, but somewhat chilling play. The wife is rather a princess of parallelograms. And too much of the plot hinges on finance. It is gold that finally weighs down the scale; even though all three adults behave with genuine altruism.

It is curious that in the last act of this early play Pirandello, who so often seems too coldly cerebral, becomes what many will feel too sentimental. None the less he is here, like Ibsen, in serious search of a morality higher than those accepted conventions of the respectable which remain so often merely cold and mean.

Some may feel, all the same, that it would have been wiser and more human not to inflict on the poor mother this horrible dilemma —either give up your child, or condemn it to hardship and poverty. One may also wonder what would have happened as the child grew up. Adoption often causes more psychological difficulties than Pirandello seems to realize. In this case the child might easily come to suffer all sorts of emotional complications—guilt at having left its mother's poverty for comfort with a stranger, or resentment at the bargain driven over its head. Pirandello, I feel, did not sufficiently think this problem out.

*   *   *

Pensaci, Giacomino (1916)
(Think, Giacomino)

'A sense of humour . . . will keep a man from the commission of a sins, or nearly all, save those that are worth committing.'

SAMUEL BUTLER

This is another paradoxical search for a morality more genuine than that of the conventionally respectable.

Professor Toti, a schoolmaster of seventy, had a grudge against the government. Therefore he resolved to marry a young wife, so that the authorities would have to go on paying her a widow's pension for many, many years to come. This would be both an annoyance to them, and a kindness to her. Two birds with one stone.

Old Professor Toti fully expects a young wife of this kind to take a lover. He does not care in the least either about that, or about public scandal. He will just make a nice girl happy, and acquire a companion.

Highly cynical? Of course. Quite Machiavellian in fact. Yet old Professor Toti has real charm. Unlike too many of Pirandello's figures, he does seem a living person; not merely a thesis in trousers. Cynicism, indeed, may prove highly effective on the stage. For there it can become as amusing as in real life, without producing those ill effects that in real life make cynicism often odious.

Accordingly Toti duly marries Lillina, daughter of the school-janitor, who used to keep reporting him to the headmaster for the bad discipline he kept in class. Lillina confesses to him that she is already with child by the young Giacomino; and Toti marries her with the calm presupposition that Giacomino will continue to be her lover.

Two years later we see Professor Toti devoted to Lillina's little boy, Nini; he has also got Nini's father, Giacomino, a job in a bank.

But Giacomino's sister and the priest Landolina set themselves to break up this tranquil but highly shocking triangle, in order that Giacomino may marry respectably elsewhere. So they persuade Giacomino to stop visiting his Lillina; and the poor girl is in despair.

In reply, old Toti marches off with the little Nini to recall Giacomino to duty. When all other pleas fail, he threatens that he will himself take the child to the family of Giacomino's fiancée, and expose the whole horrid truth of Giacomino's faithlessness.

This fantastic situation forms the central paradox of the play. Instead of the usual jealous husband at daggers drawn with his wife's lover, here is a husband resolutely dragging a reluctant lover back to his own wife's arms. A piece of neat topsy-turviness much in the manner of Bernard Shaw.

Giacomino gives in. Very well, then, he will marry Lillina after Toti's death. Meanwhile the old professor has saved Giacomino from behaving badly; has saved Lillina from going on the streets; and has saved Nini from becoming an innocent child-victim.

A most curious morality-play. But here too, like Ibsen, Pirandello could claim that he was upholding true morals against false; honesty against convention; humour and good sense against the petty malice of scandal. What matters in life is intelligence and kindness.

One recalls *La Ragione degli Altri*; but *Pensaci, Giacomino* seems to me both cleverer and more human. Its weak point is perhaps that a young man thus forced into marriage might not make a very happy husband, nor make his wife very happy.

Further, the play starts from queer premises. An old schoolmaster who marries in order to spite the state and burden it with a long pension to his young widow, seems a little farcical; and, if taken seriously, a somewhat curious kind of moralist. However, Toti is by nature a whimsically humorous eccentric; and perhaps what he says of his own motives should not be taken too seriously.

Again, it is true that Toti marries Lillina only when her parents refuse to let her marry her lover; and that he assumes she will be released by his death within two or three years. But how can he be sure of that? Old gentlemen of seventy may still live till ninety. Lillina might have to wait for her freedom twenty years. Nowhere does Toti suggest that he would carry his altruism to the point of hopping off a roof.

But perhaps this is looking too curiously and narrowly. Anyway, Toti remains a living, human character; less bounding with vitality, less incorruptibly honest, than Ibsen's Dr Stockmann; but equally resolute in his contempt of compact majorities. And, in drama, a living, human character is worth whole processions of paradoxes.

On the other hand, though Pirandello resembles Ibsen in offering a new, paradoxical morality of his own, it is hard to imagine Ibsen writing *Pensaci, Giacomino*. For Ibsen, I feel, would have judged Pirandello's piece too trifling, too frivolous. And, in fact, clever though Pirandello is, to put him beside Ibsen seems unkind. The old Norwegian is on a different scale.

*   *   *

Il berretto a sonagli (1917)
(Cap and bells)

'Quand on a été bien tourmenté, bien fatigué, par sa propre sensibilité, on s'aperçoit qu'il faut vivre au jour le jour, oublier beaucoup, enfin éponger la vie à mésure qu'elle s'écoule.'[1]

CHAMFORT

A Sicilian lady, Donna Beatrice, finds that her banker husband is having an affair with the young wife of his elderly book-keeper. So she has her husband arrested, with his mistress, in the book-keeper's house. But this proves a very Pyrrhic victory. For her brother is furious—he does not at all want a broken marriage which will leave his sister neither married, nor widow, nor single. The elderly book-keeper is also wretched. He had fully realized his wife's infidelity; but hitherto he had at least saved appearances. Now that his mask has been torn off, must he, like a good Sicilian, go and kill guilty wife and lover?

However, he suddenly hits on an ingenious remedy. Let Donna Beatrice repair her foolish intervention by going for three months into a mental home, so that her charge against her husband can be dismissed as merely an insane delusion. In this pitiable world of ours only madmen can be permitted to blurt out the crude truth—like the medieval fool with his cap and bells—'berretto a sonagli'. (Hence the title.) So finally Donna Beatrice is persuaded to go off for her spell in the mental home.

Conclusion. Acceptance of life's harsh realities works better than general upset and scandal. At least one can save *appearances*. Truth is an expensive luxury, which none can afford but the mad.

As often in Pirandello's plays and stories, the autobiographical element seems close beneath the surface. This play about a jealous

---

[1] 'When one has been thoroughly tormented, thoroughly worn out, by one's own sensitiveness, one comes to learn that one must live in the passing day, forget a lot of things and, in short, pass an obliterating sponge over life as it slips by.'

woman who in the end had to pretend she is mad, comes from a tortured man whose own wife was no less jealous, but mad indeed.

*　　　　*　　　　*

Così è (se vi pare) (1917)
(So it is, if so it seems to you—As you like it)

'What is truth? said jesting Pilate.'

BACON

'If the good Pope remains at Home,
He's the First Prince in Christendome.
Choose, then, good Pope, at Home to stay
Nor Westward curious take Thy Way.
Thy Way unhappy should'st Thou take
From Tiber's Bank to Leman-Lake,
Thou art an Aged Priest no more,
But a Young flaring Painted Whore;
Thy Sex is lost: Thy Town is gone—
No longer Rome, but Babylon.
That some few Leagues should make this Change
To Men unlearn'd seems mighty strange.'

PRIOR

Signor Ponza was secretary in the prefect's office of a provincial town. With his wife, he lived in a top-floor apartment on the outskirts; and in a flat inside the town lived his mother-in-law, Signora Frola.

Now every day the mother-in-law, Signora Frola, goes and talks from the courtyard to Signora Ponza on her top-floor. And letters are exchanged between the two by means of a basket and string. How very odd! Yet Signor Ponza is himself devoted to his mother-in-law; visits her daily; and spends with her all the leisure hours he can.

The provincial town begins to buzz with curiosity.

When pressed, Ponza explains. His mother-in-law, Signora Frola, is mad! She is really the mother of Ponza's first wife, Lina, now four years dead; but the old lady lives under the comforting delusion that Ponza's present, second wife, Giulia, is her own dead daughter, still alive. And so, to preserve her delusion, Signora Frola must be kept from too close contact.

But Signora Frola has a quite different story. According to *her*, it is Ponza that is mad. He is quite mistaken in believing his first wife, who had indeed spent a year away from him in a sanatorium, to be dead. His present wife, whom he calls 'Giulia' is simply his first wife, Lina, who has never died at all.

In its perplexity as to which of the two is really a crazy liar—Signor Ponza or his mother-in-law—the town nearly goes crazy itself.

There are no official documents to settle the problem, since the Ponza's native town has been destroyed in an earthquake.[1] It remains to question the wife, Signora Ponza—is she really Lina, or Giulia?—first wife or second?

Finally the Prefect compels her to appear. But all to no purpose. She comes, in a veil, and merely says—'I am *both* Signora Frola's daughter *and* Signor Ponza's second wife. For *myself*—no one, no one.'

The moral? Quite simple. There exists no absolute truth. What seems true to me, *is* true for me; what seems true to you, *is* true for you. And when cackling busybodies pry into their neighbours' private 'truths', the results can be cruel. Signora Frola and the Ponzas could have gone on living quite contentedly, had they only been left alone. 'Here,' says Signora Ponza, 'is an unhappiness, as you see, that must be kept hidden; otherwise, the remedy that compassion has provided, will not work.'

But Ibsen had said it all, more simply and humanly in *The Wild Duck*; Synge had said it all, more amusingly and poetically, in *The Well of the Saints*. In comparison, Pirandello's play with all its cleverness, seems an exhibition of juggling rather than a drama.

I can see only four possible solutions. Either (1) Signor Ponza is mad, and is being charitably humoured by his wife and mother-in-law; or (2) Signora Frola is mad, and being charitably humoured by

---

[1] Cf. Pirandello's Matthias Pascal who, having chosen to sham dead and assume a new identity, finds life impossible for want of official documents.

Signor Ponza and his wife; or (3) both Signor Ponza and Signora Frola are mad; or (4) Signor Ponza, Signora Ponza, and Signora Frola are all three mad.

Possibly Pirandello might have answered: 'Precisely. Documents might have proved, had they not been destroyed, that Signora Ponza was the first, or the second, wife. But life is a dream. All is illusion. The real is imaginary, and the imaginary is real. Even if, for example, the documents had proved Signora Ponza to be the second wife, for Signora Frola, in her intense conviction, she would still have remained the first, and her own daughter. And that is what Signora Ponza means when she says she is both. "Fact" makes her one; faith, the other. Two different kinds of truth. But each, in its own way, true.'

One sees how Pirandello, chained to his insane wife, could be driven to wonder whether her picture of his personality, so tragically true for her, were not just as 'real' as his picture of himself. But, natural though such doubts might become, at moments, for a hapless husband driven nearly to dementia himself, any competent detective could soon have settled whether Pirandello was or not, in fact, the faithless husband that his wife imagined.

The play reads too much like a parody of the pragmatist idea that the only test of a notion's truth is whether in practice it *works*. So that, as Bertrand Russell put it, a consistent pragmatist sitting on the jury at a murder-trial would consider, not who had really committed the murder, but whom it would best serve society to hang. For that would 'work'.

And so, despite all the ingenuity of *Così è*, three whole acts of it seem to me too much.[1]

---

[1] In audiences unaccustomed to such philosophical acrobatics the play naturally produced at first a highly novel excitement. Thus the critic of *The Outlook* (26/9/25) was amusingly tormented by a lady in the seat behind, who kept ejaculating to her husband, 'But oh, my dear, it's almost *too* interesting!' The question is how long this kind of novelty can keep its power.

*   *   *

Il piacere dell' onestà (1917)
(The pleasure of honesty)

It will already have grown clear that Pirandello is fascinated by two supreme interests—the mystery of reality and the mystery of personality. With the first he becomes a philosopher; with the second, a psychologist.

But he does not seem to me a very good philosopher. He plays with reality as a juggler with a pea; under which thimble is it? Sometimes the pea seems under all the thimbles; sometimes under none. But though jugglers and mountebanks remained in the Dark Ages the last survivors of the drama, good drama is not produced by jugglers and mountebanks, however clever. Pirandello, like Shaw, *was* brilliantly clever, a consummate juggler. He was a wizard with fireworks; yet of fireworks nothing remains next morning but charred sticks and sodden cardboard. Pirandello's pragmatism seems to me pseudo-philosophy.[1] Was Signora Ponza Signor Ponza's first or second wife? We are brilliantly tricked. But the trick is bogus. And who really cares? To be ingenious is not genius.

In literature and art there are endemic two dangerous and kindred maladies: first, the silly-clever; secondly, the false-profound. Wilde, Shaw, Chesterton seem to me to have suffered from the first; Yeats, from the second; Donne, Meredith, Pirandello from both. 'Funny fellow, Meredith,' said Hardy (so I have been told); 'he would get a good situation—and then start being *clever* about it!' 'What is the use,' wrote Christina Rossetti, 'of cleverness in matters poetic?' More, perhaps, than she realized: but less than is often supposed.

However, it is a common foible, even for the gifted, to mis-estimate their own gifts. Statesmen like Dionysius of Syracuse and Frederick of Prussia were enamoured of their own bad verse; Ingres piqued himself on his fiddling; Goethe, on his theory of colours. So Pirandello, like Proust, seems to have overvalued himself as a

[1] Croce is particularly contemptuous of Pirandello's 'philosophy' (*La Critica*, XXXIII, 1935, pp. 20-33); but perhaps with some of the professional asperity of the expert towards the amateur.

philosopher; whereas their real strength lay, not in notions, but emotions. Their philosophic ideas may have helped as scaffolding for what they built; but, for us, the value lies, not in the scaffolding, but in the edifice; not in the framework, but in the work.

It is Pirandello the psychologist, in his better plays and stories, that really counts. Few men have died as bleakly—'the horse, the hearse, the driver—and enough!' But in his tragic life there was also vast patience and generosity. Despite all his disillusioned cleverness he could, at times, also feel.

'One of the novelties,' he claimed, 'that I have given to modern drama consists in converting intellect into passion.' That was precisely the aim of the 'Metaphysicals' in poetry. But with Pirandello, as with them, the fusion of intellect into passion proves sometimes incomplete; and then the 'passion' remains frigid.

What Pope felt about Cowley, many may feel about Pirandello.

> Who now reads Cowley? If he pleases yet,
> His Moral pleases, not his pointed wit;
> Forgot his epic, nay, Pindaric art,
> But still I love the language of his heart.

The Pirandello who matters is the one with a heart. And in this next piece there is far more of the finer Pirandello.

A certain Marquis, Fabio Colli, got his mistress, a young girl of good family, with child. He could not marry her, for he was married already, though separated from his faithless wife.

So he too arranged to save appearances—those appearances that so dominate Pirandello's world of masks—by marrying the girl to a bankrupt gambler from Macerata—Angelo Baldovino.

But the new husband, being a Pirandellian character of un-compromising, logical sincerity, insists that if respectability is thus to be preserved, it must now be preserved thoroughly—in deed and fact as well as in show. Therefore he forbids his wife to see her old lover, who had counted on keeping her as his mistress. When the wife duly bears her child, the new husband feels (as often in Pirandello) obligations towards the child too. The Marquis-lover, who had also made the husband manager of a new company, now tries to get rid of him by tempting him to embezzlement. The husband, for his part, is willing to leave his wife, disappear, and pass for a thief; but only on one condition—that the Marquis-lover himself performs the actual theft. The husband's reasons for this fantastic demand are, again, quite logical. He consents to vanish, because he finds that his impassivity is breaking down. He had felt, in the aloof, impeccable integrity of his formal rôle, like a frescoed saint cloud-borne on the vault of a church-ceiling. But now he is falling really in love with his wife. Yet, on the other hand, he is resolved *not* to lose his new-found honesty.

But his wife on her side has also fallen in love with him. She sees that Baldovino is, after all, a better man than her noble lover. She refuses to let him go. And so, for once, all ends happily.

One is reminded of the dissolute Thomas Becket's transformation, when made archbishop, into a saint and martinet. The moral? In real life one's mask can sometimes become one's true face.

A play of ingenuity; but again, a little forced. Pirandello's characters succeed best when they are not too like Pirandello himself. He was at times an excellent dramatist; but he does not himself make a good *dramatis persona*. He remains too sophistical; too paradoxical; too improbable; too fond of living on split hairs, and chopped straws, to seem really alive as a figure on the stage.

*   *   *

Ma non è una cosa seria (1918)
(But it's not in earnest)

> 'Love ran with me, then walk'd, then sate,
> Then said, "Come, come! it grows too late":
> And then he would have gone . . . but . . . no . . .
> You caught his eye; he could not go.'
>
> LANDOR

This is a light-hearted farce. A rich young Don Juan, aged thirty, has already got himself engaged no less than twelve times. How is he to cure himself of this embarrassing mania, which involves duels with angry relatives? As remedy, he suggests a purely nominal marriage to the poor drudge of twenty-seven who keeps the boarding-house he inhabits. For, once married, he can no longer go on proposing marriage. In return for taking his name as a shadow-wife, the young woman shall have freedom, a home of her own, and an income. One more Pirandellian mask.

But leisure, comfort, and freedom surprisingly transform this poor Cinderella of the boarding-house into an engaging young lady. When she is wooed by an elderly gentleman among her former boarders, the young Don Juan realizes that he is himself in love with her; and, as in the preceding play, a nominal marriage is lifted into a real one.

Not 'serious', certainly; but not without human warmth and sympathy. And these comic somersaults of laughing ingenuity are in due time to lead on to the tragic world of *Henry IV* and *Six Characters in Search of an Author*.

*   *   *

Il giuoco delle parti (1918)
(Each in his rôle)

'M. D.—— L—— vint conter à M. D.—— un procédé horrible qu'on avait eu pour lui, et ajoutait: "Que feriez-vous à ma place?" Celui-ci, homme devenu indifférent à force d'avoir souffert des injustices, et égoïste par misanthropie, lui répondit froidement: "Moi, Monsieur! dans ces cas-là je soigne mon estomac et je tiens ma langue vermeille." '[1]

CHAMFORT

This is a much grimmer affair, a farce that turns into tragedy. Leone Gala, married to a light wife, lets her go her own way and

---

[1] 'Monsieur D—— L—— came and told Monsieur D—— of a monstrous injury done him, adding: "In my place what would *you* do?" His hearer, hardened to indifference by all the wrongs he had suffered, and grown egoistic in his misanthropy, answered coldly: "I, Monsieur? On such occasions I take care of my stomach, and keep my tongue pink." '

inhabits a flat apart. There he concentrates on two things only—thinking and eating. For he has found peace by killing his heart, and living merely with brain and stomach. He has become Stoic and Epicurean in one; without hope, without fear. One might think he would be better dead—indeed, that he almost *is* dead; but he still has power to kill.

To his wife's lover, Guido Venanzi, he quietly explains that he has, in fact, learnt to play the game of life—a game of desperate sadness. The secret is to abandon all hopes and illusions; to empty oneself; to become nothing but a coldly, clearly watching eye. But, when one has made oneself hollow as a celluloid figure, one needs some sort of anchor or ballast, like the weight which makes the celluloid figure spring always up again, however often it is knocked over. This counter-weight must be an interest, a hobby—in Leone's case, cookery. When fate hurls some missile at him he regards it merely as an egg, which can be caught, sucked, and swallowed—leaving only a harmless eggshell, to be played with, or crushed, at will.[1]

Leone Gala's secret, in short, is imperturbability—Chekhov's 'indifference'. And behind his witty exposition of it, one seems to feel the cold hardness of that iron Stoicism learnt by Pirandello himself, through all those agonizing years of gently humouring a mad, intolerably jealous wife. It was, indeed, in this year 1918 that, at last, she died.

Leone's wife, Silia, has overheard all his philosophizing from the next room; and with an angry laugh she hands him a symbolic empty eggshell. Silia is, indeed, a fainter cousin of Ibsen's Hedda Gabler—futile, spoilt, imperious. And she feels maddened by Leone's smiling nonchalance, fluid as water, yet invulnerable as the sea. Her husband hands the eggshell to her lover, and goes.

When he reaches the street below, the angry Silia hurls the egg-shell down at him; but hits instead (women can never throw) a

---

[1] It is worth reading, also, Pirandello's short story on the theme of this play—*Quando s'è capito il giuoco* (*When the game is understood*). Life, to Pirandello, seemed often, not only a futile game, but a cheating game where the cards were rigged against man, and the dice loaded; and therefore a game enjoyable only to dupes.

group of four drunken revellers, who mistake this projectile for an overture, and her for a Spanish dancer living next door. They mount the stairs, and insult Silia with their attentions; while for fear of compromising her, her lover Guido lurks hidden in the next room.[1]

But now Silia sees a chance of disturbing her husband's odious calm; she will make him fight a duel with the chief of these revellers, the Marchese Miglioriti.

Imperturbable as ever, Leone Gala consents; though Miglioriti is a formidable duellist. So a combat is arranged with sword and pistol, on the deadliest terms. The reluctant Guido is to act as Leone's second. But when the fatal morning comes, Leone is found not even dressed. By the etiquette of the duel, since he will not fight, his second must take his place. Perfectly logical. Leone, as Silia's formal husband, gave the formal challenge; let Guido, as her real mate, do the real fighting.[2]

Leone (*loudly*).   I have punished you both.
Silia (*as if biting him*).   But by shaming yourself.
Leone (*who has seized her arm, thrusting her far away*).   But suppose *you* are my shame!

Guido is duly killed.

A nasty ending, too much recalling the super-subtle Italian villains of our Jacobean tragedy. For, at times, the Italian mind seems to tend towards one or other of two extremes—either extreme sentiment or extreme coldness; now dove, now serpent; now Petrarch, now Machiavelli.

But one may not much like either excess.

The danger with Pirandello characters, like Leone Gala here or some of Pirandello's *raisonneurs* elsewhere, who view life with icy detachment, as merely a queer spectacle, is that they may infect the audience too. The dramatic spectator may likewise come to view the drama, with equally icy detachment, as merely a queer spectacle.

---

[1] Compare p. 360.
[2] Compare, in *Il piacere dell' onestà*, Baldovino's insistence on playing *his* rôle of formal husband with logical consistency.

The theatre may turn into a vast refrigerator. But, without emotion, no art.

*   *   *

L'innesto (1919)
(*Grafting*)

A wife, who had been married happily for seven years, was brutally violated while painting in a Roman garden. Thereafter her husband, in his furious jealousy, came to regard her with irrational aversion. In the end, he cannot bear to part with her; but his jealousy flames up afresh when his wife proves pregnant.

He insists on abortion; but the wife, maternal and idealistic, feels that even though her husband may not be physically the father, yet her unswerving love for him still makes the child, in a mystical way, *their* child. At first the pair decide to part; but finally the husband yields to her.

This solution may seem humane; the wife may be a finer character than the husband; yet one may still wonder whether the problem is quite so simple. For the doubt remains what kind of heredity that hapless child might bring with it to burden its life, and perhaps the lives of others, in this harsh world. Those who regard all abortion as wrong in any circumstances will of course find the issue clear; but not everyone (as the world has recently seen) is prepared to generalize with such rigid certainty. It may well be questioned whether this makes a very good subject for a play; still more (as with *La Ragione degli Altri*), whether all its complexities have been sufficiently thought out.

*   *   *

L'uomo, la bestia e la virtù (1919)
(*Man, beast, and virtue*)

For a writer as sensitive and subtle as Pirandello, this seems strangely crude, with an acrid touch of Machiavellian humour.

It treats of a gross sea-captain who leads a double existence, between a neglected wife and son in his home-port, and a second family in Naples. The wife has a love-affair with a professor, and finds herself with child. To save the situation, with great difficulty, the professor succeeds in administering to the captain, on one of his rare visits home, an aphrodisiac in a cream-cake, so that he performs his conjugal duties, and scandal is averted.

The same situation arose in real life when Voltaire's blue-stocking mistress, Mme du Châtelet, turned from him to Saint-Lambert and became pregnant by her new lover. A like trick was then played on her husband, M. du Châtelet. Only the unfortunate Mme du Châtelet died after childbirth. Life has its own grim ways of twisting farce into tragedy.

*   *   *

Come prima, meglio di prima (1920)
(As at first, but better than at first)

A wife, Fulvia, had deserted her husband Silvio, a surgeon, and her small daughter. After thirteen years of reckless living she is driven to suicide; but is saved by her husband's medical skill. She consents to leave her lover, Marco Mauri, and return home. But, since her daughter Livia had been brought up to believe that her mother was an angelic woman dead years ago, at Silvio's suggestion Fulvia now comes back in the guise of a new, second wife. Yet, as with Matthias Pascal, it proves very hazardous to kill off one's old personality, and feign a new one. The girl of sixteen, believing her returned mother to be her stepmother, hates her as a stepmother. Further, she worms out that this new stepmother does not seem to have gone through any marriage-ceremony; and therefore regards the baby-daughter that Fulvia has since borne, as illegitimate. The intolerable tangle is finally cut by Fulvia's going off again with her old lover and her new infant.

But it is hard to care.

It was really for the sake of her daughter that Fulvia came home. But that too ingenious artifice only alienated the girl. It is to be feared that it alienates, also, a good many readers. The characters are not pleasing, not even interesting; and they seem flattened into unreality between the rollers of this artificial machine. There was in Pirandello an element of fox. Often the fox overreached himself by being too cunning. And, in particular, this fox was over-fond of sham deaths.[1]

*　　　*　　　*

Tutto per bene (1920)[2]
(All for the best)

'The children of Alice called Bartrum father. We are nothing; less than nothing, and dreams.'

LAMB, *Dream Children*

After the somewhat artificial cleverness of its predecessors, this play seems to me a welcome return to nature—both civilized and compassionate. The plot is still ingenious; but there is less of clever trickery, more of genuine tragedy.

A young girl just married to a Marquis is about to leave for her honeymoon. Among the assembled relations and friends there is, however, one person whom she treats with studied, icy disdain— her own father, Martino Lori. He is a widower chained to the memory of a beloved dead wife, whose tomb, after sixteen years, he still visits every single day. Yet any observer would think that the bride's real father was the rich and important senator, Salvo Manfroni, who has arranged her marriage, and now dominates the

---

[1] Compare not only *Il fu Mattia Pascal*, but also *Così è se vi pare*, *Trovarsi*, *Lazzaro*; the sham madness of *Enrico IV*; and the opposite pretence, that a real death is only a sham, in *La vita che ti diedi*.

[2] Again it is of interest to compare the corresponding short story, with the same title, *Tutto per bene*; it gives a much clearer picture of Martino Lori's dead wife.

whole festivity. And indeed he *is* her real father. Everyone knows it; except, of course, the bride's supposed father, the poor widower, Martino Lori. And everyone also assumes that the poor widower knows it too, and is merely play-acting, in order to conceal his shameful obligations to his dead wife's lover. Hence, he is viewed with universal contempt. Even the bride, his daughter, shares this general belief in his ignominy, and therefore the general contempt for him. But in fact poor Martino Lori had never even glimpsed the truth. He merely went on sorrowing, in his innocence, for a false wife cold in the grave, and a supposed daughter no less cold to him among the living.

After the honeymoon the married pair return to their own house, where Senator Manfroni is a constant and honoured guest. Poor Lori, paying a visit to his daughter, is cold-shouldered worse than ever. He refuses to go in to dinner. But, afterwards, as he sits and broods alone in semi-darkness, the young marchioness returning, mistakes him for Senator Manfroni. From behind, she puts her hands under his chin and fondly says 'Papa . . .'

An excellent piece of theatre. She is stupefied to find it is not the Senator, but Martino Lori. And Martino Lori himself is no less stupefied—'Have you come even to call him *that*—alone with him!' Exasperated, she cries out to have done at last with all this hypocritical pretence of ignorance about her real parentage.

Martino Lori is stunned. Like a man whose roof has been riven by lightning he suddenly sees, stark and bare, the black desolation round him.

An illusion then, his own marriage that he had supposed so happy! An illusion, this daughter he has for nineteen years thought his own child! An illusion, the whole part he had imagined his, in a world that was all the while mocking him as a complaisant cuckold, fawning and cringing before his dead wife's lover!

Shakespeare's Othello was brought only step by step to envisage his own desolation; but Martino Lori has fallen instantaneously, like Marlowe's Barabbas, into the agony of the seething cauldron.

Hour after hour, Lori sits waiting in the Senator's house for his return; then at last, when late in the night Manfroni comes, the desolate widower rends his rival in a fury of hate. But what on earth can he do? He cannot now kill his dead wife's lover, after all these ignominious years have slipped away. He could, indeed, still ruin him; for he has come to know that the Senator's reputation as a great scientist is bogus—built on mere plagiarisms from Lori's dead father-in-law. But what use?

Lori has only two consolations left. Searching his memories, he comes to realize that his wife had at least been devoted to him during the last three years of their marriage; for she had realized, in the end, that Martino Lori was a far better man than this important Senator, who yet refused to risk his career for her.

Secondly, the daughter, understanding now that her supposed father had been genuinely ignorant, and touched by his lonely misery, turns her affection from her real father, the discredited Senator, to Martino Lori, even though he is her father in name alone.

Yet, at best, such consolations are frail and shadowy. And so the play's end becomes slightly an anticlimax after the pent-up passion released in the vivid scenes before. However, the world is like that. Even in this harassed century, life cannot be a continuous series of crises. Which is one reason why, to avoid anticlimax, so many tragic dramas prefer to end in death.

Here once more Pirandello's theme is the terrible power of mere appearances. A man seems one thing to himself; quite another thing to others. And yet it is precisely on appearances that our lives are largely built. And when one of these fantasies collapses, the effect may be as catastrophic as if the real floor suddenly fell out of a real house.

> That April should be shattered by a gust,
> That August should be levelled by a rain,
> I can endure, and that the lifted dust
> Of man should settle to the earth again;
> But that a dream can die, will be a thrust
> Between my ribs for ever of hot pain.[1]

[1] Edna St Vincent Millay.

*   *   *

La Signora Morli, una e due (1920)
(*Signora Morli, the first and the second*)

'Her person and her personality—
In the bright mirror of a lover's eyes
A woman makes them up.'

This is another work by the humaner Pirandello. Again the theme is dual personality; but it is not, as too often in Pirandello, overdone.

Evelina Morli was for five years married to the gay Ferrante, and bore him a son. Then, by bad account-keeping, her husband became involved in a scandalous bankruptcy. He had to disappear to America, and so shattered was he (this is a somewhat weak point in the plot) that he gave even his wife no further sign of his existence— for he felt, disgraced as he was, that he had best vanish, totally and untraceably, out of her life. Improbable. Still, such things remain possible. (Again one recalls the disappearance of *Il fu Mattia Pascal.*)

In this crisis a serious-minded, romantic lawyer, Lello Carpani, came to the young wife's rescue. He saved her dowry from the creditors; fell in love with her; and had a daughter by her. This liaison, so firmly and loyally established, became accepted even by respectable society in Florence.

But after fourteen years, like Enoch Arden, the husband returns. In America he has made his fortune. He frankly recognizes that he has forfeited all claims to his wife; but he craves at least to see her and his son.

The son, however, now eighteen, insists that *his* right place is with his father; and the mother, though desolated, has to let the boy go. Father and son settle down together in Rome.

But they miss Evelina. So they lure her to Rome by a false telegram, pretending that her son is ill. Arriving she finds her son at the station, a picture of health. At first she is naturally angry at being tricked; but, no less naturally, being a mother, she relents.

For eight days Evelina stays with son and husband, who stealthily intercept all the frenzied telegrams that start pouring in from Florence. And in these new surroundings she slips back into her other personality of former years. She becomes once more the gay young wife she used to be, fourteen summers back—she goes riding, she is swung on the garden swing. All is laughter and light-heartedness. For, with different persons, one becomes a quite different personality. We are chameleons that instinctively change colour to match our environment.

But when her husband, Signor Ferrante, who has now fallen in love with her all over again, tries to keep Evelina permanently with him—then her refusal is unflinching. For she cannot forget the claims of the little daughter she has left in Florence; the claims of the lawyer-lover, who did so much for her in her need; and for whom she in return can do so much, without asking herself 'Am *I* happy?'

So she goes back to Florence. But meanwhile her little daughter has been really ill. Hence the telegrams, intercepted and unanswered. Scandalized Florentine ladies of her acquaintance have been sitting up with the sick child; and Evelina's injured lover meets her return with not unnatural anger and jealousy. Only after a passionate dispute (a brilliant scene, recalling at moments the last dialogue between Nora and Torvald in *A Doll's House*) does she at last force him to understand that, if she has now returned from Rome, it was because she had done nothing there that would make her blush to meet her young daughter's eyes. She admits that she *had* felt again, for the moment, the attraction of her first love. For the old Evelina had risen again in her, after fourteen years of oblivion.

And yet, though she is thus two women, both equally real; though she is different with each of these two men who love her— gay with one, grave with the other; yet she remains still more a mother than either wife or mistress—little though her two lovers like to face that humiliating and mortifying fact.

One may be reminded of Ellida in Ibsen's *Lady from the Sea*, who resists the romantic glamour of the Stranger, for the sake of the husband who so deeply needs her; of Candida in Shaw's play who stays with *her* clerical husband because his need for her is greater than the romantic poet's who made love to her.

Pirandello's play has neither the poetry of Ibsen, nor the epigrams of Shaw; but it remains a very life-like treatment of a very convincing conflict. Further, Evelina is a more intelligent character than either Ellida or Candida. Pirandello never wrote a drama more human; and it seems to me to stand higher among his works than is usually allowed.

*　　　*　　　*

Vestire gli ignudi (1922)
(*To clothe the naked*)

'Last week I saw a woman flayed, and you will hardly believe how much it altered her person for the worse.'

SWIFT

The year 1921 produced Pirandello's two best-known dramas, *Six Characters* and *Henry IV*, which will be dealt with later in fuller detail. But, though less famous, the next in date, *Vestire gli ignudi*, is perhaps the most deeply tragic of all his plays.

Ersilia Drei was employed by the Italian consul at Smyrna as his small daughter's nurse. A naval officer arrived; became engaged to Ersilia; and seduced her on the last night before he sailed. The consul realized what had occurred; he meant well towards her; but a distrustful glance from her aroused his desire. He too seduced her. But while they were in each other's arms, the consul's little daughter fell off a terrace and was killed (compare Ibsen's Little Eyolf); and the consul's wife discovered them. Dismissed in disgrace, poor Ersilia came back to Rome, only to find her naval officer on the point of wedding another. Penniless, after a feeble and disgusted attempt at prostitution, she took poison. She was rushed to hospital; and there, waiting to die, the unhappy girl was overcome by a temptation to weave at least a last wreath of flowery romance round her forlorn and squalid end; to mould for herself at least a death-mask of high tragedy. She was dying for disgust; but she might at least seem to have died for love. 'Truth,' says the poet, 'sits upon the lips of dying men'; yet not always, even there.

So she told a journalist that she had been wrongfully and callously dismissed from Smyrna after the child's fall; and had poisoned herself because broken-hearted for her lover's marriage. In this way, the hapless, obscure creature hoped at least to get off life's stage with some of the glamour of a heroine. Poor mortals—such was one lesson of *The Wild Duck*—need often a life-lie. And even when life has reached its ultimate verge, they may need a death-lie also, to make that last step less intolerable. So Hedda Gabler too had felt; and yet fate mocked her also.

So now, with Ersilia, all went wrong. For the journalist, after the fashion of his profession, threw aside all the reticences and vaguenesses that Ersilia had employed to veil the other actors in her story. At once the Italian press resounded with this highly romantic tragedy; so much so that the consul at Smyrna and the naval lieutenant both found themselves floodlit by a blazing glare of most odious publicity. Further, instead of dying, poor Ersilia recovered.

All this has happened before the play even begins. And now comes the ruthless reckoning. Ersilia, on leaving hospital, is picked up by a novelist and taken to his flat. Then the naval officer, whose marriage has been broken off by the scandal, arrives, mad with remorse, to beg Ersilia to let him atone by marrying her. That might have been a way out. But the wretched Ersilia, frightened, caught in her own net of falsifications, utterly disillusioned, will not hear of it. Next appears the furious consul, returned from Smyrna to seek transfer from a post now made impossible for him. He taxes Ersilia with her lying fabrications; then suddenly suggests elopement. But what use? She knows too well that the ghost of the dead child would always be between them. The romantic mask she had contrived for her exit from life has been ruthlessly torn away. She is left 'naked' before the world. She poisons herself a second time; and, this time, effectively.

Pirandello has a superb gift for those scenes of passionate conflict which are the very essence of drama. Two people talking—what bores they often are! But two people violently quarrelling—at once it becomes dramatic—like the two well-dressed gentlemen I once saw smiting each other furiously with umbrellas in the Galleria Vittorio Emmanuele at Milan.

The critic may complain that here all the characters are second-rate. But the character-drawing is not. In the fate of Ersilia Drei, there remains 'the pity of it'; and for central idea, as so often with Pirandello, there is the eternal conflict between the personality imagined by others, so totally different for different observers, and that other personality which we wear in our own eyes. That conflict can be very real: it *can* become heart-rending.

This play possesses that human truth to life which is the life-blood of tragedy. Farce, of its nature, is exaggeration; comedy can often afford to exaggerate; but tragedy, unless profoundly true, sinks into travesty.

*   *   *

La vita che ti diedi (1923)
(The life I gave you)

'What senseless fools are men, who mourn the hour
Of Death, but *not* the fading of Youth's flower!'
THEOGNIS

From now on Pirandello's plays tend to relapse into excessive ingenuity. This ingenuity was still to produce in 1924 the dazzling fireworks of *Ciascuno a suo modo* (*Each in his own way*). But by 1924 Pirandello was fifty-seven; during his last dozen years his flame seems to fade, without ever recapturing the brilliance of 1920-2.

La vita che ti diedi tells of a mother, Donn' Anna, whose son Fulvio dies. But (rather like the tiresome child in Wordsworth's 'We are Seven') she refuses to recognize his death. She takes no interest in the funeral; she will not tell his mistress of his death; she has his bedroom kept as if he were alive (like Queen Victoria with the dead Prince Consort); she lets his mistress sleep there, pretending that Fulvio has gone away only for a time, she knows not where.

And for this strange attitude, of course, we are given Pirandellian justifications. 'Everything,' says Donn' Anna, 'is a dream. . . . Well then, as long as memory lives, no more is needed to turn the dream to life.' If all is illusion, an imagined son exists no less than a son whom others call 'real'.

The trouble is that, to preserve such private dreams intact, one needs to be really mad; like Joanna the Mad of Castile who for years transported everywhere with her the corpse of her husband, Philip the Fair, till it got lost in a snowstorm. For Joanna, it *was* as if he lived. But poor Donn' Anna is not mad enough; for her, reality breaks in at the end.

She argues also that even the living are mainly dead—mere con-catenations of past selves that live no more. For seven years, while Fulvio pursued a married woman, Donn' Anna kept alive in her heart the darling child he once had been. That was her real son; not the worn-out man who came home to die. But to prove that the living are largely dead is not the same as proving the dead to be still alive.

Pathetic though Donn' Anna is, as she pleads with her sister, with the priest, with her dead son's mistress, and with the mistress's mother, the play seems to me too full of sophistries. They end by arousing not so much pity as exasperation.

*   *   *

Ciascuno a suo modo (1924)

(*Each in his own fashion*)

'Tout est parade ici-bas,
Tout paroît ce qu'il n'est pas.
Voyez en haut, voyez en bas,
Autour de vous en tous états,
  Tout est parade,
  Tout est parade ici-bas;
  Tout est pantalonade.

Amant novice en amours,
Croyez-moi; craignez toujours
La masc, masc, masc, la ca, ca, ca,
  La mascarade;
Dans ce temps-ci les amours
  Sont amours de parade.'[1]

COLLÉ (1709-83)

Perhaps this is the climax of all Pirandello's clever devilries. It is constructed, with amazing virtuosity, on three different planes. For it represents:

1. A play acted on the stage in the ordinary way.
2. The audience in the passages leading to auditorium and stage during the two entr'actes.

[1]
'Parade are all things here below,
All are only seeming show.
Look, wherever you may go,
Among the high, among the low,
  All is parade.
  Parade are all things here below,
  A mere harlequinade.

Lover novice in love's school,
Beware (lest you be made a fool)
The mask-, mask-, mask-, the -er, -er, -er,
  The masquerade;
All loves today, this is the rule,
  Are loves of mere parade.'

3. The frenzied reactions of two real characters in that audience, who recognize themselves in the play; and are as badly upset at finding their troubles exhibited to the public as Laura Kieler by recognizing herself in the Nora of Ibsen's *Doll's House*.

It is an elaboration, in fact, of the play-scene in *Hamlet*, as that might be if we had:

1. The performance of the Murder of Gonzago.
2. The detailed reactions and outcries of the whole Danish court.
3. Violent outbursts of protest from King Claudius and Queen Gertrude.

The effect is like a mirror reflecting real life and reflected, in its turn, in a further mirror.

The play, says Pirandello's preface, should really begin in the public square before the theatre, with news-vendors selling a special flysheet from an evening-paper. This flysheet would be entitled— 'The Suicide of the Sculptor La Vela and this evening's performance at the —— Theatre'; and would begin:

In the theatre world there has unexpectedly spread a piece of news destined to cause an enormous scandal. It appears that Pirandello has taken the subject of his new play, to be performed tonight at the—— Theatre, from the highly dramatic suicide, which recurred some months ago at Turin, of the lamented young sculptor Giacomo La Vela.

The flysheet would then give details of that tragic event. La Vela was engaged to the actress Amelia Moreno. But, finding her in the arms of his friend, Baron Nuti, his sister's fiancé, he killed himself.

Then the spectators entering the theatre should discover standing near the box-office, an actress impersonating the actress Amelia Moreno who caused this real-life tragedy; accompanied by three gentlemen-friends imploring her to leave the theatre, and not cause a public scandal; while she refuses, nervously biting her handkerchief. In the foyer should be standing, also, an actor, impersonating Baron Nuti, the friend of the dead sculptor and the seducer of Amelia, the dead sculptor's mistress; likewise surrounded by anxious acquaintances, and trying to hide under a show of calm his frenzied emotions.

With good reason the theatre playbills would have warned the public—

It is impossible to state whether the acts will be two or three, as incidents are to be expected which may prevent the performance being finished.

The two levels of reality may be tabulated thus:

Real-life characters

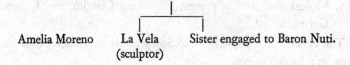

Amelia Moreno   La Vela   Sister engaged to Baron Nuti.
                (sculptor)

Characters in the play based on them

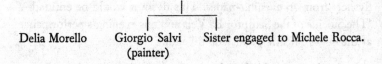

Delia Morello   Giorgio Salvi   Sister engaged to Michele Rocca.
            (painter)

ACT I

The play opens in the house of a wealthy lady, Donna Livia Palegari. She is horrified to hear that her son Doro has been defending, in a heated discussion elsewhere, the actress Delia Morello; who had been engaged to the young *painter* Giorgio Salvi; was caught by him in the arms of Michele Rocca, fiancé of Salvi's sister; and thereby caused Salvi's suicide.

Next Doro arrives. Yes, he *has* quarrelled the previous evening with his friend Francesco Savio about Delia. For Doro's friend, Savio, denounced Delia as an evil harpy. But Doro himself defended her as really an altruistic woman, who behaved as she did only in order to deter the painter Salvi from marrying her; for that, she foresaw, would mean misery in the end for both of them.

But now Doro admits that he can no longer believe his own ingenious defence of Delia's character. And much Doro's mother is relieved to hear it.

But soon after, Doro's friend Savio appears, full of apologies. For he now feels convinced that Doro was right—Delia is *not* an evil woman.

At this, Doro grows furious. Just when Savio has become converted to Doro's view that Delia is *not* an evil woman, Doro has become converted to Savio's view that she *is*. How maddening!

It is just like the *Thaïs* of Anatole France, where the holy Paphnuce converts the sinful Thaïs to righteousness; but Thaïs simultaneously perverts the holy Paphnuce to sin. Or it recalls the story of the Moslem girl who loved a Christian knight. Dying she became a Christian, so as to be with him in the next world; unfortunately, not knowing this, her lover had the same idea, and became in his last moments a Moslem.

So now Doro and Savio, having each swung round to the other's conviction, quarrel all over again. And the quarrel grows so violent as to end in a challenge to a duel. (The whole thing becomes a little farcical.)

No sooner is Savio gone, than there enters Delia Morello herself. Hearing of Doro's recent defence of her, she has rushed to thank him; though they had met only a few times before.

Doro's explanation of her motives, she explains, was so true that she has come to understand herself better. Doro, moved by her beauty, veers round again to believe in her goodness after all. (So much for popular opinion, and men's glib judgements on one another!)

Doro now tells Delia of Francesco Savio's original case against her—that she had infatuated Salvi by tantalizing him; forced him to introduce her, despite her bad reputation, to his family and sister; and then, because the sister's fiancé, Rocca, opposed her acceptance into this decent home, revenged herself by seducing Rocca and thus exposing him as merely a sham Puritan, a bogus Galahad.

To Doro's amazement, Delia exclaims, in dismay, after hearing this hostile theory of her motives, 'Who knows, my friend, that this was not really why I did it?'

So little do we understand our own impulses. All the same, these clever complications of feeling begin to seem a little too clever.

At this moment Doro's mother returns, and is appalled to

encounter the dreaded vampire, Delia Morello, under her own roof. Delia flees.

FIRST ENTR'ACTE

The stage now represents the approaches to the auditorium. A babel of confusion reigns. In the midst of it are five judiciously cautious dramatic critics; some of whom, we are told, may curse the play now, yet praise it in tomorrow's articles. 'So true is it,' adds the sardonic Pirandello, 'that a profession is one thing, and quite another the man who has to follow it for reasons of self-interest, which force him to sacrifice his sincerity (supposing he has any sincerity to sacrifice).'[1]

Similarly spectators who had violently applauded Act I will now in the interval be found denouncing it with no less vehemence.

And so from the assembled multitude there rises a perfect pandemonium of discordant cries:—'Going splendidly!' 'Nothing but dialectical traps! Cerebral acrobatics!' 'The woman is admirably drawn.' 'Petty philosophical problems at four a penny!' '*Must* there be an end of the world at *every* Pirandello first night?'

Baron Nuti, vainly restrained by two friends, shouts hysterically about 'trampling on the dead and defaming the living'. Then, as the bells ring for Act II, Amelia Moreno bursts out of her box, with three of *her* friends trying to drag her away from the theatre; whereas *she* wants to mount the stage and denounce this public infamy. Then, curious to see what comes next, she re-enters her box.

It is all fantastically ingenious and amusing. And this general riot is no worse, apparently, than the storm of fury and derision actually aroused by the first performance in Rome (May, 1921) of Pirandello's *Six Characters*.

ACT II

Savio is practising with a fencing master for his coming duel with Doro.

[1] Like Chekhov, Pirandello had no love for critics. Compare his statement, quoted by Lennox Robinson: 'Anything important I want to say in my play, I must say three times—once for the intelligent people, the second time for the less intelligent, and the third time for the critics.'

Diego, Doro's friend and the ironic mouthpiece of Pirandello himself, relates how Delia visited Doro to thank him for defending her; but then stupefied him by admitting that Savio's accusations of her were possibly true. And by all this the sceptical Diego is delighted, because the whole situation, the whole quarrel, the whole duel, have thus become ridiculous and grotesque, under that bleak light of reality which, at such moments, shows up the absurdity of all human passions and convictions. 'Sottise, sottise, toutes choses sottise!'

Diego also announces that Delia's lover, Michele Rocca, has arrived in fury from Naples, to slap Doro in the face, and fight him for his defence of Delia. But, of course, as Diego points out, Rocca ought by rights now to be fighting Savio, since Savio has meanwhile gone over to the lady's side and become *her* champion.

But now Delia Morello arrives to beg Savio not to fight Doro. And while Savio is off-stage talking to Delia, enter Michele Rocca in furious search for her.

Rocca's own version of the affair is that he wished to save his friend Salvi from marrying this bad woman. Salvi and Delia had just had a quarrel; and Rocca then maintained to Salvi, that he could himself seduce the fickle creature. Salvi accepted the challenge; then killed himself because Rocca did in fact succeed in seducing her, just as predicted.

So we have now three irreconcilable versions of the affair:

1. That the actress altruistically seduced her lover's future brother-in-law to save her lover from the disaster of marrying her;

2. that she vindictively seduced the future brother-in-law because he opposed her introduction into his fiancée's respectable family;

3. that the future brother-in-law altruistically seduced the actress to save his friend from marrying her.

But now Savio reappears, followed by Delia herself. And Delia and Rocca who, despite their own self-deception, are really infatuated with passion for each other, run straight into each other's arms. All else is forgotten—even that between them lies the death of the young painter. All their pleas of justification were mere pretences; all their reasons, mere pretexts. They simply fell in love at first sight. Just that.

SECOND ENTR'ACTE

(Its scene, again, the approaches to the auditorium)

A still worse hullabaloo breaks loose. The moment the curtain falls, Amelia Moreno bursts out of her box, bounds behind the stage-curtain, and slaps the leading lady in the face. From behind the lowered curtain come the shouts and screams of actors and intruders; and an equal bedlam ensues among the astonished audience. (It recalls the first week of Synge's *Playboy*.)

'Moreno, Moreno!'—'Who *is* Moreno?'—'They have slapped the leading lady.' 'Who? Who's slapped her?'—'Moreno! Moreno!'—'Who *is* Moreno?'—'The leading lady?'—'No, no, they have slapped the author!'—'The author? Slapped?'—'Who? Who's slapped him?'—'Moreno!'—'No, the leading lady!'—'The author has slapped the leading lady?'—'No, no, the other way about!'—'The leading lady has slapped the author!'—'Nothing of the sort! Moreno has slapped the leading lady!'

Voci dal palcoscenico. 'Basta! basta!'—'Vadano fuori!'—'Mascalzoni!' —'Spudorata!'—'Fuori! fuori!'—'Signori, facciano largo!'—'Lascino passare!'

Voci degli spettatori. 'Fuori i disturbatori!'—'Basta! basta!'—'Ma è proprio la Moreno?'—'Basta, fuori!'—'No, lo spettacolo deve seguitare!' —'Via i disturbatori!'—'Abbasso Pirandello!'—'No, viva Pirandello!'— 'Abbasso, abbasso!'—'È lui il provocatore!'—'Basta, basta!'—'Lasciate passare! lasciate passare!'—'Largo! largo!'[1]

And now appears Baron Nuti; still more convulsed with fury, he seizes by the front of his waistcoat one of the audience who favours

---

[1] *Cries from the stage.* 'Enough of it! Enough of it!'—'Out with them!'— 'Toughs!'—'Shameless woman!'—'Out! Out!'—'Gentlemen, make room!' —'Make way there!'

Cries from the spectators. 'Out with the rowdies!'—'Enough of it, enough!' —'But is it really Moreno?'—'Enough, get out!'—'No, the play must go on.' —'Away with the interrupters!'—'Down with Pirandello!'—'No, long live Pirandello!'—'Down with him! Down with him!'—'*He* is the trouble-maker.'—'Enough, enough!'—'Make room, make room!'—'Out of the way, out of the way!'

the play. Then Moreno, emerging from the stage, sees him and screams—'My God! There he is! There he is!'

Nuti. Amelia, Amelia! . . .
Moreno. Take him away! Take him away! . . .
Nuti (throwing himself upon her). No, no! You must come with me!—with me!
Moreno (tearing herself free). No! Leave me, leave me! Murderer!

So they start repeating in real life the altercations that have just been acted on the stage; till Nuti drags Amelia Moreno away with him. And then—

The manager regretfully announces that, owing to the riot, the third Act cannot be played.

It is a dazzlingly original *tour de force*—perhaps more extraordinary in its ingenuity than any play I have read. At moments it may remind us of Browning's *The Ring and the Book*, with its dozen differing versions of another Italian tragedy. Pirandello is here far less humane and idealistic than Browning; but far briefer and more brilliant.

What underlies it all?

Pirandello, I take it, was exasperated by our human passion for probing and analysing other people's private tragedies, as press and law-courts so crudely do; and by our incorrigible habit of passing slap-dash emotional judgements on totally inadequate evidence—judgements so emotional that, even if there *were* adequate evidence, they would still be falsified by prejudice; judgements so fatuously over-simplified that they cannot possibly cope with the intricacies of real life. And anyone who has read, for example, the history of the Dreyfus Case can hardly accuse Pirandello of exaggerating this form of human folly.

Secondly, Pirandello feels intensely how tragi-comic are the attempts of poor human beings to 'build themselves up'[1]; to paint themselves fancy-portraits; to wear *masks* which they end by mistaking for their own faces.

[1] *Costruirsi.*

401

The only antidotes are—mental honesty; ruthless scepticism; laughter; and compassion. One should not pretend. One should not play-act one's life. One should believe little; and judge even less. Life is a tragic farce, a farcical tragedy. Here too Pirandello becomes the Hume of the stage.

And surely there is much substance in all this. Nothing, for example, can reconcile Rousseau's picture of his own life and of his quarrels with his friends, such as Hume, on the one hand; and, on the other, the account of Rousseau given by those friends, several of whom were very honest men. To his townsfolk, again, Ibsen's Dr Stockmann became a public enemy; to his family, still more clearly, he was a public hero. Strindberg's first marriage as described by Strindberg is wildly different from the version of his daughter; his second marriage, as described by Strindberg, wildly different from the version of his second wife.

I do not believe in *complete* scepticism. Some views, after careful investigation, become much more *probable* than others. But few of us in real life are sceptical enough—especially in literary criticism. Pirandello would have amused—and, I think, pleased—the doubting Montaigne.

Ciascuno a suo modo seems to me a play extremely difficult, for technical reasons, to act (far easier, indeed, to film); but most entertaining to read. It is a piece of staggering *bravura* rather than a satisfactory play—for one does not care about a single character in it, and the essential theme is neither deep nor new. Yet it is expressed with scintillating novelty. Pirandello was never, I think, to show the same verve and vigour again.[1]

*   *   *

[1] The piece contains, however, a slight incongruity.

Its theme is the obscurity of human motives. Pirandello imagines himself as having dramatized the love-triangle of Delia Morello, Giorgio Salvi, Michele Rocca. For their behaviour various explanations are suggested— (1) Delia made love to Michele out of altruism; (2) she did it for revenge; (3) Michele made love to her out of altruism. All prove wrong. The true explanation (4) is blind passion. And so Delia and Michele just fall, finally, into each other's arms.

But this play about Delia, Giorgio, and Michele is based, we are told, on real life—on the similar triangle of Amelia Moreno, La Vela, Baron Nuti. In

From now on, the plays leave an impression of declining powers. Therefore I shall deal with them more briefly.

Diana e la Tuda (1926, in German; 1927, in Italian)—*Diana and la Tuda*—deals, like Ibsen's *When We Dead Awaken*, with the conflicting claims of life and art. Life is animated, yet mortal: art is immortal, yet dead. Death, indeed, makes statues of us all. A young sculptor, Dossi, is modelling a Diana from a girl called la Tuda, who remains, for him, (as Ibsen's Irene for Rubek) merely a model, not a human being. La Tuda desperately loves him; but *he* is captive to a worthless society woman. When, however, an artist wishes to paint la Tuda, Dossi grows jealous and marries her, in order to retain her as his exclusive model. She accepts this arrangement; but when Dossi gives his mistress the key of his studio which, at least, la Tuda feels to be her own rightful domain, then she leaves him. In a final quarrel with this girl whom he has tortured and turned to clay, Dossi is himself killed by an old sculptor, Giancano, who had loved la Tuda from afar.[1]

L'amica delle mogli (1927)—*The wives' friend*—tells of a woman

---

the second entr'acte Amelia and Nuti fall as blindly into each other's arms in the foyer as Delia and Michele had done on the stage. Here also explanation 4 —blind passion—proves the true one.

This implies that the playwright who created Delia and Michele correctly interpreted, also, the behaviour of Amelia and Nuti. Indeed he even correctly predicted it. For Amelia and Nuti's passionate reconciliation comes *after* that of their stage-counterparts. But, if so, is human motivation so inscrutable after all?

It might, then, have been more logical if Amelia and Nuti in the second entr'acte had behaved differently from Delia and Michele in Act II, so as to suggest that their own conduct needed yet a fifth explanation.

But this objection, though it does not seem unreasonable, is not important.

[1] In this play, as in *L'amica del e mogli* and *Trovarsi*, one feels the presence and influence of the beautiful and gifted young actress, Marta Abba. In her early twenties (1925) she became leading lady in the Teatro d'Arte, Rome, founded and directed by Pirandello; went on tour with his company in France, Germany, England, and elsewhere; and retired in 1938, on marrying in the United States; though later she returned to acting, both for stage and film. To her the author dedicated both *Trovarsi* and *Come tu me vuoi*. (See F. V. Nardelli, *L'Uomo Segreto*, 2nd ed. 1944, ch. xxxi, 'Marta Abba'; and photograph opposite p. 240.)

so far above the men around her that they quail at the idea of wooing her, and wed inferior women whom her gentle nobility dominates. When at last passion breaks into these Platonic altitudes, the end is only jealousy, murder, and despair.

Lazzaro (*Lazarus*), 1929, is a drama of religious fanaticism; but its plot seems marred by a fundamental absurdity.

Diego Spina, a pietistic zealot, packed off his son Lucio to a seminary, and his daughter Lia to a convent, where from neglect she became a cripple. His wife Sara, unable to control his manias, very naturally left him and went to live on one of their farms. Here, after a couple of years, she united herself to a noble rustic, with the pastoral name of Arcadi-pane, and bore him two children. All this virtuous peasantdom is made most tediously idyllic.

Little Lia has a rabbit which dies. A Dr Gionni brings it back to life by an injection of adrenalin. But the maniac father, outraged at things being brought back to life in this unorthodox fashion, ruthlessly takes the rabbit away. (A curious way of confuting inconvenient facts.) Then the son Lucio runs off to his mother's farm, resolved not to become a priest. Diego rushes in pursuit, is killed by a car, and is himself restored to life by Dr Gionni, like the rabbit.

Diego discovers that he has been dead for three-quarters of an hour. Yet his soul has no recollection of it. Therefore the soul is not immortal. He becomes frenzied.

It is hard to say of what follies the human mind is not capable. But it is hard, also, to imagine that many believers in immortality are troubled by the fact that persons whose hearts have stopped, and who have therefore been what is usually called 'dead', retain not the least remembrance of it. One fails to see why unconsciousness after apparent death should provide decisive proof of anything whatever. The whole question remains whether such unconsciousness after death is temporary or permanent. And surely most people, whether orthodox or sceptic, base their beliefs on considerations which, though often puerile, remain less completely trivial and inconclusive than this.

However Lucio decides after all to become a priest, and comforts his distressed father with a lot of rambling verbiage about the soul being really God, and in God, and about scientific miracles being still God's miracles.

O di uno o di nessuno (*Child of one or of none*), 1929, takes for its bizarre theme a couple of young men in Rome who share a mistress they have imported from their native Padua. For a few months all goes well in a happy camaraderie, until the girl Melina becomes pregnant. Then the two are tormented by the problem whose child it is. Melina refuses an abortion; she refuses also to put the child in a foundlings' home. Then she dies in childbirth, and the baby is adopted by a well-off neighbour. Melina is a charming character; and her death produces a pathos that, though it may seem to some a little facile, remains natural and real. But the wrangles of the two young men about their paternity grow tedious. And one feels that Shakespeare himself could hardly have made very much of such a subject.

Come tu me vuoi (*As you wish me*), 1930. In the First World War Cia, wife of Bruno Pieri, was violated and carried away from North Italy by Austrian or German invaders. Ten years later Boffi, a friend of her husband, thinks he recognizes the lost Cia in a Berlin dancer of Venetian origin. She is now living, amid the degraded night-life of post-war Berlin, with a decadent German writer and his daughter. Boffi persuades the dancer to come back to Italy as Bruno Pieri's long-lost wife. But there she grows to suspect that, though she has tried to redeem herself and to become really Bruno's vanished Cia, her husband remains more interested in the petty financial advantages he can gain from her resurrection. And when the German writer brings to the house a lunatic from a Vienna sanatorium who physically shows a better claim to be the missing wife, the heroine goes back to her Berlin squalor. In spirit she had tried to be Bruno's Cia; but this mercenary world cares nothing for the spirit.

An unconvincing end. The first Act in Berlin is very vivid. But the play ends disappointingly in one of Pirandello's eternal juggles with truth, identity, and personality—topics on which the heroine herself becomes a tedious she-pedant.

Questa sera si recita a soggetto (*Tonight we improvise*), 1930, is another play with a play within it, like *Six Characters* and *Ciascuno a suo modo*; but it seems to me much inferior to its predecessors.

Here Pirandello once more vents his spleen on theatrical producers—this time in the shape of a grotesque Dr Hinkfuss. But the inner play in this case is only one more study of a morbid jealousy that to northern eyes may well seem pathological and, indeed, hardly credible.

Trovarsi (*To find oneself*), 1932. As with *Diana e la Tuda*, again the theme is the clash of life and art. A great actress lives in and for her profession. She has no personal identity—only the multiple selves that she creates. Like Signora Ponza, she is, for herself, no one. But she falls in love with a young Swede, Elj Nielsen. At last she hopes to begin living a real life of her own. And yet she finds the caresses she bestows on her lover too like the imitation caresses of her acting; rather as Garrick was accused by Goldsmith of acting even off the stage; or as Talma, even while he sobbed beside his dead son, found himself listening to himself, to observe his own emotion. Acting, indeed, as Plato maintained, is a dangerous trade. So here; the actress's mask has stuck too closely to her face. She despairs of natural spontaneity. Yet she cannot give up her calling. So she returns to the stage, hoping that she may somehow contrive to merge woman and artist in one. But after her performance she finds her young lover fled. Watching her, his naturalness had revolted against all the artifice of her art. So in the end she accepts her destiny—to live only in a Platonic world of imagination, embodying characters who are only dreams. She has found herself, but only to find herself utterly alone.

A desolate conclusion; but perhaps sometimes true.

Quando si è qualcuno (*When one is somebody*), 1933. This depicts a famous writer, mummified amid his own glory, and poisoned by his own mask. Falling in love with a young woman, he tries to become young again and to begin a new poetic career in a new manner; but, of course, quite in vain. The world has relentlessly imprisoned his winged spirit in its unalterable pigeon-hole.

Now it is quite true that the critical world tends to resist an established author if he attempts to strike out on a new line. But Pirandello seems to exaggerate the difficulty. Writers of sufficient power and will have overcome the world's resistance. Scott, for example, changed most successfully from a poet to a novelist; Hardy, from a novelist to a poet. Indeed, Pirandello himself had turned at fifty from fiction to the stage.

Non si sa come (One knows not how), 1934. This seems a needless tragedy, inspired by Pirandello's feeling that, whatever demure masks civilized men may wear, each carries within him a wild beast of instinct, capable of suddenly smashing the polished bars of its cage. We can be swept into doing something that would normally shock us—

> 'Tis done, and in the after-vacancy
> We wonder at ourselves like men betrayed.[1]

And then, if we are neurotics with the sedulously cultivated sense of guilt that has so often been mistaken for morality, we continue to brood and agonize over the past instead of simply taking steps to do better in future.

Such a neurotic is Count Romeo Daddi, married to Bice. They are guests of Romeo's friend, the naval officer Giorgio Vanzi and his wife Ginevra. One morning, left alone in the villa, Count Romeo and Ginevra fall into each other's arms. It was a mere fit of momentary madness; and Ginevra wants to do the only sensible thing—forget it. But Romeo cannot.

As a boy, in a similar fit of passionate emotion, he once hurled a stone at a peasant-lad who had been tormenting a lizard, and killed him. He was never found out. But now his old sense of guilt is redoubled by this new crime; and he madly craves self-punishment. Accordingly he torments not only himself, but also his wife Bice. Has she too these dark impulses? He wrings from her an admission that once, in a dream, she had given herself to Giorgio Vanzi. She too, it follows, is as bad as himself. For it was, essentially, in a waking dream that he and Ginevra gave way to their desire.

[1] Wordsworth, *The Borderers.*

407

But, instead of leaving it at that, this mystical noodle, with his longing for atonement, is finally driven by his obsession to confess to Giorgio; who, being a man of action, promptly shoots him.

'Pirandello,' says Vittorini, 'has never revealed the tragedy of being human more powerfully than in this play.' But I cannot feel that such praise, were it true, would do much credit either to Pirandello or to humanity. For one thing, this Sicilian frenzy of jealousy that overshadows so much Pirandellian drama, like a poisonous evergreen, ends by becoming a deadly bore. Life has surely finer tragedies than that. Further, Pirandello's attitude to sex in general seems to me one of his less healthy sides. He was not a prude—indeed he could be crude, as in *L'uomo, la bestia e la virtù*; but he tended to become a sort of mystical puritan. Perhaps his own unhappy life had left him warped—'too full of choler with living honest'. Often, at all events, he sees physical love, not with the sanity of many Greek poets when they praise the golden, laughter-loving Aphrodite, and Eros the bitter-sweet; not with the exaltation of Blake when he celebrates that 'on which the soul expands its wing'; but with the grudging, guilty distaste of the later Plato, or Tolstoy, or some religions. Often he treats physical desire as a necessary evil, but an evil necessity—the opposite extreme to Buffon's cynical observation that 'in love there is nothing good but the physical'. Buffon seems to me excessive; though many a disillusioned lover looking back may own, if honest, that those bleak words are only too often true. Still they are not the whole truth. Little to envy in the desolate ennui of figures like the ageing Louis XV. None the less Pirandello's air of slight disgust seems to me slightly disgusting. Chekhov was wiser.[1]

Non si sa come was Pirandello's last play except for the unfinished *Giganti della montagna* (*Giants of the Mountain*), a wild fantasy about giants and a magician, which was produced posthumously in 1937. But there seems nothing worth dwelling on either in this, or in *La nuova colonia* (*The New Colony*), 1928, or in *La favola del figlio cambiato* of which something has been said already.[2] Piran-

---

[1] See p. 18 (letter on marriage).
[2] p. 363.

dello's best dramatic work was done by the early nineteen-twenties, and before his fifty-eighth year.[1]

It is time now to turn in more detail to the two plays that have won international fame—*Six Characters* and *Henry IV*.

[1] I have also omitted some other pieces of Pirandello's that seem less important or less interesting—such as *La Morsa*, 1910; *Lumie di Sicilia*, (*Sicilian Limes*), 1910 (a moving little play about a peasant-lover whose love becomes a successful singer, and is lost to him); *L'uomo dal fiore in bocca*, 1923 (about a victim of cancer); and *La sagra del signore della nave* (1925).

Sei personaggi in cerca d'autore (1921)
(Six characters in search of an author)

'My notion always is that, when I have made the people to play out the play, it is, as it were, their business to do it and not mine.'

DICKENS

'Often my characters astonish me by doing or saying things I had not expected—yes, they can sometimes turn my original scheme upside down, the devils!'

IBSEN

'There is a regular army of people in my brain begging to be summoned forth, and only waiting for the word to be given.'

CHEKHOV

Why this should be Pirandello's most renowned work (it is said to have been translated over five hundred times) I cannot quite understand. When first seen or read it is, indeed, intriguingly odd—full of ingenious surprises and surprising ingenuities; but, once this first wonder has worn off, one may wonder how much of lasting value remains.

For the play seems far less human than, for example, *Vestire gli ignudi*. *Six Characters* is a most adroit piece of Pirandellian thimble-rigging. There may be some real truths under the thimbles; but truths not, perhaps, very startling.

These are, apparently, as follows:

1. Fictitious characters, rising phantom-like in an author's imagination, can pester him to give them form and life; just as Samuel Butler's Erewhonians believed that the unborn pestered the living to bring them to birth. This had been Pirandello's own experience, recorded also in his *novelle*, *Colloqui coi personaggi* and *La tragedia di un personaggio*. And again, when once conceived, an author's characters can become so lively and wilful that they force him to give them a different destiny from what he had intended. So Ibsen also found.

But of course this idea of wilful independence on the part of fictitious characters is nothing unfamiliar. Turgenev, for example, put the matter excellently when he said that an author must cut the navel-string between himself and the offspring of his imagination.

2. Imaginary characters can have a more vivid and lasting reality than real ones.

But this too is nothing new. It is only an adaptation of Plato's 'ideas'; and, again, of Aristotle's view that creative literature is more philosophical than factual history; so that imaginary beings like Hamlet, or the Wife of Bath, can live in our minds with a more intense and enduring vitality than historic figures like Charles I or Beau Brummell.

It was a similar feeling that made Balzac, for instance, after a perfunctory inquiry about the health of some relative, say impatiently to Jules Sandeau, 'Now, let's get back to *reality*—who shall marry Eugénie Grandet?'

So too those who sit decade after decade at college high-tables, while generations grow up and pass away around them, may come to feel that the college portraits of statesmen and ecclesiastics which watch them immutably from the walls, are more real, though only paint-and-canvas, than the fleeting pageant of flesh-and-blood that rises up and vanishes again under the gaze of those impassive, changeless eyes.

3. Stage and actors give, very often, only a crude, incomplete, and distorted embodiment of an author's conceptions. They blunt, simplify, and coarsen the delicate subtleties and nuances of the poet's dreams.

In *Six Characters*, however, neither plot nor persons offer any very enchanting dream. Their drabness is no fault of stage-conditions—it is already present in the plot. Evidently Pirandello was fascinated by the idea of making certain imaginary characters materialize in visible shape; force their way into a real rehearsal; and demand forthwith to be acted. But one may wonder what he found so fascinating about these particular six characters, that they should haunt him. Yet they did. He had first thought of them, it seems, seven years before, in 1915.

Their story is simple; and sordid. A somewhat intellectual man, possessed by a demon that tempted him to experiment with life, chose to marry a naïve and stupid woman of the people. The pair had a son. But this doctrinaire father, wishing his son to grow up robustly healthy, packed the boy off to be reared by country peasants. The poor, simple mother, left lonely and at a loose end, grew attracted to her husband's humble secretary. And the husband noting with irritation the mutual sympathy in their looks, and perhaps bored by now with this socially unsuitable wife, took the unconventional step of settling her with the secretary in a home of her own. There she bore her lover a daughter; then, four years later, a son; then, after ten years more, another daughter.

For a long time the husband still kept his protective eye on this alien family. He even used to meet the elder little girl, as she came out of school, and give her presents; much to the indignation of the mother, who mistrusted his intentions.

Then wife, lover, and family disappeared to another town. There, in the end, the secretary died. And the mother, reduced to poverty, returned with her three children to her husband's neighbourhood, though without her husband's knowledge. Her elder daughter, now eighteen, went to work for a milliner, Mme Pace; who employed her young assistants in the additional rôle of prostitutes.

To Mme Pace's establishment the father, now about fifty, one day betook himself; and, in ignorance, was about to make love to his own stepdaughter, when the mother chanced to enter and with a passionate cry revealed their true relationship.

The husband then brought his wife and her three children back into his own home. But such a home naturally became a hell.[1] The elder son, now twenty-two, being the only legitimate child, loathed and despised both the mother he had so long been separated from, and also the bastard half-brother and sisters that she had borne to her lover.

[1] There is a slightly confusing passage where the Elder Daughter speaks of 'the squalor of the horrible room where we all four slept together'. At first the reader, or hearer, may take this to refer to the four *children*; and wonder why they had to pig together like this in the house of a father comfortably off, whose garden contained such amenities as a garden-pool, with ducks and bamboos. But evidently the Elder Daughter is referring to the time of poverty *before* they moved to the father's home, when she, her mother, her brother, and her sister slept all four in one room.

The elder stepdaughter, after her sordid experiences at Mme Pace's, had developed into a brazen minx, redeemed only by affection for her little sister of four. The younger boy of fourteen was utterly miserable. And the poor mother was gnawed by hopeless fondness for her elder son, who would not even look at her.

In the upshot, the youngest child of four got drowned in the garden-pool; and her brother of fourteen, staring at his little drowned sister, shot himself with a revolver.

A ghastly ending, like the children's deaths at the end of *Jude the Obscure* or *The Wild Duck*. But, though horrible, it does not seem terrible in a really tragic way. It is more like some hideous paragraph in the crime-column of a newspaper. One is sorry for these victims simply as human beings; but not as characters one has come to know and care about.

It is hard then, as I say, to see why Pirandello found these particular characters so hauntingly irresistible. The two youngest do not even speak. The elder son can only grunt, in chronic sulks. The poor mother does little but emit noises of anguish. The elder stepdaughter is a hussy; her father, a seedy semi-intellectual. Only these last two show much character of any kind.

The real originality of *Six Characters* lies in its technique—a novel series of tricks, which begins with the audience finding that the curtain, instead of rising before them, is raised already. A stage-director and his cast are starting a rehearsal of Pirandello's other play, *Il Giuoco delle Parti*.

Here of course there is full scope for Pirandello's ironic humour when the actors complain that the play in question is ridiculous, and the Director retorts: 'What do you expect me to do, when we get no more good plays from France, and have to act pieces of Pirandello's that are a perfect feat to understand, and are carefully composed in such a way as to satisfy neither actors, nor critics, nor public?'

At this point enter the Six Characters. Pirandello suggests that their essential contrast with the living actors should be emphasized by special lighting; by their stiffly statuesque clothes; and by masks that leave free their eyes, noses, and mouths. The Mother, in particular, should have wax tears fixed on her cheeks, like a Mater Dolorosa in a Roman Catholic church.

To the astonishment of Director and cast, the Father now explains that he and the other characters are wandering in quest of an author. For their original author, after conceiving them, had abandoned them; will not the Director, then, take the author's place, so that these poor orphans may at last taste existence, for a moment, on the stage?

This need not be difficult. First, they can enact what befell them; then the actors can take over. The Stepdaughter, who is beautiful, throws out hints of alluring and sinister passion—of domestic tragedy of the most glaring kind. Both Director and cast begin to grow interested in these strange phantoms wafted from a Platonic world of ideas, and to forget that these shadows are not real flesh and blood (especially as the Characters now commence a bitter wrangle among themselves about their past). Indeed the Leading Man starts flirting with the spectral Stepdaughter.

Little by little, as the Characters dispute, their history begins to take shape. Finally the Director agrees to try what sort of script can be made for performance.

After an interval, the play proceeds in what is virtually a second Act. The required stage-properties are arranged, and the prompter prepares to take down the dialogue in shorthand; though the professional actors, with their professional pride, still remain a little restive at having to watch the acting of mere amateur phantoms, instead of doing it all themselves. But suddenly, when the interior of Mme Pace's shop has been set up, there appears, as if conjured thither by magic, the odious, middle-aged, peroxided Mme Pace herself—a Seventh Character. In a pidgin Italian, garbled with Spanish, she begins coaching the Stepdaughter for her profession. Then follows the crucial scene between Father and unknown Stepdaughter.

Next the Leading Man and Leading Lady repeat this encounter; but their histrionic mannerisms move the original Characters to derisive laughter. (Pirandello seems to have viewed producers, stage-directors, and actors in general with a persistent irony.) Then Father and Stepdaughter continue their scene up to the instant when the Mother bursts in to find the girl half-unclothed, with her head on the Father's breast; and drags her away with the cry—'Beast! Beast! She is my *daughter*.'

The Director is delighted with this strong 'curtain'. Next, the scene changes to the Father's garden with its little pool. And there follows a long passage of tiresome Pirandellian debate, in which the Father argues that he and the other Characters are really more real than the Director himself.

Then we see the vain appeal of the Mother to her elder son to give her some touch of affection; the drowning of the small daughter; and the suicide of the fourteen-year-old boy. After which the characters, except the Father, disappear behind the back-curtain, which represents the sky.

Leading Lady (re-entering from right, in misery). He's dead! Poor boy! He's dead! Oh what a thing to happen!

Leading Man (re-entering from left, laughing). Dead indeed! Illusion! Illusion! Don't believe it!

Other Actors from right. Illusion? No, reality! Reality! He's dead!

Other Actors from left. No! Illusion! Illusion!

The Father (rising and crying out among them). Illusion indeed! Reality, gentlemen! Reality!

Then he too disappears behind the back-cloth.

Director (at the end of his endurance). Illusion! Reality! Devil take the lot of you! Light! Light! Light!

(*All at once the stage and the whole auditorium are ablaze with the most dazzling illumination. The Director breathes again, as if delivered from a nightmare; and all the rest look in one another's eyes, tense and bewildered.*)

Director. Never knew anything like it. They've wasted a whole day!

He tells the electrician to put out the lights. A green reflector reveals behind the back-cloth the shadows of Father, Mother, Son, and Stepdaughter. Then the reflector goes out. Father, Mother, and Son reappear on the stage, like dream-figures—the Mother with arms still outstretched in vain appeal to her obdurate first-born.

Last, the Stepdaughter emerges, and dashes with shrill laughter, down from the stage, up the theatre-gangway and, still laughing, out through the exit.

An effective close. But the play still seems to me to contain more juggling than real drama. The Six Characters may be in search of an author; but I still wonder why an author should go in search of six such characters.

In conclusion, it is hardly necessary to point out that the whole scheme is perhaps stranger to us than to the Italian theatre with its old tradition of the *Commedia dell' Arte*, where the actors, provided with the outline of a plot, would then improvise their own dialogue, as they went along. Here, already, were characters more independent of an author than those of our own stage could ever be.

Enrico IV (1922)

'Visions, you know, have always been my pasture; and so far from growing old enough to quarrel with their emptiness, I almost think there is no
wisdom comparable with that of exchanging what is called the realities
of life for dreams. Old castles, old pictures, old histories, and the babble
of old people, make one live back into centuries that cannot disappoint
one. One holds fast and surely what is past. The dead have exhausted
their power of deceiving—one can trust Catherine of Medicis now.'

HORACE WALPOLE

This play has been likened to *Hamlet*; its hero likewise treads on the
brink of madness. But there remain vital differences—in Hamlet
there are characters that excite vivid sympathy, and poetry that
is magnificently moving. *Enrico Quarto* rouses, I think, not so much
sympathy as curiosity. Perhaps it plays better as a film than on the
stage. Yet it remains a highly artificial form of drama—bearing, I
feel, the same sort of relation to the best of Shakespeare, or Ibsen,
as Metaphysical poetry to the best of Milton or Wordsworth.

A wealthy young Italian loved a certain Donna Matilda. The
pair took part in an elaborate pageant, where the young man
impersonated the Emperor Henry IV (1050-1106), famous for his
long struggle with Pope Gregory VII, and for that hour of historic
humiliation when he came to the castle of Canossa (1077), shivered
three days in the hair-shirt of a penitent, bare-footed amid the
January snows, and meekly held the stirrup for the Holy Father to
mount his mule. For her part, Donna Matilda represented the
Countess Matilda of Tuscany (1046-1115), Châtelaine of Canossa,
and Gregory's ally against Henry.

But another young man, Tito Belcredi, also loved Donna
Matilda. And during the pageant, as he rode behind her and his rival,
he pricked 'Henry's' charger with his sword-point, so that the beast
reared and threw its rider on his head. The victim seemed unhurt;

but his brain was injured; and so it became his fixed idea that he really *was* the medieval Emperor, Henry IV.

As his family was wealthy, they could at least afford to humour the unfortunate young madman. His sister arranged for him to live in a secluded villa, surrounded by four hired companions dressed in clothes of the eleventh century. There year after year, in cloistered isolation, continued this tragi-comic make-believe.

After twelve years the imaginary Emperor somehow regained his reason. Yet he saw with horror that life had passed him by. Why, then, go back, as a middle-aged Rip Van Winkle, to the so-called world of modern reality? Why not remain, like a figure on a Grecian Urn, a timeless part of art's eternal masquerade? Why not live on like a Lady of Shalott forbidden to look out of her window or embark on time's all-devouring stream?

That any sane being could really stand the boredom of pretending, all day and every day, year after year, to be a medieval Emperor, seems hard to swallow. But it may perhaps be argued that 'Henry' was still only partly sane; though less mad than before.

Eight years more crawled by. 'Henry's' old love, Donna Matilda, had long since married a Marchese Spina, and borne him a daughter. Then, widowed, she became the disdainful mistress of her old admirer, Tito Belcredi. And now at last the play opens, with a visit by her to 'Henry's' retreat, accompanied by Belcredi; by her daughter Frida; by the son of 'Henry's' sister, the Marchese di Nolli (now betrothed to Frida); and by a mental specialist, Dr Genoni. Their object is to see if 'Henry' can be cured. For his sister, before her recent death, had come to suspect from certain strange remarks of his that he was regaining his reason.

The tragedy begins, effectively, on a light note. The scene is the Emperor's medieval throne-room, with four young men dressed as German knights of the eleventh century. A new attendant for Henry has just been engaged, in replacement for an old one who suddenly died; and to play his exacting part, this new-comer naturally had to cram the history of the period. But, by some stupid misunderstanding, he has been laboriously learning up the history, not of Henry IV, Emperor of Germany, in the eleventh century, but of Henri Quatre, King of France, in the sixteenth. Now his three colleagues laugh-ingly reveal his catastrophic mistake. Things will certainly be awkward; for Henry grows furious if they are faulty in their parts.[1]

Next appears Matilda, with her companions. She herself is now about forty-five; still handsome, but heavily made-up. Yet her vanished beauty of twenty years ago has flowered anew in her daughter Frida. On the other hand, her old lover Tito Belcredi, though younger than she, is more deeply scarred by the years; prematurely grey, he has grown to resemble a grotesque bird. A chief actor, indeed, throughout this tragedy is Time.

Now comes the exposition of the past. Dr Genoni is given details, by Donna Matilda and Belcredi, of that fatal pageant, and its accident, twenty years ago. Here, however, the machinery slightly creaks. These details have an air of being given less for the benefit of the Doctor than of the audience. For surely any doctor would have insisted on hearing the full story at a far earlier stage. He would not have waited to be briefed in this throne-room where the patient may irrupt at any moment. More of these facts, which an audience needs, could have been explained by 'Henry's' three attendants to their new colleague earlier in the act. However . . .

In order to talk with this madman who, living immersed in the eleventh century, would be dumbfounded by modern clothes, the party now disguise themselves in medieval attire. The Doctor dresses up as Abbot Hugh of Cluny (the monastery of Pope Gregory's earlier years); Belcredi, as one of the Abbot's monks, so that he looks like a cowled ostrich; while Matilda impersonates the Emperor's mother-in-law, the Duchess Adelaide.

Then (an excellent dramatic moment) Henry enters. He is now fifty; but to preserve the illusion that time stands still for him, his greying hair is dyed (but only in front); and his cheek-bones are rouged. Over his imperial dress he wears penitent's sackcloth, just as when Henry IV came to humble himself before Pope Gregory at Canossa.

---

[1] The new employee begins to realize his mistake from looking at the furnishing of the room and the costumes of his colleagues. But if he had really learnt anything about Renaissance France, it seems a little odd that he should not have suspected something wrong when he was first given his own medieval German dress to wear, before entering the room at all.

Like Hamlet, Henry talks with a kind of rambling hysteria. And, bitter as Hamlet, he calls malicious attention to his old love's tinted hair. He also plays, by sinister innuendoes, with the hated Belcredi. For he has at once recognized his rival, beneath that monkish disguise.

ACT II

The same afternoon. Matilda, Belcredi, and the Doctor discuss their recent interview with 'Henry'. The Doctor is made by Pirandello's satirical pen to utter with scientific pomp a deal of absurd pseudo-science. But woman's intuition can at times possess a sharper penetration than scientific reason. Matilda feels convinced that the patient *knew* her. In his eyes there shone a glint of recognition; and he talked of her hair as having once been dark—which it *was*, though now dyed blond. She is sure, too, that he detected Belcredi.

The Doctor has prepared a curious kind of shock-treatment. In 'Henry's' room there hang two portraits painted twenty years ago, at the time of the fatal pageant—one of 'Henry' himself; one of his beloved Matilda, as Countess of Tuscany. The Doctor now plans that Matilda's daughter Frida shall wear her mother's old pageant-costume, as the living image of her mother's portrait—of her mother as she *was*, twenty years ago. Thus 'Henry' shall be confronted simultaneously with Frida in the semblance of Matilda as she was then, and with Matilda herself, as she is now. This shock, like shaking a refractory watch, shall set ticking again the patient's arrested sense of time.

But 'Henry', after a second brief interview with Matilda, again dressed as Adelaide, and with the Doctor disguised as the Abbot of Cluny, suddenly loses patience. The moment they have left him, he rounds on his astonished servitors—'Enough! Have done! I'm sick of it. By God, the impudence! To come here with her lover! . . . And they pretended to do it out of compassion!'

All the same one may wonder how sane 'Henry' really is, even now—so hysterical grows his manner, as he pictures the horror of this real world where one thing seems true today, another tomorrow; where we are always alone, because the picture of oneself that forms in the mind of another will always be a mere phantom that one can never know. Why not, he argues, go on living safely in the remoteness of eight centuries ago, away from the men of today who must eternally torture themselves about what the morrow will bring?

ACT III

The throne-room is now in darkness. Where previously hung the portraits of Henry IV and Matilda, there now stand, in the same dresses, the Marchese di Nolli and his fiancée, the young Frida. 'Henry' enters with an oil-lamp. Frida whispers 'Henry!' And again, 'Henry!' He sees her head stretch forth from the picture-frame, and with a wild cry, lets fall his lamp.

There rush in Belcredi, the Doctor, and Matilda who is now dressed, like her daughter, as Matilda of Tuscany. The light is turned on—'a strange light, coming from lamps hidden in the ceiling'. Already, warned by the attendants, these three are aware that 'Henry' has admitted his sanity. Yes—so he himself now confesses to the Doctor—after twelve years his reason did begin to return. Then it dawned on him that 'not only my hair, but I too must inwardly have grown all grey. Everything fallen! Everything finished! And I should have arrived, ravening as a wolf, at a banquet already cleared away.'[1] Therefore he deliberately chose to continue seeming mad. After all, life is only a masquerade anyway; whenever and wherever it is lived. 'The pity is for you who in such agitation,

---

[1] It is not, I think, fanciful to catch here the bitter accents of Pirandello himself. Indeed, he is said to have called the play 'my testament'. Chained through his thirties and forties to a mad wife, he too, when at last released in 1918, may well have felt like 'Henry' that through those twenty silent years he had 'grown all grey', only to find the feast of life now over; with no choice but still to remain prisoned, like 'Henry', in the dreamworld of art and imagination. (Compare the old sculptor Giuncano in *Diana e la Tuda*, the actress in *Trovarsi*, the old poet in *Quando si è qualcuno*.) Goethe or Victor Hugo would not have resigned themselves, even though middle-aged, to so austere a surrender; but in Pirandello there was something of a self-mortifying ascetic. 'I have forgotten to live,' he once wrote, 'so totally forgotten, that I can say nothing, literally nothing about my life, except, perhaps, that I do not *live* it, I *write* it.'

without knowing it and without seeing it, live out the madness that is yours.'

Matilda, he points out, has lived with time these twenty years, and faded; while he has stayed constant to his timeless dream. Then, turning to the young Frida, in whom he sees the love of his youth still everlastingly young, with mad laughter he suddenly crushes her in his arms. Belcredi rushes to the girl's rescue. But 'Henry', snatching a sword from one of his servitors, runs his detested rival through the body—a flash of deadly reality amid all these mists of dream.

Then, as Belcredi is carried out to die, 'Henry' gathers his medieval servants round him once again—'Ah now! . . . inevitably . . . here together, here together . . . and for *always*!'

Amazingly ingenious; and—far more than ingenious—dramatically tragic. The whole play seems to me less chilled by rather showy sophistry, more illumined by a mournful poetry, than the drab realism of *Six Characters*. Some may object that they are still wearied, here too, by the eternal Pirandellian quibbles about what is 'reality'. Or that they cannot care much about any of the characters; and cannot care much what happens to characters they do not care about. Or that 'Henry's' peculiar and bizarre insanity has less appeal than the simpler pathos of Ersilia Drei in *Vestire gli ignudi*, with its more human theme of a poor girl who so passionately feels, like Ibsen's Ekdals or Hedda Gabler, the hunger for romantic illusion, that she cannot live, and hates to die, without it. But such cavils seem a little thankless. The main theme of *Enrico IV* is general enough—simply pity for mankind, caught in the web of Illusion by the spider Time.

The play lives, I find, very vividly in the memory. Its daring of conception gives it, not perhaps a place of the highest rank, but still a place apart.

CONCLUSION

Between the wars Pirandello's work was translated into at least twenty-five languages—even into Arabic, Lettish, Hebrew, Japanese. His plays were performed all over the world—in North and South America, in Russia, in China. Freud's fuller discovery of the Unconscious was becoming for the twentieth century what the discoveries of Copernicus and Columbus were for the sixteenth. And so science and psychology, by undermining old beliefs and assumptions, had prepared for Pirandello just the type of audience that he needed—a public ready to take an intrigued, disillusioned interest in his scepticisms and his paradoxes. What, then, are the essential ideas running through Pirandello's plays; and what is their lasting value?

Much of our mental and emotional life goes on unseen; we lead, perforce, a double life—part conscious, part unconscious. Therefore the old picture of man as a creature with a single rational soul, an individual self, has given place to a new vision of individuality as individual no longer. 'Individual' meant originally, like 'atom', an ultimate unit, impossible to divide. But today both individual and atom are split. And the study of neuroses has shown that one person can have several personalities, like Dr Moreton Prince's Sally Beauchamp, who had half a dozen. Hume had doubted the individual self. That doubt Pirandello brought to the footlights of the public stage. Indeed, as I have said, the sceptical Pirandello can be seen as a kind of dramatic Hume.

Matthew Arnold had already written half a century before (1869):

> Below the surface-stream, shallow and light
> Of what we *say* we feel—below the stream
> As light, of what we *think* we feel, there flows
> With noiseless current strong, obscure, and dark
> The central theme of what we feel indeed.

Earlier still Wordsworth had written in *The Borderers*—

Action is transitory—a step, a blow,
The motion of a muscle—this way or that—
'Tis done, and in the after-vacancy
We wonder at ourselves like men betrayed.

Earlier still, about A.D. 1010, while here in England reigned Ethelred Evil-Counsel, in remote Japan the Lady Murasaki, writing her strangely civilized *Tale of Genji*, had made a mistress reply to the reproaches of a forsaken lover—'What in waking hours I may have promised, I know not; but now I wander in the mazes of a dream; or someone wanders, for I scarce think it can be I.' Earlier still, the Chinese sage Chuang Tzu, after dreaming he was a butterfly, had debated whether he was then a man dreaming himself a butterfly, or now a butterfly dreaming itself a man.

None the less, to ordinary men before the twentieth century such notions would have seemed merely the crazy maunderings of eccentrics. Only with modern psychology did themes like these gain a wider currency and interest.

It follows, secondly, that if our own characters are such unstable compounds, we can know very little of one another. Everyone becomes to everyone else a moon with its further side for ever hidden. When A talks to B, it is really a mask of A talking to a mask of B. How much can masks really communicate? Signora Morli with her husband is quite a different person from Signora Morli with her lover. Which is the real Signora Morli? Life becomes a dream-world of phantoms. We are like billiard-balls, rushing hither and thither, colliding, clicking, kissing, recoiling—but only an infinitesimal fraction of their surfaces can ever be in contact. A bleak view—but Goethe's; as bleak as Spinoza's description of love —'Amor est titillatio, concomitante idea causae externae'—'Love is a tickling, attended by the *idea* of an external cause.'

Thirdly, if we are such mere simulacra, such shifting wisps of vapour, how relative become all our moral codes! Merely a kind of collective masks. That truth, too, is old—old as Herodotus, whose King Darius confronted, to their mutual amazement and disgust, Indians who thought it their duty to eat their dead fathers, and Greeks no less convinced that it was their duty to burn theirs. But such moral relativity had never found any wide acceptance, or even understanding.

Fourthly, Pirandello came to feel the relativity and subjectivity, not only of Good, but also of Truth. Thinking makes it so. For Signora Frola, Signora Ponza *is* her daughter, and Signor Ponza is mad to question it; for Signor Ponza, Signora Ponza *is* his second wife—the first Signora Ponza is dead and Signora Frola, her mother, is mad to question it. 'So it is, if to you it seems so.' In short, pragmatism.

Life, it would appear, is much more confused and chaotic than men can bear to admit.

But at this point, I think, we should grow careful how far we let Pirandello lead us on. Life turns out, and *we* turn out, to be far less rational than was once assumed. But from that notion men may draw quite opposite conclusions.

They can cry—'Reason proves a mere delusion. So let us cultivate the irrational, and abandon ourselves blindly to instinct and impulse.'

That has been, and still is, a widespread answer in our time. But I believe it a dangerous and disastrous self-surrender—the answer of degeneracy, decadence, and barbarism.

Or, again, there is the answer of the unheroic hero of a recent novel about New York—'We just don't know why we're here, or where we came from, or where we're going. . . . We can only shrug.'

Very well, one can 'shrug'. But in that case it may be only a very few years before the Russians take over—or the Chinese. Today Western Man has often only three gods—games, girls, good living. But that decadent Trinity will hardly save us from Nature's ruthless purgings of the unfit.

Alternatively one can answer as, in effect, did Freud: 'Yes, we *are* all far, far less rational than we assumed. But that makes reason all the more—not less—important. A man wandering in a lightless catacomb will do well to treasure and protect his own poor little candle as dearly as his life. For his life depends on it. Candles become only the more indispensable in a naughty world of darkness. We have, indeed, discovered the Unconscious; then let the conscious mind make use of this discovery (made, after all, by scientific reasoning) to control these blind unconscious forces that welter within us. Mental health is to be attained and kept, not by letting go—not by accepting stupid intoxications—but by patient pursuit of understanding and self-control.'

After all, though reality is highly confused and confusing, it is the weaklings that like to make this confusion seem even worse confounded than it is. They stir every muddy puddle, hoping to fish in such troubled waters—to find plenary indulgence for their own lack of backbone or principle. Just as drunk people like everybody round them to be equally drunk.

Life would be duller were we never intoxicated by ideas, or persons. Yet, in the long run, intoxication seems a precarious and perilous remedy; the head-ache follows. It may be desolating to think, like Pirandello, that we live so isolated from one another; that every observer forms a different picture of us from that of every other observer, and from our own picture of ourselves. Yet one can grow resigned to it. A considerable degree of loneliness must be accepted by the honest; and can be accepted by the brave. And affection can bridge many gaps, even if the closest affection must be, not seldom, blind.

And again, granted that our personality thus shifts and varies, not only from observer to observer, but also from moment to moment, from mood to mood; still why be so upset by it? Why not be content, like Walt Whitman, to 'contain multitudes'? The harm lies less in containing multitudes—indeed, it can add variety to life—than in developing a sense of guilt about it. With some self-knowledge and some self-control, the 'multitudes' can, to some extent, be limited, and managed. One need not become a drifting derelict; one can try to remain a ship that is sea-worthy, with engines and anchors, charts and compasses, even if there are many shoals uncharted, many currents incalculable. It would be a foolish navigator who lamented that his keel was not fixed immovably upon some stable rock.

No doubt, we all do things, and say things, and write things, which make us wonder afterwards how on earth we could be capable of them. But if much in human character is strangely fluid, there remains also much that is strangely solid. There *are* men and women who do more than 'shrug'. Pirandello himself, in practice, was one of these—a man of inexhaustible generosity and indomitable will.

Pascal may have said, 'There is no man who differs more from another than he differs from himself in the course of time.' But Pascal seems here to exaggerate; as epigrammatists are too apt to do.

We still expect characters in drama, or fiction, as Aristotle pointed out long ago, to be consistent; even if some are consistent only in inconsistency. 'Believe a mountain has moved,' says the Arab proverb, 'but not that a man has changed his character.' Dryden might paint his Zimri as 'everything by turns, and nothing long'. But Dryden makes it equally clear that he therefore regards Zimri as extremely odd and exceptional. Pope's Narcissa 'paid a tradesman once, to make him stare'. But that implies how constant Narcissa usually remained to her firm principle of *not* paying tradesmen. If the tradesman had shared the views of Pirandello, a thousand Narcissas could not have made him stare—or even blink. Many people may, indeed, have more personalities than one; but even they seem usually restricted to three or four. They may change often; but the range of their changes remains tolerably limited. And there *are* people on earth—fortunately—of whom one knows that they will *not* give in to the world, or betray one's trust. There *is* force in the old Stoic ideal—'*unum* hominem agere'—'to act a *single* part'—to be consistent. There remains truth, as well as eloquence, in the words of Churchill on the great Marlborough—'He won his way up from grade to grade by undoubted merit and daring. But thereafter was a desert through which he toiled and wandered. A whole generation of small years intervened.' And yet—'His sword never rusted in its sheath. . . . There it lay, the sword of certain victory, ready for service when the opportunity should come.'

A splendid tribute; still truer of Winston Churchill himself. For, once Churchill had matured (which was late), one could feel pretty sure, in *any* crisis, how he would react. It was by this that he became, during the Second World War, like a great rock in a weary land.

Plato saw the charioteer of the soul as driving a white horse of goodness and a black horse of evil. Today we realize that we have to drive a whole team of invisible horses, or forces. But that is no reason for feebly throwing the reins on their necks, and letting ourselves be torn in pieces by these uncanny creatures. One can learn, rather, to know oneself better and to cope, in some degree, even with invisible powers. So Signora Morli went back to her true lover in the end; in that, *not* in return to her legal husband, lay the true morality.

Similarly with men's relations to each other. From modern psychology one may indeed see more clearly what has always been obvious to the sensible—that most of our worldly contacts are mere masquerades of noise and twaddle; most of our social gatherings just empty Vanity Fairs. Yet life is not all Vanity Fairs. Though our relations to others turn out more complex and difficult even than we thought, people do contrive, all the same, to live together in loyalty and trust—understanding all the better, just because they realize better how hard it is to understand at all. In the same way, science has revealed that men's own solid-seeming bodies are constellations of whizzing particles; and yet even with these insubstantial limbs they contrive to build pyramids, to storm fortresses, to penetrate outer space.

As for Pirandello's relativity of ethics, sensible men have known for thousands of years that of course ethics, like aesthetics, are relative—that the crimes of one land, or age, can be the virtues of another. Yet it remains true, always and everywhere, that wise men can cope better with life's problems than fools—can foresee what means are likely to gain their ends, and what will not; what ends will probably be worth gaining, and bring contentment; what will probably become mere dust and ashes in the mouth. And though it might be rash to say that mental health, good sense, and loving-kindness can never be harmful, it is not easy to imagine how they can.

Again, if the freedom of the will begins to seem perhaps an illusion, like the flatness of the earth, here too the weak-minded and the strong will draw opposite conclusions. The weak will abandon themselves; the strong are likelier to recall that men like Mohammed and Calvin, though disbelievers in human freedom, were yet men of consuming energy; and will decide that such philosophic concepts as determinism make no practical difference in life, except to increase charity and tolerance; because we see that men do not make themselves, and even Hitler and Stalin were doomed to be what they were, and to do what they did.

On the other hand, Pirandello's idea of the relativity of truth itself, seems to me pernicious verbal juggling. For the Chinese sage dreaming himself a butterfly, it may have been for the moment *as if* he really were a butterfly. There is much in those two small words— 'as if'. But, had the Chinese sage tried fluttering out of an upstairs window, one could predict with some probability that he would have speedily awakened to the facts, or never have awakened at all.

Relativity itself was confirmed by astronomical observations; had they failed to give the predicted results, Einstein would have concluded that his thinking was somewhere wrong. I believe that, whereas our *feelings* of Good or of Beauty are indeed subjective, it can be absolutely true that A is the case, or that B is not. Truth is usually consistent; Error, in the long run, not.

> But play no tricks upon thy soul, O man;
> Let fact be fact, and life the thing it can.

Pirandello, like many clever men, was at times too fond of tricks. But tricks, as Johnson observed of Butler's *Hudibras*, tend to be amusing only so long as they are novelties; in the end, they are apt to bore or irritate; to seem, in Johnson's phrase, 'either knavish or foolish'. Pirandello's popularity, for all his diabolical cleverness, seems in England, at least, far today from what it was. Such, at any rate, is my impression; which my bookseller confirms.[1]

---

[1] In the twenties, however, from 1923 on, Pirandello's impact on the French stage in particular, was immense; in 1925 Paris was performing five plays of his at once. 'Pirandello,' it has been said, 'shone in the French sky, and there is not a single satellite which did not retain his rays even long after the passing of the meteor.' 'Satellites' retaining the rays of long-past meteors may be odd astronomy; but for the next three decades French dramatists did continue to cook up Pirandellian recipes, and to harp on Pirandellian strings, such as plays within plays, plurality of personality, the relativity of truth, the power of illusion, the fixity of art in contrast to the fluidity of life. See T. Bishop's interesting work, *Pirandello and the French Theatre* (English ed., 1961), which discusses his influence on such playwrights as Sarment, Gantillon, Pellerin, Gabriel Marcel, Bernstein, Denys Amiel, Lenormand, Bernard, Ghelderode, Achard, Salacrou, Giraudoux, Crommelynck, Guitry, Cocteau, Anouilh, Sartre, Camus, Adamov, Ionesco, Beckett, Neveux, Genet.

From his philosophy of life Pirandello was able to pluck paradoxes like strings of rabbits from a hat. Characters go looking for actors, instead of actors for characters. A husband pushes his wife into a lover's arms, or a lover pushes his mistress into her husband's arms. A wife who has revealed her husband's infidelity, has to undo the harm by shutting herself three months into a madhouse, to cancel her own accusation. Or a madman, recovering his sanity, yet prefers to pretend he is still mad. And so on.

Pirandello lines up his characters beside his stream of thought, and shows us his reflections. For *us*, the images mirrored there look, of course, topsy-turvy. And these images are, no doubt, in a sense as 'real' as flesh-and-blood. But move away from the deceptive stream of Pirandello, and you see your fellow-creatures the right way up, as before—or almost as before. For a little more of healthy scepticism may have been added to one's view of life.

I do not say at all that Pirandello was an insincere mountebank. His view of life filled him with a deep and disconsolate pessimism. And with many of his conclusions one *can* heartily agree. It *is* ridiculous that men should so wear masks, to deceive each other and themselves. It *is* desirable that we should try to stop play-acting towards others, or being duped ourselves by *their* self-dramatizations. Perhaps one essential moral of Pirandello is that life requires plenty of action, but a minimum of acting; though, for many, that minimum may yet become an indispensable necessity.

Again, it *is* absurd that people should rush in futile curiosity to discover scandals, and pass judgements for which they lack either evidence or intelligence. And one can heartily agree that the only choice lies often between hating, scorning, or pitying people; and that pity is far preferable to hate or scorn.

But, when all this is granted, there remains, I think, about many of Pirandello's plays something unsatisfactory. Like Machiavelli, he has often too much Mephistophilean cleverness, too little human good sense.

Possibly the logical, ironical reasoning of Pirandello is often more congenial to the French temperament; whereas the English mind feels more sympathy with the melancholy-humorous sincerity of Chekhov.

Too few of his characters seem to me really sympathetic—with a few exceptions, such as the honest Signora Morli, the humorous Professor Toti, the pathetic Ersilia Drei. Because of this, his dramas tend to become interesting rather than moving. The marionettes dance on wizard strings; but marionettes, too often, they remain.

Yet it would be very unfair to judge Pirandello only by his plays. It is arguable that, like Chekhov, he rose highest, not in plays (or in full-length novels), but in short stories.[1] With these, like Chekhov, he was amazingly productive. During the nineties he turned out over a hundred *novelle* within three years; by 1919 there were fifteen volumes. And in this field (again like Chekhov) he could reveal more of his own personality—the deep pity that went with his pessimism, the sympathy that could soften his sharp dissections of the human soul; just as a doctor may better show his real humanity at a bedside than in a public lecture-theatre.

For the drama remains a specially difficult form for a writer preoccupied, like Pirandello, with ideas. It offers, no doubt, enormous attractions. Its effects are more intense; its successes more spectacular; its rewards often richer. But the drawbacks also are serious.

The dramatist must work through middlemen—producers and actors—who often blur or distort. He must work as a ventriloquist hidden behind his characters; he cannot come before the curtain to explain; and though he may sometimes use a *raisonneur* as spokesman, this artifice tends to become too artificial, stale, and inadequate.

Further, the dramatist must address an audience, a herd, subject to herd-psychology—cruder, more emotional, more conventional, less intelligent than the solitary reader may often be. That can be vividly exemplified by comparing some of Pirandello's plays with the subtler, more sensitive *novelle* on which they are based.

Lastly, in the glare of stage-lighting and the presence of a public, the dramatist can easily become less his true self, less simple and sincere. Like his actors, he may begin to act. Even Shakespeare could speak bitterly of 'public means which public manners breeds', and of growing stained, like the dyer's hand. And Victor Hugo has

[1] Nearly two-thirds of Pirandello's dramas are based on what he had first written in story-form.

described how the rising theatre-curtain seemed to lift 'the skirt of his soul.'

But for the writer with general ideas the drama can prove particularly treacherous. Easy to talk impressively about the stage becoming a pulpit for ideals. But in practice. . . . Not that the influence of drama may not be immense. But this influence remains largely emotional. The playwright who wants really to put across ideas, must make them pretty simple. When Figaro says to Count Almaviva, 'Vous vous êtes donné la peine de naître',[1] the lowest minds in the pit could understand. Beaumarchais had driven the tumbrils of the Revolution one stage closer. Whether or no that was a good idea, it was not a deep or difficult one.

But it is another matter with notions more abstruse and abstract, such as Pirandello's view of reality. Euripides was called the philosopher of the stage; but his fondness for arguing about ideas often damaged his plays; and what his ideas really were, was wildly misunderstood in his own Athens, and remains disputed still. There are interpretations by the dozen of the real meaning and intention of *Hamlet*; yet the public enjoyed *Hamlet* long before critics began to fuss and buzz about it; and still enjoys *Hamlet* in spite of them. For the play provides what the public really wants—not so much ideas as an exciting plot, vivid language, and characters it can admire, like, deride, or hate. Even Ibsen, who did so much to make the theatre think, still gets misinterpreted in contradictory ways; and had constantly to repeat that he was concerned, not to preach, but to depict. Even Shaw who specialized in problem-plays, had to explain his plays in prefaces; which were often not much clearer than the plays. To use the stage for imparting ideas of any subtlety or complexity can prove as clumsy as playing the piano in thick woollen gloves. Theatre audiences, like church congregations, may enjoy being mystified. They can feel that they are walking on mountain-heights, even though lost in cloud. But how many spectators, after seeing *Six Characters* or *Così è* (*se vi pare*), could write next morning a coherent sketch of Pirandello's philosophy of life?

But to open Pirandello's short stories is to enter quite a different world, and see him far less disguised and masked. The irony still

[1] 'You just took the trouble to be born.'

remains as biting, the melancholy as deep, or yet deeper; but the pity and sympathy become far more unmistakable. There is, for example, the story *Lontano*[1] with its picture of a simple Norse seaman, Lars Kleen, set ashore sick at Porto Empedocle in Sicily, near Pirandello's native Agrigento, and trapped there into lifelong homesickness by marriage with a Sicilian girl—a Calypso who holds him captive among strange faces and incomprehensible ways. Even the child she bears him remains for him a little stranger, wholly of this alien south. Or there is *Con Altri Occhi*[2] (a tale that Hardy might have made into a poem), where a second wife, finding a photograph of her predecessor, reads in that vanished woman's eyes a kindred sadness to her own—a sadness till now unrecognized by her in her own face—the sadness of marriage to a loveless egoist. Or there is *Come Gemelle*[3] where a kindly mistress nurses, along with her own infant, the daughter of a cold wife dead in childbirth, despite the horror of outraged relatives. Or there is *Il Fumo*,[4] with its picture of a ruined sulphur-mineowner driven to a sudden frenzy of despair by the injustice of the world; or *Prima Notte*,[5] where a young girl weds an old sexton, and both spend their bridal night sobbing beside the graves of those they had really loved—he by his dead wife, she by her young lover lost at sea; or *Tra Due Ombre*[6] where an ill-married husband, gnawed by jealousy at seeing on shipboard the successful rival who has married his old love, finds his rancour fade for a moment to insignificance before the indifferent stars above the eternal sea.

Or, again, there is *Il lume dell'altra casa*,[7] which tells how in the evenings Tullio Butti used to gaze from his window at a happy

---

[1] *Far away.*
[2] *With other eyes.* Compare Hardy's poem 'The Rival', where a wife jealously destroys the photograph of her younger self, cherished by her husband in his desk.

> Could you ever have dreamed the heart of woman
> Would work so foolishly!

[3] *Like twins.*
[4] *Smoke.*
[5] *First night.*
[6] *Between two shadows.*
[7] *The light in the other house.*

433

family opposite, till one day the landlady's daughter saw him through the keyhole, and told her mother their lodger must be in love with the lady over the way, and the mother must needs tell the lady herself. So began a romance, which ended in an elopement. But some months later Tullio Butti and the lady revisited his old lodging, so that she might beg leave at least to watch for once, from the same window, the room opposite, where now sat in solitude the husband and three children that she had, like Ibsen's Nora, left forsaken. The old irony of the tragic reversal, of the intention that produces the opposite result to that intended.

But even more typical, in its blending of farce and tragedy, of pity and futility, is *Canta L'Epistola*.[1]

Tommasino Unzio, the sub-deacon, lost his faith and left the Church. After being beaten by his infuriated father, who accused him of losing his faith merely from a desire 'a fare il porco'—'to play the pig'—the disconsolate young man took to wandering the countryside, and acquired a sort of gloomier Wordsworthianism. In this he found, at last, his only peace—

To have no more consciousness of existence—like a stone, like a plant; no more to remember even one's own name; to live just for living's sake, without being aware that one lives—like the animals, like the plants; with no more emotions, nor desires, nor memories, nor thoughts; with nothing, henceforth that would give sense and value to one's own life.

Non aver piú coscienza d'essere, come una pietra, come una pianta; non ricordarsi piú neanche del proprio nome; vivere per vivere, senza sapere di vivere, come le bestie, come le piante; senza piú affetti, né desiderii né memorie, né pensieri; senza piú nulla che desse senso e valore alla propria vita.

How beautiful Italian is, in the hands of a master! This haunting sadness of Pirandello's prose takes the mind back to that Venetian composer of the eighteenth century who could chill even the buoyant optimism of Browning, and inspire one of the most moving of Browning's lyrics, 'A Toccata of Galuppi's'—

---

[1] *He intones the Epistle.*

Yes, you, like a ghostly cricket, creaking where a house was burned—
Dust and ashes, dead and done with, Venice spent what Venice
earned!
The soul, doubtless, is immortal—where a soul can be discerned.[1]

In Pirandello's world to discern that soul becomes more difficult
still. Poor Tommasino's reflections are very close to Pirandello's
own.

To mutilate the mountains, to fell the trees, for the sake of building
houses. More houses in this mountain village. Toil, trouble, weariness
and pain of every kind—why? Just to achieve a chimney, and then make
issue from that chimney a little smoke, at once dispersed in the vanity of
space.

And, as with that smoke, so with every thought, every memory of
men.

But before the vast spectacle of nature, of that immense green plain of
oaks and olives and chestnuts, sloping from the folds of the Ciminian
Forest[2] down to the Tiber valley far below, he felt himself slowly grow
tranquil, in a gentle, unremembering melancholy.

All the illusions, all the disappointments, and griefs, and joys, and hopes,
and desires of men appeared vain and transitory, in the face of the feeling
that breathed from those things which endure and outlast them—
impassively. Like changes of the clouds appeared to him, in the eternity
of nature, the single acts of men. Enough to gaze on those high peaks
beyond the Tiber valley, far, far away, smoking on the horizon—smooth,
almost ethereal—in the light of the setting sun.[3]

Mutilare la montagna; atterrare gli alberi, per costruire case. Lí, in
quel borgo montano, altre case. Stenti, affanni, fatiche e pene d'ogni
sorta, perché? Per arrivare a un camignolo, e per fare uscir da questo
camignolo un po' di fumo, subito dispersa nella vanità del spazio.

E come quel fumo, ogni pensiero, ogni memoria degli uomini.

Ma davanti all' ampio spettacolo della natura, a quel immenso piano
verde di querci e d'ulivi e di castagni, degradante dalle falde del Ciminio
fino alla valle Tiberina laggiú laggiú, sentiva a poco rasserenarsi in una
blanda smemorata mestizia.

[1] Compare, too, the melancholy of the Roman landscape in Browning's
Two in the Campagna.
[2] South of Viterbo, and north of Rome.
[3] This passage, like the one quoted just before, must have specially appealed
to Pirandello himself; for both recur, little altered, in his novel *Uno, Nessuno e
Centomila*, with its similar philosophy.

Tutte le illusioni e tutti i disinganni e i dolori e le gioje e le speranze e i desiderii degli uomini apparivano vani e transitorii di fronte al sentimento che spirava dalle cose che restano e sopravanzano ad essi, impassibili. Quasi vicende di nuvole gli apparivano nell' eternità della natura i singoli fatti degli uomini. Bastava guardare quegli alti monti di là della valle tiberina, lontani lontani, sfumanti all' orrizonte, lievi e quasi aerii nel tramonto.

What stage-painter could paint a scene so well?

To Nature, and the simple folk of the natural countryside, Pirandello came back, like Wordsworth, Synge, or Hardy, when sickened with the hollow ironies of sophisticated city-life.

And so poor Tommasino in the end fixed his affection on a blade of grass—a type of all those little lives that are born into this enormous world, and live their little space, and pass away, never, never to return. A blade of grass between two grey boulders, behind the deserted church of Santa Maria di Loreto.

For a month Tommasino watched maternally while his blade of grass rose up timidly, and gazed out over the great green plain, and put forth a little reddish pennon, like the crest of a cock. Every day he visited it, anxious lest a gale might break it, or goats eat it, on their daily journey past the ruined church.

Then, one day, coming to visit his pet, Tommasino saw sitting on one of the boulders Signorina Olga Fanelli. He waited, watching, at a distance; till, annoyed by his attention, the young lady rose disdainfully to go. Then, quite absent-mindedly, she picked that sacred blade of grass, and popped it in her mouth. Beside himself with fury, Tommasino cried out 'Stupida!' And Olga's fiancé, Lieutenant De Venera, came up and slapped his face.

A duel followed. Tommasino insisted on the deadliest conditions. He fell, mortally wounded. At his mother's prayer, he allowed a priest to be sent for. Perseveringly the holy man asked him—'But what was it *about*, my son? What was it *about*?' Yet Tommasino could only reply—'Padre, per un filo d'erba'—'Father, about a blade of grass'. It was concluded that poor Tommasino died in delirium.[1]

---

[1] Fantastic? Yet my newspaper recorded in March 1960 the murder of a Mr Rawlins in Florida by his lodger, Sam Human, because Mr Human wanted

Pirandello, the bitter 'humorist', was never more his essential self than here.

The title of another of his stories *Pena di vivere così—The pain of living so*—might well be the motto of his whole works. Indeed the motto of one work of his does run—'I see, as it were, a labyrinth where our soul wanders through countless conflicting ways, without ever finding an issue. In this labyrinth I see a two-headed Hermes, that with one face laughs, and with the other weeps; it laughs with one face at the other's weeping.' Pirandello's real Muse was Maya—Illusion.

'We are all puppets,' repeats a character in *Cap and Bells*. And 'to that puppet,' Pirandello continues, 'each of us adds another puppet he *believes* himself to be.'

Or there is the grey conclusion of Don Cosmo in the novel *I Vecchi e i Giovani*: 'Only one thing is sad, my friends; to have understood the game.[1] I mean the game of that jesting goblin which each of us has inside him—which amuses itself by showing to us, outside ourselves, as reality, what a moment later it shows us to be only our own illusion; mocking us for all the toil we have given ourselves to gain it, and mocking us also, as happens to me, for not having known how to illude ourselves, since apart from that illusion there is no other reality at all. . . . Do not complain, then. Toil and torment yourselves, without reflecting that it all brings no conclusion. If it brings no conclusion, it shows that it is not meant to bring a conclusion, and that it is therefore vain to seek one. We must live—that is, illude ourselves; we must let that jesting goblin inside us play on till he is tired; and reflect that all of it will pass away—will pass away.'

And in the letter to Vittorini, printed at the beginning of Vittorini's book on him, Pirandello adds—'As a man, I have tried to tell men something, with no ambition, except perhaps to revenge

---

some turnip-tops cooked with the stems on, but Mrs Rawlins persisted that she *would* cook them, as always, with the stems off. Not so much difference between being killed over a blade of grass or over a turnip-top.

[1] The identical phrase used by the frozen Leone Gala (p. 381)—'Ah, my dear, it's a sad business when one has *understood the game* . . . the whole game! This game of life!'

myself for having been born. And yet life, despite all it has made me suffer, is so beautiful. (And *there* is another statement without even a shadow of logic; yet all the same as true and truly felt.)'

One is surprised to find Pirandello making this admission that he finds life 'beautiful'. He did not often admit it. But his best writing is itself one more example of that beauty.

His plays sometimes lend themselves to misunderstanding. But one understands them far better when one has also read his stories; and his life. For then one knows that, if he may seem at times callously clever, this too was only a mask—that Pirandello's deeper self was a spirit very unhappy, but at times heroic—and very far from unkind.

EPILOGUE

The six dramatists, Ibsen, Strindberg, Chekhov, Synge, Yeats, and
Pirandello, throw a fascinating sidelight on the intellectual history
of the last hundred years—the more fascinating because they are all
so different, and yet in their different ways so typical.

Our world is bitterly divided between those who long for more
rationality, and those who crave for less. It has become so common,
and so easy, to exclaim—'Oh, you are being too logical, too
rational!' But one may suspect the accusation to be far commoner
than the fault. Our human future may be threatened by an excess
of science; but hardly by any excess of intelligence.

Of the final outcome Freud took no very rosy view. He saw a
sardonic appropriateness in the advertisement of an American
undertaker—'Why live, when you can be buried for ten dollars?'
Freud, indeed, like Swift, though loving individuals, could not love
mankind. 'In the depth of my being I remain convinced that my dear
fellow-creatures—with individual exceptions—are riff-raff (*Gesin-
del*).' Two qualities above all he saw as impeding, perverting, and
endangering humanity's progress—'that they have no spontaneous
love of work, and that arguments are powerless against their
passions'. Or, as Benjamin Franklin put it, 'Passion governs, and
she never governs wisely'. Reason and unreason seem to me more
and more the Ormuz and Ahriman, the good and evil spirits, that
battle for the future of our world.

Typical anti-rationalists—though in extremely different ways—
are those gifted figures, Strindberg and Yeats. The first threw an
angry glare into the bottomless abysses of the human soul; the
second projected dream-figures on to the drifting vapours of the
human imagination. But both seem to me too self-centred and self-
hypnotized to excel in drama. Strindberg remained, above all, an
autobiographer; Yeats, a lyric poet, who could sing like Ariel, but,
like Ariel, rode often by owl-light on the wings of bats.

In contrast, the sceptical and pessimistic Pirandello exemplifies,
like the dogmatic and optimistic Shaw, the dangers of reasoning to

unreasonable excess. Pirandello was so over-clever as to make reason itself seem at times absurd. Under the dissection of that razor-mind, his characters could become bloodless. Often they seem mere puppets dancing on frail strings of sophistry. Chekhov would have told him he was not simple enough. Yet, though too clever, Pirandello could also be shrewd; sometimes, even, wise; sometimes deeply human. As a writer of plays (and, still more, of stories), he was, I feel, more effective than Strindberg, and far more effective than Yeats; less lost in nightmares than the one, in dreams than the other. His view of life fades into grey vistas of desolation unutterable; yet it would not be very easy to prove it false.

Synge, Chekhov, and Ibsen, on the other hand, seem to me healthier, saner, more balanced, more humane—men both of good sense and of good will. Synge, even more than Chekhov, was a spirit cramped and frustrated by a frail body. The life he depicted was constricted and primitive, on the uttermost edge of Europe, and fast fading even while he wrote. Yet by his sincerity and integrity, by his zestful delight in human character, by the lilt of a style where art even bettered nature, he drew from that obscure, romantic corner of the Western World a volume that has become, in its own way, a classic.

Chekhov is far more of a world-figure than Synge—one of the most charming, wisest, and best of men (which writers are quite often far from being). His finest stories seem as perfect of their kind as Ibsen's finest plays. Yet Chekhov's dramatic characters, though so living, lack perhaps the pungency and poignancy, the daemonic energy or incisive irony of Ibsen's. Chekhov has left us an Ivánov, but no Peer Gynt; an Uncle Vanya, but no Hjalmar Ekdal; a Helen Serebryakóv, but no Hedda Gabler; a Sonia, but no Hilda Wangel or Rebecca West. And Chekhov's ideas seem more limited—the need for irony, for compassion, for hard work, for stoic indifference. The questionings of Ibsen are more revolutionary and more passionate; on a dozen still contentious themes his answers, whether or no we accept them, have still to be reckoned with. Finally, his dramatic structure has more the architecture of a master builder, the precision of a master engineer.

Since these last three dramatists died, in the brief five years between 1904 and 1909, over half a century has passed; but one may doubt whether it has produced any successor even approaching them. They were never vulgar, nor Philistine, nor barbarous, nor brutal; believing in little, they yet believed in individuality, in human dignity, in grace, in intellect. They were not mere providers of an evening's entertainment; they remain, to those who value them, friends for life.

A FEW SUGGESTIONS FOR FURTHER READING

In a book of this kind for the general reader it seems senseless to burden him (and his pocket) with a fat bibliography, which would begin going out of date forthwith. It will, I hope, be more practical to propose a few works that may prove rewarding.

CHEKHOV

Texts (Letters etc.)

Garnett, C. (trans. by). *Letters to his family and friends*. Chatto and Windus, 1920. *Letters to O. L. Knipper*. 1926.

Hellman, L. (editor; trans. by S. Lederer). *Selected Letters*. Hamish Hamilton, 1955.

Koteliansky, S. S. and P. Tomlinson (trans. and edited by). *Life and Letters*. Cassell, 1925.

Magarshack, D. (trans. by). *The Seagull, Produced by Stanislavsky*. Dobson, 1952. (Interesting notes by Stanislavsky.)

Personal Papers. New York, 1948.

Biography and Criticism

Avilov, L. (trans. by D. Magarshack). *Chekhov in My Life*. Lehmann, 1950.

Bruford, W. H. *Chekhov and his Russia*. Faber, 1947.
Chekhov. Bowes, 1957.

Erenburg, I. G. *Chekhov, Stendhal, and other essays* (trans. by A. Bostock and Y. Kapp). MacGibbon and Kee, 1962.

Gorky, M. (trans. by K. Mansfield, S. S. Koteliansky, L. Woolf). *Reminiscences of Tolstoy, Chekhov and Andreev*. Hogarth, 1934.

Katzer, J. (edited by). *A. P. Chekhov 1860-1960*. Moscow, 1961. (A collection of essays.)

Koteliansky, S. S. (trans. and edited by). *Literary and Theatrical Reminiscences*. Routledge, 1927.

Laffitte, S. *Tchékhov par lui-meme*. Paris, 1955. (Admirably compendious.)

Magarshack, D. *Chekhov; A Life*. Faber, 1952. (Excellent.)
Chekhov, the Dramatist. Lehmann, 1952.

Triolet, E. *L'histoire d'Anton Tchékhov*. Paris, 1954.

SYNGE AND YEATS

General

Coxhead, E. *Lady Gregory*. Macmillan, 1961.

Ellis-Fermor, U. M. *The Irish Dramatic Movement*. Methuen, 1939, 1954.

Fay, Gerard. *The Abbey Theatre*. Hollis and Carter, 1958.

Gregory, Lady. *Our Irish Theatre*. New York, 1914.

(edited by L. Robinson). *Journals* 1916-30. Putnam, 1946.

Moore, George. *Hail and Farewell*. Heinemann, 1911-14.

Synge

A new complete edition is in progress, edited by R. Skelton; Vol. 1, Oxford U.P., 1962.

Greene, D. H. and Stephens, E. M. *Synge*. Macmillan (New York) 1959. (The standard biography.)

Price, Alan F. *Synge and Anglo-Irish Drama*. Methuen, 1961.

Yeats, W. B. *The Death of Synge*. Dublin, 1928.

(Also 'Preface to Synge's Poems' and 'Synge and the Ireland of his Time' reprinted in *Essays*, 1924.)

Yeats

Here there is embarrassing abundance; many variant selections might be made.

Ellmann, R. D. *Yeats, The Man and the Masks*. Macmillan, 1949.

The Identity of Yeats. Macmillan, 1954.

Gibbon, W. Monk. *The Masterpiece and the Man*. Hart-Davis, 1959.

Henn, T. R. *The Lonely Tower*. Methuen, 1950.

Hone, J. M. *Yeats*, Macmillan, 1942, 1962. (The standard life.)

Jeffares, A. N. *Yeats, Man and Poet*. Routledge, 1949.

Yeats, His Poetry and Thought. Camb. U.P., 1961.

Macneice, F. L. *The Poetry of Yeats*. Oxford U.P., 1941.

Melchiori, G. *The Whole Mystery of Art*. Routledge, 1961.

Wilson, F. A. C. *Yeats and Tradition*. Gollancz, 1958.

Yeats's Iconography. Gollancz, 1960.

Pirandello

Bishop, T. *Pirandello and the French Theatre*. P. Owen, 1961.

Nardelli, F. V. *L'uomo segreto*. Mondadori, 1932, 1944. (Biography.)

Siciliano, I. *Il teatro di Pirandello*, Turin, 1929.

Vittorini, D. *The Drama of Pirandello*, Philadelphia, 1935.

INDEX

*(Main entries in **bold** type)*

INDEX

Yeats, William Butler—*continued*.
292*n*; *Senate Speeches*, 277; *Vision,
A*, 255-6, **264-70**, 272, 277;
Wheels and Butterflies, 273, 333*n*;
(3) *Characteristics:* aristocratic
sympathies, 269, 273-4, 312-13,
337-40; dreaminess, 243-5, 325;
generosity, 243, 321, 355; hatred of
old age, 270, 291*n*; hatred of
rationalism and science, 242, 269,
276, 323; individualism and introversion, 269-70, 278-80, 344; lyric
rather than dramatic, 247-9, 278-
280, 344-5, 353-5; moral courage
and liberalism, 205-6, 277-8, 332*n*;
nationalism, 251, 294-8; occultism,
251-2, 257-72; sceptical side, 271-2,
276; wearing of the 'mask', 290,
325, 346-52, 355; contrasted with
Hardy, 351-2; with Synge, 164-6,
171, 228, 237*n*, 249, 353, 355

Zola, 45, 222
Zonas of Sardis, 188